The dBASE Book
Developing Windows Applications
with dBASE PLUS

Ken Mayer

Third Edition

Volume 1

The dBASE Book
Developing Windows Applications with dBASE PLUS
Volume 1
by Ken Mayer

Copyright © 2005, 2007, 2013 by Kenneth *(Ken)* J. Mayer
ISBN: 978-0-9892875-0-0 (sc) print

First Printing, 2005; Second Printing, 2007; Third Printing, 2013
Printed in the United States of America

Trademark and Copyright acknowledgments:

- *Visual dBASE, dBASE, dBASE PLUS, dQuery* and variations of these product names and words are registered trademarks of dBase, LLC.
- *Borland Database Engine, BDE, Paradox, InterBase* and *Delphi* are registered trademarks of Borland International, Inc. and/or Embarcadero.
- *Firebird* is a registered trademark of Firebird Foundation Corporation.
- *Microsoft, Windows XP, Vista, Windows 7, Windows 8* (and all other forms of the names of the Windows operating system), *Word, Excel, FoxPro* are registered trademarks of Microsoft Corporation.
- *Quicken* is a registered trademark of Intuit, Inc.
- *Inno Setup* is copyrighted to Jordan Russel and Martijn Laan
- *Apache* is copyrighted to the Apache Software Foundation

No attempt has been made to designate as trademarks or service marks all personal computer words or terms in which proprietary rights might exist. The inclusion, exclusion or definition of a word or term is not intended to affect, or express any judgement on, the validity or legal status of any proprietary right which may be claimed in that word or term.

Disclaimer

The author and publisher have used their best efforts in preparing this book, and the programs contained herein. However, the author and publisher make no warranties of any kind, express or implied, with regard to the documentation or programs contained in this book, and specifically disclaim without any limitations, any implied warranties of merchantability and fitness for a particular purpose with respect to program listings in the book and/or the techniques described in the book. In no event shall the author or publisher be responsible or liable for any loss or profit or any other commercial damages, including but not limited to special, incidental, consequential or any other damages in connection with or arising out of furnishing, performance, or use of this book or the programs.

Table of Contents

About the Author

Ken Mayer has used dBASE both as a hobbyist and as a professional coder for many years, starting with dBASE III+ and working up to dBASE PLUS.

Ken worked for Borland, Intl. for two years as a Senior Quality Assurance Engineer on the Intrabuilder and dBASE products (Intrabuilder 1.0, Visual dBASE 7.0 and 7.01), and also worked for five years for dBASE Inc. as a Senior Quality Assurance Engineer, also working on dBASE (Visual dBASE 7.5, dB2K and dBASE PLUS, as well as dQuery). Ken was a contributing editor to dBASE Advisor magazine for the one and a half years or so it was in publication.

He served on Borland's TeamB (volunteer technical support) when Borland owned dBASE, and has helped many in the dBASE developer community. At this time he is a member of the dBVIPS for dataBased Intelligence, Inc., doing the same things he did with TeamB. He authored a good portion of the Knowledgebase articles that ship with dBASE PLUS, and authored the original dBASE PLUS tutorial. Some of the material in this book will look suspiciously familiar to any who have used the Knowledgebase.

Ken has also been the librarian of a freeware library of code made available to all dBASE developers called the dBASE Users' Function Library Project (dUFLP) for so long he's lost count. He has been a speaker at Borland and other conferences on dBASE, speaking about coding techniques.

Ken's current job is as a full-time instructor at Heald College (in Concord, CA) for over 5 years, teaching Microsoft Office courses, and other Business classes (e-Commerce, Entrepreneurship, Human Resources, etc.).

When not working, Ken is very active in the Society for Creative Anachronism, Inc. (http://www.sca.org), and enjoys cooking, movies, games, and reading.

Ken lives in Walnut Creek, CA with his wife Carolyn Eaton and their two cats Rebo and Zootie *(named after a pair of comedians from the science fiction TV show Babylon 5)*.

(Photograph of the author is by Sandra Linehan, December, 2012)

Introduction

Between dBASE II and Visual dBASE 5.x, a great number of books were written about dBASE. With the 32-bit versions of dBASE (Visual dBASE 7.x, dB2K and dBASE PLUS), even data became objects, ruled by object-oriented programming. In order to deal with these new data objects (data modules, queries, rowsets, and even field objects) a new language was created: OODML. This has created a steep learning curve for developers fluent in the 16-bit versions of dBASE, as well as those new to dBASE. When books were needed more than ever, only one book was published until now about the 32-bit versions of dBASE (Ted Blue's courseware book The dBASE Developer – Book 1: Getting Started).

The dBASE Book: Developing Windows Applications With dBASE PLUS is a bridge to those coders who are having a difficult time with the OOP model of dBL (the dBASE Language), and will help them develop solid Windows database applications. In addition, many dBASE coders are self-taught or have learned from those who were self-taught, and in the process have picked up a lot of bad coding techniques that can cause problems in their own code. This book will attempt to put dBASE developers on the "right path" to better coding techniques as well. Understanding object oriented development is essential to designing a proper Windows application, and this book will focus heavily on this aspect of dBASE.

Attempts have been made to make this book usable by developers using dBASE PLUS ranging from beginner to advanced.

The 3rd Edition of this book *(the one in your hands or on your screen)* is an update with fixes to the text and some of the code samples as suggested by a variety of folk from the first and second editions, and attempts have been made to include as many important updates to the software as possible at the time of printing. In addition, as the folk at dBase, LLC have been working on improving the software, I have attempted to update various parts of the book that deal with those improvements, enhancements and changes through release 2.8 of dBASE Plus *(released in the spring of 2012, with upgrades/bug fixes up until the time of this printing)*. The chapters that deal with deploying applications have been completely re-written/overhauled to deal with Windows Vista and Windows 7/8 and UAC issues, in order to make your applications work better with Windows itself. A new chapter (2) was added that explains the Windows UAC requirements for applications, and how dBASE has been modified to work with it *(rather than fighting with Windows and the UAC as dBASE developers have tended to do)*.

Why Did I Split the Book into Two Volumes?
Faithful readers will note that the first two editions of this book were a single volume. This is a HUGE book, as you know. There are two problems with it all being in one book – the first is just plain weight. The printed version is very large and a bit unwieldy. The publisher, AuthorHouse also has a page limit issue. You may recall – for the 2nd Edition I had to remove a chapter so that it could be printed. By splitting this into two volumes, the page count issue will go away for each of the two volumes, and the general weight of the book will be smaller for the individual books. While it does mean purchasing two books to obtain the set, I think the benefits outweigh the cost. I hope you agree.

Acknowledgments and Thanks

I would like to thank the people who have helped make this book possible. While I cannot thank by name every single person who may have contributed indirectly to the writing of this book, I would like to thank the following specifically.

The dBASE Community
Thanks to the dBASE community for the encouragement which helped me to decide that writing this book was a good idea. I cannot possibly name everyone who sent me "Please do this!" messages, either in private email or in the newsgroups, but my thanks to you all.

In addition, when I posted messages asking for ideas or specific information in the dBASE newsgroups many people came forward with their thoughts, advice, and assistance, sometimes providing code samples. Some of these folk are mentioned by name in the book, where I have referenced posts by them in the dBASE newsgroups, code I am using of theirs, etc. Again, thanks to you all.

Contributors
Others who have contributed to this book, and who have given me permission to use or reference materials of their own – in no specific order: Lane Coddington, Rich Muller and Peter Rorlick. A special thanks to Ivar B. Jessen for helping fine-tune the book title from what I had posted in the newsgroups, and to everyone who responded to requests for ideas for a title for the book. It was an interesting series of discussions, and I learned a lot from them.

Editors
I wish to thank **Jean-Pierre Martel** and **Professor Michael Nuwer**, who helped immensely from the beginning of this process right up to publication of the first two editions – their work permeates the book in many places, and I couldn't have done this without them.

These two gentlemen helped with the book proposal, table of contents *(which continues to evolve right up to publication)*, and much more. In addition to basic editing, they helped with the explanation of concepts, and to ensure that the sequence of the content made sense. They were great as sounding boards – being ready and willing to field questions and concerns I had, and were not shy about telling me when I was going in the wrong direction. The reason they did this is that they agreed with me that a good book on dBASE was needed.

In addition to the above, Jean-Pierre created the cover for this book *(he came out of retirement to do a new cover for me for the 3rd edition!)* – and what a great job he did, too! I cannot thank him enough for his generosity and the excellent job he has done!

Additionally several others stepped up to the plate for specific chapters that they had expertise in. Jim Sare kindly rewrote the Windows API (Chapter 22). Frank Polan helped with the chapter on Working in a Shared Environment (Chapter 9) having recently dealt with several of the issues covered by that chapter. These two did this with no thought of any reward or even mention in this book, but I have always believed in "credit where credit is due", and I owe them a debt of gratitude.

For the Second Edition of this book, I have to thank Frank Polan for stepping up and helping edit the chapters that were heavily modified, which meant walking through a bunch of exercises, and telling me what didn't make sense, etc.

For the Third Edition of this book:

James Peterson has over 10 years' experience in the analysis and development of enterprise computer systems. He joined The M Corporation in 2005 as an analyst / programmer and in 2008, was promoted to product manager - Subscribe systems with responsibility for the support and ongoing development of our subscription management systems. Prior to joining TMC, he developed his skills implementing and supporting ERP & CRM systems with UBA-Unicomp. James has a Bachelor of Science (Information Technology) and a Bachelor of Business from The University of Technology, Sydney. James has been invaluable in helping fix the grammar and sentence structure throughout the book.

Gerald Lightsey's career in management spanned 39 years in automobile Assembly Plant operations. He learned dBASE 3 in the early 80s, writing applications for his department. He has worked with dBASE through dBASE IV, dBASE 5 ... When he retired in the mid-90s he got involved with Visual dBASE 5 and has continued working with the dBASE community testing the software, and helping users. He was extremely helpful with this book in the latter chapters (in Volume 2), where he made me re-think some of my approaches and explanations.

Michael Rozlog, CEO of dBase, LLC

Michael worked with me to produce and make available the 2nd Edition of the book as a PDF, which is being distributed with dBASE Plus 2.8. This process included my rebuilding the book completely in Word™ (2010), and avoiding using a third party tool to produce the book. I had to re-do all the screen shots for that version, as Word didn't like the ones I was using for earlier versions. This started me thinking that since the book was converted to Word, maybe I could just work on a 3rd Edition, which is where we are now.

With the plans for moving forward into the future that Michael has presented, I would expect a 4th Edition of this book at some point. Once I complete the third edition, I anticipate starting right in on changes for the 4th Edition. I cannot speak to most of these changes as they are under NDA *(non-disclosure agreement)*, and some of them are still being worked out as I write.

Also at dBASE, LLC

Marty Kay, head of R&D has always been pretty straightforward, although quite politic, when dealing with issues. I worked with Marty when the company was dBASE, Inc., and I was still there. The interesting thing is that I have never met him. Suffice it to say that when I bring an issue to his attention he is usually very fast to turn things around, even it if it means telling me I forgot something or made a stupid error in my own code.

Kathy Kolosky, a woman of many talents. Again I have never met Kathy, but she's always tried her best to be helpful, whether in a Tech Support position, QA (my old job), or working on the Project Explorer and trying to provide as much help as she can. She has tried hard to provide assistance as I stumbled through aspects of this edition of the book.

My Wife

Last, but far from the least, I need to thank my wife of nineteen years *(as of the time this version of the book becomes available)*, Carolyn Eaton, for being supportive of pretty much everything I do. When I wrote the 1st and 2nd Editions of the book, it was a tough time financially. However, she supported this effort despite the difficulties with nary a complaint. All the time I worked on the book I was also looking for work, and trying to pick up some paying contracts. Now she puts up with me muttering and mumbling while I work on the text, and sometimes cursing and swearing when a code example doesn't work. She has always been supportive – how can you ask for more? There are simply not enough words to thank her ... except to say "I love you!"

Terminology

A minor note about terminology throughout the book ...:

When I write I tend to sound things out in my head. When I discuss things like file extensions, I tend to pronounce the period as "dot". Hence you will see interesting syntax such as:

"A .INI file"

In this case, if you pronounce the period as "dot", using the letter "A" is correct. If you do not, and instead pronounce it without, then correct English would be to state:

"An .INI file"

I prefer the former option. My editors questioned this in various places throughout the book, and I chose to leave the text as is in these cases. I hope this does not offend anyone's sensibilities *(although if it does, well, it's my book ...)*! And many thanks to my editors for putting up with my quirks and helping me correct my English, making this book easier to read.

Sample Code

It should be noted that throughout the book there are code samples. The sample code can be found on my website for this book, through my main dBASE webpage:

> http://www.goldenstag.net/dbase

If you go to this page, and find the information about my books, the page for the 3rd Edition of the books will have a link for the source code. This is contained in a .zip file with all of the code samples provided in folders, one folder per chapter, with a few folders as they are suggested in specific chapters of the book.

NOTES:

Part I: Getting Started

dBASE PLUS is a large and complex software package with a lot of options, often with more than one way to accomplish any given task.

In this section of the book we will take a look at the environment and setting up dBASE in a way that will meet your specific requirements.

Chapter 1: Setup and Parts of the Environment

When dBASE PLUS arrives the CD (if you didn't download the installer from dBase, LLC) comes with a <u>User's Guide</u> (in PDF format), a <u>Language Reference</u> (in PDF format), and then in the DOCS folder a set of PDFs. In addition, you will have received *(with dBASE Plus 2.8 or later)* the 2nd Edition of this book, titled (in the DOCS folder) <u>The Complete Book</u>.

Installation of dBASE PLUS is pretty well covered in the manual, so there is no need to discuss it in this book *(except for notes below)*. If you follow the instructions in Chapter 2 of the <u>User's Guide</u>, you will have installed dBASE successfully.

This chapter is aimed at getting you started, so – away we go.

Using "Modern" Versions of Windows

It should be noted that there are some changes in this chapter from the 2nd Edition, based on dBASE Plus 2.70 – which was modified to work with the Windows User Account Control (UAC).

When you install dBASE Plus, it assumes on Windows Vista and later versions of Windows (Windows 7, etc.) that you are using the UAC, and it installs accordingly. This book, starting with the 3rd edition, assumes that you are using a newer operating system. If you are using Windows XP (and many people still do), all of the items that deal with the UAC are not something you need to worry about, until you get to the issues dealing with deploying your application *(because you don't usually know what your end-users will be using for their operating system)*. We will discuss those challenges in Chapter 2 and other parts of the book.

One trick for dBASE developers is that the file PLUS.INI (used to store many dBASE Plus settings) is not necessarily where you expect it to be, nor are the Samples folders. You will see copies in:

```
C:\ProgramData\dBASE\PLUS
```

However, these are just copies, and may not be the files used by dBASE *(depending on which version of dBASE and which version of Windows are being used)*. The files being used may be in your private users' folder structure:

```
C:\Users\<username>\AppData\Local\dBASE\PLUS
```

This will take some getting used to on your part.

Using Windows XP?

If you are installing dBASE Plus 2.7 (or later) on a Windows XP computer dBASE is installed differently than described above. It basically is installed as it was before, it assumes the useUACPaths setting is false, the manifest file assumes dBASE will be run with "requireAdministrator" rights, and the path for the .INI file will be in the same folder as the file PLUS.EXE.

> **NOTE**
>
> If you have an installation of dBASE Plus earlier than 2.70 on Windows Vista, Windows 7, Windows 2008 R2 or later operating systems, you may wish to uninstall it first before installing the newer version. The reason for this is that the files that are installed with dBASE Plus may be installed in multiple places. Uninstalling will help clean things up. You will want to check the folder structure:
>
> ```
> C:\Program Files (x86)\dBASE\Plus
> ```
>
> After you uninstall dBASE for various files that were not uninstalled. The BIN folder will contain "PLUS.INI" for example, and you may want to hold onto that if you have any Source Code Aliases you were using before the uninstall. But the other files should probably be deleted if they were left behind. dBASE (2.7 or later) installs files in a very different way on modern versions of Windows than it did before.

Starting dBASE Plus

When you start current versions of dBASE Plus (2.7 and later) on "modern" operating systems (Windows Vista and later), it ensures that the user (whoever is logged in to the computer at the time) has a specific dBASE folder in the private user folder tree (C:\Users**username**\AppData\Local\dBASE\PLUS\) to hold private copies of configuration, sample programs and databases, converter files, and any temporary files that may be created when running dBASE.

The first time dBASE is run by a user, a "new user setup" utility is run to set up sample and converter files, create all the default Source Aliases, and default User BDE Aliases. This program is one that you, as a developer, will be able to use if you so wish. It will be discussed in more detail in later chapters of this book. One thing to note, the BDE Aliases that used to be stored in the IDAPI.CFG file in older versions of dBASE are now being created as User BDE Aliases. These are mentioned below, and will be discussed throughout the book.

In addition, during startup, dBASE checks the user's PLUS.INI file for any User BDE Aliases, and if found, loads them into the default BDE session so that they are available for use right away.

User BDE Aliases are new to dBASE Plus 2.70 and later. These are private aliases and stored in each user's PLUS.INI file. New BDE Aliases can be created using the Database Wizard in dQuery, through code, or manually editing the PLUS.INI file. *(BDE Aliases can be created using the BDE Administrator – see Chapter 2 and Chapter 4, importantly, the BDE Administrator requires Administrator rights to create or delete aliases. This can cause some difficulties, and in those chapters of the book as well as others, we will discuss different methods of creating BDE Aliases ...)*

When starting dBASE, the User BDE Aliases and Source Code Aliases (including any you have created) are loaded into the appropriate places.

There is more detail on what happens the first time you start dBASE Plus, and where files are stored, in the Online Help for dBASE.

dQuery – the Startup Program

When dBASE starts, briefly you may see the area that this book will be focusing on – namely the Navigator and Command Windows. However, dBASE by default starts a program called dQuery. This is a nice, graphic front-end for dBASE PLUS. You can do a lot with dQuery and there is a chapter in this book dedicated to it, although that chapter only barely scratches the surface of this tool.

As a developer, you will want to use dQuery to create and modify data modules. However, you may find that there are times you may need dQuery to do other things (such as importing data from another source, and so on).

My point here is that while dQuery is useful, as a programmer you may not want dBASE to start with dQuery. Most of this book assumes that dQuery is *not* running, unless you are told otherwise. We will discuss how to modify your setup so that dQuery does not start automatically *if you wish to turn it off*. Preferences are preferences, and some users of dBASE prefer to start with dQuery, while others prefer otherwise. There is no "one true way."

Some Basic Setup

dBASE PLUS has quite a few defaults that are set up for you when the program is installed. You may wish to alter the behavior of dBASE, however.

To that end, you should become familiar with the Desktop Properties Dialog, which we are now going to look at. If you wish to follow along and look at this dialog at the same time, feel free to do so.

For the time being, start dBASE PLUS, and then close dQuery if it is open. (Use the "x" in the titlebar, or use the "File" menu, and "Close" to close dQuery itself.)

To get to the Desktop Properties, click on the "Properties" menu in dBASE, and select "Desktop Properties". Note that you can also type the word "SET" in the Command Window and press the Enter key, and you should see the same.

The Desktop Properties dialog box has several tabs at the top of the screen, each for different categories of properties.

When you first bring this dialog up, it should start on the first tab "Country". The screen should look like:

Figure 1-1

Many of these options can be set in dBASE using various commands such as "SET SEPARATOR TO", and so on, but it is useful to see the various options here. Most of these are pretty self-explanatory.

It should be noted that while you can change the language dBASE uses for menus and responses (UI Language), this does not affect language drivers for tables. You will need to use the BDE Administrator for that, which is covered in another chapter.

If you click on the next tab, "Table", you will see something like:

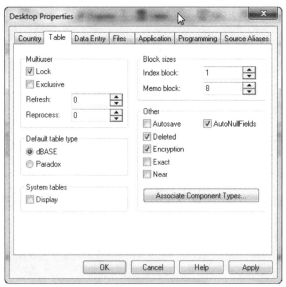

Figure 1-2

One very useful thing to examine here is the "Associate Component Types ..." dialog *(which can also be gotten to if you are in the Form Designer, but we will look at the Form Designer in later chapters ...).*

If you click that button, you will see:

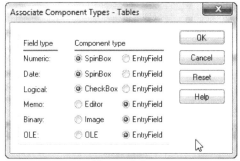

Figure 1-3

This particular dialog tells dBASE what the default control should be for specific field types. I recommend *(but you can ignore that recommendation)*, that you set Memo, Binary and OLE to the other setting, and personally I don't like to have date types default to a Spinbox, but rather to an Entryfield. If you make any changes, click "OK", if not, or you don't wish to save any changes, click "Cancel".

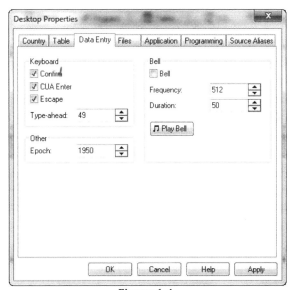

Figure 1-4

The "Data Entry" tab allows you to change settings that are specific to data entry.
The one thing I always change is the "Bell" setting – basically this is not all that useful, the idea is that when an entryfield is full, as a user types values into it, it will beep – as a user I find that annoying. Under Windows this doesn't always work, either – that would depend on how your sound card is configured.

The "Files" tab looks like:

Figure 1-5

I don't usually do very much with this particular tab. One recommendation: leave "Sessions" unchecked. It is unnecessary and can cause problems.

The "Application" tab has several things that I tend to turn off:

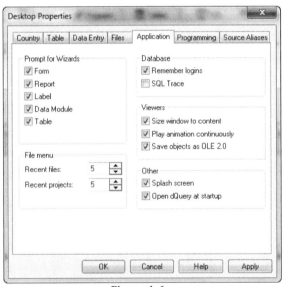

Figure 1-6

Very specifically, and this is personal preference, I turn off all of the Wizards, and I go to the bottom right and uncheck the "Open dQuery at startup" checkbox. These choices are left to you, as always – these are personal preferences or suggestions only.

The "Programming" tab shows the following options:

Figure 1-7

I don't usually do much here, as the defaults work fine for me.

Finally, the "Source Aliases" tab is one that we will revisit later in this book several times, when we start talking about "Source Code Aliases".

Figure 1-8

There are some entries shown in the list in Figure 1-8 that may not appear in yours – this is because I have been using dBASE PLUS, and have added some "Source Aliases" that I use for my own application work. It is a good idea to leave the ones that were installed with dBASE, because removing them may cause you some problems (for example, if you removed the "dQuery" Source Alias, dQuery itself would not run). dBASE may, if you delete some of these entries, re-create them the next time it starts, but only ones that are vital to dBASE itself.

If you have made any changes, clicking "Apply" will cause them to go into effect now, and "OK" will do the same and close the dialog. If you have not made any changes, you can click "OK" and have no effect, or you can click "Cancel" to close the dialog, and you can click "Cancel" if you made changes you don't wish to save.

The dBASE Desktop

Now that we have gone through the Desktop Properties dialog, let's take a closer look at the actual Desktop area of dBASE PLUS.

The Desktop for dBASE PLUS, without dQuery running, looks like this:

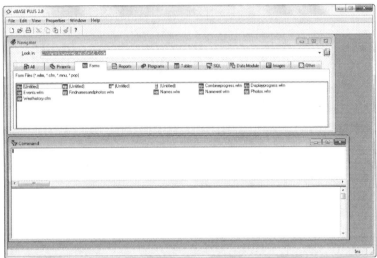

Figure 1-9

The desktop can be broken down into multiple parts, which we will examine in the following pages, in a little detail. If you are familiar with Windows applications in general, some of this will be pretty much the same as what you are used to with those other programs.

The "Desktop" is often called the "IDE" or "Integrated Developer's Environment" (this term also refers to the complete developer's environment, including the design surfaces).

The Title Bar

At the top of the main window, is the Title Bar. The Title Bar displays an icon, and some text. The Title Bar by default looks like:

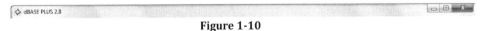

Figure 1-10

This shows the dBASE PLUS icon, the words "dBASE PLUS", and on the far right are some buttons, the first to minimize the application, the second to maximize or restore the window, and the third to close (the "x").

In your own applications, you will have the ability to change the text and the icon displayed in the title bar.

The Menu Bar

The Menu Bar is where the menu will reside. If, in the text of this book, I suggest you use the "File" menu, this is where it will be. The Menu Bar is always just below the Title Bar.

The standard, default menu in dBASE PLUS looks like:

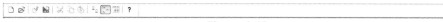
Figure 1-11

The menu in dBASE is dynamic – it changes based on what tools you are using at the time. If you were to start the Form Designer, the menu would change and different options would become available to you. Once you closed the Form Designer, the menu would revert back to what it was before.

The Tool Bar

The Tool Bar is where a series of tool buttons will go. The Tool Bar is always below the Menu Bar. The default Tool Bar in dBASE PLUS looks like:

Figure 1-12

As with the menu, when you work with different tools in dBASE the Tool Bar will change appearance, adding some buttons, removing some buttons, depending on what you are doing.

The Navigator Window

The Navigator in dBASE PLUS is a way of organizing your files, by grouping them appropriately. You can also edit files from this location, and more. You can navigate through Windows by selecting working folders, database aliases, and a lot more. As you work with the product you will become quite familiar with this part of it. The Navigator Window looks like:

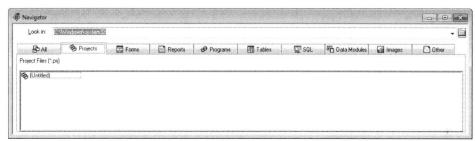
Figure 1-13

You can resize this, you can move it around to where you want, and dBASE will remember these settings the next time you start the program.

The Command Window

The Command Window is very useful for a programmer. One of the great aspects of dBASE is that you can actually type program commands into the Command Window, and have them execute. You can test program statements without having to write a program to do so!

The Command Window is a very important tool in dBASE PLUS, and throughout this book we will use it quite often. It looks like the following, although you can change it:

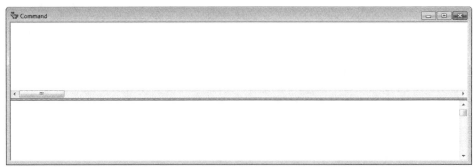

Figure 1-14

The default settings for the Command Window are for the actual Commands to be typed in the top (the "Command Pane"), and for the results to be output into the bottom (the "Results Pane"). However, if you right click on the Command Window, there is a dialog ("Command Window Properties") that allows you to change the Command Window appearance. You might want the Commands on the left, and the output on the right, for example.

You can also modify other settings that affect both the Command Window and the Source Code Editor from the "Command Window Properties" dialog. I suggest that for starters you leave things as they are – but you can always come back to it.

It should be noted that you can change the fonts that are used in either pane of the Command Window. For readability it is a good idea to use what is called a mono-spaced font – one such as the default of Courier. The reason is that your code lines up better, your output is easier to read because some things assume columns that will be all out of alignment if you use a font that is not mono-spaced.

The Status Bar

The status bar is useful for a variety of things. It appears at the bottom of the desktop window. It looks like:

Figure 1-15

This may not look like much, but, based on various keyboard settings (Caps Lock, Insert/Typeover, etc.), you can see the status. If you use the XDML commands to manipulate tables, you will see the table name that is currently in use, the number of rows, and other useful information in the status bar. Some menu options may display information in the status bar as well. You should look at it periodically as you work with dBASE, to see what shows up there.

Important Tools in dBASE PLUS

dBASE PLUS, being a programming environment and a useful tool for manipulating data, forms, reports, and so on has a lot of useful tools built in. We will look at a few of them and then of course as we work through later chapters of the book, we will see more and more of these tools.

Speed Menus

Most or all Windows in dBASE PLUS have a context-sensitive "speed" menu, or what is called in dBASE a Popup Menu. If you right click on the Window (or press the "Application Key" on your keyboard, or press Shift+F10), a popup menu will appear. The contents of this menu will be context-sensitive – in other words, the contents of the menu will depend on what window currently has focus.

Getting Help

dBASE PLUS has a fairly extensive HELP system, that includes the Online Help and the Knowledgebase.

Using the Online Help (OLH)

The Online Help (or OLH), is available in many different ways in the product. In many cases pressing ⌨ will bring up a context-sensitive version of help. What this means is that if you are working in a specific area of the product, and press ⌨, dBASE will attempt to bring up the most useful information it can. That said, there are of course, other ways to use Help in dBASE.

One method of using Help that I use all the time, is to simply go to the Command Window, and type the word "Help" followed by a topic. I can never remember all of the properties of the various objects in dBASE for example, so if I wanted to look at the properties of an Entryfield, I might type:

```
help class entryfield
```

Doing this, dBASE will take me straight to the help information about the Entryfield class and I can then attempt to find what I am looking for.

You can also go to Help from the main menu in dBASE at any time. This menu gives you several options, including:

Context Sensitive Help

Contents and Index

User's Guide

Language Reference

How To Use Help

We've discussed the first. The second is useful, because you can scroll through the list, you can type part of a topic title and have Help try to find it as you type, and more. This looks like:

Figure 1-16

There is a lot more. The "Contents" tab will show you a variety of options:

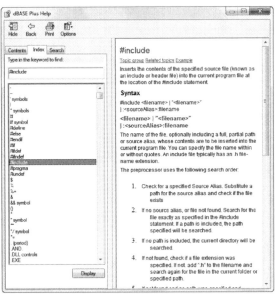

Figure 1-17

This includes the User's Guide, the Language Reference, and a lot more. It is worth taking some time and delving into this, just to get a feel for what is there.

> **NOTE**
> The User's Guide includes a chapter on converting applications from older versions of dBASE to the 32-bit versions, including converting from dBASE for DOS to dBASE Plus.

Using the Knowledgebase

The Knowledgebase is a series of articles written by various people to assist the user with parts of the software that may or may not be confusing. They go into more depth than the manuals and help do and included in the Knowledgebase is a very nice, complete, tutorial.

If you select the "Help" menu, and "Knowledgebase", a web page is displayed. In dBASE PLUS version 2.8, the Knowledgebase is not installed to the local hard drive, and the web page points you to the dBASE LLC Website. *(In earlier versions of dBASE PLUS prior to 2.5 you could install the Knowledgebase, but dBASE, LLC decided to only keep the Knowledgebase up to date online.)*

The Knowledgebase will display a menu. This includes "Beginner" topics, "Intermediate" topics, and "Advanced" topics. There are also "Frequently Asked Questions", and links to the Bug Report and Wishlist Request databases, allowing you to help support the product and make it even better.

It should be noted that the Knowledgebase, to the best of my knowledge, has not been updated in several years. There have been a lot of changes to dBASE since most of the articles were written, and while many of these articles are incorporated here, and this book has been updated, the Knowledgebase itself has not.

You should spend some time looking at some of the information there. The Tutorial is useful, and after you have gone through this book, you may find that you can get even more information from there. As you go through the Knowledgebase you will see my name on many articles there. Indeed, I did write much of the content of the Knowledgebase, and some of that information is included in this book.

Other Tools

dBASE has many other tools built into it that we will examine as we go through the chapters of this book. These tools are usually specific to whatever part of the product you are currently working with, whether it be the Table Designer, the Form Designer, etc. These tools will be discussed in appropriate chapters.

Summary

As you have seen, dBASE PLUS is a complex software package. If you are not already familiar with it, this chapter should give you a bit of a start in the basic layout and such. The rest of this book is aimed at teaching you how to develop applications either for your own use or as a commercial software developer. Take it a bit at a time as there is a lot to learn!

NOTES:

Chapter 2: Items to Consider When Developing an Application

This chapter was inserted into the book to provide dBASE Developers with an overview of a variety of issues and items that a developer needs to be aware of before even starting to develop an application.

Administrator Rights for an Administrator Account?

This is important enough it should be discussed early before we get into other information in this and later chapters of the book. Marty Kay at dBASE responded to a request for some information by helping understand this issue, as it is a frustrating aspect of working with current versions of Windows (Vista, Windows 7 and Windows 2008 Server R2).

If you log into one of these operating systems with an account that has administrator rights, Windows creates two sets of permissions. One has all of the administrator permissions, the other has standard user permissions.

Windows starts the Desktop with the standard user permissions. Any program launched (including from the Start menu) receives the standard user permissions. If the program being launched has a manifest file with the setting of "requireAdministrator", you will be prompted by the UAC (if it is turned on) for permission to run the program with administrator rights. If you click "Yes", it is launched with full administrator permissions. This is important for programs such as the BDE Administrator, or install routines.

If you launch the program with a lower setting of "asInvoker", you will not be prompted by the UAC. This is important for your application as a developer, the BDE Administrator, or for dBASE Plus itself.

If you need to start the dBASE Plus IDE or your own dBASE application with administrator rights, you should right-click the shortcut or menu option and select "Run as Administrator". This overrides the manifest file's "asInvoker" setting for dBASE Plus (and dBASE executables using the Runtime engine) for dBASE Plus 2.7 through current versions on these operating systems.

If your own application is written properly, you shouldn't need to have your users use the "requireAdministrator" option, or have them run "As Administrator" – using the correct folders (as described here).

The Environment

When discussing this chapter of the book with other dBASE developers, a few topics came up I hadn't considered. This chapter started out concerned mostly with Windows Vista, Windows 7, and the UAC, and has evolved quite a bit since I started working on it (with help from said other dBASE developers).

The Development Environment

One issue is the actual development environment, and then the environment your application will be deployed to.

To start the discussion, from my own experience there are basically three types of database application developers who use dBASE:

1) Independent developers (ISVs – Independent Software Vendors), who work at home or in their own office, writing applications for various clients, or perhaps having specific software package that they develop and sell to others
2) Developers who work within a company, either as part of the IT department or as part of a separate department within the firm;
3) Hobbiest/student developers – people who use dBASE for fun, not so much for profit *(this may seem an odd concept to some people, but they do exist).*

One could nit-pick and come up with a lot of variations *(for example, my first professional programming job was creating dBASE IV applications for the U.S. Department of Energy as a subcontractor – the company I worked for contracted to the DOE … strictly speaking my job didn't really fit any of the above, but it was mostly the 2nd item in the list).* Obviously the developers that need a lot of what is in this book the most are the ones who make a living developing applications. However, all developers can use advice, help, and all that.

In an ideal world an independent developer would be able to duplicate the environment as closely as possible, that an application will be deployed to. This is particularly useful for multi-user networked applications. That may not be easy, or even possible in some cases. However, if you have two computers and a network (wireless routers are pretty common and not expensive) you can duplicate *(or emulate if you will)* a multi-user environment to test applications.

If the developer is working within a company, or for a company, then they will need to work closely with the IT department to determine the correct locations for files being deployed, and how to get parts of their application to work.

The Deployment/Application's Environment

There are, of course, many possible configurations for your client or end-user. This is what can make a developer a bit crazy. Are they using Windows XP only? Are they using a networked environment? Do they have a mix of operating systems *(very likely these days – new computers come with the most recent version of Windows on them)*?

In a company environment or a corporate environment (in this case I am using the term "corporate" to describe a fairly large company, typically with their own IT department, often with very specific rules for security and such) things can get more complicated.

As a developer, you need to be aware of what the location of things will be and be sure that you know how to make your application work within that environment. If you are working with a corporate IT department, you will want to create a positive relationship with the IT team as soon as possible.

With a good understanding of where everything will be deployed, and with what specific obstacles, security requirements, etc. will be used, you, as the developer will be well-armed and ready to write the application. If you know the environment your application will be deployed to, it is my opinion that you do not need to completely replicate that environment to develop for it. You can plan ahead. Your code can be set up to find the appropriate files in the correct locations and interact with them as needed both in the developer environment and the deployed environment.

Windows Folder Structures

If you are going to create applications that work *with* Windows, rather than working around Windows and all the various permutations, the first thing to understand is the folder structure. Where should a "well-behaved" application deploy the executable, the tables, and other files?

In order to be truly Windows compliant, your application should store the various files used in specific locations. All of the following assumes you are using Windows Vista or Windows 7 for your deployment. Windows XP (still popular as an operating system at the time I am writing this) does not difference 32-bit and 64-bit application folders, among other things. I will compare the settings used by Windows XP to the ones used by later operating systems.

The Windows API (Application Programming Interface) uses special folder paths defined internally by values named CSIDL (Constant Special Item ID List). These paths are referred to in the OLH (Online Help) for dBASE (2.7 and later, under _app.UseUACPaths and related topics), as well as other documents when discussing the UAC options, it is helpful to know more about them.

Use of these paths can save a developer a lot of effort, as the terms do not change much between versions of the operating systems, even if the actual paths change. The CSIDL paths are not easy to find, however, Andrew Shimmin created a routine that is available in the dBASE Users' Function Library Project (dUFLP). This routine can be used to find these paths in your code if you need to. *(This example assumes you have set up the dUFLP properly – see the appendices in Vol. 2 of this book for details on obtaining the dUFLP and setting it up.)*
For example:

```
set procedure to :dUFLP:MiscAPI
? getWindowsCSIDLPath( "CSIDL_LOCAL_APPDATA" )
```

Which on my Windows 7 computer returns:

```
C:\Users\Ken\AppData\Local
```

The paths we are specifically interested in right now are *(there are a lot more)*:

- CSIDL_LOCAL_APPDATA *(private user folder structure)*
- CSIDL_APPDATA *(roaming user folder structure)*
- CSIDL_COMMON_APPDATA *(shared data folder structure)*
- CSIDL_PROGRAM_FILES *(program files folder structure)*

It should be noted that Microsoft is changing from "CSIDL" to "KnownFolderID" *(added in Windows Vista, and intended to replace CSIDL, as explained in documentation found online)*. Andrew Shimmin intends to create a routine that will return the information for KnownFolderIDs at some point in the future, and Marty Kay from dBASE notes that the documentation and code for dBASE will start using KnownFolderIDs in future releases of the software.

Hidden Folders?

If you cannot see folders on your computer, such as the C:\Users\<username> folder structure, you may need to modify settings in Windows Explorer.

In Windows 7 (the options have been moved from earlier OSes, of course):
- Open Windows Explorer
- Click "Organize"
- Click "Folder and Search Options"
- Click the "View" tab
- In the "Advanced Settings" treeview list, under "Hidden Files and Folders" click "Show hidden files, folders, and drives"
- Click "OK"

From this point forward with Windows Explorer you should be able to see everything.

The Program and Other Files (CSIDL_PROGRAM_FILES)

The program (.exe) and other files used to execute the application, including .DLL files, should be placed in the "Program Files" structure of the computer.

Using Windows XP

Windows XP uses the location:

```
C:\Program Files
```

Using Windows Vista, and Later Versions

As dBASE is still (at this time) a 32-Bit application, on a Windows 7 64-bit computer with Windows 7 64-bit Windows installed (you can install 32-bit version of Windows on a 64-bit computer), the folder structure is typically (on an American/English computer – the path will be different for other language installations):

```
C:\Program Files (x86)
```

If you are using the 32-bit version of Windows (whether on a 32-bit computer, or have chosen to put a 32-bit version on a 64-bit computer), the path will be:

```
C:\Program Files
```

If dBASE eventually creates a 64-bit version (which I anticipate will eventually happen), then the path used will be the same as above, but without the " (x86)" in the path. 64-bit applications are typically stored in this folder structure:

```
C:\Program Files
```

At this time, when looked for (within dBASE Plus anyway), the CSIDL_PROGRAM_FILES setting points to the 32-bit program files path. If dBASE becomes a 64-bit application I assume this will change to the path shown above. If you wished, you could use CSIDL_PROGRAM_FILES32 instead to be sure that you were using the absolutely correct path.

In either version:

When you plan to deploy your application, it is recommended that your application have a folder that uses your company name, or something of that nature (so that if you install multiple applications on the same computer, you group them together), and then the individual application in its own folder. For example:

```
C:\Program Files (x86)\MyCompany\MyApplication
```

One of the most frustrating aspects of the "standard" Windows UAC compatible/compliant application is that once installed in this folder, your users should *only* have read and execute rights to this folder, but not modify. Therefore, your data, and other files that you expect to modify need to be somewhere else, INCLUDING the .INI file! *(See information later in this chapter on what happens with the .INI file.)*

You should be sure to deploy a proper Manifest file into the same folder as the executable. *(More on Manifest files in chapters dealing with deployment of your applications.)*

While it is acceptable to place the executable in folders off the root of the hard drive (i.e., C:\MyApplication, or variations …), it is recommended that they be placed as shown above.

Shared Configuration and Non-Updateable Data Files (CSIDL_COMMON_APPDATA)

Files that will not be modified by the user, but are not required by the executable at the time of execution can be placed in the ProgramData folder tree.

Using Windows XP:

```
C:\Documents and Settings\Users\MyCompany\MyApplication\Config
```

Using Windows Vista, Windows 7, etc., American/English installation:

```
C:\ProgramData\MyCompany\MyApplication\Config
```

If your application is set up to use DEO files (this will be discussed later), the references in the .INI will need to point to the correct location. This can be in the ProgramData folder structure, or some other location. The installer can create the appropriate settings, and this will be discussed when we get to the chapter on deploying your application.

Master Copies of Files Used by Each User (CSIDL_COMMON_APPDATA)

If your application has files that are used and modified by individual users *(for example, for user preferences)*, you should use the ProgramData folder tree structure, you might wish to create a folder containing these, and then copy to the users' private folder structure the first time the application runs. Something like:

Using Windows XP:

```
C:\Documents and Settings\Users\MyCompany\MyApplication\UserFiles
```

Using Windows Vista, Windows 7, etc., American/English installation:

```
C:\ProgramData\MyCompany\MyApplication\UserFiles
```

Your install routine should ensure that the users have the correct permissions.

Shared/Updatable Data Files (CSIDL_COMMON_APPDATA)

This references your primary data. For a single-user application either these files should be placed in the ProgramData folder tree structure, or off the root directory of the hard drive *(although the ProgramData structure is preferred)*, with permissions allowing users to modify the files:

Using Windows XP:

```
C:\Documents and Settings\Users\MyCompany\MyApplication\Tables
```

Using Windows Vista, Windows 7, etc., American/English installation:

```
C:\ProgramData\MyCompany\MyApplication\Tables
```

As with the topic above, your install routine should ensure that the users have the correct permissions when the folder is created.

For a networked application the primary data files would need to be placed on a file server. In those cases you will want to work with the network administrator and/or your client to determine the appropriate location.

For these data folders, a User BDE Alias should be created in the .INI file *(for each, if you use more than one)*. Some details on what is meant by this below and more information will be given in later chapters.

Getting the Folders Set Up

One of the tasks that you need to do is to put all your folders (referenced above) in the correct locations. The install routine for the application can set up these folders with appropriate rights.

The developers at dBASE use some code when dBASE is first run on a computer that you may want to consider using to help (InitNewUser.prg). They have made the code available to developers so that if you wish to use it, you can. When we get to the chapter on deployment, we will take a look at how to use this program to get your folders where you need them to be.

Referencing These Folders in Your Application

The developers at dBASE, LLC have added (in dBASE Plus 2.7, and available in current versions of dBASE) a few properties of the application object to make it easier to access and use these files and paths. It should be noted that these properties will be correctly set under Windows XP, Windows Vista, Windows 7, etc., based on the CSIDL paths as described above.

The initialization file (.INI) file can be referenced by using:

```
_app.IniFile
```

If your application needs to modify the .INI file, this should be the one in the users' private folder structure *(unless installed on Windows XP, in which case it will be the one in the same folder as the .exe file)*. If your application needs to make changes to a .INI file anywhere else will need to be explicitly referenced. Using this property to reference the location of the .INI file can make it easier in your code, rather than checking to see which operating system is being used, and so on.

The folder where shared files are stored may be found using (data, etc.):

```
_app.allUsersPath
```

This can be used if you need to copy files to another location.

The path to the users' private folder can be found using:

```
_app.currentUserPath
```

If your application is set up to work for roaming users, the users' private folder can be found here:

```
_app.roamingUsersPath
```

INI File

As noted above, the initialization file must be in a specific location for the application to find it. If it is not there, the runtime engine will create a very simple .INI file with just the items required for the runtime to work. There is a discussion on the location of the .INI file later in this chapter.

You can modify the .INI file within your application to store preferences for how the application works, to store information required by the application for various reasons, and so on. You can create your own routines to read/write to the .INI file, but you can also use code in the dBASE Users' Function Library to do the work (ini.cc). Using the path stored by the runtime in the application object as shown above (_app.IniFile) will make it easy to modify the correct version of the file.

It should be noted that you can have your application load a specific .INI file by passing a parameter (-c) when you run the application. See the OLH for more details.

User BDE Aliases

User BDE Aliases take a bit more work understanding. Up until the current versions of dBASE, BDE Aliases were added through the BDE Administrator to the IDAPI.CFG file – either by your installer, or by code in the application to update the file.

The problem with this now is that the standard installation of the BDE, stores the IDAPI.CFG file in a folder that may be read-only *(or require administrator rights to modify)*. Unless the aliases are created in your installer, once everything is installed, your application will have a hard time modifying the IDAPI.CFG file because the user may not have permission to write to that folder in program code without some extra effort.

To avoid those issues there are a couple of ways your application can create what are called *User BDE Aliases*. These were created by the developers of dBASE in order to make it possible to bypass the rights issues with the BDE.

As a developer, one useful aspect of User BDE Aliases is that while you can have, on your installation, a standard BDE alias defined via the BDE Administrator (or code) and stored in the IDAPI.CFG file, User BDE Aliases actually take precedence. What this means is that in your test environment you can have a path to the data that is stored in the "old" way, and in your deployed application User BDE Aliases will be used, despite anything set up in the .CFG file.

To help explain a little better – when testing User BDE Aliases myself, I have an application on my computer that I was testing with. The application uses a couple of BDE Aliases, both stored in the usual way, via the BDE Administrator in the IDAPI.CFG file. However, when testing the actual application, my .INI file has User BDE Aliases with the exact same alias names, but different file paths *(I was testing the standard Windows file structure)*. The executable ignored the settings in the IDAPI.CFG file, and modified data in the paths specified by the User BDE Aliases.

If you install dBASE Plus (itself, not a deployed application) to Windows XP, the default BDE Aliases ("Samples", "Contax", etc.) will be stored in the IDAPI.CFG file. On Windows Vista, Windows 7, etc., these aliases are created as User BDE Aliases.

An application deployed to a Windows XP computer using the dBASE Plus Runtime engine for dBASE Plus 2.7 and later can use User BDE Aliases stored in the application's .INI file (or using the other method shown below). This means that you do not have to write your code differently if your application may be deployed to different operating systems.

Using the .INI File

One method to create User BDE Aliases is to add information into the application's .INI file. These can be added to the .INI file in a few ways, the Inno Setup program has the ability to add information to a .INI file, including paths used during the installation.

The following is the basic structure of how you define your aliases in the .INI file:

```
[UserBDEAliases]
0=MyAlias
[MyAlias]
Driver=DBASE
Options=PATH: "C:\ProgramData\MyCompany\MyApplication\Tables"
```

The first section heading (UserBDEAliases) is where you define each alias you need. If you need more than one, the second would start with the number 1 instead of the number 0.

```
1=MySecondAlias
```

Repeat for as many aliases as you need to define, incrementing the number.

The second section is the definition of the specific alias. It must have both lines – which database you are using (the default is "DBASE"), and then the "Options" line, which gives the path to the database.

If you have a second alias, you would have a second section in the same format as shown above, repeating for any others.

One difficulty is that dBASE itself does not have a way to get the path to the database, if you need it. This can be dealt with and when we get to it later in this book, it will be discussed.

User BDE Aliases can be created in your installer, and when we get to the chapter on deploying your application we will look at this in more depth.

It should be noted here *(this will be discussed in later chapters as well)* that User BDE Aliases added via the application's .INI file are loaded when the application (or dBASE Plus) loads and reads the .INI file to the default session object (_app.session). If you need to use these in another session, you need to add them to the session object as described below.

Using the Session Object's addAlias() Method

The _app object has a default session object, and the session object has a new method called *addAlias()*. This method requires three parameters, the name of the alias, the database type, and the path to the data. An example, using the alias shown in the example for the .INI file:

```
_app.session.AddAlias( "MyAlias", "dBASE",;
  "PATH:C:\ProgramData\MyCompany\MyApplication\Tables" )
```

(The above would be either one statement, or the semicolon can be added – as shown – in your program code to break the line-up but be treated as one statement. More details on that in the chapter on programming …)

If your application uses session objects besides the default, you can use the *addAlias()* method in the same fashion. These alias references would disappear once the session object is deactivated and released.

The *addAlias()* method can be used "on-the-fly" in your application if you need a temporary BDE Alias to reference a folder, for placing temporary tables or for specific processing for your application.

Windows Vista, Windows 7 and the UAC

The biggest change in Windows from Windows XP was the addition of the User Account Control (UAC) in Windows Vista. The UAC became a bit less intrusive in Windows 7, but is still there.

The UAC was created by Microsoft to add security to Windows, to protect users from poorly designed applications causing corruption, to protect users from programs designed to wreak havoc on their computers (malware, viruses, etc.), and so on.

In order for this to work, basically even a standard "Administrator" user does not always have full control of the computer, requiring an administrator to respond to prompts that were not required prior to using Windows Vista. *(See discussion at the beginning of this chapter on Administrator rights.)* This can be very frustrating to an application developer who is used to writing applications that work in certain ways, as Windows often now prevents some things and makes others much harder.

dBASE developers have been struggling with the UAC ever since Windows Vista was released *(and continuing into Windows 7)*, including turning off the main UAC routine itself as a solution to some of the problems. Interestingly, there are aspects to Windows security that turning off the UAC did not resolve, which made things even more interesting for developers. It is likely that Windows 8 *(and later versions of Windows)* will continue to use the UAC. While I am not a big fan of the UAC, my recommendation is to stop turning it off.

The R&D team at dBASE, LLC have been working to make it easier for the developer, starting with dBASE Plus 2.7.

In the first and second editions of this book I put some effort into showing how a developer could work *around* the UAC (including registry changes, permissions on folders, and more).

I decided when updating the book for the 3rd Edition to take a different tack, and instead show how to use the new abilities provided by the dBASE R&D team to make your applications work more smoothly *with* the Windows UAC, rather than work around it.

What Happens When a dBASE Application Starts?

In the first chapter I described the basics of what happens when dBASE itself runs the first time. The following is what a compiled dBASE application (e.g. "MyApp.exe") using the dBASE Runtime engine does when it is run for the first time. *(All of the following are based on Windows Vista and later – Windows XP does not have the UAC, and so a dBASE application acts like it did previously – it does not copy the .INI file as noted below. There is a brief discussion of what happens with Windows XP after this.)*

It should be noted that the following assumes the application is deployed to the appropriate folder structure you have determined. *(There is more discussion of the expected / suggested locations of files earlier in this chapter.)*

When your application starts the following sequence of events occurs:

1. If one does not exist, it creates a private user folder for the application (referenced by the path CSIDL_LOCAL_APPDATA). On a typical installation, this will be *(using the American/English folder structure for Windows)*:

    ```
    C:\Users\<username>\AppData\Local\your_application_structure
    ```

    "<username>" is the name of the user logged in to Windows, and "your_application_structure" is the path to your .exe from the root of the hard drive, or from the Program Files location.

    What is meant by this last statement is if your application is run from:

    ```
    C:\MyCompanyName\MyApplication
    ```

    The structure that will be created under the user's private folders will match inside the "Local" folder – in other words:

    ```
    C:\Users\<username>\AppData\Local\MyCompanyName\MyApplication
    ```

    If your application is run from:

    ```
    C:\Program Files (x86)\MyCompanyName\MyApplication
    ```

    The structure under the user's private folders will be the same as the previous example.
2. Look in the folder containing the executable (.exe) file for an application's .INI file (CSIDL_PROGRAM_FILES), for example:

    ```
    C:\Program Files (x86)\MyCompanyName\MyApplication
    ```

    and if it does not exist there, look in the folder your data is in, e.g.:

    ```
    C:\ProgramData\MyCompanyName\MyApplication\Data
    ```

    In any case, the following will occur:
    a. If found and there is no matching .INI file in the users' private folder (CSIDL_LOCAL_APPDATA), copy to the user's private folder as above.

    b. If not found, and there is no matching .INI file in the users' private folder, create a .INI file in the user's private folder as above.

    c. The path to the .INI file is stored in the application object's (_app) *IniFile* property, so that it can be referenced as needed by your application.

3. If there is already a .INI file that matches the name of the executable in the private user's folder path, then the runtime engine will not do any of the options in step 2 above.

4. If your .INI file contains User BDE Aliases, these will be read and set up according to internal mechanics, and used with your application. These are not stored in the IDAPI.CFG file, which is interesting.

It should be noted that if your .INI file has a switch set to not use the BDE at all, then any User BDE Aliases would not be loaded, etc.

 NOTE

If, when creating the application, the BUILD command is given the option *INI ROAM*, the path used for the "users' private folder" will be in the Windows roaming path instead. The *roaming* option is useful for a network application where a user may log in to different computers on the network, as opposed to on an individual workstation.

For this to work properly, the network has to be configured to allow for roaming users, and you will need to work with the network administrator for this.

What About Windows XP?

As Windows XP does not work with the UAC, the steps mentioned above (specifically dealing with looking for and copying the .INI file to the appropriate folders, and checking for private user folders, etc.) will not occur.

The application will look in the folder containing the .EXE for the .INI file by the same name (i.e., "MyApp.exe" will look for "MyApp.ini" in the same folder) and if it does not exist, the executable will create a simple .INI file with just the items needed by the runtime.

If User BDE Aliases are used and stored in the application's .INI file, they will be loaded when the application reads the .INI file on startup. User BDE Aliases are not specific to applications run on versions of Windows that use the UAC, and dBASE applications can use them no matter what operating system they are installed on *(starting with dBASE Plus 2.7 and later, of course)*.

Speaking of the BDE

The Borland Database Engine under the UAC causes some interesting issues. Some of these can be dealt with, with the information given above. Developers used to using code in the dBASE Users' Function Library (dUFLP) to work with the BDE (BDEAlias.cc) will find that some of that doesn't work as well under the UAC *(see discussion at the beginning of this chapter on Administrator rights)*. However, the developers at dBASE have included code that you can use in your application that will work with the BDE Aliases (qBDEMgr.cc), and end-user developers have created code in the dUFLP that can work around these limitations (ccs_BDE.cc). Use of this code will be discussed in greater detail in various chapters of this book.

To manually create BDE Aliases you would use the BDE Administrator. To ensure it is run "As Administrator" every time, from the Start Menu, open the dBASE Plus folder, then right click on the "BDE Administrator" icon. Select "Properties" from the popup menu, and click on "Compatibility". On that tab at the bottom is a checkbox that says "Run this program as an administrator" – check this box, and click "OK". If you deploy the BDE Administrator with your application, you may want to be sure the Manifest file deployed has the "requireAdministrator" setting.

As noted throughout this chapter and this book, there are other methods of working with the BDE and aliases.

On another note, some applications do not rely on using the BDE at all. If that is the case, you can place a setting in your application's .INI file:

```
[DataEngine]
DefaultEngine=NONE
```

When your executable runs, the runtime engine will see this setting and not load *(or even attempt to find)* the Borland Database Engine.

It should be noted that if your application uses tables at all (local tables or other), you must use (for now).

Code Signing

Current versions of Windows (and the UAC specifically) look for digital signatures stored in the applications being run. This is called "Code Signing". The idea is that this provides more security, as the developer has to pay for a certificate, which is checked against a database of "authorized developers" by Windows. The UAC will run an application that has been Code Signed without asking the end-user if it is safe to run. If the application has *not* been Code Signed, then the UAC will require that the user confirm they wish to run the application and that they trust the developer. This can be annoying.

dBASE itself has been modified so that if you choose to Code Sign your executable, it will store the appropriate information in the way the UAC is designed to look for it. If you choose not to, it will build the executable without that information, which means it will not cause issues. However, as noted, if the UAC is enabled on the computer the application is being run on, the user will be required to confirm the application is "safe".

This topic will be discussed a bit more in the chapters dealing with deploying an application.

Windows Registry Settings

If your application needs to write to the Windows Registry, any changes should be in the HKEY_CURRENT_USER node in the registry. Changes to other locations may not be accepted by the registry and may cause some issues with your application. We will discuss this in later chapters of the book as well. If your application writes to the SOFTWARE key, you will want to be sure to use the WOW6432Node:

```
HKEY_LOCAL_MACHINE\SOFTWARE\Wow6432Node\...
```

as mentioned elsewhere in this chapter.

Installing Your Application

The chapter of the second volume of this book that deals with deploying an application gets into very specific details, and gives examples from a working installation.

Inno Setup (a free installer used by the Project Explorer, as well as many dBASE developers to deploy applications) is very flexible and very powerful. It allows your installation to set up the .INI, even set up registry settings (although there may be some issues with that).

This will be discussed at some length in the appropriate chapter(s).

Don't Wish To Use the UAC?

When you deploy your application, it is possible to place an entry in the Windows Registry for the "useUACPaths" setting. If you do *not* wish your application to work with the UAC, you can do so *(this is not recommended, but ...)*. The installer can create this key, or you can set it yourself. It should be noted that if your application is installed on a Windows XP computer, the useUACPaths setting will be automatically set to "N" (per below). All of this is according to the R&D team at dBASE.

The key to be used is:

```
HKEY_LOCAL_MACHINE\SOFTWARE\dBASE\PLUS\RuntimeApps\app
filename\useUACPaths
```

If your application's .exe file is named: MyApp.exe, then the key would be:

```
HKEY_LOCAL_MACHINE\SOFTWARE\dBASE\PLUS\RuntimeApps\MyApp.exe\useUACPaths
```

It should be noted that the path will vary depending on the version of Windows you are using – if you are using a 32-bit version of Windows, the path will match what is shown above. If you are using the 64-bit version of Windows, the path will include an extra bit:

```
HKEY_LOCAL_MACHINE\SOFTWARE\Wow6432Node\dBASE\PLUS\RuntimeApps\MyApp.exe\u
seUACPaths
```

This occurs for 32-bit applications running on the 64-bit version of Windows. (WOW in this case stands for "Windows on Windows", which as Marty Kay from dBASE tells me is the compatibility layer that runs 32-bit function calls from applications into native 64 bit function calls on 64-bit versions of Windows.)

The value stored in the key is either "Y" (or "y") or "N" (or "n"). Using the letter "Y" (the default value) will set the value of the application object (_app) property useUACPaths to *TRUE*. If the value stored in the registry key is "N", the value in the _app.useUACPaths property will be set to *FALSE*.

You can achieve the same thing by passing a parameter to your executable (when you run it) – the parameter is –v, and if followed by the number 1 it will set the _app.useUACPaths property to *TRUE*, if set to zero, it will set it to *FALSE.* This would be done by calling your application this way:

```
MyApp.exe -v0
```

There is more information on this by using the OLH (Online Help) and searching for "useUACPaths".

This is useful in the case of a developer deploying multiple applications on the same computer, where some may be using the UAC and one doesn't.

Other Considerations

Partitioning of Hard Drives

One developer, when discussing this chapter, mentioned how important it is to partition the hard drives you are working on. Honestly, the first two types of developers *(mentioned at the beginning of the chapter)* have little control over this in a lot of cases. For your own computers, of course you have that kind of control. You can decide to partition your drives, to set up one partition that is data-only, and so on. But you have little control over your clients' setup if you are an independent developer (you may be able to suggest some things as "best practices") if you work for a company, then the IT department is in charge of this kind of thing. I am not real sure how much it affects the development of applications exactly, except perhaps for where your data is stored.

The primary reason this was brought up was data security. If the data is stored on a partition that *isn't* the operating system and other programs, then data recovery becomes easier in the case of a disaster. You can also back up the partition if the operating system needs to be recovered you do not need to worry about losing the data.

Data Execution Prevention (DEP)

Windows for some time has had built into it a program called DEP (it is actually in many operating systems, not just Windows, and it is in a lot of hardware these days as well). This is a security measure that is meant to prevent applications accessing protected memory on the computer. The concern is an application overwriting important data stored in memory. There is a lot of detail on the web about this, if you care to research it.

You need to at least be aware of it, because on some computers, you need to deal with DEP. Some computers will incorrectly block dBASE from loading properly. (According to the dBASE support website, this is largely due to the use of the Borland Database Engine's language driver protocol, which is integral to the use of the BDE.)

To modify the DEP to allow for your application, dBASE, etc., to work with the DEP:

- Click the Start Button
- Right Click on "Computer" (or "My Computer" for older operating systems)
- Select "Properties" in the popup menu (you may need to click "Advanced Properties" to get the next dialog)
- Click "Advanced" on the "System Properties" dialog
- Select the "Settings" button in the "Performance" section
- Click the "Data Execution Prevention" tab in the "Performance Options" dialog

Under Windows 7 (at least on my machine) the option that is currently the best one is:

"Turn on DEP for essential Windows programs and services only"

This works fine with dBASE, dBASE executables (applications using the dBASE runtime engine), and the BDE. I have not had issues with DEP on this computer. On some OSes you may need to do the following:

- Click "Turn on DEP for all programs and services except those I select:"
- Click the "Add" button
- Add the individual programs necessary (such as: plusrun.exe, plus.exe, bdeadmin.exe)
- Click "OK" to close the dialog (repeat for each dialog ...)
- If necessary reboot the computer

Application Compatibility Toolkit (ACT)

Another security issue you may want to be aware of is the Application Compatibility Toolkit (ACT). This is available from Microsoft's website. I hesitate to give a specific URL as things shift around a lot on the web. If you search for "Application Compatibility Toolkit", you will find quite a few entries. At this time, I am unclear as to how much you may need to rely on this.

Summary

As you can see, there is a lot that needs to be considered when creating an application and deploying it. A good portion of the changes in this edition of the book *(besides layout and appearance)* are specifically aimed at these issues, and as you work through the book, hopefully between this overview and the examples and information given throughout the book, your application will be more compatible with Windows and the UAC.

Special thanks to the following for their feedback, ideas, and help with this chapter *(in no particular order)*: Bruce Beacham, Ronnie MacGregor, Gerald Lightsey, Andrew Shimmin, Rick Miller, Christopher F. Neumann, Emilio Vilaro, Marty Kay (of dBASE, LLC).

NOTES

Part II: Data

Working with data is what a database software package such as dBASE is all about. The next few chapters will take a look at working with data in dBASE PLUS.

Chapter 3: Table Types

dBASE has always used a specific table format called a .DBF (DataBase File). Through the use of the Borland Database Engine (BDE), the Windows versions of dBASE have always assumed the Paradox table type (.DB) to be a native table type. With the 32-bit version of the BDE, Borland added FoxPro table support (also using a .DBF file extension), which is treated as a local table type, although there are some problems with the implementation of support for the index format (.CDX). It should be noted that to use FoxPro tables in dBASE, you will be better off using the ODBC drivers provided by Microsoft for Visual FoxPro tables. While the BDE accepts these as "native" tables, the implementation is not good.

As we will see in later chapters, dBASE can, via the BDE, access many types of tables. However, the dBASE, Paradox and FoxPro table types are the only three that are considered to be "native" to dBASE, meaning that no special drivers are necessary to use them.

This chapter and for the most part, this book will focus largely on the native DBF table format. There is information available in several places, including the online help for dBASE, the Knowledgebase at the dBASE website, and the online help for the BDE about other table formats.

Over time, the DBF table has gone through some changes in capability. The BDE can work with level 3 (dBASE III/III+), level 4 (dBASE IV), level 5 (dBASE 5.0 for Windows, Visual dBASE 5.x) and level 7 (Visual dBASE 7.0 through dBASE PLUS) versions of the DBF table format. The only one that it can't work with is the level 2 (dBASE II) – the original dBASE table format. There is information in the appendices (in Vol. II) showing differences between the various table formats.

By default when you install dBASE, it assumes you will want to work with the latest version of the DBF table as the default, so it sets the level to 7. You can change this, using the BDE Administrator, if you need to. As the DBF table format is the real native table type for dBASE, we will focus on this. By default when you create a table in dBASE it is a DBF table, and when you tell dBASE to open a table, it assumes it will be a DBF, unless it is told otherwise.

Should I Change the Table Level?

The only reason you might be concerned with changing the table level in the BDE is if an application you are working on, or some tables you wish to modify, MUST remain at a specific level if you alter the table structure (or create/modify indexes). Notice however that you can edit data, add new rows, delete rows, etc., in a table that is of a lower level without ever having to change the settings in the BDE. As an example, if the BDE is set to level 7, and you are working with a table that is level 4, you may need to change the level setting in the BDE, depending on what you wish to do.

The only commands or actions that you take on a table where it is necessary to force the settings to a different table level are:

- Changing the field structure of a table – adding, removing, renaming fields (using the table designer or the ALTER TABLE command).
- Adding a new index tag, modifying an index tag, removing an index tag.

If you are creating an application that may need to perform either of the actions above on tables of a level lower than the current setting, you should make sure that the BDE table level is set properly before performing those actions. However, if all your application does is create, read, update and delete (CRUD – the four basic functions of persistent storage) data in tables, then you should not be real concerned with this.

Terminology

When discussing tables sometimes the terminology can get confusing. This can often be attributed to some poor documentation in early versions of dBASE and some other software. The term "database" was sometimes used for what are really tables, which causes some difficulty when developers talk to each other.

A *database* is a collection of tables. When discussing local tables, a database is a reference to the folder that tables are in. When discussing SQL Server tables, the term "database" references the file that contains the tables. In either case, the term "database" should not be confused with the term "table".

A *table* consists of *rows* or *records*. These rows or records contain information about a single entity, such as a person, place or thing.

Each *row* or *record* is broken down into *fields*. A field is one piece of information, such as a last name, a phone number, a zip code, the individual price of an item, etc. A field can be considered a *column*, as well.

Each *field* is defined by a *type* – this describes the kind of information, such as a date, a character value, a numeric value, etc. that is stored in the field.

Each field is also described in more detail by the *width* of the field, and in the case of numeric values, the number of digits to the right of the decimal point.

The dBF Field Types

dBASE has defined quite a range of field types. The following is a short description of each of the types of fields that can be used in a DBF. This chart is taken from the dBASE Help with a few additional notes:

Field Type	Default Size	Maximum Size	Index Allowed?	Allowable Values
Character	10 characters	254	Yes	All keyboard characters, and characters in the ANSI/ASCII character set.
Numeric	10 digits, 0 decimal	20 digits	Yes	Positive or negative numbers the maximum size must include the digits to the right of the decimal, the decimal point itself, and if necessary, a minus (-) sign to show the number is negative.
Float	10 digits, 0 decimal	20 digits	Yes	Positive or negative numbers. Identical to Numeric; maintained for compatibility
Long	4 bytes	N/A	Yes	Signed 32 bit integer, range approximately +/- 2 billion. Optimized for speed.
Double	8 Bytes	N/A	Yes	Positive or negative number. Optimized for speed.
Autoincrement	4 bytes	N/A	Yes	Contains long integer values in a read-only (non-editable field, beginning with the number 1 and automatically incrementing up to approximately 2 billion. Deleting a row does not change the field values of other rows. Be aware that adding an autoincrement field will pack the table.
Date	8 Bytes	N/A	Yes	Any date from AD 1 to AD 9999
Timestamp	8 Bytes	N/A	Yes	Date/Time stamp, including the Date format plus hours, minutes, and seconds, such as HH:MM:SS
Logical	1 Byte	N/A/	No	True (T, t), false (F, f) yes (Y, y) and no (N, n)
Memo	10 Bytes	N/A	No	Usually just text, but all keyboard characters; can contain binary data (but using binary field is preferred)
Binary	10 Bytes	N/A	No	Binary files (sound and image data, for example)
OLE	10 Bytes	N/A	No	OLE objects from other Windows Applications

Other table types will have different field types available to them, and they may have different limitations on the field types.

Field Properties

The Table Designer in dBASE (which we will get to in a bit) allows you to define values for some field properties that affect the field for all rows in the table.

As many other table types do not use these properties, it may not be a good idea to rely on them yourself, particularly if you are planning on making your application one that can be upsized to other database formats. However, the warnings aside, the following are the properties that you can define for a field in a dBASE level 7 DBF table:

default – allows you to set a default value – this value is what is stored in the field when a new row is added to the table. The user can change it, but if they do not choose to do so, the value defined here will be stored in the table. One special thing that can be done is with date and timestamp field types – you can use the words TODAY or NOW to specify that the current date or date/time is stored in the field by default (meaning that when a new row is added, the current date or date/time value will be stored in the field).

maximum – you can define a maximum value for a field. This could be in the case of a character field a value of "Z" which would not allow a user to enter any character with an ANSI value greater than that of the letter "Z" (in a single character field – for more characters, you might want to place the number of letters here that match the length/width of the field). For a numeric field, you could store a maximum numeric value here.

minimum – the smallest value that can be stored in the field. This is very much like the *maximum* above, except that it sets a lower boundary to what can be entered into the field.

required – this can be null (the default), *true* or *false*. If this is set to *true*, it means that a user *must* enter a value in this field – it can never be left empty.
Custom – you can create custom field properties for a field. These have limited use in a table, and should most likely be avoided. While some developers have found them to be useful, as the chances are great that other table formats (or other software that might use your table) will not recognize these, it is probably best to not create a lot of custom properties for a field, and instead rely on custom code *(a topic that will be discussed in great length in later chapters of this book)*.

Null Values

When the dBASE level 7 table format was created by the folk at Borland, International, they decided to do something that has flummoxed many dBASE developers over the years. Some developers have argued it was a bad idea, but it is "the way things work", and whether you think it is a bad idea, a good idea, or don't really care, it is part of the definition.

When a new row is added to a table, most of the field types default to a value of *null*. If you are not really familiar with this concept, you might simply assume that this is not any different than what was done with earlier versions of DBF tables, which was to default to a value of "blank" in the case of character and date fields, or other values (*false* for logical, zero (0) for numeric ...) in the case of other field types.

"Blank" is not the same as "null". "Blank" in the case of a character field is as if you stored "" to a field. If you do that, you still store a value to the field. The value *null* is literally "nothing".

This gets even more confusing, because in older DBF formats, a new row would default to "zero" (0) for a numeric field, and *false* for a logical type, and an "empty" date for a date type.

The DBF 7 table format stores *null* in character, numeric and logical field types by default when you add a new row, while date and datetime fields are still empty.

This causes difficulties if your programs try to do something with these values, such as combining two character fields. For example, if you have the fields "FirstName" and "LastName" in a table, and you want to combine the two values in a report, you could try:

```
FirstName+LastName
```

However, if one (or both) of these fields contain a *null* value, what is returned is a *null* value. If, instead, they had a "blank" value, you would get the contents of the non-blank field. The phrase that is often used in the dBASE community is:

"Any-value plus *null* returns *null*."

This is similar to the mathematical concept that any value multiplied by zero is going to return the value zero.

There are ways around this issue that will be discussed in later chapters of this book, but you should be aware of it early on.

A *null* value in a numeric field can cause difficulties in some cases, but actually resolve some issues in others. If using older DBF table formats, and performing a calculation such as an Average on the values in a field in a table, the value zero (0) would actually throw the calculation off. However, using a *null* value means that the average might actually be more accurate, because the software sees *null* and doesn't add it into the calculation at all.

A *null* value in a logical field often confuses programmers – up until the level 7 table format, a logical value was either *true* or *false*. Now a logical field can be *true*, *false*, or *null*.

Dates (and now timestamp fields) still default to a blank value, because there is no way to set a *null* for those field types. Memo fields are a bit confusing on this, because testing for *null* in a memo can return unexpected results.

So, how do you, as a programmer, deal with the null value in a field? One way around this issue is to set a default value for each field type – as noted earlier in this chapter, that can be a bad idea as some software that might use your table(s) will not recognize the default property; and if you are planning on upsizing to a different database engine, again that engine may not recognize the default property.

Some functionality was added to dBASE that can change the behavior of the automatic filling of fields with *null* values (SET AUTONULLFIELDS ON/OFF or using the rowset's *autoNullFields* property). You may wish to examine these in the online help if you need this behavior.

The last and as a programmer probably best solution is simply to be aware of this issue, and know that it can come up. There are many ways to deal with each situation, and you may find in the long run that the automatic null can work in your favor.

Field Names

dBASE allows you to use field names in a DBF7 table with very few restrictions – you can use spaces, you can use underscores, and you can use letters and numbers. Your fieldnames can be up to 31 characters long in DBF7 tables. Other table types may have different restrictions. However there are some limitations.

- The first character must be a letter.
- Some characters may cause difficulties, and require the use of the colon (:) delimiter around the fieldname, including spaces in the fieldname in some parts of your code:

  :My Field Has Spaces:

  In some parts of your code you will need to reference the field differently, see Chapter 4.

- You should not use reserved words in dBL and SQL as the names of fields in a table. This can cause some difficulties. While the designer may allow you to create a field named "Date", for example, "Date" is a key word in dBASE (used for the name of a class, and also as the name of a function). If you have tables that use keywords already, you may want to modify the way you use them in your code. Such things as:

  :Date:

Will not necessarily work, but:

```
q.sql := "select FirstName, Lastname, MyTable.'date' from MyTable"
```

should work.

A complete listing of reserved words for local SQL that should be avoided when naming tables is in the online help, one under Reserved Words. For dBL, you should avoid using words that are commands, but otherwise you may be okay.

Table Language Drivers

A language driver is used to tell dBASE, the BDE, and applications that use your table(s) more about how to work with the tables based on the characters that are (or may be) stored in the table. This is most important when creating *indexes* and sorting data. We will discuss indexes shortly ...

What gets confusing about language drivers are the vast quantity of them. This is because there have been attempts to create as many useful language drivers as possible. Why so many? Mostly because different languages have different requirements for sorting characters, and some languages use characters that other languages do not.

For example, English does not use characters such as Ü, but German and many other languages do. Some of the ability to work with these characters comes from Windows, but it was possible to work with many of these language-specific characters in the older DOS programs.

This confuses the issue even more. DOS programs use what is called the ASCII character set. Many programmers got to be quite familiar with this character set, and how the characters were "mapped". Each character has a numeric value associated with it, from 0 to 255.

When Windows came along it introduced the ANSI character set *(see the Appendices for an ANSI chart)*. This is a bit more flexible, and while still using numeric values from 0 to 255, the characters that were mapped to the numbers from 128 through 255 are often different than those in the ASCII set.

In addition, in order to handle languages that have more characters such as Japanese (Kanji, etc.), Chinese, and others, there is what is called UNICODE, which doubles the size of the character set available if using those languages. *(As I am completely unfamiliar with issues dealing with these languages, I will not be discussing them here, other than to make you aware of them.)*

The language drivers contain very specific information about how characters are sorted. For most of the language drivers a programmer will see very little difference, but some have *very* specific rules for what characters sort where in a list.

What has all this to do with DBF tables? Well, everything really. When you installed dBASE, it installed the BDE, which has some default values. The default language driver for dBASE tables is either 'W Europe' ANSI, or it is 'ASCII' ANSI, depending on how the installer is set up.

While it is fine to use the default driver in most cases, if your application will be used primarily Spanish speaking people with Spanish characters, you might want to use the language driver "'Spanish' ANSI". This would ensure that any special requirements for the Spanish language were met and possibly some characters would be mapped to the keyboard appropriately.

When you create your tables for your applications, you should determine what language driver is most useful for your situation. For most of my own applications I have found that 'W Europe' ANSI works perfectly fine for my needs, and there have been no complaints from my users. However, most of the users of my applications are in the U.S.

Indexes

The DBF table format uses a means of sorting the information in a table called an *index*. What is an index? It is a way of sorting the data, allowing for automatic updates of the sort sequence, without having to re-sort the data all the time.

With the old DOS .NDX files, you still had to "reindex" the data – this would rebuild the index files – after you modified the data (added data, edited fields in the indexes, or deleted data).

When dBASE IV for DOS came along, the developers added what is called a Production or Master Index. This is a way of storing up to 47 index *tags* in one file. An index *tag* serves the same purpose of a .NDX file, but with the ability to store these in a single index file (with an extension of .MDX), we also have the ability to not have to rebuild the index tags or be concerned about the index tags being updated *(most of the time, anyway – there may be times you need to do this, but they should be rare)*.

This means that we can keep all of our associated indexes in one place, and not have to automatically rebuild them each time the data is modified.

Now, all of that said, what exactly is the purpose of an index?

It is a means of telling dBASE to display the data in a specific sequence, based on, among other things, the language driver *(see the discussion earlier in this chapter)*, and a field or fields, or a dBL expression involving fields in the table.

An index tag can be ascending or descending in sequence, it can be based on a single field in a table, multiple fields in a table, or indeed, as mentioned earlier, it can be a dBASE Language (dBL) expression. One thing to note about ascending and descending: a dBASE index tag can either be one or the other, not a combination. It is possible when using the Paradox table type (specifically when using Paradox itself, as the table designer in dBASE does not allow this) to define an index that has one field ascending, and another descending. While there may be perfectly good reasons for doing this, dBASE indexes cannot be set this way.

What kind of expression would you want to use for an index? The simplest one, and probably most common, is to index the data on the upper case version of the contents of a field. The reason? If the data contains values that begin with lower case letters and with upper case letters, the data will actually sort in a way you might not expect. Most language drivers place upper case letters first, then lower case letters. Hence, you could have a series of names such as:

> Adams
>
> Clarke
>
> vanVogt
>
> Zelazny

However, if you sort the data, rather than "van Vogt" being *before* "Zelazny", it would end up after it:

> Adams
>
> Clarke
>
> Zelazny
>
> vanVogt

This is because the last name starts with a lower-case letter *(if you examine the ANSI chart in this book, you will see that "v" has a higher ANSI number than "Z", so it ends up after "Z")*. If you told dBASE to use an expression that said to convert the contents of the field to upper case, and sort on *that* version of the data, it would place "van Vogt" before "Zelazny" as in the first version of the list.

> **📒 NOTE**
>
> By definition a dBASE index can only be either *ascending* or *descending*, and not mixed. However, a clever dBASE coder could create an index tag that gets around this. It does take some work. For example, you could create an index that was descending on the lastname, and ascending on numeric value with an expression like:
>
> ```
> lastname+str(1000000000 - ;
>     ANumericField,10,0,"0") descending
> ```
>
> Or you could create an index that was ascending on the lastname field, and descending on a date field:
>
> ```
> lastname+str({01/01/3000} - ;
>     ADateField,10,0,"0" ) ascending
> ```

There are many ways that we can create index tags, and this is just an overview.

Note that you can have 47 index tags in a production .MDX file. Each index tag expression must evaluate to no longer than 100 characters wide, although the expression itself can be up to 220 characters.

In addition, it is possible to use a .MDX index file that is not the default .MDX (which by definition has the same filename as the table – for example, if you have a table named AddressBook.dbf, the default MDX file is AddressBook.mdx), but for the most part this is not necessary, and the dBASE PLUS object model does not understand a production index that does not have the same name as the table.

Using BLOB Fields

A BLOB field is a "Binary Linked Object" field – a memo, a binary, or OLE field in a DBF. These values are actually stored in a .DBT file that is associated with the table – it has the same name as the table. So if your table was named "MyTable.dbf", and you used any of these types of field, you would also have a file called "MyTable.dbf".

It should be noted that even if you delete rows in a table that have memos or other BLOB fields associated with them, the values may still remain in the .DBT. This causes what is sometimes called "dBloat" – files that appear to just keep growing. One solution is to copy the table to a new table. The following code would work for a file in the current folder:

```
use MyTable
copy to NewTable with production // copy index tags
use
drop table MyTable
rename table NewTable to MyTable
// and if you had created a _dbaselock field - this is
// not necessary, otherwise:
use MyTable excl
convert
use
```

DBF Table Limits

There are some limits to table sizes, and such, the following list comes from a variety of sources, mostly it has been gleaned from the BDE help *(a more complete version of this information is in the appendices for this book)*.

dBASE Limitations

512	Open dBASE tables per system (BDE 4.01)
100	Record locks on one dBASE table
100	Records in transactions on a dBASE table
1	Billion records in a table
2	Billion bytes in .DBF (Table) file
32767	Size in bytes per record
1024	Number of fields per table
47	Number of index tags per .MDX file
10	Open master indexes (.MDX) per table
220	Key expression length in characters
31	Characters in a fieldname
254	Characters (letters, numbers, characters) in a character field

Table Design Guidelines

There are of course many ways to design tables, including having one huge table that has all your data in it. Pretty much anyone will tell you that this is the least efficient design. Here are a few things to consider:

Identify the Type of Information You Need to Store

It is a good idea to determine what is relevant data, and what is unnecessary. Many times an application ends up storing information that is not needed, and often distracts the user from the purpose of the application.

Take a good look at what is necessary, and what is not. For example, when dealing with a purchase from a store, do you really need to store the exact time of purchase? Do you need to know the name of the salesperson?

Break the Information Down

After you have determined what data is needed, it is a good idea to review the data, and break it down into groupings (such as persons, places and things). Identify the activities (events, transactions, etc.). In general, each table should contain one kind of entity or activity. The fields in each table would identify the parts of that entity or activity.

For example, if you are creating an ordering system for a store, you would need information about the customer, including name, address, etc., credit card(s), notes, etc. You would need to have information about the orders (order date, order number, sales, date, amount paid). For an individual order you might have multiple items, so you might need a table specifically listing the items ordered (product name, price, quantity ordered, etc.).

Determine the Relationships Among the Tables

You need to know how your tables relate to each other, and determine how you will make the relationship between the tables occur.

Each table should have a specific purpose. It is usually considered good form to have smaller tables and link them together, rather than storing everything in one large table. Keeping all the data in one table will mean having redundant data, and can become a bit of a maintenance headache for a developer or end-user.

In the case of an ordering system as noted above, storing everything in one table would mean that for each order that a customer made, you would be storing the customer name, address, etc. It gets even worse, because if *everything* was in one table, then for each line item – each item sold, you would be storing the customer name, address, etc., AND information about each order for each item sold.

Using multiple tables reduces the redundancy, by storing the information about each customer *once*, and the information about each order *once*, and so on. If you need to update the customer information, you only have to change it in one place, rather than for each item the customer ever ordered.

Relationships Between Tables

There are two types of relationships between tables: One-to-one and One-to-many.

Continuing with the ordering system concept, a customer can place several orders, and each order can contain one or more items. The relationship between the customer table and the order table is a one-to-one relationship, in that for each order there is only one customer. However, looked at from the other direction, each customer may have more than one order, so it could be called a one-to-many relationship.

Moving on, each order can have one or more items, which creates a one-to-many relationship.

There is a theoretical "Many-to-Many" relationship, but to make it work you have to have an "intermediate" table, which really ends up creating a "Many-to-One" relationship, and then a "One-to-Many" relationship.

Parent and Child Tables

When you create a relationship between two tables, one of those tables is called the *parent* table, and the other becomes the *child* table. As you select a row in the parent table, you see the corresponding child row or rows. When discussing a complex relationship you could take this too far and start talking about "grandparent" and "grandchild" tables, but that gets a bit silly.

By creating a link between the two tables, you can easily find rows in the child table that match the parent table. As an example, you can set up the customer table as a parent table, and the order table as a child table. This means that as you look at the customer data, you can see all of the orders from that customer.

In order to accomplish this, there is a unique field in the parent table, called the *linking field*, which is *linked to* from the child table. The link is established by creating an index on the linking field in the child table, and then establishing the link to the parent table.

In the example we've been discussing, a customer record will have a field that is unique – the customer number. For each order, we would then store the customer number in a field in the order table. For this to function properly there must be an index on the customer number in the order table. When the link is established, navigating in the customer (parent) table will show only the matching orders in the order (child) table.

This can be taken a step further, because the order table can also be a parent table, if a link is established between it and the line item table, which then becomes a child table of the orders table.

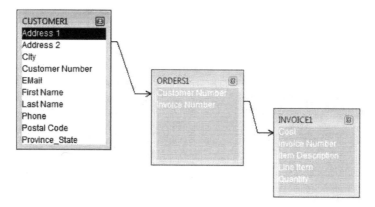

Figure 3-1

Normalization
This whole concept of reducing redundancy by using multiple tables is called *normalization*. There are many books out there on this concept and it is one that can easily confuse a developer. The main thing to remember when designing your tables is that you can keep the amount of redundant data to a minimum by using multiple tables, and creating links between the tables.

Other Terminology
When dealing with normalization there are terms that are often used. Some of these terms will be used in this book, and some may not, but you should at least be aware of them.

Entities – an entity is an element of the database, such as a person (a row in the Customer table), and Order (a row in the Order table), an Invoice Item (a row in the Invoice table), and so on. The important aspect of this is that each table contains in a single row information about a single entity.

Attributes – in more simple terms, the columns of the data that define an entity, or the fields of a row.

Primary Key – This is the primary field used to uniquely identify any given row in a table. Typically this is indexed. The two aspects that truly define a primary key in any table are:

1. It must have a unique value; and
2. It cannot be null or empty.

Primary Keys are typically indexed, and are sometimes referred to as Primary Indexes. In dBASE you can define a Primary Key on a dBASE level 7 table or a Paradox (.DB) table. Doing this will allow dBASE (through the database engine) to enforce the two rules defined above. You can optionally manually write code to enforce the integrity.

The easiest way to create a Primary Key on a table is to use an AutoIncrement field – by definition the field must contain a value, and by definition it must be unique. You can only have one AutoIncrement field in a table.

Foreign Key – This is a key in another table, used to link two tables together. In the sample shown in Figure 1, when referring to the Customer table, the foreign key would be the Customer ID field in the Orders table. A properly designed system will enforce the rule that the Foreign Key matches a value in the Primary Key of the parent table, or is null. If this is done, then you have Referential Integrity. Good RI rules ensure that it is impossible for a child row to point to a non-existent Primary Key in the parent table. (The way this normally happens is by deleting a parent row, but not removing any child rows associated with the parent row – called a *Cascading Delete*).

Referential Integrity

Referential Integrity (RI) is a way of stating rather concisely that your application ensures that the links between the tables (the references) are enforced.

dBASE tables (.DBF) can have some of this built in, but the way this was written into the BDE is apparently really flawed and setting referential integrity in the tables themselves can cause data corruption.

For the most part, as a programmer you would want to define what RI rules you needed, and then write the code to enforce them. This is where a data module can be very useful, because you can create your RI rules and the code that enforces them in one location, and not have to rewrite that code. *(We will discuss data modules in a later chapter of this book, and we will discuss referential integrity again there, with some code examples.)*

Making it Possible to "Upsize" to Other Platforms

As a developer, you may need to create applications that work on database platforms that you may not actually have (for example, the cost of Oracle is rather steep, so you may not own a copy yourself). However, you do not need to panic. You can develop an application using DBF tables and if designed properly, migrate directly to the Oracle tables for your client without having to change one line of your code.

Designing Your Tables and Application Appropriately

How is it possible to design an application that can work with native tables and with a SQL platform?

Some careful planning and design of your application will allow you to do what you need with minimal, if any, changes to your application.

One thing that will help is knowing what you can about the table format your application will "upsize" to. Do not use any features in your own tables that are not available in the other application. For example, dBASE has a field type called *logical* – many table formats do not have this type of field. If you know in advance that the database engine you will be working with does not have a logical field, you can work around this.

Field Morphing
There is a technique called Field Morphing that allows you to change the value used for a field based on the field's type.

A good example of this would be, as noted, the logical field. If you know that your client is using a database that does not use a logical field, you can simulate one, using Field Morphing. All databases use numeric data, so you could create a 1 digit wide numeric field. You could store in it only zeroes and ones. A zero would be *false*, a one would be *true*. Then, using field morphing, you could hook that field up to a checkbox on a form. The checkbox value can only be true or false, so you could use special code that told dBASE to treat a numeric value of zero as false, and a numeric value of 1 as true. When saving data back to the table, you could reverse that, telling dBASE to treat false as zero, and true as one.

Other Ways of Handling Different Fields
This kind of thing is great for some types of fields. For others, such as the dBASE AutoIncrement field, you may have to do something different. One technique that works is to actually use a second table to store a value in. When you save a row to the main table, you go to the secondary table, increment the value (add one), return that new value to your table, and store that in the field. We will look at some of this in a later chapter.

Some *(many)* SQL Server databases also use what are called *triggers*, which are basically similar to dBASE events. The problem is that since those triggers do not exist in the DBF table format, you can't simulate them with DBFs, so it may be easier to design your application without assuming the trigger functionality. Combining a trigger with a *stored procedure*, which is a way of creating specific code that is executed when a trigger fires, you can simulate an autoincrement field without *too* much effort.

All of the above assumes that you, the developer, do not have access to the database software while developing your application.

If you do have access to that software, then you can much more easily design your application to work with that format.

Summary

We have only briefly *(really)* covered quite a few concepts about tables, mostly the DBF table format as this is the default table type used in dBASE. We discussed table design concepts, normalization of data, and creating tables that can be *upsized* to a different data server than the one in dBASE. This should get you thinking about the next application you need to develop. Before you leap in, you might want to spend some time going back over some of the concepts in this chapter.

NOTES:

Chapter 4: SQL - A Different Language

What Is SQL and Why Is It Important?

SQL is a fairly universal and standardized language used to manipulate table, with commands that allow you to select the data, create tables, create indexes for tables, and more.

> SQL (correctly pronounced "ess cue ell," instead of the somewhat common "sequel") is a *data sublanguage* for access to relational databases that are managed by relational database management systems (RDBMS). Many books and articles "define" SQL by parenthetically claiming that the letters stand for Structured Query Language. While this was true for the original prototypes, it is not true of the standard. When the letters appear in product names, they have often been assigned this meaning by the product vendors, but we believe that users are ill-served by persuasions that the word "structured" accurately describes the language. The letters, by the way, don't stand for anything at all. They are not an abbreviation or an acronym, merely the result of the evolution of research projects. (Understanding the New SQL: A Complete Guide, Melton and Simon)

Most database software uses SQL in some fashion or other. You may find that some data engines have added their own enhancements to SQL, creating some non-standard commands or options for commands. However, at the base is a standard, the ANSI-92 definition of SQL.

Over time these standards have been ratified by the International Standards Organization as standard ISO 9075 (SQL92 - ANSI92) and extended via ISO 9075 Parts 1 thorough 10 (SQL2003, SQL2006, SQL2007, SQL2011). In addition complimentary standard ISO 13249 has been established to define structures & interfaces for Framework, Full-Text, Spatial, Still image & Data mining functionality.

dBASE uses, via the BDE, what is called Local SQL, which is a subset of the ANSI-92 standard definitions of SQL. The commands used in Local SQL can be used on all local table types, either in your programs, from the Command Window, or with the database objects that are defined in dBASE itself.

The reason that SQL is important in dBASE is that the database objects (which will be discussed in a later chapter) use local SQL to open tables, and extract data. In addition, a basic understanding of SQL will help if you, as mentioned in Chapter 2, need to "Upsize" your application to a SQL database server.

In addition to the discussion here, there are many other sources available that discuss SQL. When dBASE is installed, the Borland Database Engine folder (typically: Program Files\Common\Borland\BDE) has a file called "localsql.hlp", which can be used to learn both more about SQL and how it is implemented via the BDE. The book that I found the most useful when first learning SQL is: Understanding the New SQL: A Complete Guide, by Jim Melton and Alan R. Simon, Morgan Kaufmann Publishers, San Francisco, 1993, ISBN: 1-55860-245-3. *(This book may be out of print, but if you can find it, it is well worth the money, in my opinion.)*

The SQL SELECT Statement

The SELECT statement is the single most important command in SQL, because it is how you open tables, create connections between tables, set filters on tables, etc., in SQL. There are other commands used to create tables, modify table structures, create indexes, etc., but the SELECT statement is the one that actually allows you to open the table(s).

SQL commands, like dBASE's XBASE commands, are not generally case sensitive. In this chapter they are usually shown in all caps to differentiate them from the data, fields, etc., but you can use them in mixed case, all caps, all lower case, etc. You will find in most of this book that the commands tend to be all in lower case.

In this chapter you will see "Syntax" listings. When you do, brackets are shown (< and >) around the name of a value. For example: SELECT * FROM <tablename> – if you wanted to use the "FISH" table in the samples folder, you would replace "<tablename>" with "fish" (without the quotes) – the resulting command would look like: **SELECT * FROM fish**

When referring to Paradox tables, you may need to include the .DB table extension, and in some cases you may want to, or need to include the extension anyway.

When executing most of these commands, the table does not need to be opened. The examples should be fairly clear and most of them have been tested against the samples tables that ship with dBASE PLUS.

Many of the SELECT statement options return a result query, rather than opening the table directly as you might expect. This query is opened in dBASE as a temporary table, in the form of an alias with the name of SQL_<num>. Any table opened this way is not updatable *(it is read-only)*. If you are not sure, you can use code along these lines to find out:

```
// issue your select statement and then
// (replace <tablename> with the
// name of your table:
if ( <tablename> $ DBF() )
   // do whatever you want to do – it's updateable
else
   // it is read-only
endif
```

The term *columns* is used to reference the fields in a record and the term *rows* is used to reference records in a table (these are standard SQL terms).

If you see a pipe (|), it means you have an option for what to use (for example: "* | <fieldlist>" will mean that you can use either the wildcard for "all fields" or a list of specific fieldnames separated by commas).

If you see a command option in square brackets ([]), it means that this is optional, and is not required. This is often shown with the "WHERE" clause, i.e.,

```
SELECT * FROM <tablename> [WHERE <condition>]
```

In many of the examples below, in order to actually use the samples tables, their database aliases are used. The database alias is a pointer to a "database" and precedes the table. As an example, you may want to manipulate the FISH table in the DBASESAMPLES database.

To reference this table, it must be preceded with the database reference: ":dBASESamples:", i.e.,

```
SELECT * FROM :DBASESAMPLES:fish
```

Some columns in tables may have spaces or use SQL reserved words as the field names – in those cases, you need to reference them with the table name in front of them with a dot separator, and quotes around the field name. Example:

```
SELECT name, fish."length cm" FROM :DBASESAMPLES:fish
```

Now we have the basics of the syntax worked out, let's take a look at the way the SQL Select statement works in dBASE PLUS. If you wish to follow along, the commands shown can be typed into the Command Window in dBASE.

In order to shorten the command syntax a little, we are going to apply a trick that works in dBASE, both in code and in programs, using SQL Select statements and other commands (such as the XDML command "USE"), which is to open a database, allowing us to work with it without having to specify it each time (as in the examples shown above).

The command OPEN DATABASE <database> will open a database – you should use this command if you wish to follow along in this chapter and test the sample statements shown:

```
OPEN DATABASE DBASESAMPLES
```

This will open the database, but we can also point dBASE to that database, by using another command:

```
SET DATABASE TO DBASESAMPLES
```

This is particularly useful if you want to work with more than one database, you can issue the OPEN commands for each and then as you move from database to database, you can then issue the SET DATABASE command.

As noted earlier, the basic syntax of the SELECT statement is:

```
SELECT <column list> FROM <tablename>
```

If we wanted to open the FISH table, which is in the DBASESAMPLES database, with all the fields in the table, we would want to type:

```
SELECT * FROM FISH
```

In this case, the "*" acts as a wildcard – it tells the database engine that we wish to use all of the fields in the table. If you are following along and typing commands in at the Command Window, you will not have seen much happen. However, if you look at the status bar at the bottom of the screen, you will see: 

| fish.dbf | Row: 1/10 | Ins |

Figure 3-1

This tells us that the table is open, and that currently we are "on" (or pointing to) row 1 of 10 rows in the table.

How can you see the data? Various dBASE XDML commands will work here, such as LIST:

```
LIST
```

This will list the contents of the table on the screen. You should see something similar to:

```
Record#              ID Name                         Species
 Length CM Description Fish Image
         1              1 Clown Triggerfish              Ballistoides
conspicillu
     101.00 MEMO            BINARY
         2              2 Giant Maori Wrasse           Cheilinus undulatus
     228.00 MEMO            BINARY
         3              3 Blue Angelfish               Pomacanthus nauarchus
      30.00 MEMO            BINARY
         4              4 Ornate Butterflyfish         Chaetodon
Ornatissimus
      19.00 MEMO            BINARY
         5              5 California Moray             Gymnothorax mordax
     150.00 MEMO            BINARY
         6              6 Nurse Shark                  Ginglymostoma
cirratum
     400.00 MEMO            BINARY
         7              7 Spotted Eagle Ray            Aetobatus narinari
     200.00 MEMO            BINARY
         8              8 Yellowtail Snapper           Ocyurus chrysurus
      75.00 MEMO            BINARY
         9              9 Redband Parrotfish           Sparisoma
Aurofrenatum
      28.00 MEMO            BINARY
        10             10 Bluehead Wrasse             Thalassoma
bifasciatum
      15.00 MEMO            BINARY
```

Notice that the lines "wrap" inside the width of the command window.

If we only wanted to see two columns, such as Name and Length CM, we would do the following. Notice the syntax used for the Length CM field – because there is a space in the fieldname, we have to do it differently than the Name field:

```
select name, fish."length cm" from fish
```

Now if you issue a LIST command, you will see:

```
Record#   Name                      Length CM
       1  Clown Triggerfish            101.00
       2  Giant Maori Wrasse           228.00
       3  Blue Angelfish                30.00
       4  Ornate Butterflyfish          19.00
       5  California Moray             150.00
       6  Nurse Shark                  400.00
       7  Spotted Eagle Ray            200.00
       8  Yellowtail Snapper            75.00
       9  Redband Parrotfish            28.00
      10  Bluehead Wrasse               15.00
```

Of course, this is all nice and simple. What if you wanted the data to be in a specific sequence based on a fieldname? Local SQL doesn't directly recognize index tags, although because we are using the BDE, if an index tag exists that matches the expression we use to order the data, dBASE will use that index tag, which will speed up the process *(this is more noticeable on a large table with thousands or more rows)*.

> **NOTE**
> SQL commands generally work faster when the rowset's *indexName* property is <u>not</u> set.

We could order the data by name, for example:

```
select name, fish."length cm" from fish order by name
```

This would give us a LIST that look like:

```
Record#  Name                        Length CM
      3  Blue Angelfish                  30.00
     10  Bluehead Wrasse                 15.00
      5  California Moray               150.00
      1  Clown Triggerfish              101.00
      2  Giant Maori Wrasse             228.00
      6  Nurse Shark                    400.00
      4  Ornate Butterflyfish            19.00
      9  Redband Parrotfish              28.00
      7  Spotted Eagle Ray              200.00
      8  Yellowtail Snapper              75.00
```

We can do it the opposite way and order by the "Length CM" field and we can even combine them ...

We can also filter the data, using a WHERE clause. The WHERE clause requires an expression that evaluates to a logical value (*true* or *false*), and only those rows that the expression evaluates to *true* for will be returned. For example, what if we wanted to list all rows that had a Length of less than 100 CM?

```
select name, fish."length cm" from fish where fish."length cm" < 100
```

And a LIST would look like:

```
Record#  Name                        Length CM
      3  Blue Angelfish                  30.00
      4  Ornate Butterflyfish            19.00
      8  Yellowtail Snapper              75.00
      9  Redband Parrotfish              28.00
     10  Bluehead Wrasse                 15.00
```

We can also set the ORDER for the select statement, giving a command that looks like:

```
select name, fish."length cm" from fish where fish."length cm" < 100 order
by name
```

If a LIST command were issued, this would return:

```
Record#  Name                        Length CM
      3  Blue Angelfish                  30.00
```

```
10  Bluehead Wrasse                    15.00
 4  Ornate Butterflyfish               19.00
 9  Redband Parrotfish                 28.00
 8  Yellowtail Snapper                 75.00
```

As you can see, this can be quite powerful. When we start working with the database objects of dBASE in a later chapter, we will come back to the SQL SELECT statement, and of course you can also look at various sources as noted at the beginning of this chapter.

Calculated Fields

It is possible to create calculated fields as part of the SQL statement. We are only going to briefly look at one *very* useful example – creating a "full name" field by combining or *concatenating* a first name and a last name field. To do this, we have to use a special syntax.

```
open database dBASEContax
// the following would have to be typed in as a single
// statement in the Command Window
select FirstName || ', ' || LastName as fullname, Company, ContactType
from :dBASEContax:contacts
// followed by this:
list
```

This command tells the data engine to get the FirstName field, concatenate it using the || symbols for that purpose with a comma and a space, then to concatenate that with the LastName field, and using the keyword "as", to call it "fullname", then it is also getting the Company and ContactType fields, from the table "contacts" in the database alias "dBASEContax".

This can be useful when creating reports, and such, because the calculated field is already created and ready to go.

It should be noted that you can select a combination of wildcard and calculated fields in a query, if you need to do so. The syntax is a little more complicated, but not horribly:

```
open database dBASEContax
// the following would have to be typed in as a single
// statement in the Command Window
select contacts.*, FirstName || ', ' || LastName as fullname,
Company from :dBASEContax:contacts
// followed by this:
list
```

The extra part of the command in bold says to select "from the contacts table, all fields", followed by the calculated field.

It bears mentioning that when you select character fields from a table using the SQL SELECT command that there is no need to "trim" the fields (remove the extra spaces) – whether in a calculated field as shown here or just using the wildcard character to select all fields, the BDE trims the fields automatically. While SQL has a TRIM() function it is not necessary in dBASE.

SQL Joins

SQL Joins can be useful when creating reports, although since a join creates a readonly result set, it is not really useful for forms and such.
The following is from the InterBase Tutorial:

> Joins enable a SELECT statement to retrieve data from two or more tables in a database. The tables are listed in the FROM clause. The optional ON clause can reduce the number of rows returned, and the WHERE clause can further reduce the number of rows returned.
>
> From the information in a SELECT that describes a join, InterBase builds a table that contains the results of the join operation, the results table, sometimes also called a dynamic or virtual table. InterBase supports two types of joins: inner joins and outer joins.
>
> Inner joins link rows in tables based on specified join conditions and return only those rows that match the join conditions. If a joined column contains a NULL value for a given row, that row is not included in the results table. Inner joins are the more common type because they restrict the data returned and show a clear relationship between two or more tables.
>
> Outer joins link rows in tables based on specified join conditions but return rows whether they match the join conditions or not. Outer joins are useful for viewing joined rows in the context of rows that do not meet the join conditions.

The WHERE Clause

WHERE clauses work fine for filtering data, but there are some caveats.

- Dates must be character strings, in US MM/DD/YY or MM/DD/YYYY format — note that this is an ANSI SQL requirement, not dBASE or the BDE. It is possible to use a date in a European date format, if the separator is set to the dot (.) character *(see SET SEPARATOR in the online help)*.

```
                                         // January 1, 1999
select * from parts where date_field = '01/01/1999'
        // or, to use the current date:
cCmd = [select * from parts where date_field = ']+date()+[']
&cCmd.
// etc.
```

This second set of commands may appear a bit odd, but due to the fact that SQL does not understand the "date()" function in dBASE, we have to build the command as a character string. Then, using a special process (which will be discussed later) called *macro substitution*, we can execute the command that we built as a string.

The reason dates must be enclosed in SINGLE quotes is to differentiate them from mathematical operations. This allows the BDE to know that 04/15/1998 is a date and not the literal value 4 divided by the literal value 15 divided by the literal value 1998. It is very important to note that you must use single quotes as delimiters in many cases with local SQL.

- Boolean literals TRUE and FALSE may be referenced either with or without quotes. The older .T./.F. notation is not recognized by the BDE when used with SQL statements. You must use the words "TRUE" or "FALSE".

Read Only Queries

Local SQL (SQL statements used on local tables) will often generate read only queries. The following will generate read-only queries:

- ORDER BY with more than one field.
- Aggregate calculations (AVG, SUM, etc.)
- GROUP BY clause
- HAVING clause
- Subqueries (see SQL references)
- Joins of two or more tables

Other Useful Local SQL Commands

In addition to the SQL SELECT statement that we have been discussing, there are several other "local SQL" commands that a dBASE developer should be aware of. All of these commands are discussed in the dBASE online help in more detail, they are discussed here to make you aware of them. You can use these commands on local tables (.DBF or .DB), you can use them on tables in a SQL Server database, dBASE doesn't really care, as long as the connections to the data are correct.

Creating a Table

If you wish to create a new table, you can use the CREATE TABLE command. To use this you need to know some specifics, such as the field names you wish to create, and the sizes of the fields, and for numeric fields, the number of decimal places. Luckily, the online help in dBASE has all the information you need for this. If you type the word "HELP" (or go to the Help menu and select "Contents and Index"), and then enter in the entryfield "CREATE TABLE", you will be given an option to look at help about the command "CREATE TABLE", or "Data type mappings for CREATE TABLE". This gives a listing of the keywords that should be used for the Create Table command.

There are a few caveats for this command – there is a line-length limit built into dBASE for commands, of something like 4096 characters. If you are building a large table, you may want to combine the CREATE TABLE command with the ALTER TABLE command (discussed below).

If a fieldname either has spaces or is a SQL or dBL *(or sql)* keyword, you may need to use the syntax:

```
Tablename."fieldname"
```

Otherwise, an error may occur. This syntax makes the statement longer, but allows you to be sure that there will be no errors in the process. In general it is a bad idea to use keywords such as "date" for a fieldname, but if you absolutely must, this is one way of getting around any errors when creating the table.

The syntax for field types when using this command and when using ALTER TABLE can be found in the online help. Type "create table" in the search dialog, and then when given an option of topics, select "Data type mappings for CREATE TABLE". Decide what field type you need, and use the information in the *first* column ("SQL syntax"). For example, if you wanted to a field in a table with a type of LONG, you would use the word "INTEGER" in the chart in the help topic.

Add/Remove Fields

If you wish to add or remove fields in a table, there is the ALTER TABLE command. This is useful for adding or removing fields in a program. The discussion on Creating a table above is important for this command – particularly the caveats for dealing with fieldnames and the line length issues for commands.

Deleting a Table

If you simply issue a command such as:

```
erase mytable.dbf
```

dBASE will do exactly what you told it – it will delete the single file "mytable.dbf". What if there is a .MDX and a .DBT file? Or more fun, if you are using a Paradox .DB table, there may be a large number of files associated with it. None of those files will be deleted.

The DROP TABLE command in dBASE allows you to erase the table and associated files without having to think about it.

Renaming a Table

The dBASE RENAME command has the same problem as the dBASE ERASE command – if you wish to delete a table and all of its associated files, you have to do them one at a time, and the big problem is that some of the information about a .MDX or .DBT file, for example, are stored in the header of the .DBF file – if you just change the name of one of these files, it does not update the information in the .DBF file, and dBASE may not be able to find them.

The local SQL RENAME TABLE command will handle all of that for you.

Creating an Index Tag

It is possible to create an index tag programmatically using local SQL using the CREATE INDEX command. There are a lot of caveats as to what can be done and what cannot be done using this command in the online help for dBASE, you should be careful when using it. There are other ways *(discussed in later chapters)* to programmatically create index tags that will give you more options.

Deleting an Index Tag

Just like you can create an index tag, you can delete one using local SQL – the command is DROP INDEX. Again, this is discussed in more detail on the online help.

Adding Data to a Table

You can programmatically add data to a table using the INSERT INTO command. The syntax is very specific (and again discussed in the online help). The nice thing is that you can add data for just specific columns, or for all columns in a table.

Update a Set of Data

You can update a column or more of data based on specific criteria with the local SQL command UPDATE. This command is actually quite useful, as it can change a large amount of data fairly quickly. If you wanted to update a logical field based on a date for example:

```
UPDATE myTable SET LogicalField = false WHERE DateField <= {01/01/2004}
```

This would change the value of the field named "LogicalField" to *false* in the table "myTable", if the field "DateField" has a value that is less than or equal to the January 1,

2004. You can add more fields to the SET, and if you leave off the WHERE condition, all rows in the SET will be updated.

Cleanup

If you've been following along, you will want to issue the following command – the reason for this is that if you do not, dBASE will remember (by storing a setting in the PLUS.INI file) what database alias was open when we closed dBASE, and it will attempt to open that database alias when we start it up the next time. This may be fine for some purposes, but it can often be frustrating if you don't realize it did that (especially if you were working with a password protected database – starting dBASE and having a login dialog appear is a bit confusing at best!). The command shown below will close any open tables and any open database aliases:

```
CLOSE DATABASE
```

Summary

This chapter briefly discussed SQL, and why it is important, and gave an overview of the most important SQL commands available to you, the SELECT statement. While this was not explored in full depth, it did give a feel for some of what can be done. I do want to thank Mervyn Bick for pointing out some pieces of information that were not in this chapter previously.

Chapter 5: Working with Databases – SQL and Local

This chapter will give an overview of concerns working with data, databases, BDE Aliases, and so on. This includes a quick run through installing InterBase, which used to come with the installation of dBASE. If you wish to access data through an ODBC driver (which may be necessary for more recent versions of some of the SQL Server data engines), then once you have the ODBC driver installed and configured, the BDE should recognize it, so the details in this chapter should still work.

What Is SQL Data, versus dBASE or "Local" Tables?

In Chapter 3 there were three types of tables mentioned as "Local" tables – dBASE, Paradox and FoxPro. However, one of the advantages to working with dBASE is that because of the BDE a developer can work with many more table types. Most of these table types are accessed through the BDE and special drivers, which can then pass commands to the data engines and can pass data back to the BDE and then to dBASE itself. As this book is being updated the engineers at dBASE, LLC, are considering several new options. As these have not yet been implemented at the time the author is writing the book, very little can be said about them here.

These are called SQL Server databases. Don't let the term SQL Server confuse you with MSSQL (Microsoft SQL Server), which is only one of the many SQL engines available. Of the ones that have drivers that ship with the BDE, sometimes called "Native" drivers (because they were written specifically for the BDE) are Oracle, MSSQL, InterBase (now Firebird), DB2, Informix, Sybase, and Microsoft Access.

Unlike local tables, which *can* use a database alias via the BDE, these servers *require* a database alias, which is a pointer created in the BDE to the database itself. We will discuss this process shortly.

In Chapter 3 we briefly discussed the term "database" versus the term "table", in an attempt to clarify a misconception or misuse of terminology that has occurred among dBASE developers for years – this will be more important as we go. In Chapter 4 we discussed the SQL select statement and SQL in general.

Database Aliases

Database Aliases are the way that we connect to databases via the data engine. In this case, the data engine is the Borland Database Engine (BDE). Database aliases can be used both with local tables and with SQL Servers. You should consider using database aliases in general.

A database alias is a way of assigning a name that points to a database. When using the database in your code, all you have to use is the name that you assigned to the database.

In the case of a SQL Server, a database is a specific file that contains the tables (and in some cases other objects). As we will see shortly (in this chapter), for example, a .GDB file is what is used for an InterBase/Firebird database – it contains a set of tables. When using a SQL Server you *must* use a database alias.

> **📝 NOTE:**
>
> InterBase *used* to be available with the dBASE installer. This is no longer the case (probably due to many changes over the years in different companies). However you can still get InterBase from Embarcadero (the company that now owns the rights to it develops the software). Or you can get Firebird which is based on InterBase (the source code was "forked" to another company) who named it Firebird. This is an open source version of InterBase. I cannot speak to this in more detail as I have not worked with it.

In the case of local tables, a database is the folder on the hard drive *(or network drive)* that contains the tables for your application. When working with local tables, a database alias is optional. If you are working only with local tables, why should you consider using a database alias and therefore a database object?

- Your user may want to move (or install) the data to a different directory than the one you plan on it being installed to. All that would be needed in that case is to change the Database alias' pointer to the directory, and your application will run without any modification to the source code.
- You may need to deploy the application to a network, and not know exactly where it will go. Again, changing the path in the Database alias is all that is necessary.
- You may eventually move the data to a SQL server such as InterBase, Oracle or one of the others. The best part of this is that you could design your whole application using local tables (if you have the alias set up), move everything to the server when you deploy it, and again no internal changes to your application would be necessary, you would just need to modify the properties of the database alias.
- You are working with dBASE Plus 2.7 or later and Windows Vista or later and now dealing with the security measures added to Windows.

Most of the rest of this chapter deals with connecting to a SQL Server database, but the steps to create a database alias for local tables are very similar to the ones for a SQL Server database (and mentioned below).

User BDE Aliases

User BDE Aliases were created for dBASE Plus 2.7, in order to assist with working with the Windows Vista (and later) UAC and folder structure and user permissions. There are some interesting and frustrating issues involved with permissions and User BDE Aliases are a way to avoid those issues. This is detailed in Chapter 2 of the book, and expanded a bit here.

There are two methods of creating a User BDE Alias:
- Via the Session object and the method *addAlias()* – this might be useful for temporary tables, for example. *(Hint, you can remove the alias added to the session object by using the* deleteAlias() *method).*
- By placing information in the .INI file for your application. These will be treated as a "regular" BDE Alias, but are not stored in the BDE's IDAPI.CFG file. As a developer this means you do not have to use special code to modify either the Windows Registry or the .CFG file used by the BDE, you do not need to have your end-users run the BDE Administrator, etc.

More interesting is that if you perform a test deployment of your application on your development computer *(this is from personal experience)*, the User BDE Alias override the settings for ones used in the BDE. For example, to test an application in the dBASE IDE I created two aliases. But my application when compiled and deployed on the same machine uses two User BDE Aliases defined in the .INI file for the application, the application used the paths defined in the .INI file for the same aliases, but the source code used the ones defined in the BDE.

User BDE Alias Specifics

In order to create User BDE Aliases there are a couple things you need to know. The first is the Driver name, and the second are the options that you may need. I worked with the developers at dBASE to get the following information.

Driver Names

The Driver name references the driver used by the Borland Database Engine (BDE) to access the tables. There are quite a few database servers on the market. Below is a list taken from the BDE Administrator:

Driver Name	Database
ASCIIDRV	ASCII Text files (Native)
DBASE	.DBF Tables (Native)
FOXPRO	.DBF Tables – FoxPro (Native)
PARADOX	Borland's Paradox Tables (Native)
DB2	IBM's DB2 database (SQL Links)
INFORMIX	Informix (SQL Links)
INTRBASE	InterBase (SQL Links)
MSACCESS	Microsoft's Access (SQL Links)
MSSQL	Microsoft's MSSQL database (SQL Links)
ORACLE	Oracle (SQL Links)
SYBASE	Sybase (SQL Links)

The first four are the drivers that are considered "Native" – built in to the BDE. The others are "SQL Link" driver names.

If you use ODBC drivers, then the BDE normally automatically finds the database – there is no need to create the alias for the BDE. It may be possible to add an alias using the methods shown here (in the .INI file or using the *addAlias()* method of the session object noted below), but according to the developers at dBASE this should not be necessary *(and some of the options can actually cause difficulties)*.

Options

The Options name sets up any specific options, with one being specifically the path to the table, with the keyword "PATH:" as part of the option, followed by the path. The path should be included in quotes, especially if there might be a space anywhere in there.

The various options that you *may* need, depending on the driver, are:

SERVER NAME:
DATABASE NAME:
USER NAME:
SQLQRYMODE:
PATH:
ODBC DSN:
DB2 DSN:

Each of these would be followed by a specific string, depending on the purpose.

For local databases, the only option you should need is the path to the database, something like:

```
PATH: "C:\ProgramData\MyCompany\MyApplication\Tables"
```

To understand the other options shown above, you will want to examine qBDEMgr.cc, a file that should be in the source code alias defined in dBASE Plus as "NonVisual". To view this source code, you could issue this command in the Command Window:

```
modify command :NonVisual:qBDEMgr.cc
```

You would want to click (in the treeView on the left of the Source Editor window) on "QBDEManager", and then on the "CreateAlias" method. You can then view which options are needed for a specific database alias.

If you need to use more than one option, separate them by semicolons, i.e.,;

```
"Database: C:\SomePath\DatabaseName.ext; User: username; Password:
somepassword"
```

Creating a User BDE Alias Via the .INI File
A .INI file is loaded when you start your application, and information can be read from and written to this file. More details on this will be discussed in a later chapter of the book. Here we are focused specifically on User BDE Aliases.

User BDE Aliases are loaded by dBASE Plus or your application from the .INI into the _app.session object when the application loads *(details on Sessions and Session Objects are in Chapter 10)*. If your application needs to use a database loaded this way in another session, you will need to use the session object's *addAlias()* method (see below).

A .INI file is simply a text file with a special file extension (.INI for "Initialization"). This means we can add whatever we need to into it. The .INI file has sections, and then name/value pairs of information that are used. To create a User BDE Alias, you need two sections and a few specific name/value pairs. The first is this:

```
[UserBDEAliases]
0=MyAlias
```

The section is in square brackets, and the name/value pair uses an equal sign (=) as an assignment. User BDE Aliases are numbered starting at 0. If your application needs more than one alias, then you would add something like:

```
1=MySecondAlias
2=MyThirdAlias
```

where the value to the right of the equal sign is the name of the alias itself.

After that, you create a section for each alias you need. Each section here defines the alias, and needs two name/value pairs:

```
[MyAlias]
Driver=DBASE
Options=PATH: "C:\ProgramData\MyCompany\MyApplication\Tables"
```

If you need another User BDE Alias, as noted above, you would add the same information as necessary:

```
[MySecondAlias]
Driver=DBASE
Options=PATH: "C:\ProgramData\MyCompany\MyApplication\TempTables"
```

Creating a BDE Alias Using the Session Object's addAlias() Method

You can add User BDE Aliases in code in your application, which some developers may find particularly useful for a temporary alias. Using the table provided above, you can use this method for the database drivers listed in that table.

In a case such as that, you would use the session object (there is a default session object if you are not using your own in the application – more on session objects in later chapters of the book). The basic syntax and command requires the same information the .INI file does:

This example uses the default session object that is always available in a dBASE application (or in dBASE itself):

```
_app.session.AddAlias( "MyAlias", "dBASE",;
"PATH:C:\ProgramData\MyCompany\MyApplication\Tables" )
```

Once this code has been executed, the database alias is available in your application as if it had been added to the IDAPI.CFG file. Note the difference in the syntax, but the above code should work fine, assuming that path exists with tables in it.

SQL Server Databases and User BDE Aliases

The examples above assume that you are working with local tables, in which case the database is the folder that contains the tables.

In SQL Server databases, as noted earlier in the chapter, the database is a single file that contains the tables. *(This includes Access databases.)* As such, the path needs to include the name of the file itself, such as:

```
_app.session.AddAlias( "MyAlias", "INTRBASE",;
"PATH:'C:\ProgramData\MyCompany\MyApplication\Tables\employees.gdb';
SERVER NAME:''; USER NAME:''; SQLQRY MODE:'LOCAL'" )
```

Or (using the .INI file):

```
[MyAlias]
Driver=DBASE
Options=PATH:
"C:\ProgramData\MyCompany\MyApplication\Tables\employees.gdb"; SERVER
NAME: ""; USER NAME: ""; SQLQRYMODE: "LOCAL"
```

In either case you will want to include whichever options are needed for the database you are using.

Making the Connection

When you wish to work with a SQL Server database, you have to add an extra layer in the process of working with the data. For dBASE and/or your application to work with the SQL Server, you have to have the SQL Server engine running. When this book was originally written, the CD that dBASE came on had a free version of InterBase available to install. The instructions given here are based on that.

The "Follow Along" part of this was written when InterBase was available to be installed on the CD that dBASE came on. This has changed, and InterBase is no longer available. You can read the following, and if you have a SQL database installed, can actually follow along making appropriate changes.

(Note: If you do not wish to Install InterBase or do not have the installer, it is not required to understand what this chapter is about.)

Start the Data Engine

To start the data engine, you will need to bring up the Control Panel in Windows. There is an icon that says "InterBase Manager" – double-click on that.

Note that the Start-up Mode may be set to "Automatic", in which case the Status may say "Started". This is a preference issue – if you don't use InterBase regularly you should probably leave this as Manual, so that it is only active when you need it to be.

If the Manager is set to "Stopped", click the "Start" button. The line "The InterBase Server is currently Stopped" will change to say "The InterBase Server is currently Running".

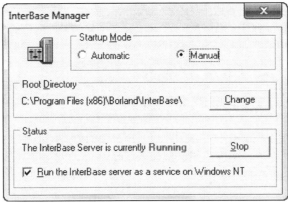

Figure 5-1

Create the Database Alias

To create a "permanent" Database Alias, you need to start the data engine's administrator – since currently we are using the Borland Database Engine (BDE), we need to start the BDE Administrator. As noted in Chapter 2, you may need to run the BDE Administrator "as administrator". *(As also is noted all the way through this book, it is recommended that you us User BDE Aliases instead of the following method – these instructions are left here for thoroughness, more than anything else ... see earlier in this chapter for details on User BDE Aliases.)*

When the BDE Administrator starts, you need to click on the "Databases" tab, and you may need to expand the tree by clicking on the "+" by the word "Databases" in the window.

When you do this, you should see a list of all available aliases.

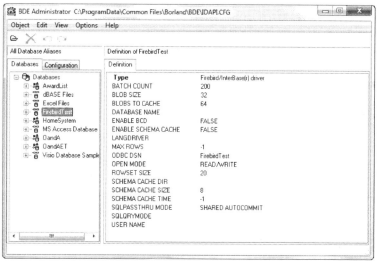

Figure 5-2

To add a new database alias, press the keys ⌨Ctrl⌨+⌨N⌨ (hold Ctrl and the letter "N").

Change the word "STANDARD" to "INTRBASE" and click "OK".

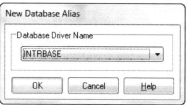

Figure 5-3

Where you see "INTRBASE1", type "IBEmployee". This is so we are working with the same alias. On the right, we need to change the "SERVER NAME" entry – this is the location of the database we want to associate with the database alias.

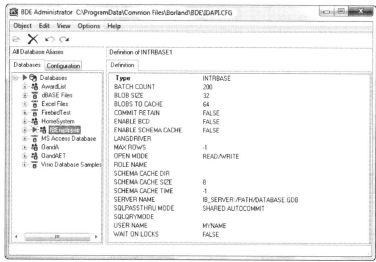

Figure 5-4

InterBase databases all end with the extension ".GDB". Click on the entryfield next to "SERVER NAME", and a button will appear with an ellipsis on it (...). Click on that, and a dialog appears allowing you to find and select the database. You will have to move through several folders to get to this, but the path by default will be (on Windows Vista or later):

```
C:\Program Files (x86)\Borland\InterBase\examples\Database\employee.gdb
```

Select this.

To save all of this so far, press ⌨Ctrl+A *(apply changes)* and you will get a confirm dialog, click "OK". You should be able to close the BDE Administrator now.

Start dBASE

Start dBASE PLUS, and we can now open the data and look at it. To do this, go to the Navigator, and select the "Tables" tab. Click on the down arrow of the combobox next to the words "Look In". You will see a list of folders you may have worked in, but more importantly, a set of icons for all of the database aliases that are currently defined by the data engine.

Select "IBEMPLOYEE", and notice that a dialog appears, asking for a username and password! You didn't set those! InterBase has a default username and password *(which if you decide to create your own databases using InterBase you should change)*.

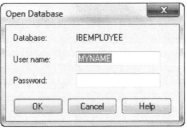

Figure 5-5

The default username for InterBase is: **SYSDBA**
The default password for InterBase is: **masterkey**
Note that the password is case-sensitive.

Once you click "OK", assuming you entered the username and password correctly, you should now see a set of tables in the Navigator.

From here you can open tables in dBASE as if they were native to dBASE. If you double click on a table, you can open it, edit the contents, etc. If you are familiar with XDML commands, such as USE and so on, you can open tables that way, you can work with these in code using the OODML data objects (covered in a later chapter of this book), and you can work with these in dQuery (a topic we will discuss later in the book) to design datamodules, and so on.

For what it's worth, the version of InterBase that was on the CD with older versions of dBASE does not load the database (possibly due to the fact that the database is in the Program Files folder structure). You can obtain a newer version of InterBase from the internet, there is a free version, but the driver with the BDE may not work with it. If you are looking for a free SQL Server you may want to look for Firebird or MySQL.

Other Data Engines

If you wish to work with a SQL Server other than InterBase, the steps will be similar, although not identical to those shown here. If the SQL Server is not one of those native to the data engine (DB2, Informix, InterBase MS Access, MS SQL, Oracle or Sybase), you will most likely need to go through the extra steps of setting up an ODBC connection first. Most or all of the SQL Server engines out there you might wish to use will have ODBC drivers (such as MYSQL).

A very popular database engine some dBASE developers are currently using is MySQL. This is because there is a free version, as well as a paid version. The one difficulty is that there is a communication issue with current ODBC drivers for MySQL and the BDE. It is recommended to use version 3.51 of the ODBC driver for MySQL (at least for now).

It should be noted that this author makes no recommendations for specific SQL Server databases. At this time I have very limited experience with them and do not wish to make any recommendations.

ODBC Drivers

ODBC is a commonly used acronym for a Windows standard called "Open DataBase Connectivity". If you use a database server such as MYSQL, you will need to install, if it was not automatic, an ODBC driver. Once that is installed, you may need to do some setup. This is normally done by going to the Control Panel in Windows, and finding the ODBC applet. On Windows XP this may be under "Administrative Tools", where you will see it as "Data Sources (ODBC)". On Windows 7 you may need to double-click "Administrative Tools", then you will see "Data Sources (ODBC)".

If you have installed a data engine that uses an ODBC driver, you will want to configure this driver. Once you have done so, it should be recognized in the BDE Administrator automatically.

One recommendation: through experimentation, you may need to set a language driver for an ODBC database before the BDE Administrator will recognize it. It is suggested that you use an ANSI driver as mentioned elsewhere in this book.

It should also be noted that for Microsoft Access you most likely will want to use the ODBC drivers. In the dUFLP you will find a program and a custom class that can help you set up both the ODBC drivers and the BDE Alias. The program is called: "CreateODBC.prg", and the custom class is "BDEAliasEX.cc". Read the documentation in the source code carefully and you should be able to use those Access tables easily.

dBASE Plus 2.61 (released in July, 2006) included new ODBC drivers to connect to many of the most popular databases out there.

In General

If you wish to (or need to) work with SQL Server databases, once you have the connections set up, you should find that most of what you can do with local tables can be done just as easily with the SQL Server data.

There are a few things to be aware of:

- SQL Server databases often have different field types than the native tables do. There is some discussion of this in chapters of this book comparing programming commands (XDML, OODML, SQL ...).
- Some SQL Server databases have in their documentation SQL commands, or options to commands that do not work in dBASE. This is usually because the BDE does not recognize them, but be aware that not all options will work. (Note: It is possible with a database object to pass some of these options through directly to the SQL Server engine through the use of the *executeSQL()* method.)

Creating a Database Alias for Local Tables

A database alias can, and should, be used with local tables as well as SQL Server tables, for reasons given elsewhere in this chapter.

The instructions are the same as they are for the InterBase example as given earlier in this chapter, except that rather than selecting "INTRBASE", you would simply use the default "STANDARD" selection. When you want to select the database, rather than changing "Server Name" and selecting a .GDB file, you would select "Path" and the folder that contains the tables for your application. Otherwise, this process is the same as with SQL Server tables. The instructions for a simple application might be:

- Click on the "Databases" tab
- Click the "+" by the word "Databases"
- Select the menu "Object", and Select "New" (or Ctrl+N)
- Click "OK" for "Standard"
- Note that in the list on the left you should see "STANDARD1" and it should be in an "Edit" mode – allowing you to type
- Change the name to the name you wish to give the database, such as "MyApp" and press the Enter key
- Click on the right: "Default Driver" and select "DBASE"
- Click (on the right): "Path:" and use the tool button to point to the path that the tables are in (such as "C:\ProgramData\MyCompany\MyApplication\Tables)".
- Select the menu "Object", and Select "Apply" (or Press Ctrl+A)
- If a dialog appears about closing all BDE Applications, click "OK".

Now a database alias exists for your application, and you can use it as described here and elsewhere.

It should be noted that if you wish to use the UAC settings to make your application more compliant with Windows Vista, Windows 7 and later, you should be using a BDE Alias for your local tables, and that User BDE Aliases are actually a better way to go. Trying to set up a BDE Alias on a Windows Vista or later computer may run into Administrator Rights issues, if you try to store these in the IDAPI.CFG file *(as described in Chapter 2)*.

Cleanup

Before you close dBASE, it is a good idea, especially if you have been following along, to issue the command (in the Command Window):

```
CLOSE DATABASE
```

This will ensure that the database engine does not attempt to connect to the SQL Server you were using when you start dBASE up. This can be particularly confusing if a login is required, because normally dBASE does not require you to login to anything when it starts. However, if you had a connection to a SQL Server open when you closed dBASE, it will try to reconnect when you start it back up.

Summary

In this chapter we took a brief look at the steps involved in actually connecting to a SQL Server database, using the free InterBase 6, which used to be on the dBASE PLUS CD (with several notes about other database servers). We discussed a few issues involved in working with SQL Server databases, and noted that most of the time you can use these tables exactly the same way you can work with local tables in dBASE.

NOTES:

Part III: Object Oriented Code and dBASE

The following chapters will take a good hard look at the dBASE object model in the dBL language, including the OODML (Object Oriented Database Manipulation Language) objects.

Chapter 6: Introduction to Objects and dBASE PLUS

dBASE has always had a programming language. Over the last few years this language has been given an acronym of "dBL" (for dBASE Language). Developers who have worked with earlier versions of dBASE are probably more accustomed to what is usually called Procedural Code or Procedural Programming – particularly if you programmed in dBASE for DOS *(any version)*. This type of coding works from the top of a program down to the bottom and then stops. Inside the code there may be calls to other code, or loops, but ultimately the code goes from the top to the bottom.

Object Oriented Programming (OOP) changes this way of coding completely. With a new way of coding comes many new terms. These terms can be confusing, but when looked at a bit at a time in the right sequence, it all comes together and starts to make sense.

In Volume 2, Chapter 21, we discuss "generic" programming techniques. I felt that a general overview of OOP given earlier in the book would help as we examine other aspects of dBASE, specifically objects (database objects, forms, reports, etc.) and how they work. This chapter is largely aimed at programmers who started writing code in Procedural software (such as dBASE for DOS), and need to understand how OOP works.

One of the great features of dBASE and dBL is that there are multiple ways to perform most tasks and you can combine old coding techniques with new. While this book will focus heavily on OOP, if your code works and you feel no need to update it to OOP coding techniques, there is no reason to feel you *have* to change your code.

In this chapter you will be exposed to some code in order to understand basic OOP concepts. Some commands may actually be ones that are not directly related to OOP, but are necessary just to show how it works.

In order to assist, many examples in this chapter are based on some visual objects in dBASE, but there are some examples that are not visual, just to help explain some of the terms and ideas being demonstrated. If you wish to actually try the examples, most of them can be executed from the Command Window of dBASE PLUS.

OOP Concepts and Terminology

OOP code uses various terms that can be confusing. We will discuss the terms briefly below and then in the following pages discuss some of them in more depth. Some of the terms will start to make even more sense in later chapters, as you read through this book.

Any proper object oriented programming language has these characteristics: *encapsulation*, *inheritance*, and *polymorphism*. The dBL version of OOP has all three of these.

As the expression suggests, *Object*-oriented programming is based on *objects*. These objects can be visual controls (like the forms, the pushbuttons, the comboboxes, etc), or can be non-visual objects (for example, the data objects). dBASE offers many prototypes of objects. Each of these prototypes are called a *class*. Under dBASE, the *class* or *prototype* of an object are synonymous. The objects already prototyped and offered with dBASE are called the *stock classes*.

- *Encapsulation* is one of the cornerstones of Object Oriented Programming. This term often causes consternation in developers just getting used to OOP, but it's a relatively simple concept. Encapsulation simply means that an object is "self-contained" – meaning that all the *properties*, *methods* and *events* needed for the object to function properly are *encapsulated* in that object's *class definition*. Encapsulation is important because it means that each object functions independently of each other object. Even multiple instances of the same object remain independent. If you have worked with xBASE code, you would never open the same database table in two work areas. But with OOP design this is no longer a problem. Tables are opened in an encapsulated object and each is treated by dBASE as completely independent of the other.

  Encapsulation also means that once your code is debugged, you can use the object in different contexts or programs and never need to worry about making changes.
- *Inheritance* refers to a class or object that is *subclassed* from another and the fact that the *derived* class *inherits* the *properties*, *events* and *methods* of the *superclass*. Inheritance is the way to reuse existing code in a very efficient manner. With inheritance you can change or extend code from a parent class by making a child (or *derived*) class. In the child class you write only the changes or enhancements, everything else is handed down (*inherited*) from the parent. Moreover, the child remains linked to the parent, which means that whenever the parent is changed the child is also changed. If you enhance the parent, all the children are also enhanced. To fully understand inheritance, you should also understand:
- *Subclassing* is creating a class that is based on, or *subclassed* from another class or prototype. A class that is subclassed from another class can also be referred to as being *derived from* that class. The class that another is subclassed from is often called the *superclass*.
- *Overriding* refers to changing the way code that is inherited from a superclass works. Overriding is commonly done to properties, methods and events of a class.
- *Polymorphism* (from the Greek meaning "having multiple forms") refers to the ability of an object to change its meaning or purpose based on a set of conditions. One way that polymorphism is manifested is in is the ability of objects to alter inherited behavior. In a parent class, for example, a mouse click might cause a special form to open. But in the child class that behavior is replaced (overridden) by a routine that sends a report to the printer. Another way that polymorphism is manifested is when a named action changes depending on the *parameters* it is given. If a specific condition evaluates to true, the object might do something totally different than if that same condition evaluates to being false. For example, an object may have the ability to output to a printer, to a disk file or to the internet. A polymorphic method named "output" might handle this depending on whether a report object is passed, a string is passed or an HTML file is passed. This makes objects very flexible. This will be seen in later chapters of this book.

There are of course other terms that need to be discussed when talking about object oriented programming. Other terms that you need to be at least passingly familiar with, and will be covered in more depth as we go are:

- The following three items make up what are called the *members* of a class, and are how we define a class or prototype:
    - *Properties* are similar to memory variables – they the characteristics of an object. When talking about a visual object such as a form, these could be things such as where the top edge of a form displays, where the left edge displays, the height and width of the form, the color (*colorNormal*) of the form, and so on. There are other properties that affect how the form behaves.

- *Events*: an event is a single action – usually initiated by the user – such as clicking a button or pressing a key on the keyboard. If a pushbutton is clicked, this is an event (*onClick*). If the mouse is moved, that is another event (*onMouseMove*). Objects are designed to respond only to those events addressed specifically to them. In addition to the default behavior that a control has in response to an event, developers can write their own *event-handlers*. Adding these event-handlers allows *event-driven programming*.
- *Methods*: while events are usually the action that an object is submitted to, methods are the actions that an object can perform. In other words, methods are the things that an object knows to do by itself. For example, to open a form, the form's open method is called: once it is called in a single line of code, all the tasks needed to be done to open the form are performed. Very often, a method will perform its tasks only after an explicit call is made.

- When you create an object, you are creating an *instance* of a class (the term *instantiating* an object is often used for this process). When you define a form, you are creating an instance of the form class. When you define a pushbutton on a form, you are creating an instance of the pushbutton class.

- Each instance of a class (or each new *object*) should have its own name. That name identifies that object and is called an *object reference* or *object reference variable*. The reference is a pointer to an object and you can have multiple references to a single object. When you create a second object reference to the same object, you are not creating a new object, but two different ways to reference the same object. dBASE treats an object reference as a memory variable *(a topic that will be covered in depth later)*. This means you can overwrite an object rather easily. Object references should be treated as memory variables (which they are), which includes being concerned with such things as *scope* (this will be discussed in a later chapter).

- *Containership* refers to the fact that an object can contain other objects. This requires that one object be a *container*. This *container* object is also called a *parent* object. It is possible for container objects to contain other container objects. A form is a container object – it can contain other objects such as a text object, or a pushbutton object. In this context, the form is the parent of the text or pushbutton.

Working with Simple Objects

To get a better feel for the way this works in dBASE, we will start looking at one of the most commonly used objects in dBASE, the Form. The advantage to this is that the form is what is called a User Interface (UI) object, which means it is visual – you can see it, and you can see changes made to it. When working with non-interface type objects, it is harder to see and understand some of what is happening.

Creating a Form Object

The form object is created in dBASE based on the stock class definition built into dBASE itself. To create a form object, in the Command Window, type:

```
f = new form()
```

There are three *very* important things to know about this command.
1. The letter "f" is arbitrary – we could use "oForm", we could use the letter "x". It doesn't really matter. "f" is a convention used to help understand what we are looking at, it is not required that you use that specific letter.
2. The letter "f" in this command is a *variable* and an *object reference*. An object reference variable is a pointer or handle used to identify that specific object.
3. The word "new" is required in order to create a new instance of an object.

So, what did this single command do? As soon as the Enter key is pushed, dBASE has created two things. First, an *instance* of the form class and secondly, a *variable* called *f* in which the address in RAM where the instance of the form class is stored. So the variable *f* is the name of the new form (in other words, a reference to the form) and a pointer (or a variable pointing to the address in memory where the form is stored).

All this was done in a single line of code. Yet nothing has changed on your screen. Didn't we create a form? Why can't we see it? Simply because we didn't open it. Now that the instance of the form is created, we can open it by making a call to the open *method*:

```
f.open()
```

You should see something like:

Figure 6-1

We can get an understanding of properties by looking this. For example, if you want to change the place that the form displays on the screen, you could issue code such as:

```
f.top = 5
f.left = 10
```

📝 **NOTE**

We could issue a command such as:

```
new form().open()
```

This has a serious problem: How do you reference the form you just created and opened? This kind of syntax is useful for some quick tests and in a few cases can be useful when you need to execute a method of a stock class. For the most part it's not the best way to instantiate an object, mostly because there is no way to access or manipulate the object – in other words, no object reference variable is created.

When you pressed the Enter key after typing the first command shown, the form moved vertically on the screen and when you pressed the Enter key after the second command, the form moved horizontally on the screen. You just changed properties of the object referenced by "f".

The form itself has many more properties, some of which will be discussed in this book, all of which are described in detail in the online help (OLH).

Creating Objects On A Form

To create objects on a form, such as text, you need to use slightly different syntax.

```
f.text1 = new text( f )
```

In the line above, we have created an instance of the text class and a custom property (called *text1*) of the form *f*. We could have called this simply *text1* instead of *f.text1*, but it is easier when viewing the code to realize that *text1* belongs to the form. When we create a visual object that has to be contained in a container (like the text object is contained in a form), the containership (i.e. the parenthood) must be passed as a parameter in the parentheses at the right end. *(In this example, you cannot create a text object without a parent – dBASE will return an error.)* Containership is not defined at the left side of the equation but passed as a parameter in the right side of that equation.

> **NOTE**
> dBASE coders most often store object references in memory variables. However, you can store them in arrays, or as properties of other objects (as seen here with "f.text1"). Much depends on how you need to use the object, and what the scope of the object will be.

When you created the text object, you didn't see anything happen on the form. Why not? The reason is that the text object's default for the *text* property is an empty string. So, how do you modify the text? You do this by assigning a value to the *text* property:

```
f.text1.text = "This is some sample text."
```

If you are entering the sample code as you read this book, you now see *part* of the text. The text is attempting to wrap inside the width of the text control, based on the default *width* property. Because the text control's default *width* is shorter than the text we have given it, you need to modify the width of the text control to see all of the text *(we could change the height instead, but let's do it this way for now)*:

```
f.text1.width = 25
```

You can change other properties of the text object, such as the color:

```
f.text1.colorNormal = "red"
```

And so on. This is a very simple example and as we move on through this book we will get more complex.

At this point you should know that to create an object you must use the NEW keyword; that memory variables and properties can be pointers to new objects; and that some objects are contained inside other objects.

Dot Notation

The separator used to separate an object reference from a property, method, or event in a command is called the "dot" operator, or a period (.). It is easier to simply call this a dot and you will hear coders talk about "f dot text1 dot text".

An example is the code we looked at previously when creating and modifying a form. To reference the form, we were using the letter "f". To reference the form's *top* property, we used:

```
f.top
```

The dot tells us and dBASE that the property *top* belongs to the object referenced by "f". Similarly, to reference the *top* property of the text object "text1" from the example shown in the previous section, we would use:

```
f.text1.top
```

You can query any property using dot notation, for example if you want to know what the *top* property is currently:

```
? f.top
```

You can change the value as well:

```
f.top = 15
```

As we go, you will see that we can do much more with this notation, including long references to get to specific objects from within code associated with another object.

Containership

We've just done some work with *containership*, as well as discussing dot notation. Most user-interface classes in dBASE require what is called a *parent* object – that is to say, they are *contained* by another object.

If you place controls onto a form, those controls are said to be *contained* by the form. The form is the *container*, or the *parent*.

You can refer to the parent of a contained object with a special reference:

```
this.parent
```

> **NOTE**
> It is important to understand that some objects that can be contained are also containers. For example, there are visual controls like the Notebook or Container objects. These are designed to be containers, but they are also contained on a form. Indeed, a Notebook object can contain a second Notebook object. This is very much like the folder structure on your hard drive, where you might have "C:\Folder1\Folder2\Folder3" and so on. This can lead to some fairly complex object structures, as you might imagine.

If the property *parent* does not exist, then the object cannot be contained by another object. For example, a form does not have a *parent* property.

This may seem silly, but it shows that you can modify the parent of the text control:

```
f.text1.parent.left = 15
```

This is of course the same as saying:

```
f.left = 15
```

There are reasons that we will discuss later where this can be a useful thing to be able to do, however, believe it or not, that is all there is to the concept of containership!

There are controls that are containers that have to have *parent* controls. We will come back to this concept again later in this chapter.

Understanding the Object Inspector

The Object Inspector is a very useful tool in dBASE – it allows you to inspect and even change, properties *(as well as work with Events and Methods – we'll come back to these later)*.

To see the Object Inspector in action, we'll start with a fresh form:

```
f = new form()
f.text1 = new Text( f )
f.text1.text = "This is some text"
f.text1.width = 25
f.open()
```

This should overwrite the previous form associated with the letter "f" and start over.

To see the members of the object referenced by "f", you can type the following in the Command Window:

```
inspect( f )
```

You will see a new window open up in the design surface that looks like:

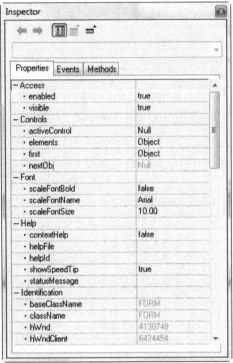

Figure 6-2

This Inspector is interactive, in that you can change properties of the form object referenced by "f".

The Object Inspector is one of many useful tools in dBASE, and is accessible from the different design surfaces (Form Designer, Menu Designer, Report Designer, etc.). It allows you to view and modify the various properties of an object and when in the design surfaces will allow you to work with events and methods.

By default, the Object Inspector *(or simply "Inspector")* opens with the categories of properties in a "closed" position, although it appears that Version 2.8 opens with the categories "open". You can open individual categories by clicking on them, and you will see all properties of a specific category. You can also open (or close) all categories with the two buttons on the top right (if you hold your mouse over them a speedtip will appear that shows you which is which). There is a button that changes the view from category to property view as well. This is useful if you cannot find a specific property, or do not know what category the property belongs to.

If you wish to change the top or left properties, find the "Position" category, and click on it. You will see that open up and if you click on "left" you will see a number on the right that you can change. You can use the spinbox control (the up/down arrows) or change the value directly by typing over what is there. If you change the left property to 15, when you press the Enter key the form will jump to the new position.

Notice that there are many other properties displayed in the inspector. We did not define these properties when typing the code to create this form. So where did all these values come from? The answer is *inheritance*. When we created this specific form, it inherited all of the properties of the stock form class.

The Inspector is interactive with the object being inspected. As we work in the various design surfaces we will find the Object Inspector to be very useful.

If you have been typing commands in as you read this, it is suggested that you close the Inspector for now. You can do that by clicking on the 'x' in the titlebar of the inspector.

Understanding Events

Windows is Event-Driven

Windows is an event-driven software package. What exactly does that mean?

Windows, once it loads and is sitting on your desktop looking nice and pretty, is not actually *doing* anything except looking and waiting for specific events to occur. Those events are things such as the mouse moving. When the mouse moves, the mouse pointer must be moved, so Windows has events to deal with the mouse moving. Basically it is a reactive operating system. It reacts to what the user does. If you type on the keyboard, depending on what keys are clicked, something may happen – even if you don't have any specific software running – Windows looks for keys being pressed. If they are, it looks to see what keys were pressed, and if it knows that specific keys are supposed to do specific things it tries to actually do those if needed.

When Windows "hears" that an event has occurred, it sends messages to some or all of the existing objects. Thus when the user clicks the mouse on a button, Windows detects this event and sends a message to the button object. The button object's *onClick* event handler is then told to fire because the message was received from Windows that the button was clicked. In order to do this (this will be discussed in more detail in a later chapter), these objects have a handle (*hWnd*) property that uniquely identifies the object to Windows. Some dBASE developers use the Windows API (Application Programming Interface) to capture messages that are not captured by dBASE and thereby add functionality to their objects.

What is Event-Driven Programming?

Event-Driven programming is literally writing programs that work similar to Windows by hooking into Windows events. Basically, if you need your form to do something specific when the mouse is moved, you would have to use an *onMouseMove* event that hooked into the Windows event so that your code knows that the mouse has moved and what you want it to do when that happens.

The significant aspect to event-driven programming that tends to cause developers the most difficulty is that the user controls the order of events, not the code. DOS programmers are used to designing screens (for example) that are very linear – a user moves from one control to the next and it is always in the same sequence. In Windows applications the user can jump around. Data Validation is a more interesting task, because you cannot guarantee that a user is going to move from one control to the one that you want them to. A user could, using the mouse, click on one control, then jump to something in the middle of the screen – there is no way for your code to know what the user will do and it is considered bad programming to try to force the user to a specific place.

dBASE Events

dBASE has many controls that have events that talk to Windows. The form, a pushbutton, etc., all tie into Windows itself, and you can take advantage of those events.

In addition, the data classes have their own events that are built in to them that you can work with in your own code, such as adding a new row (*beginAppend()* or *onSave()*) and so on. The report engine has events that are designed specifically for working with reports and labels.

Using the dBASE Form to See How This Works

If you want to see what events are built in to dBASE for a form, do the following:

```
f = new form()
inspect(f)
```

Rather than looking at the Properties, as we did earlier in the Inspector, let us look at the Events. To do that, simply click on the "Events" tab.

You should see a list of possible events that you can hook code into. Since we are not currently in the dBASE form designer, we cannot actually use the inspector to hook code up to these events. But we can see the names of them, which will give you some idea of what is possible.

Events that begin with the word *can* (as in *canClose()*) are special events that can be used to prevent a method from being allowed to fire or to be fired only when certain conditions are met. So if you set an event such as *canClose()* to return a value of *false*, then when the user tried to close a form, they would not be able to. Why would you want to do that? There are probably quite a few reasons, one that immediately comes to mind is if you have a data validation routine – you would want all data to be valid before the user could close the form. You could set the form's *canClose()* event to return a value of *false* unless your validation code returned a value that said the data was all valid. At that point, the event could be changed to return a *true* value and the user would be allowed to close the form.

Events that begin with the word *on* (as in *onClose()*) fire **after** the method referenced has been executed. For example, if you have code that you want to fire after the form has closed you would use the *onClose()* event, once the form has been closed that code will fire. This could be used to do some memory cleanup, close a temporary table you might have opened, or whatever else might be necessary.

If you look at the "Methods" tab for a moment, you will see Methods (we'll come back to these) such as "Open", "Close" and so on. The Events on the other tab are often, but not always, tied to those methods.

Event Handlers

An *event handler* is the code that is assigned to fire when an event occurs. If you examine the events in the inspector for the form, you will see that all of them have the word "Null" in the second column. That is because no code has been assigned to event handlers.

As we haven't gotten very deeply into working with dBL at this point, we are going to only look at some very basic things we can do here.

First, since the Inspector will be useless in the next steps, we should close it (use the 'x' in the top right). Next, let's create a new form using the Command Window, and then we're going to add a pushbutton to the form, set the text, and then open the form:

```
f = new form()
f.PB = new Pushbutton( f )
f.PB.text = "Close Form"
f.open()
```

At this point, you have a form with a pushbutton on it, but what does it do? Well, nothing. You can click on that pushbutton all you want and nothing will happen.

Assigning Event Handlers

To assign code to the event handler, you must know what it is called how to reference it. In this case, the event we wish to create is an event handler for the *onClick()* event – this event fires after the pushbutton is clicked *(a "click" event is one where the mouse button is pushed down and let up once – this is different from onLeftMouseDn(), which fires when the mouse button is in the down position, or onLeftMouseUp(), which fires when the mouse button is in the up position)*. Since what we want it to do is close the form, we can do something fairly simple here and that is to call the Method of the form called *close*. This will cause the form to close when the pushbutton is clicked.

We're going to use what is called a *codeblock* for this. We'll come back to codeblocks and explain them in more detail shortly, but for the moment, let's just do a simple call:

```
f.PB.onClick = {; form.close() }
```

Does it work? The only way to tell for sure is to click on the pushbutton. If you typed this correctly, clicking on the pushbutton should cause the form to close.
You can see it again by typing:

```
f.open()
```

> **NOTE**
> Why can you re-open the form at this point, without re-declaring it? The form referenced by the letter "f" is an object that is still in memory. Even though the form was *closed* it was still in memory. This is an important concept to remember. Unless you release the form, the form will still exist in memory and you can reopen it without having to recreate it or create another instance of it. This is true of objects in dBASE in general – in order to completely get rid of an object you need to release it.

And then clicking on the pushbutton again.

Working With Methods

As mentioned earlier, methods are code associated with a class. We have already used two methods that were built in to the form – *open* and *close*. A method is code that is pre-defined for the class, and is available to any object instantiated from the class.

You can call a method by referencing the object, using dot notation and then the method. So for example, we used a codeblock earlier to close the form with:

```
form.close()
```

There are other means of calling methods that can be used, but we will discuss those in later chapters. We're looking at the basics here.

Codeblocks

What is a Codeblock? Quite simply, a codeblock is a block of dBL code that executes as if it were a function or procedure. They are useful when doing simple tasks because you don't have to write a specific function or procedure to do the code.

We used one earlier when we defined code for the event handler of the pushbutton's onClick event. This looked like:

```
{; form.close() }
```

A codeblock must begin and end with braces *(or "curly braces")* { }. Everything inside of that is normally considered a codeblock *if* the next (non-space) character is either a semicolon (;) or pipe (|). The OLH says that a codeblock cannot span multiple lines, although it's been found to work. When we start looking at the source code editor, it should be noted that a program with a codeblock that spans lines will appear as an error, even if it is valid code.

📓 NOTE

You should understand that the curly braces ({ }) are used for more than one thing in dBL. You can also use them to define a literal date or a literal array as well as a codeblock. dBASE itself has to look at what is contained inside the curly braces to decide what exactly is contained in them and therefore how to treat it. For example, a literal date is defined as *(assuming US Date format of MM/DD/YYYY)*:

```
{08/20/2004}
```

And a literal array is defined as:

```
{"element 1", "element 2", "element 3"}
```

As a codeblock always begins with either a semi-colon or a pipe symbol, dBASE understands what it is looking at. dBASE can do this because it looks at the context and the content of what is contained in the braces.

There are two types of codeblocks: *statement* or *expression*. A *statement* codeblock acts like a dBL function – it contains standard dBL commands, multiple commands are separated by a semi-colon (;), and may accept a parameter. If the codeblock accepts a parameter it must use the pipe symbols (two of them) with the parameter between them. An *expression* codeblock contains a single dBL command, and may also accept a parameter.

Expression Codeblocks

The following are valid examples of *expression* codeblocks:

```
{ || false }
{ || date() }
{ |x| x * 2 }
```

The first two do not have parameters. The first returns the value "false". That's all it does. The second returns the value returned by the date() function. The third returns the value of a parameter named "x", multiplied by 2.

To use these, you could assign them to a variable, such as MyCode:

```
MyCode = {|x| x * 2 }
```

And to use that code:

```
? MyCode( 2 )
```

Where "2" is a parameter passed to the codeblock. This should return a value of 4 in the output pane of the Command Window.

Statement Codeblocks

A *statement* codeblock may begin with the | or || symbols, but each statement in the codeblock must begin with a semi-colon. The following are valid examples of *statement* codeblocks:

```
{; return false }
{||; return false }
{; return date() }
{|x|; clear; ? x*2 }
```

The first two codeblocks are functionally the same, as the second does nothing with the parameter. In both cases they return a value of *false*. The next returns the date and the last clears the output pane and then displays the value of the parameter multiplied by 2.

So what is the actual difference between *expression codeblocks* and *statement codeblocks*? An expression codeblock by definition must return a value, whether that value is a logical *true* or *false*, a value that is evaluated based on a parameter, or whatever. A statement codeblock by definition is designed to execute dBL commands or statements. These commands always begin with a semi-colon (;) character to show dBASE that this is a dBL command, not a value to be returned and you can have multiple commands in a single codeblock (each starting with a semi-colon). If a statement codeblock is to return a value, it must explicitly use the word "return" to do so.

You can assign statement codeblocks to variables as was shown previously with expression codeblocks.

Using Codeblocks as Event Handlers

As seen earlier, it is possible to use codeblocks as event handlers. This is really useful for relatively simple code. Once you start getting into more complicated code, you will want to create a more complex event handler. This will be discussed in later chapters.

Using Custom Properties and Methods

Custom properties and methods allow a lot of flexibility in dBASE code. By using these we can extend the capabilities of one of the stock classes in dBASE, or we can create our own special purpose custom classes.

dBASE does not allow us to create custom events – this is because we would have to tell dBASE what Windows event to wait to occur for our event to fire, or we would have to have the ability to tell dBASE how to define a new event – in either case this is not currently possible.

The Object is Built From the Class

While we discussed this a bit earlier in this chapter, it is time to delve into this concept in more detail. As mentioned earlier, the *class* is the description or *prototype* of an *object*. It is used to define the members of the object – the *properties*, *events* and *methods*.

Parts of a Class

In order to understand a class properly, you need to know what the different parts are.

A dBASE class has a *class declaration*, *constructor code*, *methods* and an *endclass* statement. A class may also have *parameters* – information passed to the class that is used in the constructor code.

Some special variables are created that are used in a class. These are *this*, and *form*. When used in a form, report, or datamodule, the word *form* refers to the top level container. The word *this* refers to the current object and is a shortcut to that object, rather than using the full *dot notation* syntax to refer to the object.

The Class Declaration Statement

When we used the form class earlier in this chapter, we really weren't defining a class. What we were doing was creating an instance of the stock form class, by using the command:

```
f = new form()
```

If we want to create a form that is reusable, we would want to define the characteristics of that instance of the Form Class. This is most often done using the Form Designer, but that's a different topic. A basic form class would start with a *declaration* statement:

```
class MyForm of Form
```

This statement tells dBASE that we are defining a class and that MyForm is subclassed from the stock Form class. From this point, all code until dBASE sees the word endclass, it is assumed that we are defining the class.

> **NOTE**
> There is more that can be done with the CLASS declaration statement, we are only looking at it briefly at the moment. We will come back to this later in more depth.

The Class Constructor Code

Next we have the *constructor code* which is the definition of the properties, and assignment of event handlers for the object, and then any *contained* objects. Remember that a form is a container for objects such as text, pushbuttons, and so on. So, the class's constructor might include commands like the following:

```
with( this )
   top = 4
   left = 6
   width = 40
   height = 10
endwith
```

What does that mean? Well, simply, dBASE PLUS has a special command used to make coding objects a little easier. The "with" and "endwith" code simply says "with the object used as a parameter" (that's what the word *this* means, remember?). It's a way of making code like the following easier to write:

```
this.top = 4
this.left = 6
this.width = 40
this.height = 10
```

Imagine if you have a lot of properties you want to modify – typing the word "this" followed by a dot and *then* the property could get tiring very quickly. However, there is nothing in the coding rules that says you *must* use the with/endwith structure, if you would prefer not to, dBASE doesn't care!

 NOTE

It is important to note that the with/endwith construct of dBL does not allow you to create new/custom properties of a class, whether you are working with a stock class or a custom class.

If your form has a text object and a pushbutton object, you might write code like the following *(the Form Designer does write code like the following)* to define those as part of the constructor for your form:

```
this.text1 = new text( this )
with( this.text1 )
   left = 2
   width = 25
   text = "This is some text"
endwith

this.pushbutton1 = new Pushbutton( this )
with( this.pushbutton1 )
   left = 2
   top = 3
   text = "My Method"
endwith
```

 NOTE

You might wonder why we couldn't define these objects using the same sort of code we did in earlier examples, such as:

```
f = new form()
f.text1 = new text( f )
```

This is because when we were creating the form object "f" earlier, we were doing so "on the fly" – we were creating a very simple object with an object reference. We were not defining a reusable class. We could get similar results, but each time you want to use an object like that, you have to issue all of the commands necessary to build it and any contained objects. By defining a class, we do not have to define the properties, events, methods, and contained objects each time we want to use it.

Any other objects that might be on the form would be defined in a similar fashion. All of this is the *constructor* of the form – it is used to build or construct the form and the objects contained by the form. The constructor code ends when the first method is encountered or when the word endclass is encountered.

Class Declaration of Methods

Once the constructor code is done, if your class has any methods, this the place to define them.

A method in a dBASE class is defined with either the word *function* or the word *procedure*, followed by the name of the method. After that, any code that you wish to execute when the method is called and then an optional *return* statement. What is the difference between the words "function" and "procedure"? In older versions of dBASE, there was a difference in the way the code was called and in the way the code worked. In more recent versions (including dBASE PLUS) this changed, and the terms are interchangeable. Basically both were left in the software to keep from "breaking" older programs.

The *return* statement used to be required in earlier (DOS) versions of dBASE at the end of a method, but when dBASE PLUS is executing code in a class's method, when it sees the beginning of a new method, or it sees the *endclass* statement, it knows that the method is complete and stops processing.

Many developers feel that every method should always have a *return* statement. This is a philosophical question more than anything else. The only time it is required is if you need your method to return a value back to the user, or to the code that called it. We will discuss this concept later on when we get into more complex coding. However, for code documentation and readability it is a good idea to always use a return statement. If you get into good coding habits now, you can avoid frustration later, so all examples in this book will include a return statement for each and every method.

You could create a method called "MyMethod" that simply displayed some text in the output pane of the command window:

```
function MyMethod
    ? form.text1.text
return
```

The command inside the method tells us to go to the form object and the contained object named "text1", and display the contents of the "text" property of that object.

This is perfectly valid. It is obviously possible and often necessary to do a lot more. One example might be that you would want to create code that validated your data before saving it to a table – you could do all of it in one method, or even in multiple methods of the form.

Once you have a method, how do you call it from somewhere in your form?
There are multiple ways to call a method in a class:

```
this.MyMethod
form.MyMethod
class::MyMethod
MyForm::MyMethod
```

The words *this* and *form* were briefly discussed earlier. These are automatically created when you create an instance of a class (an object). The word *form* is specifically used for forms, reports, and datamodules (high level containers), even though the latter two are not actually forms – the word *form* in this case refers to the top-level container.

The word *class* is used in some cases to reference code that is associated with a specific class. The "::" operator is called the *Scope Resolution Operator* – we will come back to this in more detail later.

MyForm:: uses the scope resolution operator again and *MyForm* refers to the Class that we want to execute the method of.

So what is the best way to reference the method from inside the form? It depends on where we are calling the method from. Let's say that you want to call the method *MyMethod* from a pushbutton's onClick event. If you used the command:

```
this.MyMethod
```

What do you think will happen? Remember that the word *this* refers to the current object. If you click the pushbutton, the current object is the pushbutton! The problem is that if you tell the pushbutton that when it is clicked to execute "this.MyMethod", it won't find that method, because it is not associated with the pushbutton.

The safest way, at least for now, is to use the second option listed above:

```
form.MyMethod
```

Now, how would we hook this up to the pushbutton? By using an *event handler*, defined in the constructor code. We would want to add this line to the constructor code for the pushbutton:

```
this.pushbutton1 = new Pushbutton( this )
with( this.pushbutton1 )
   left = 2
   top = 3
   text = "My Method"
   onClick = form.MyMethod
endwith
```

As you will see in other code, sometimes when we want to call a method we use the parentheses, sometimes we do not. Why is that?

We use the parentheses at the end of the name of a method when we want the method to execute *right now*. If we put the parentheses at the end of the statement in the constructor code, the method would fire as if the user had clicked the mouse when the form was being constructed. In some cases this may be harmless, but most of the time we don't want the code to execute when the form is being created, only at the appropriate time, in this case, when the user clicks the pushbutton.

The ENDCLASS Statement

Each class requires the statement *endclass* at the end. This is required by dBASE and will cause your code to fail to compile if it is left out. Its purpose is to let dBASE know that we are done defining the class – that's all it does.

With all of that discussion, how do we actually use such a class? In order to use this, we have to put it in a file, save the file, and then work with it from there.
To create a file in dBASE, in the Command Window type:

```
create file MyForm.cc
```

This will open the dBASE Source Code Editor. We will discuss this in greater depth in a later chapter of this book.

> **📄 NOTE**
>
> Why are we using the file extension of ".CC", rather than ".WFM", which is the one used for a form in dBASE? The ".WFM" file extension assumes some code that is generated automatically by the form designer, making it possible to execute a form by double-clicking on it in the dBASE Navigator window, or by typing in the Command Window (or in code):
>
> ```
> do MyForm.wfm
> ```
>
> As we are not including this startup code, the form we have created is not an executable dBASE program by itself. We will look at forms created by the form designer later in the book.

In the main pane of the window *(the big open space)*, type the following as closely as possible to what you see here:

```
class MyForm of Form
   with( this )
       top = 4
       left = 6
       width = 40
       height = 10
   endwith

   this.text1 = new text( this )
   with( this.text1 )
       left = 2
       width = 25
       text = "This is some text"
   endwith

   this.pushbutton1 = new Pushbutton( this )
   with( this.pushbutton1 )
       left = 2
       top = 3
       text = "My Method"
       onClick = form.MyMethod
   endwith

   function MyMethod
       ? "This is MyMethod of the form class MyForm"
   return
endclass
```

Once you have the above in the source editor, you will want to save it and exit. You can do this in one of many ways, the simplest for now is to hold the Ctrl key and type the letter "W" and let go (`Ctrl`+`W`).

Now that we have our class, how do we actually create an instance of the form, and use it?

You can do this from the Command Window using the following commands:

```
set procedure to MyForm.cc
f = new MyForm()
f.open()
```

If you click on the pushbutton, you should see output in the output pane of the command window because we hooked up an event handler to the pushbutton's onClick event. Each time you click the pushbutton you will see the same thing (because our code is *really* simple). To close the form, since we don't have a pushbutton for it in this example, use the 'x' in the titlebar of the form.

One term we haven't used so far, but which describes what we just did is *subclass* – we have created a subclass of the form class called "MyForm". This is also called *subclassing* and we could say that we have *subclassed* the form class.

The *className* and *baseClassName* Properties

When you create a class that is derived from one of the stock classes of dBASE, it automatically inherits two properties that can be *very* useful in your code. These are: *className* and *baseClassName*. These should not be confused with the object *name* which is created when an object is instantiated.

If you instantiate a form object using the code below:

```
f = new form()
```

"f" is the object *name*, and the *object reference*. The *className* and the *baseClassName* would be "FORM".

The *className* property is used to tell you the actual name of the class. If your class declaration statement says:

```
class MyForm of form
```

Once you have instantiated a form object from this class, you can check to see what the *className* or the *baseClassName* is. You could do this using code like:

```
set procedure to MyForm.cc additive
f = new MyForm()
? f.className
? f.baseClassName
```

This should display in the output pane:

```
MYFORM
FORM
```

This information can make your code more flexible, as you could write a method that did specific things based on what object was calling the method.

dBASE provides a wide variety of stock classes that already follow OOP design. A developer using dBASE most often builds their objects based on the stock classes and then extends or customizes them for their own needs. Because most classes the developer will create are subclassed from the stock classes, these will all inherit the properties, events and methods of those stock classes. Because dBASE supports polymorphism, any of these properties, events and methods can be overridden (or replaced) with your own customized version. And because dBASE supports encapsulation, each subclassed object operates independently from any other object.

When you need to create a class that is not derived from any of the stock classes, dBASE provides you with the Object class (a kind of empty class), that you can subclass and add any properties or methods that you need. We will discuss this class shortly.

Working with Object Reference Variables

In order to work with an object, whether it is a query, a form, or a control on a form, we must always work with a reference variable. In a later chapter we will discuss memory variables in more detail. Most or all of that discussion pertains to the way that object reference variables work. A simple example is to create an instance of a form:

```
f = new form()
```

"f" is the object reference variable. This is the way that we reference the object, its properties, events and methods. Through the use of this variable name (or object reference), we can open the form, change the position and size of the form (either before we open it or after), and so on.

Things to remember are the scope issues of memory variables *(these are discussed in more depth in later chapters)*, because an object reference variable is really just a memory variable – a reference to a place in memory, the contents of which may vary.

If you need your object to be public, wish to instantiate it either as a public variable:

```
public f
f = new form()
```

or you may wish to instantiate it as an object reference that is contained by the _app object:

```
_app.f = new form()
```

You should remember that if you define an object reference variable inside of a program without defining a scope, it is *private*.

The dBASE Object Class

dBASE has a class built in called "object". The purpose of this class is to give the developer a way to create an object "on-the-fly", in their own code. It works like this:

```
o = new object()
```

This is functionally equivalent to defining an empty class, such as:

```
class MyObject
endclass
```

and then instantiating this class:

```
o = new MyObject()
```

In either case you are creating an object that has, by definition, no properties, no events and no methods. In addition, the class definition of "class MyObject" is quite literally, by default, using the internal object class of dBASE.

There are advantages to either way of doing this.

The first way ("on-the-fly") allows you to create a simple container object – one that you can add your own properties to, you can add arrays to it (which can be useful for some coding operations), and so on. You cannot create methods for it, because the syntax to do that doesn't exist.

When designing an application, *most of the time* you are better off creating a class as code and storing it in a file. This allows you to define custom properties and to create your own methods as part of the class definition.

One serious difference between defining your own classes is that if they are not subclassed from the other stock classes (in other words, not from the *object* class) in dBASE, they do not have the *className* or *baseClassName* properties. If you wanted to, you could add your own, but you would most likely want to set the *baseClassName* property to the word "OBJECT".

All of this said, having discussed this with members of the dBASE Developer's Community, there certainly are times that using the object class in your code can be handy for a quick way to create an object. As you will see, dBASE's programming language (dBL) is a very flexible and powerful language.

Types of Classes

There are types of classes in dBASE, as you might imagine. However, there aren't that many types in the overall scheme of things. There are *stock classes*, *custom classes* that are based on (or *derived from*) the stock classes and *custom classes* that are completely user-defined.

Stock Classes

Stock Classes are the classes built into dBASE. We have already briefly looked at the form, text, and pushbutton stock classes, creating instances of them in the sample.

dBASE has a large quantity of stock classes, many of them visual for use on forms, reports and labels. However, dBASE doesn't stop there, it has a lot of other stock classes designed for working with data. dBASE has an excellent data object model that allows a developer to use object-oriented coding down to the field level of a table. dBASE also has non-visual classes such as the array, date, string, and file classes that are not specifically data related.

Stock Classes have their own built in properties, events and methods. You can use these, you can modify them, and you can create subclasses of them. You can also add your own custom properties and methods to your subclasses or custom classes.

User-created Custom Classes

User-created Custom Classes, are really of two types – the first is a subclass of a stock class – something we have already looked at *(although only briefly so far)*. You can create complex subclasses that can do things such as display calendars and so on. We are only getting started!

The second type of user-created custom class is completely defined by the user, and it does not have any events.

A custom class that is not based on a stock class can be quite useful and very powerful because you can do pretty much whatever you want to with it. Members of the dBASE developer's community have created custom classes that can read from and write to a .INI file using calls to Windows' API; that can read and write information used by the BDE; and much more.

Building Custom Classes from Scratch

To get an idea of what can be done to create a custom class that is not derived from a stock class, let us imagine that we want to put together something quite simple. *Note that the following is not the way that I would recommend actually doing the following for a real application, as everything is hard-coded – this is just an example of a simple class.* This is a simple little class that will provide details about a CD by one of my favorite a capella singing groups:

```
class BobsCD
    this.title = "My, I'm Large"
    this.label = "Great American Music"
    this.year = "1987"
    this.tracks = new array()
    this.tracks.add( "You Really Got A Hold On Me" )
    this.tracks.add( "Johnny's Room" )
    this.tracks.add( "Please Let Me Be Your Third World Country" )
    this.tracks.add( "Valentino's" )
    this.tracks.add( "Banana Love" )
    this.tracks.add( "Little Red Riding Hood" )
    this.tracks.add( "My Shoes" )
    this.tracks.add( "My, I'm Large" )
    this.tracks.add( "Helmet" )
    this.tracks.add( "My Husband Was a Weatherman" )
    this.tracks.add( "Mopping, Mopping, Mopping" )
    this.tracks.add( "Bulky Rhythm" )

    // Method to display the track list:
    function getTracks
        local i
        for i = 1 to this.tracks.size
            ? this.tracks[i]
        next
    return
endclass
```

Without getting into all of the specifics of this class, we are using an array object as a property of this class to store the tracks on the CD. *(This makes our class a container, as it contains another class ...)* We have a method in this class called "getTracks" that will, when called, return a list of the tracks of this CD. We could use this by creating an instance of the class, and then query different properties by displaying them, and so on. The following code assumes that the class as given above was saved to a file called BobsCD.cc:

```
set procedure to BobsCD.cc additive
oBobs = new BobsCD()
? oBobs.title
? oBobs.label
? oBobs.year
```

```
oBobs.getTracks()
```

You should see, in the output pane of the Command Window the title after you press the Return key for the command:

```
? oBobs.title
```

And so on. When you issue the last command, note that you see all of the tracks. You could be quite specific, say you wanted the title of the third track:

```
? oBobs.tracks[3]
```

Which would list the third track. We will discuss arrays later in this book, but this is a *(very)* short introduction to them.

General Syntax for Custom Classes

Custom Classes should all follow a similar syntax. Some of this is by coding conventions, others are required by dBASE and the language dBL.

Every custom class must have a CLASS statement that tells dBASE that this is a class definition. This is also called a class *declaration*:

```
class className
```

The above is the simplest variation on this statement. If the class you are defining is not subclassed from any of the stock classes of dBASE, this is all you absolutely need.

 NOTE

dBASE allows any length to a class name, but it only recognizes the first 32 characters. If you need to define a class with a name that is this long, you should reconsider your design.

However *(you knew that was coming, didn't you?)*, the declaration statement for a class can be more complex than this. For example, you could do something like:

```
class className( parameters ) of superclass( parameters ) custom
```

First, note the parentheses, with the word *parameters*. It is possible to pass values to a class when it is instantiated. Parameters defined in this fashion are *local* in scope (more about *scope* will be discussed in later chapters of this book). You may create a list of parameters and you may pass parameters to the superclass. If you pass parameters to the superclass, they need to be named the same as they are in the derived class – in other words, if you want to pass a parameter such as "oParent" to the superclass, it needs to be named "oParent" in both the first part of the declaration and in the parentheses for the superclass. A good example of this would be if you had created a subclass of the pushbutton stock class, which requires a parent as a parameter:

```
class MyPushbutton( oParent ) of Pushbutton( oParent ) custom
```

The keyword *custom*, while not required, is important if you are using the designers that are built in to dBASE. What this means is that if you have a custom class such as:

```
class MyPushbutton( oParent ) of Pushbutton( oParent )
```

```
        this.width = 15
        this.height = 2
        this.colorNormal = "white/red"
    endclass
```

And you try to use this with the Form Designer, if you don't use the "custom" keyword, then those properties will most likely be streamed out to the form. This is not really good OOP design, because if you change the properties in the custom class, and they are streamed out in the form, the form will use the ones in its own constructor code rather than in the class prototype. However, if you use the "custom" keyword:

```
    class MyPushbutton( oParent ) of Pushbutton( oParent ) custom
```

these properties shouldn't be being streamed out to the form. This will make more sense after we start looking at the Form Designer in a later chapter.

And to make things even more complex, we can add to this statement a pointer to another file. This is useful if you wish to subclass another custom class contained in a different file *(the following is one line, it wraps here, as there is not enough room …)*:

```
    class MyPB( oParent ) of MyPushbutton( oParent ) from "MyPushbutton.cc" custom
```

Basically the statement above says that we are creating a class called "MyPB", which has a parent referenced by "oParent", and is a subclass of "MyPushbutton". The class definition of "MyPushbutton" is stored in the file "MyPushbutton.cc". *(We will discuss this in more depth in later chapters.)*

Next we have the *constructor code*. We examined constructor code earlier, it is literally a definition of the properties of the class, as well as the assignment of event handlers, and then if the class is a container, the information needed to construct any contained classes.

After the constructor code, we have any methods that are defined. Methods must begin with the keyword "function" or "procedure", the name of the method, and any parameters (they can be passed in parentheses). It is a good idea to always end your methods with a "return" statement. Your methods would generally look like:

```
    function MyMethod( myparameter1, myparameter2 )
        // any code to be executed
    return
```

Finally, we have the required statement:

```
    endclass
```

If you leave this last statement out of your class definition, you will cause dBASE to return an error when you attempt to compile your custom class file (this occurs when you attempt to use it).

Declaring Class Parameters

We briefly discussed *parameters* in the previous section of this chapter, when looking at the declaration statement. Parameters are an important part of code for dBASE, it is how you pass information from object to object, making it possible for objects to communicate with each other. It is also a way for functions and procedures to be able to work with specific information and so on. When we get to later chapters of this book we'll look at parameters in conjunction with functions, procedures, and programs. For now, let us look at parameters used with custom class definitions.

When you define a custom class, sometimes there are required parameters. This is particularly important for custom classes that are derived from the visual stock classes – any control that is contained by a form or a report. These controls must always have a parent property, and the parent property is always a container object's object reference. An example might be a pushbutton class that you wanted to define:

```
class MyPB( oParent ) of Pushbutton( oParent ) custom
```

In this case, you must have a parent object reference passed to the class and it must be passed on to the superclass (Pushbutton). This is called a *passthrough* – which means that your code does not have to actually do anything with this parameter. This is because the constructor for the superclass requires the *parent* property to function properly – indeed, it actually assigns the object reference for the parent to the *parent* property of the class.

 NOTE

If you use the Form Designer to create a new custom class *(something we will discuss in a later chapter)*, the Form Designer streams out a second parameter – the name. Your class declaration might look like:

```
class MyPB( parent, name ) of Pushbutton( parent, name )
```

This actually can cause problems, because a pushbutton that is derived from this on a form will inherit a default name that doesn't make sense. This will be discussed in more depth later.

You could set in the constructor code for a simple pushbutton something like:

```
class MyPB( oParent ) of Pushbutton( oParent ) custom
    ? this.parent.className
endclass
```

When you created an instance of this (note that you would need to create an instance of a form object), that you would get the *className* of the parent object:

```
f = new form()
f.PB1 = new MyPB( f )
// will display: FORM
```

You didn't do anything to assign the *parent* property directly, but by passing the object reference 'f' to the declaration, it was passed on to the superclass, and in the superclass' constructor code the property was assigned the object reference.

What happens if you leave the *parent* reference out of the instantiation code?

```
f = new form()
f.PB1 = new MyPB()
```

An error occurs:

```
Error: Data type mismatch. Expecting: Object
```

This is because the object reference was left out and dBASE requires it for most of the stock visual objects.

If you are creating your own custom classes, you can do more with parameters. You can define whatever parameters you wish. You can check to see if a value was passed to them and more. As we examine various classes throughout this book, you will see examples of parameters, and parameter error checking and a lot more.

Using Class Hierarchies

A Class Hierarchy is multiple classes, derived from other classes. Sound complicated? It can be, but the concept is relatively simple.

Keeping it simple, let us assume that for a project you want to define a set of pushbuttons that perform specific tasks, but you only want to define some properties once. You could define a base pushbutton that had specific properties such as *height*, *width*, *fontName*, and *fontBold* properties defined. Then, you could define pushbuttons that are derived from your base pushbutton class that have properties specific to them, such as different *onClick* event handlers and whatever else might be needed. This would be a simple class hierarchy – your base pushbutton class would be derived from the stock pushbutton class. Then the other pushbuttons would be derived from your base class. To get a feel for it, we could do something like the following:

```
class MyBasePB( oParent ) of Pushbutton( oParent ) custom
   this.height = 1.5
   this.width = 20
   this.fontName = "Times New Roman"
   this.fontBold = true
endclass
```

This pushbutton would be your base pushbutton. Note that it is derived from the stock class and that we are using the *oParent* parameter, as discussed earlier.
Next, you could define two pushbuttons that did something specific:

```
class MyPB1( oParent ) of MyBasePB( oParent ) custom
   this.text = "Pushbutton 1"
   this.onClick = class::PB1_Click

   function PB1_Click
      msgbox( "This is MyPB1!" )
   return
endclass

class MyPB2( oParent ) of MyBasePB( oParent ) custom
   this.text = "Pushbutton 2"
   this.onClick = class::PB2_Click

   function PB2_Click
      msgbox( "This is MyPB2" )
   return
endclass
```

If you saved all three of these in a custom class file (.cc) such as "MyButtons.cc", you could then place these on a form:

```
set procedure to MyButtons.cc
f = new Form()
f.PB1 = new MyPB1( f )
f.PB2 = new MyPF2( f )
f.PB2.top = 2 // so we don't appear on top of PB1
f.open()
```

If you click the first button, you'll get a message box with one bit of text, if you click the other button, you'll get different text. If you close the form, we will move on to the next bit.

Now, here's one of the best things about writing custom classes in this fashion – what if you want to change the *fontBold* property of all pushbuttons derived from the base button class?

There are two ways to do it – the first is the hard one: we could set the *fontBold* property for each button derived from the base class. OR we could do this the simple way: we could change the *fontBold* property for the base pushbutton, which would affect any pushbuttons derived from it!

If you bring the file back into the source code editor (in the Command Window: MODIFY COMMAND MyButtons.cc), you can change the colors used in the base pushbutton class:

```
class MyBasePB( oParent ) of Pushbutton( oParent ) custom
   this.height = 1.5
   this.width = 20
   this.fontName = "Times New Roman"
   this.fontBold = false
endclass
```

Then you could save the class file, and exit the source code editor ([Ctrl]+[W]) and then do the same thing we did before:

```
set procedure to MyButtons.cc additive
f = new Form()
f.PB1 = new MyPB1( f )
f.PB2 = new MyPF2( f )
f.PB2.top = 2 // so we don't appear on top of PB1
f.open()
```

Notice that the text of the pushbuttons is now displayed as NOT having boldfaced text on the pushbutton! And we only had to change it in one place, rather than in both of the pushbutton class definitions! This hopefully will get you realizing some of the great power behind properly designed objects and an object hierarchy. We'll come back to this example code in a bit, so you might want to make sure you've saved it someplace handy.

Using the Scope Resolution Operator

We briefly mentioned the Scope Resolution Operator earlier. This needs to be looked at in more depth to really understand it.

The *scope resolution operator* is really the :: symbol (two colons) and the word that comes before it defines where to get the code that needs to be executed. There are at least three different ways to use the scope resolution operator.

The first way to use this operator is to point to the current class definition, using the word CLASS.

An example of this might be from the MyButtons.cc we defined earlier in this chapter:

```
class MyBasePB( oParent ) of Pushbutton( oParent ) custom
   this.height = 1.5
   this.width = 20
   this.fontName = "Times New Roman"
   this.fontBold = true
endclass

class MyPB1( oParent ) of MyBasePB( oParent ) custom
   this.text = "Pushbutton 1"
   this.onClick = class::PB1_Click

   function PB1_Click
      msgbox( "This is MyPB1!" )
   return
endclass

class MyPB2( oParent ) of MyBasePB( oParent ) custom
   this.text = "Pushbutton 2"
   this.onClick = class::PB2_Click

   function PB2_Click
      msgbox( "This is MyPB2" )
   return
endclass
```

In this example, note that the onClick event handler for MyPB1 uses the syntax "class::PB1_Click". This tells dBASE when the pushbutton is clicked, to look in this class for the method called "PB1_Click". If that method did not exist (or you misspelled it), you would get an error when a form was run and you clicked on the button.

The second way to use the scope resolution operator is to reference the super class. If we modified the example above, we could do something quite different:

```
class MyBasePB( oParent ) of Pushbutton( oParent ) custom
   this.height = 1.5
   this.width = 20
   this.fontName = "Times New Roman"
   this.fontBold = true
   this.onClick = class::MyBase_Click

   function MyBase_Click
      msgbox( "This is "+this.className+"!" )
   return
endclass

class MyPB1( oParent ) of MyBasePB( oParent ) custom
   this.text = "Pushbutton 1"
   this.onClick = super::MyBase_Click
endclass

class MyPB2( oParent ) of MyBasePB( oParent ) custom
   this.text = "Pushbutton 2"
```

```
      this.onClick = class::PB2_Click

   function PB2_Click
      msgbox( "This is MyPB2" )
   return
endclass
```

Note that in the base pushbutton, we have added a method called "MyBase_Click". Also note that we changed the event handler in MyPB1 so that it points to the code used by MyBasePB, by using the word "SUPER" and the scope resolution operator: "this.onClick = super::MyBase_Click".

The last way of using the scope resolution operator is by a direct call to a class and its method. In the code for MyPB1 we could have used: "MyBase::MyBase_Click", and it would have worked just as well. This can be useful if you wanted to call code from another class. For example we could have, for the event handler of MyPB1, the onClick event that is in MyPB2: "this.onClick = MyPB2::PB2_Click". Rather than the message from the base pushbutton, we would get the one from MyPB2 (which is not very different in appearance in this code).

It is important to note here that we didn't really need to assign any event handler to MyPB1. Since this pushbutton is derived from MyBasePB, by default it *inherits* the behavior of the superclass. Since the superclass has an onClick event handler, any pushbutton that is derived from it, inherits that event handler. A more efficient way to write this code would then be:

```
class MyBasePB( oParent ) of Pushbutton( oParent ) custom
   this.height = 1.5
   this.width = 20
   this.fontName = "Times New Roman"
   this.fontBold = true
   this.onClick = class::MyBase_Click

   function MyBase_Click
      msgbox( "This is "+this.className+"!" )
   return
endclass

class MyPB1( oParent ) of MyBasePB( oParent ) custom
   this.text = "Pushbutton 1"
endclass

class MyPB2( oParent ) of MyBasePB( oParent ) custom
   this.text = "Pushbutton 2"
   this.onClick = class::PB2_Click

   function PB2_Click
      msgbox( "This is MyPB2" )
   return
endclass
```

Note that MyPB1 has *no* event handler defined for the onClick event? It isn't really necessary, unless we want to overwrite the event.

Overriding Methods and Events

We should look at the term: *overriding*. You can change the behavior of a method or event of a class from that of the superclass it is derived from. In the example above we are changing the behavior of MyPB2 from the default behavior of the superclass by defining a new behavior. That's really all there is to overriding a method or event! If we didn't change it, MyPB2 would inherit the *onClick* event of the superclass.

Object Containership

One of the most important aspects of working with objects is that an object may contain another object. You can create class libraries *(we will discuss this in a later chapter)* that are a single object that contain instances of other objects that interact with each other. Some of this material was covered briefly earlier in this chapter – we're going into a little more depth now.

The most obvious example of this is the form itself. A form that contains no objects is just a blank window in dBASE. You can work with it and manipulate it, but unless you have more objects contained within the form object, there is not a *lot* you can do.

When an object is created that is contained by another object, it must have a reference to that object. If you examine the way a form is created that has an entryfield on it, the entryfield will be created as:

```
this.ENTRYFIELD1 = new ENTRYFIELD(this)
```

"this.ENTRYFIELD1" is creating an object reference variable ("ENTRYFIELD1") that is contained by the form because of the use of "this." at the beginning. More importantly, however, notice that the word "this" is used in the parentheses for the instantiation of the object: "new ENTRYFIELD(**this**)".

When the entryfield is actually instantiated (when an instance of the form object is created), the *parent* property of the entryfield is given the object reference "this", which in this case is a reference to the form object. Thus dBASE knows what object is the parent of the entryfield and you can query that property.

The Keyword *This*

The keyword "this" now becomes very important to your vocabulary. The keyword "this" when working with the dBL object model **always** refers to the current object. This will become more and more important as you work with event handlers in your code, because if you are not clear what "this" refers to, you may find your code getting confused, you may get confused when examining the code, and so on.

In a form, the keyword *this* refers to the same object as the form's *activeControl* property.

The Keyword *Form*

When working with Forms, Reports, and Datamodules there is a special keyword that can be used to reference the top-level class. This object variable is created when a Form, Report or Datamodule is instantiated, and always refers to the class defined in the main CLASS statement. This is not available if you create your own subclasses unless they are Forms, Reports or Datamodules.

By using the FORM variable, you can write re-usable code that can be used to reference specific properties, events and methods of the container class, without having to be concerned with the name of the container class. This is useful for custom classes, as well as for code that might be referenced by more than one class. It is common to use calls such as the following:

```
form.close()
```

Which would call the *close()* method of the form – there is no need to know the name of the form class for this to function properly.

 NOTE

It is important to understand that the database objects, because they may be used outside of a form or report, even while the form or report do not have focus, and even if their object reference (i.e., their name) has been passed to them as a parameter when they are instantiated in the constructor code, they do not recognize the keyword *Form* in any event handlers, methods, etc. This includes the database object, session object, query object, rowset object, etc.

The Keyword CLASS

dBL allows you to use the keyword CLASS to reference the current class, most commonly to execute the methods and event handlers of the class. For example, if you created a form that used the *onOpen()* event to call an event handler in the form, you might see code in the constructor that looked like:

```
with( this )
   onOpen = CLASS::Form_onOpen
endwith
```

The separator here, rather than the dot notation you normally see, is the scope resolution operator. It is important to note that in this case, the code shown is telling dBASE to assign the event handler named "Form_onOpen" (a function that would be defined later in the class definition) to the event so that when the form opens it would execute the code in the event handler.

You can also use CLASS:: to run or execute an event handler or method of a class. The following would execute a method of the class named "Init".

```
class::Init()
```

The big difference between this and the assignment shown above is that in this case we use the parentheses to tell dBASE to execute the method now (when it reaches the statement in your code).

The most difficult part of understanding and working with object containership is how you reference objects – the main object and the contained objects often need to pass information back and forth in order to perform whatever it is that they need to do.

For example, a form might need to have entryfields. The entryfield objects would need to know what field they are datalinked to. In order to do that, the entryfield objects would need to be able to query the form's *rowset* property, to find the *fields* array and then the individual field objects contained by that array. A pushbutton that navigates in the form's rowset would need to be able to also query the form to know what rowset to affect when it is clicked.

There are many ways of moving back and forth in the object hierarchy. First, there is always a main or *parent* object. Most classes in dBL have a *parent* property that can be used to reference the parent object. So if you have a form object and you place an entryfield object on the form in the Form Designer, the entryfield object's *parent* property will be an object reference to the form. If, however, you placed a notebook object on the form, and then placed the entryfield onto the notebook, rather than directly onto the form, the *parent* property of the entryfield would point to the notebook instead.

This is called the object hierarchy and it is important to be able to navigate through this hierarchy to find what objects you might need.

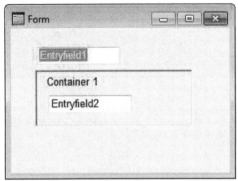

Figure 6-3

In the example shown in Figure 6-3, Entryfield1's *parent* property will point to the form. Entryfield2's *parent* property will point to the Container. The Container's *parent* property will point to the form.

The syntax would be:

```
form.entryfield1.parent
```

or

```
form.container1.parent
form.container1.entryfield2.parent
```

In all three of the following statements, if we asked dBASE to return the value of, say, the *parent* object's *className* property, we should get "Form":

```
? form.entryfield1.parent.className
? form.container1.parent.className
? form.container1.entryfield2.parent.className
```

Or should they? In the last statement shown above, you would get the word "Container" instead of "Form" – why? Because we asked for the *className* property of the *parent* of the **entryfield**, not of the container. In order for the last statement to return a reference to the form, we would need to add another "parent" into the statement:

```
? form.container1.entryfield2.parent.parent.className
```

As you can see, this object hierarchy can be a little confusing.

The important thing to understand at all times is what level you are in the hierarchy. The examples given are not the most useful, because we already actually know what the parent of each of those objects is going to be. However, we could create code for each object that told us.

To do that, we would use the object reference *this* to refer to the current object. We could create a form class that had a method that simply told us the *className* property of object, and call it for each object when the form is opened (using the object's *onOpen()* event). This might be placed in the form's class definition as:

```
function ShowParent
    // Show the className of the parent object
    // of the object that calls this method:
    ? this.parent.className
return
```

Then for each control we wished to show this, we could set, in the control's *onOpen()* event, code similar to:

```
function ENTRYFIELD1_onOpen
    class::ShowParent()
return
```

When you run the form, you would see something like the following in the output pane of the Command Window:

```
CONTAINERSHIPEXAMPLEFORM
CONTAINERSHIPEXAMPLEFORM
CONTAINER
```

(To show this, I created a simple form as shown in Figure 6-3, and then added the code as mentioned above ...)

Using Objects as Parameters

In later chapters of this book we will discuss using parameters to get information from one program to another and to get information from one function or method, etc., to another.

It is possible to pass object references as parameters. If you wanted to create a report that uses a specific set of options that you have defined, perhaps for use in a filter, you might create an array to contain all of those options and pass them at once to the report:

```
aParameters = new array()
aParameters.add( form.rowset.fields["FirstName"].value )
aParameters.add( form.rowset.fields["LastName"].value )
do MyReport.rep with aParameters
```

Then in the report you could check in, say, an overridden *render()* method to see if the array was passed to it and if so work with that array's values to filter the report.

Another example might be a simple function that would show the className of an object, you might make this a method of a form:

```
function ShowClassName( oObj )
```

```
       ? oObj.className
return
```

And to use it:

```
form.ShowClassName( form.Entryfield1 ) // returns "ENTRYFIELD"
```

Making Objects Go Away

Objects, like memory variables, use memory. It is often desirable to release them from memory so that you properly clean up after yourself.

dBASE does a lot of automatic "garbage collection" – cleaning up after itself. For example, if you have a container object and you release the container object properly, any objects contained by it are also released – you don't have to do more cleanup there.

However, some objects do not have a *release()* method and even if you release an object, the object reference variable still exists in memory. For example, if you do something like:

```
f = new form()
f.entryfield1 = new entryfield(f)
f.mdi := false
f.readModal()
f.release()
```

The (form) object referenced by the variable "f" is released, as is the entryfield that is contained by this object. But the object reference variable "f" is still in memory. You can see this by issuing the commands shown above in the Command Window (closing the form after it opens), and then in the Command Window typing:

```
display memory
```

(Click the "Cancel" button after it displays one screen of information.) You will see something like the following in the output pane:

```
            User Memory Variables
F              Pub    O
```

This means that the memory variable "F" still exists in memory and that it is public (because we did this in the Command Window) and finally that it is an object reference.

If you type:

```
? f.entryfield1.value
```

You will get an error that says "Attempt to access released object". So how do you get rid of this memory variable? It is suggested that you "null it out" – assign a value of "null" to it:

```
f = null
```

If you then try to examine the value of "entryfield1" you will get a different error: "Data type mismatch. Expecting: Object". This is because "f" no longer is an object reference variable, it contains the value of "null". You can go one step further and release the memory variable itself:

```
release f
```

If you do this and then type the "display memory" command again, you will see:

```
            User Memory Variables
       0 variables defined,        0 bytes used
```

Multiple References to the Same Object

All of the above is well and good, but what if you have more than one reference to an object? This often trips up developers of dBASE applications.

If you have a form defined:

```
f = new form()
```

And then you have another object reference variable that points to the form:

```
g = f
```

If you then use the DISPLAY MEMORY command in the Command Window (and click the "Cancel" button the first time you are asked), you should see in the output pane:

```
            User Memory Variables

F                 Pub    O
G                 Pub    O
       2 variables defined,        0 bytes used
```

When you issue a set of commands such as:

```
f.release()
f = null
release f
```

There is still a reference to the form that was originally defined as "f", but the object reference variable is "g".

If you issue the DISPLAY MEMORY command again, you will see:

```
            User Memory Variables

G                 Pub    O
       1 variables defined,        0 bytes used
```

"G" references a released object, which you can see if you try to open it or query any of the properties, but the object reference is still there. You would want to release the variable:

```
g = null
release g
```

Multiple Instances of the Same Class

This sounds like it would be the same thing as the previous section titled "Multiple References to the Same Object", but really it is quite different.

It is possible to open the same form more than once, for example. This would create two different *instances* of the same form class. Let us say that you have defined a form called "MyTest.wfm". In an application, you might allow the user (assuming this is an MDI application) to open the same form more than once, which might allow them to examine two totally different records in the same table(s). If your code releases one instance of the form, the other instance is still out there in memory.

You may want to find that instance and release it as well, just to make sure that everything has been cleaned up in memory. There is a means of finding an object reference in memory and allowing you to manipulate the object – the *findInstance()* function. This function needs to know the name of the class and returns an object reference, which can then be used to close a form or release an object. Assuming the example, you might want to create a loop along these lines:

```
o = findInstance( "MyTestForm" )
do while not empty( o )
   o.release()
   o := findInstance( "MyTestForm", o )
enddo
```

The *findInstance()* function has other uses as well, including the ability to find out if there is an instance of an object in memory and either create one or not as needed in your application.

Protecting Members of a Class

There is a school of thought that with a custom class you should protect some of the members of the class, to avoid a developer overwriting or modifying those members, or accessing some of the code in a class that it is not necessary for them to access.

Personally I seldom use this ability, but if you have a need to protect some of the members of your own classes, you can do so with a command called PROTECT.

This command *(when used in an object's constructor code)* is used to tell dBASE that the only way the properties that are protected may be modified is through code in the class, and the only way a developer can use methods of the class that are protected is through other methods of the class – no direct access to the protected members of the class is available.

You would use the PROTECT command in the constructor code of a class, along these lines:

```
class MyClass
   protect FirstName, Birthdate, Age
   this.FirstName = ""
   this.Birthdate = {} // empty date

   function Age()
      local dReturn
      dReturn = ( floor( ( val( dtos( date() ) ) ) ;
                  - val( dtos( this.Birthdate ) ) ) / 10000 ) )
   return dReturn
endclass
```

The problem with this now becomes the fact that any developer (yourself included) cannot directly access or modify the properties, nor can they use the method *Age()* that is part of this class.

If you tried to use this class (the following assumes that the code above is saved to a file named "MyClass.cc"), then change a property or access the method, the following will happen:

```
set proc to MyClass.cc
oC = new MyClass()
oC.FirstName = "Fred"
```

If you tried to execute the *Age()* method:

```
? oc.Age()
```

You would get the same error. So, how do you then allow access to these? You would create what are called *setters* and *getters* – methods that allow you to set a property value, get a property value, or access a method of the class.

You would want to add methods to the custom class such as:

```
function setFirstName( cName )
   this.FirstName := cName
return

function getFirstName
return this.FirstName

function setBirthdate( dDate )
   this.Birthdate := dDate
return

function getBirthdate
return this.Birthdate

function getAge
return this.Age()
```

Then to use them, you would issue command such as:

```
set proc to MyClass.cc
oC = new MyClass()
oC.setFirstName("Fred")
? oc.getFirstName()
oC.setBirthdate( {03/29/1963} )
? oC.getBirthdate()
? oC.getAge()
```

To be more practical, you would most likely want to add error checking to be sure that you were assigning a date value to the Birthdate property and that you were assigning a character value to the FirstName property, but this gives you the basic idea.

When we get to the discussion of Custom Classes in a later chapter of this book, we will examine this again, as the PROTECT command is important for Encapsulation (see below).

Encapsulation

By protecting members of a class (properties, methods, etc.), and then using getters and setters, you are encapsulating your class – making it completely self-contained. This is considered to be the "ideal" method of creating custom classes and then using them in your applications. To that end, I will attempt to use proper *encapsulation* in the various classes created as examples in later chapters of the book, unless it is meant to be a very simple, quick example of some concept being shown at the time.

Knowing What the Members of a Class Are

Normally a developer would know, or have access to information about the members of a class. However, your programs may need to know specific information. How do you know what the members of any class are?

As a developer, you can use the Inspector in your code to check out the properties, events and methods of any object. However, in a compiled and built executable that uses the dBASE PLUS Runtime, the Inspector is not really an option.

There is a function in dBASE that can be used with any object, called *enumerate()*. This function returns an associative array (these will be discussed in detail in a later chapter of this book), which stores the name of the member as the key and the value is either a "P" (for Property), "E" (for Event) or "M" (for Method).

To use this on class you have to have an instance of the class, pass the object reference variable to it and give a place to store the information:

```
aMembers = enumerate( _app )
```

(The _app object is always available, so is useful for this test.)

This will create an associative array called aMembers, which you can then examine using the properties and methods of an associative array. For example you might wish to loop through the various members of the _app object and display their name and type:

```
local aMembers, cKey, i
aMembers = enumerate( _app )
cKey = aMembers.firstKey
for i = 1 to aMembers.count()
    ? cKey + " - " + aMembers[ cKey ]
    cKey := aMembers.nextKey( cKey )
next
```

This can save you a lot of difficulties. You could check to see if a specific property, event or method existed:

```
if aMembers.isKey( "MyCustomProperty" )
```

Or if the member exists, you could check to see if it is, perhaps, a property:

```
if aMembers[ "MyCustomProperty" ] == "P"
```

And once you know if it is a property, you could then of course query that property, modify it, etc.

Summary

In this chapter we have discussed the basic concepts of Object Oriented Programming, shown examples that you may or may not have tried in dBASE PLUS and tried to get you used to the basics. At this point you should have a basic grasp of what a *class* is, what its *members* are and the standard OOP terms *encapsulation*, *inheritance* and *polymorphism*. Armed with knowledge of these concepts, you are now ready to start seriously looking at what it takes to build an application in dBASE PLUS.

NOTES:

Chapter 7: Working with the Data Object Model (OODML)

This chapter will focus on one of the most important parts of dBASE PLUS – the Data Object Model, or "OODML" (Object-Oriented Database Manipulation Language).

In Chapter 6 we learned about objects and how to work with them. Here we are going to learn how to use the Data objects that are built in to dBASE to work with data. In Chapter 8 we will compare using OODML and SQL versus XDML to get a good idea how it all combines.

A general note about the code samples in this chapter *(and in Chapter 8)* – rather than confusing you as a programmer and trying to incorporate completely proper OOP design at the same time as trying to teach you the basics of how individual objects work, we are going to focus on individual objects. There are more OOP ways of doing some of what I am showing in the code samples and as we get more in to programming techniques we will move more and more into proper OOP coding techniques.

An Overview

Borland, and now dBASE, LLC have taken the world-class object model that was created for Visual dBASE 5.x, and moved it over to the tables and the databases. What this means is that you can now use tables, records, and fields as objects, with each having its own set of properties, events, and methods. This gives the developer a lot of control over the code and allows the developer a lot of the object oriented power and reusability that you can get from other objects in dBASE.

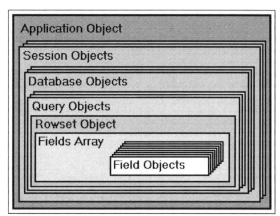

Figure 7-1
(Image by Gary White, used with permission)

So, what are all these objects and how are they related? Before we get into the "in-depth" discussion, let's step back and take a look at the bigger view of the data objects in dBASE.

Most of these objects are containers. This means that they can hold other objects. An example which you will see a lot of is the query object. This object holds a rowset object, so it is a container for the rowset object. Unlike some containers, there can be only one rowset object for each query object. The rowset object is a container for a fields array. The fields array holds pointers to each field object that is contained in the rowset. Hence, you might draw out a diagram something like Figure 7-1.

The rowset object would have a parent, which is the query, the fields array would have a parent, which is the rowset object, the field objects have a parent, which is the fields array.

Note that you cannot define a rowset object independent of a query object, but you can define a field object independent of a fields array or rowset *(this is not really a good idea, as it will have limited use)*.

Now, to make things more interesting, a database object refers to a database or database alias. A database, by its very nature, contains tables. In a way, the database object is a reference to an object – the database itself. However, that is rather simplifying matters.

A session object is used to handle simultaneous database access. (The most likely scenario would be an MDI application where multiple forms accessing the same tables might be opened – however, note that most developers using dBASE do not use the session object all that often, if ever.)

Stored Procedures can only be used with SQL Server tables and are used to access a stored procedure on the server database (a stored procedure is a collection of SQL statements that run independently on a server, usually triggered by a pre-programmed event). Local tables do not recognize these and attempting to use them on local tables may cause heartburn or at least mild frustration.

A data module can be used to contain: database objects, stored procedure objects, session objects and query objects. Rowsets are, as noted previously, contained automatically by queries, hence, if you wish to access a rowset contained in a query in a data module, you have to work through the object hierarchy to get to the rowset.

While the image above *(Figure 7-1)* shows the relationship of the various objects, it makes more sense to discuss functionality and as we go we can discuss the relationships as needed, so some of this is not going to be in a sequence that might make sense from looking at Figure 7-1.

Creating and Coding Query Objects

The query object is used to reference the individual tables of your database and is required if you are going to do any work with tables using the OODML.

As such, it is very important that you understand this. It is the container *(or parent object)* of the rowset, which is where most of the data manipulation methods and events are, as well as the rowset being a container for the fields.

How Do I Use a Query?

We will keep coming back to this topic, but at its most basic, and assuming that you are starting with local tables, you need to instantiate the query, assign the SQL property, and then set the *active* property to true.

```
q = new query()
q.sql = "SELECT * FROM mytable"
q.active = true
```

Before we move on there is one aspect of this that it is vital you understand: before you set the *active* property to *true* for the query object, the rowset object is not instantiated. What this means is that if you try to set properties or access the rowset before setting the query object's *active* property, the rowset effectively does not exist and either you will get errors, or just nothing will happen. Once you set the *active* property to *true*, the rowset is instantiated and any properties you changed are reset to their default values! One very deceptive thing that dBASE developers mistakenly do is:

```
q = new query()
q.sql = "SELECT * FROM mytable"
q.rowset.indexName = "someindex"
q.active = true
```

No error occurs, but the *indexName* property of the rowset is not set, because the rowset has not been instantiated. When you then try to work through the table you will see that the index was not set and the data is in natural order. If you set the *indexName* property after setting the query's *active* property to true it would work:

```
q = new query()
q.sql = "SELECT * FROM mytable"
q.active = true
q.rowset.indexName = "someindex"
```

NOTE

It should be noted that there are many "shortcuts" that may be used in OODML and it is possible in some cases to shorten several lines of code to a single line of code. There are reasons this may be useful and other times when you may need to use the "long" version. For example:

```
q = new query()
q.sql = "SELECT * FROM mytable"
q.active = true
```

Could be shortened to:

```
q = new query( "SELECT * FROM mytable" )
```

The problem with this might be if you needed to access a database object or a session object *(see later in this chapter)*. In those cases you need the longer form of the code. The longer form is more readable, so that is what will be used throughout the book.

It sometimes worries new users of dBASE is that they "have to know SQL"... no, you don't. The above command is the most SQL you absolutely have to know to create some very complex applications in dBASE PLUS. Most of what you might want to do is covered by properties, events and methods of the rowset object, which we will get to presently.

The program statements shown above are all fine and dandy if you are creating a program that needs to manipulate data, but what if you want to use a form or a report?

It couldn't be more simple. Bring up a form in the Form Designer, click on the navigator "Tables" tab and drag the table you wish to use onto the form (or report) surface. You will see an icon used to represent the query object. This has the letters "SQL" on it. The designer surfaces automatically fill in the required information, although the code looks different if you examine the source code:

```
this.CUSTOMER1 = new QUERY()
this.CUSTOMER1.parent = this
```

```
with (this.CUSTOMER1)
   left = 52.5714
   top = 2.5
   sql = "select * from customer"
   active = true
endwith
```

The designers stream out the *left* and *top* properties so that every time you open the form, the query icon is in the same location. When you run the form, the query icon will not appear on the form – it is there only during design mode. We will look at this again when we get to working with data on forms in a later chapter of this book.

The first statement creates an instance of a query object, but note that rather than "CUSTOMER1" you see "this.CUSTOMER1" – "this" refers to the form. Note also that the parent property is being assigned for you and again "this" refers to the form.

You could write the same code that was originally shown in a similar fashion in your program:

```
q = new Query()
with( q )
   sql = "select * from mytable"
   active = true
endwith
```

This is just as valid as the previous way of writing the code.

Next ...
Once you have the query set and it is active, what can you do with it? It mostly depends on what you need to do. To work with the data, you have to work with the rowset and field objects as discussed later this chapter. Here are a few caveats:

If you are working with local tables, a SELECT statement like that shown here is probably going to be okay. If you are working with a SQL Server (such as Oracle, etc.), you may want to consider adding filters (using the WHERE clause), as SQL Servers that feed a whole table across to the application will be much slower. If you limit the amount of data that is fed to the application, you will see a huge speed difference *(in most cases)*.

Setting relationships may be different with SQL Servers than with local tables – this is discussed in later chapters.

It should be noted that you can change the *sql* property of a query on the fly – after the query is active. This can be useful if you need to add a WHERE clause to the SELECT statement, or modify the WHERE clause based on something the user is doing.

There are other ways to manipulate the query object itself – specific events that can be used, such as *canOpen()*, *canClose()*, etc., and some methods such as *execute()*, *prepare()*, etc. but those are a bit more advanced than we need to deal with here.

When we visit this object again in a later chapter we will see some other things that can be done with the query object as well.

Query Objects and SQL Server Databases

If you are using a database backend engine such as InterBase (Firebird), Oracle, etc., then you may want to tell dBASE that you wish to pass the SQL Query directly to the SQL Server. In order to do that sort of thing in versions of dBASE prior to release 2.61, you had to use the database object's *executeSQL* method, which isn't exactly optimal - it does not allow you to use the returned rowset with a query object. With dBASE Plus 2.61 a new property has been added to the query object itself, called *usePassThrough*, which has a logical value. The default is *false*, which tells dBASE to act like the data is a local database table, but if you set this property to *true*, the SQL statement of the query is passed directly to the SQL Server data engine.

Of course, setting this property to *true* when using a .DBF or .DB table is not going to do much good, since there is no SQL Server data engine running. The purpose of this property is to allow the developer access to functionality that might not be available through the BDE.

Rowset and Field Objects – The Heart of the Data Object Structure

When we work with data, one of the most important objects to understand is the rowset. The rowset object determines how we move through our data (navigation), what the state the data is in (browse, edit, append, etc.), how to filter and search the data, and more.

The rowset is contained by the query object, which we discussed above. While you can create your own query objects, including custom query objects, a rowset does not exist until a query object exists and is active. It is important to note this – the query object not only has to exist, but the *active* property of the query must be set to true for the rowset object to exist.

Along with the rowset object, you also get the field array object, which is an array that allows you to work with the individual field objects for each field.

Remember the discussion of objects in earlier chapters – objects can have properties, events and methods. Events can have custom event handlers assigned to them and methods can be overridden if needed. All of this is quite useful to know and we will start to see how some of this works.

Some Basic Information about Rowsets

When you work with data in a rowset, there is a concept that is very useful for the developer – that of the row buffer or record buffer. What exactly is this? In the older XDML code, many developers created code that stored the contents of the fields in a record (row) to memory variables or arrays and then they set up links to the entry areas of a screen that were not linked to the record directly, but to the memory variables. They were creating a record buffer – this meant that the user was not editing the actual data, but a copy of the data. The developer would then have to write more code to save the contents of the memory variables back to the table, if the user decided to save their changes. This allowed a lot of flexibility for the user, but it was a lot of coding for the developer.

Using the rowset object, the record buffer is *automatic*. The user makes changes to a copy of the data, and it is not saved until a call to the rowset's *save()* method is made *(we'll talk in more depth about implicit calls to the* save() *method later)*. If a call to the rowset's *abandon()* method is made, then changes to the data are not saved and the data is restored on screen to its previous status, with the developer (you) having to write very little actual code.

This is an important concept and must be remembered. There are a few "gotchas" in here, that we will discuss later (such as the aforementioned implicit calls to the *save()* method of the rowset), but as a whole, if you understand the record buffer you can save yourself a lot of work.

Rowset Events and Event Handlers

Rowsets are quite literally the control for navigating in data, modifying data, etc. This is similar to working with records and record numbers in the old XDML code *(if you're familiar with that)*. However, the rowset, as you will see, gives us a huge amount of flexibility and control, all built in to the object itself.

Much of that control comes from the use of events and the ability to assign event handlers to the events. One example of such is the ability to perform data validation by assigning an event handler to the ability to save a row to the table.

The rowset object has a set of events that begin with the word "can" – such as *canSave()*. What this means is that if you have an event handler assigned to the *canSave()* event and you then make a call to the *save()* method of the rowset, a call is made to the *canSave()* event *before* the save occurs. A *canSave()* event handler must return a logical value of *true* or *false* – if it returns a value of *false*, the rowset is not allowed to actually call the *save()* method.

You may be starting to see the usefulness of this, but let's take it a step further. You can create an event handler associated with *canSave()*, which will return a logical value and in that code you can perform data validation. You can check to make sure that fields that need to have values have values, if fields that have specific ranges for the data entered fall within the correct ranges, and more. If any condition evaluates to false, you can then return a false value for the event handler and dBASE will not allow your user to save the data.

If the *canSave()* event handler returns a value of *true*, then dBASE will allow the user to save the data.

In addition to the *canSave()* event handler, there is an *onSave()* event handler. This event allows you to execute code *after* a save is completed. So what happens if your code makes a call to save changes to a row?

The *canSave()* event checks to see if an event handler is assigned. If so, any code associated with this is executed and a *true* or *false* value is returned.

IF an event handler was assigned to *canSave()*, and it returns a *true* value, OR if no *canSave()* event handler was created, then the *save()* method is executed and the data is saved to the rowset from the rowset buffer.

The *onSave()* now checks to see if an event handler is assigned. If so, any code associated with this event is executed. Note that the *onSave()* event handler does not return a value.

This same sequence occurs for various rowset (and some other objects as we'll see in other parts of this book) methods that have *can*MethodName and *on*MethodName events assigned to them.

So far we've just talked about this, let's look at validating a row's data just to get a better feel for it. To do this, we are going to use the samples database that is installed with dBASE. If you wish to follow along, then you will want to make a copy of the table we are using.

First let's open the samples database. We're going to do this using the Navigator in dBASE. Click on the "Tables" tab in the Navigator. Now click on the down arrow for the combobox next to the words "Look in:". In the list you see, should be "DBASESAMPLES". Select this, and now note that you should see two tables – "Fish.dbf" and "Sample.dbf".

 NOTE

The combobox mentioned here in the Navigator can confuse a user who has never dealt with it before – especially if you have database aliases with the same names as folders on your hard drive(s). When using the "Look in:" combobox on the Navigator window from the Tables Tab, you will see items listed with either a folder, or with a database icon. If you open a folder, you may get a list of tables, but they will act differently than if you open a database alias. The databases will all be listed *after* the folders. In this example, make sure you select the *database* called "DBASESAMPLES".

The drop down list might look like:

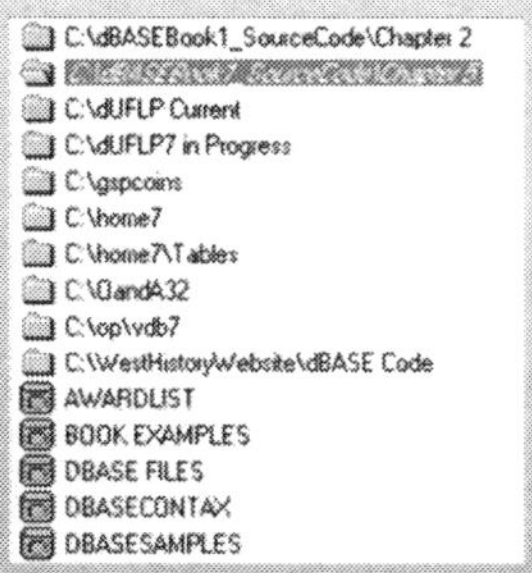

Figure 7-2

In the Command Window, type:

```
COPY TABLE FISH TO MYFISH
```

And now note that you should see "Myfish.dbf" in the tables shown.

 NOTE

You could use the command:

```
COPY FILE FISH.DBF TO MYFISH.DBF
```

But this would *only* copy the .DBF file. This table also has a .MDX and a .DBT file and while you could also issue the same command for each of the other file types, there are other issues. The both of these files are referenced in the table header and would expect to find "FISH.MDX", not "MYFISH.MDX", etc. This can cause problems. It is safer to always use the COPY TABLE command as shown above when copying tables.

Rather than change the data in the sample table, we are going to be working with a *copy* of the data.

We will be creating a small program (because it is easier to show this using a program, than trying to do some of this in the Command Window directly) and we will be using some code that I will not explain in much depth here (if at all), but in either this chapter or even later chapters of the book. If you pay attention, much of this should start to make sense, even if I don't explain it all.

First we need to create a program, and to do that we will be using the Source Editor for dBASE. In the Command Window, type:

```
create command TestFish
```

This will bring up the dBASE Source code Editor, and it will assume that when you save, that you are creating a program called "TestFish.prg".

In the editor, type the following:

```
open database DBASESAMPLES
q = new query()
q.sql := "select * from :DBASESAMPLES:MyFish"
q.active := true
```

So far, this code will create a query object (we'll discuss this more later), will tell dBASE what data to use (the sql statement), and then will make the query active. (Until we run the program, this code has done *nothing*, it's just sitting there, waiting for us to do something.) We will discuss the use of ":=" versus "=" for assigning values in a later chapter of this book, but suffice it to state that it is a good habit to get into and I try to use that syntax throughout the book where it is appropriate.

With the query object created, our code will create a rowset automatically, along with the fields array and the field objects.

We can access the data in the field objects by using the object hierarchy:

```
? q.rowset.fields["name"].value
```

This will output the contents of the name field in the first row of the table to the output pane of the Command Window. We will see this when we execute the program. Note the syntax shown above. 'q' is the name of the query object, the query object is the parent of the rowset object, which is the parent of the fields array object. In the square brackets we have placed the name of the field (in quotes). Finally we are looking at the *value* property of the field object. *(We will look at the fields array and field objects in a bit more detail later in this chapter.)*

Now, let us assign some code to the event handler for the rowset's *canSave()* event:

```
q.rowset.canSave := ValidateData
```

The code shown above will create a reference to an event handler named "ValidateData" that is assigned to the rowset's *canSave()* event. However, the actual event handler code "ValidateData" does not yet exist. Where do we put it?

For our purposes, we will put it at the end of the program. Despite all of the discussion in the previous chapter of object oriented coding, a dBL program still runs from the top to the bottom. If it reaches a command such as RETURN, it stops functioning because it has been told that the program is done executing. If it reaches a command such as PROCEDURE or FUNCTION, it stops executing, because this tells it that any code following is not part of the main program. This will be discussed in more depth in later chapters. *(As noted at the beginning of the chapter, we could write this code in a more OOP fashion, but I am concerned that you learn how the objects work and then in later chapters we will put together "proper" OOP examples ...)*

So, the first thing we need to know is what kind of validation we wish to create? We are going to go for simple for the time being, so let us say that the name field cannot be empty. To create the code we want for the validation, press the ENTER key twice or more, so we have some blank space, and then type in the source editor:

```
function ValidateData
   local bReturn
   bReturn = true
   if empty( q.rowset.fields["name"].value )
      ? "Name is empty - this is not valid!"
      bReturn = false
   endif
return bReturn
```

This little function will check to see if the value of the name field is empty and if it is, tells the user that the name field is empty and that this is not valid, so the row is not saved – any changes made are still in the row buffer, but it has not been saved to the rowset. If however the field is not empty, the value will be saved.

Next we want to add some code that will test this. So to do that you will need to move back to those blank lines we added, and type in code that looks like this:

```
q.rowset.fields["name "].value := ""
q.rowset.save()

q.rowset.fields["name"].value := "This is a test"
q.rowset.save()

? q.rowset.fields["name"].value
```

This code will first attempt to change the value of the name field to a blank value (nothing inside the quote), and then attempt to save the data. If we did everything correctly, this will not work, and our error message will display in the output pane of the Command Window. It will change it to something else, and again it will attempt to save the data. This time, since we actually put a value inside the quotes, the save will be successful.

The complete program should look like:

```
open database DBASESAMPLES
q = new query()
q.sql := "select * from :dbasesamples:MyFish"
q.active := true

? q.rowset.fields[ "name"].value

q.rowset.canSave := ValidateData

q.rowset.fields["name"].value := ""
q.rowset.save()

q.rowset.fields["name"].value := "This is a test"
q.rowset.save()

? q.rowset.fields["name"].value
```

```
function ValidateData
   local bReturn
   bReturn = true
   if empty( q.rowset.fields["name"].value )
      ? "Name is empty — this is not valid!"
      bReturn = false
   endif
return bReturn
```

Check your code for typos. Try the code – to run it, save and exit the Source Editor using
⌨Ctrl+⌨W. Then in the Command Window:

```
do TestFish
```

If there are no errors in the code, the output pane should show:

```
Clown Triggerfish
Name is empty — this is not valid!
This is a test
```

Now granted, this is actually a fairly simple situation hopefully it shows you some of what can be done using these events and event handlers.

Navigation in a Rowset

It is often necessary to navigate through the rows in a table, either to find a specific row or to process the data for some reason or other.

We will take a look at doing this with a form in a later chapter, here we are looking at basic code concepts.

The simplest way to navigate is to use the *next()* method of the rowset object. However, there are some other methods that can be used as well.

If you have set the *indexName* property of the rowset object, the table will be navigated based on whatever sequence is set in the expression of the index.
There are some things you should note:

* If the user modifies the data, then navigates, the changes to the data are automatically saved. The only way to avoid this is to have the user "abandon" their changes.
* Some methods and events of the rowset cause navigation which you might not expect:
  * The standard navigation: *first()*, *last()*, *next()*, *goto()* methods will, of course cause navigation, and save changes to the row.
  * *filter*, *applyFilter()*, *applyLocate()*, *findKey()*, *findKeyNearest()*, *setRange()* will all cause navigation and will save changes to the row. Navigation caused by these events or methods is called implicit navigation (the navigation is implicit in the event or method's code and will affect your application by saving the data in the record buffer and so on)

If you decide to write your own navigation code, here are some things to consider:

* Never let your user navigate beyond the first or last rows of the rowset – otherwise errors will occur. The best way to handle this is to check the *atFirst()* or *atLast()* methods of the rowset before allowing them to navigate.

- It's probably a good idea to keep the user from navigating if they are in the middle of adding a new row or editing a row, because changes will be saved automatically. This can be done by checking the *state* property of the rowset.

A simple example of navigating in a rowset with a query is shown below. If you wish to type along, you will see a query, and then navigating in a rowset:

```
clear // clear the output pane of the Command Window
// create query object
q = new query()
q.sql := "select * from :DBASESAMPLES:MyFish"
q.active := true
// set index for table
q.rowset.indexName := "name"
// make sure we're on the first row
q.rowset.first()
// display value of name field
? q.rowset.fields["Name"].value
// move to the next row
q.rowset.next()
// display value of name field
? q.rowset.fields["Name"].value
// jump five rows from where we are
q.rowset.next(5)
// display value of name field
? q.rowset.fields["Name"].value
// jump backward 6 rows
q.rowset.next(-6)
// display value of name field
? q.rowset.fields["Name"].value
```

And so on – there is much more that can be done. We can check to see if we are at the first row (using the *atFirst()* method), the last row (using the *atLast()* method), if we have gone beyond the rows in the table (in either direction) with the *endOfSet* property (which always returns a true or false value), etc. As we get further into this book we will examine more of these methods, events and properties.

Programmatically Stepping Through a Rowset

There are several ways to perform what is called a loop in your application (we will look at some of these in more depth in a later chapter of this book), and these can be used to "traverse" a rowset, working through all the rows. This is a very common procedure. In XDML there was a SCAN/ENDSCAN construct. In OODML, we can loop through a rowset by use of a FOR/NEXT loop, but that requires knowing how big the table is. This can be done, but counting the rows in a large table using the rowset's *count()* method can actually slow down a process. Instead, it is recommended that you use one of the following forms of code to loop through a rowset's rows:

```
do
    // some process
until not queryname.rowset.next()
    OR
do while not queryname.rowset.endOfSet
    // some process
    q.rowset.next()
enddo
```

The first version is less "wordy", but reading it is a bit confusing. The DO/UNTIL command structure literally says that dBASE must loop through the code *UNTIL* some condition is met. The condition shown is "not queryname.rowset.next()". The *next()* method returns a boolean value letting the coder know if it is successful, so if it returns *true* it was successful, if it returns *false* it was not. I find that putting the condition at the end of a loop a little confusing, but this may simply be a "style" issue. Because we are putting the code that causes the navigation to occur in the loop code, it's a little less code to write.

Easier to read, but a bit more complex, the second example says to loop while we are not at the end of the rowset marker. Inside the loop we have to make sure that we actually navigate, or we can find ourselves in an infinite loop (dBASE will continue processing the same row forever, or until the user presses the escape key, etc.).

To see the contents of the name field in the fish table, we could write:

```
clear // clear the output pane of the Command Window
// create query object
q = new query()
q.sql := "select * from :DBASESAMPLES:MyFish"
q.active := true
do while not q.rowset.endOfSet
   ? q.rowset.fields["name"].value
   q.rowset.next()
enddo
```

If we had not had the second statement inside the loop, we would end up repeating the same fish name over and over.

Editing Data in a Rowset

You can set a rowset to be not editable until the user explicitly decides to edit (I find this to be a good idea – it is very easy to accidentally change the value of a field) by setting the rowset's *autoEdit* property to false (it defaults to true). This has the effect of disabling all controls that are dataLinked to the fields of the rowset when using a form (the term *datalink* will make more sense when we discuss form controls). Note that *autoEdit* is only effective when working with a form and datalinked controls.

A quick example of editing a row:

```
clear // clear the output pane of the Command Window
// create query object
q = new query()
q.sql := "select * from :DBASESAMPLES:fish"
q.active := true
// set index for table
q.rowset.indexName := "name"
// show the current value - "Clown Triggerfish"
? q.rowset.fields["name"].value
// change the current value
q.rowset.fields["name"].value := "Fred Smith"
// show the current value - "Fred Smith"
? q.rowset.fields["name"].value
// abandon the change
q.rowset.abandon()
// show the current value - "Clown Triggerfish"
? q.rowset.fields["name"].value
```

If we had chosen to save or to navigate, the value of the field would have been changed to "Fred Smith" and saved to the table. Why does the *abandon()* method work the way it does? Remember that record buffer mentioned earlier in the chapter? When the change to the name field was made, changing the *value* to "Fred Smith" as shown in the code above, the changes are only stored <u>in the rowset buffer</u>. No changes made in the buffer are saved to the table unless a call to the *save()* method is made OR a call to *abandon()* will tell dBASE to refresh the row buffer from what is in the table.

Deleting Rows

The OODML does not support the XBASE "soft delete" (this is the ability to continue to display a deleted row on the form) directly. It is possible to do this via the BDE's API, but we will not be getting into that in this book.

The reason for this is that the .DBF is the only table format that allows this functionality – all others basically assume that a deleted row is gone (and they are – you cannot undelete rows from any other table type that this author knows of). Don't panic, however – if your user decides to delete a row, it is actually still in the table, but you cannot show it to the user and you cannot (using the OODML) allow the user to recall (undelete) that row. You can still use the older XDML commands (RECALL, etc.) to find and "undelete" the row if necessary.

Deleting a row is done by using the command (well, calling the rowset method) you might expect:

```
queryname.rowset.delete()
```

Once you do that, to all intents and purposes the row is deleted because the OODML data objects will not see it.

Fields Array and Field Objects

The field object is the way the programmer connects directly with the data in a table. So far we've looked at working with a query, which opens a table and allows us some options for manipulating it. The rowset, which is how we interact with the individual rows, navigate in the table, and so on. But we need to look at the field object itself.

In order to reach a field, you must use the fields array. The fields array is contained by the rowset object. To access a field, we must know either the fieldname, or use a number to reference the field in the order it is laid out in the table's structure.

In the code we've examined before, we have actually spent a bit of time working with the fields array and field objects, but only in a limited fashion. In a program statement like:

```
queryname.rowset.fields
```

We are referencing the fields array. We can determine the number of fields in a table, by a statement such as:

```
? queryname.rowset.fields.size
```

And we can get the value of any field by a reference such as:

```
? queryname.rowset.fields[ "fieldname" ].value
```

```
      // or
? queryname.rowset.fields[ fieldnumber ].value
```

Note that the fieldname must be in quotes, whereas the fieldnumber is not placed in quotes. As we look at various aspects of the software, we will come back to this over and over again and you will see a lot of examples in the book because the field is where the actual data resides.

If we had an instance of the fish table:

```
? q.rowset.fields["name"].value
   // or
? q.rowset.fields[ 2 ].value
```

would return the same information because the "name" field is the second field in the table's structure.

dBASE includes several field object types, and the following are a brief listing of each.

Field Class

This is the base or "super" class for all the other classes. It is also one way you can create a "calculated field" for a rowset *(this will be discussed in a later chapter of this book)*.

DBFField Class

This is the default class used when you use a .DBF (dBASE) table. Most DBF fields will use this class, with the exception of the _DBASELOCK field, which uses the LOCKFIELD Class, this will be discussed in later chapters.

PDXField Class

When you open a .DB or Paradox table, the PDXField Class is used automatically by dBASE for those fields.

SQLField Class

If your query uses any other table type, the SQLField Class is automatically generated by dBASE for the fields of the table.

LockField Class

This is used only with .DBF tables and has a very specific purpose – it is not something you can add to a table through the OODML commands. As noted above, this will be discussed in later chapters.

Why are there this many field classes? Because different tables types (and data engines) have different ways of defining fields. Therefore these classes have different properties.

Looping Through All Fields in a Table

There are occasions when you, as a programmer, may need to work through all the fields of a table to perform some sort of process. One way of doing this is to know the name of all the fields, but this can get quite tedious, and can create more complicated code than is necessary.

It is possible, because the field objects are stored in an array, to loop through them. For example, if we were working with the FISH table:

```
clear // clear the output pane of the Command Window
// create query object
q = new query()
q.sql := "select * from :DBASESAMPLES:fish"
q.active := true
for i = 1 to q.rowset.fields.size
    ? q.rowset.fields[ i ].fieldName
next
q.active := false
release object q
```

This code will loop through and show the *fieldname* property for each field object contained in the fields array of the rowset. This may not seem a particularly useful thing to do, however, you could do something where you wanted to copy the contents of the current row to memory so that you could make a COPY of that row for some reason (perhaps to emulate the XDML command SET CARRY, for example). Instead of displaying the *fieldName* you might want to obtain the *value* property and store that. You can do it without knowing the names of the fields, or writing a long and complex routine to do this.

Other Field Object Events, Methods, etc.
Like most objects in dBASE, the fields objects themselves have properties, events and methods. We will be looking at the use of the *beforeGetValue()* and *canChange()* events to "morph" the value of a field to some other type of value in the next chapter of this book. Other interesting events that can be very useful include *onChange()*, an event that fires when the user makes a change to the value (the *value* property) of a field. There is an example in the online help (HELP ONCHANGE()) and then click on the *example* link), that shows a lot of the power of OOP. You can store code of this sort in a datamodule *(we will take a look at these starting in a later chapter)* and it can then be used by any forms in an application that use that datamodule – this is proper OOP design, creating reusable code.

OLE, Binary and Memo Fields
These fields may be used to store files in a table. In order to do so, there are two methods of the field object you need to be aware of:

copyToFile() – This method copies the contents of the field to a file.
replaceFromFile() – This method allows you to store the contents of a file in a field.

There is no way to empty one of these fields unless you create an empty file of the type being used and use *replaceFromFile()* to do replace the contents. (For example, if you use a binary field to store images in a DBF, you could create an empty image file and then use the *replaceFromFile()* method to replace it. When viewing the field it would appear empty.)

Another issue you should be aware of is that the *empty()* function in dBASE does not always return a useful or meaningful value when used on a BLOB field (Binary Linked OBject) such as one of these – it often returns a value of *false* (meaning the field is NOT empty) when indeed it is. It is best to not rely on this function when working with these field types.

Creating and Coding Database Objects

The database object is used when you use database aliases to handle your databases. We discussed creating database aliases in an earlier chapter.

An alias is absolutely required when working with SQL Server tables (such as InterBase, Oracle, etc.) and is optional but useful & highly recommended when using local tables. If you opt to use an alias, you should use the database object in your code, on your forms, reports, datamodules, etc.

It should be noted that if you wish to create applications that are compliant with the Windows Vista, Windows 7 (or later) UAC (User Account Control) security, you will *need* to use database objects for your tables, even if you are using local tables. This is because the UAC requires that the data not be in the same folder as the program. There will be details on this in the chapters that deal with deployment of your applications.

The Default Database
It is important to note that dBASE has a default database, which points to the "current directory". This can always be accessed via the application object:

```
_app.databases[1]
```

and any methods of the database object can be called:

```
_app.databases[1].packTable( "MyTable" )
```

for example.

The default database objects's *active* property has no effect – you can attempt to set it to *false* but nothing will happen. The default database has a default session as well *(see below)*.

Creating a Database Object Reference
You can create a database object reference easily enough. There are only a few properties you must set:

- The *databaseName* property is the name of the database alias.
- The *loginString* if you need one (particularly for SQL Server databases) and wish to login automatically, rather than through the default dialog.
- The *active* property must be set to true.

```
// for local tables
d = new Database()
d.databaseName := "DBASESAMPLES"
d.active := true
// create a query object
q = new query()
q.database := d
q.sql := "select * from fish"
q.active := true
```

If you compare this example to earlier ones where we included the database alias name in the SQL Select statement of the query object, you will see that this is not needed now. In addition, you could create multiple query objects for the same or different tables, all using the same database object.

Table Maintenance
The database object has built into it some methods that are very useful for the dBASE developer – they are alternates to the XDML commands to empty a table (ZAP), rebuild the indexes (REINDEX), pack a table by removing the deleted rows (PACK), and so on.

The database object does these using methods that are built in (the following assume that there is a database reference named simply "d"):

```
// empty a table:
d.emptyTable( "tablename" )

// rebuild indexes:
d.reindex( "tablename ")

// pack a table:
d. packTable( "tablename" )
```

In addition, you can use methods built in to do quite a few other table maintenance options – you can copy a table (*copyTable()*), delete a table (*dropTable()*), rename a table (*renameTable()*), add indexes (see the discussion on the index objects later in this chapter, using the *createIndex()* method), delete index tags (*dropIndex()*), and see if a table exists in the database (*tableExists()*).

All of these work only inside the current database, it is not recommended to try to use the database object to do something such as copy a table from one database to another.

Transaction Processing

One of the things that you may wish to use the database object for is transaction processing. Many applications these days no longer use this, but it is still something that you may need for your own application(s) or your users may prefer it. *(This will be discussed in a later chapter in more depth.)*

Transaction processing is a method of posting transactions at a specific point, rather than performing interactive processing. This is sometimes called "batch" processing.

When you activate your database, you can start a transaction set with the database's *beginTrans()* method:

```
// for local tables
d = new database()
d.databaseName := "MyAlias"
d.active := true
d. beginTrans()

// do whatever — start the application,
// or load the form and allow the user to
// do their work ... etc.

d.commit()    // will save the transactions, and update
              // the table(s) appropriately.
// OR
d.rollback() // will cancel all transactions since
              // the beginTrans() method was called.
```

Using the Index Object(s)

The index object is the way you create indexes in OODML. There are actually two different index objects, one of which is a subclass of the other. The primary index object is called INDEX, the other is called DBFINDEX which is specifically aimed at the .DBF table format.

There are minor differences between the two, basically because the dBF index tag is different from many other databases.

To define a.DBF index, and then create it, you must do the following:

```
i = new DBFIndex()
i.indexName := "MyIndex"
i.expression := "field1 + upper(field2)"
// use the default database object:
_app.databases[1].createIndex( "tableName", i )
```

That's really all that is required. If you want to do more, you can set the *type* property to "1" for a .NDX (note however, that the OODML doesn't know what to do with a .NDX file), you can set the *unique* property to true, you can set the *descending* property to true and so on. Remember that the expression must be a proper dBASE expression.

If you have a database object that points to a specific database alias, this will affect a table in that database:

```
d = new database()
d.databaseName := "MyData"
d.active := true
i = new DBFIndex()
i.indexName := "MyIndex"
i.expression := "field1 + upper(field2)"
// use the default database object:
d.createIndex( "MyTable", i )
```

More on Expressions

This discussion assumes you are working with .DBFs, as they are the native table type for dBASE. As such, let's briefly discuss a few things.

Numerics

Numeric indexes are not generally a good idea. You should index on character strings for most situations. A former "dBVIPs" member made the following observation:

"Most key fields are essentially character, even if they contain numerals. For example, telephone numbers, zip codes, part numbers and social security numbers have nothing numeric about them. A good rule of thumb is that if you don't have to do arithmetic with it, it should be character." – Gary Thoenen

Dates

Dates can be interesting. If you are using the American date format of MM/DD/YYYY and you set an index on the date "as is", what happens if you have dates that span several years? Your sorting will be by month, rather than by year and month.

Let us say you set your date format to YY/MM/DD, which is logical (Year, Month, Day). What happens when the year to dates before 2000? You end up with all dates that are in (or after) 2000 appearing in your index before 1999. This is probably not desirable. The best way to index on dates is to include the DTOS() function. DTOS() returns dates as a character string, in the format: YYYYMMDD (YearMonthDay – for example, 20120716 (July 16, 2012)).

The handy thing is that this works for all international date formats.

DateTime/Timestamp

The DateTime or Timestamp field type is an interesting one – it stores the date and time in the field – and there is one difficulty – the BDE sometimes ignores the time part of the data when indexing on it. This can be frustrating if you need to sort the data on that value. There are ways to ensure that you get the correct information, but they may take a bit of work.

The method that appears to be the best is to use something like the following:

```
DTOS( timestampfield ) + TTOC( timestampfield )
```

According to Ken Chan *(a former TeamB member, who did some research and testing with this)*, when displaying TTOC(timestampfield) in a program, it appears to rely on the value of SET HOURS (12 hour or 24 hour time), the BDE always assumes 24 hour time if this is used in an index expression.

Expression Lengths

The actual length of the expression can be 100 characters, but that is a really long expression. If you are working with multiple fields and you combine them into an expression that is longer than 100 characters, dBASE won't let you do it. How to get around it? Use the left() function to extract enough of each field so that you have unique values and you should be fine. Example, if you are working with a CD collection, many album titles can get pretty lengthy (one that comes to mind is: "The Myths and Legends of King Arthur and the Knights of the Round Table" by Rick Wakeman). You might want to index on the artist name and then the album title. But if the artist field is say, 40 characters and the title field is 100, you get into problems (a combined width of 140 characters, which is illegal in dBASE index expressions). To create an expression for this, you can probably get the whole artist name and then just the first 40 or so characters (or maybe less) of the title:

```
i.expression := artist+title.left( 40 )
```

Case Sensitivity

DBF index expressions have always been case sensitive. You never really know what a user will do with your software. Your safest bet is to make your expression case insensitive. *(In addition to the issues noted here, by doing the following you can save some trouble when searching the data.)* How do you do that? Index on the upper-case of your character strings and make sure that your search routines always search on the upper-case of the value entered by the user. To create the expression, you might use:

```
i.expression := upper( artist+title.left( 40 ) )
```

A Few Misc. Things

Keep in mind that the more index tags you have for a table, the longer it takes to update a table, which includes adding new rows, editing rows (especially if the user is allowed to modify fields used in the expressions for your index tags) and so on. If you are doing programmatic changes to your tables, this can get worse. There are ways around some of this, but we're not going to get into them just yet. The important thing here is that you should create indexes that you will actually be using, rather than just deciding to create a bunch of them, with the attitude of "maybe I'll use them ...".

While the discussion has been mostly about using the DBFIndex object, the use of the Index object is pretty much the same, except that some of the properties will be different, as will some of the limitations on expressions *(if you can use expressions at all)*. The Index object should be used with tables that are not .DBF tables and vice versa, the DBFIndex object should only be used with .DBF tables.

Creating and Coding Session Objects

A session object is sort of like a container. It can be used with either a database object or directly with a query object (however, if you are using a database object, you should use the session with the database, not the query).

In earlier versions of dBASE sessions were necessary when an application allowed multiple access to the same tables within one "session" of the application. If you opened the tables up in their own sessions, you avoided some conflict issues (not all).

In dBASE PLUS, the only real purposes for using a session object are if you want to use the *onProgress()* event (to hook into a progress bar), if you are using encrypted tables (you can "auto login"), or perhaps if you are creating a full MDI application allowing the same form to be opened more than once. Other than that, they really just confuse the issue and add an extra layer to what the developer is doing. Session objects can be used if your application needs to create a temporary User BDE Alias "on-the-fly", as well. They can be useful if you need to test on a local computer that is not connected to a network to be sure that any multi-user issues are resolved, but it is still more complex than you might want. You can see all of the different properties, events and methods of this (and other objects discussed here) in the online help for dBASE.

To create a new session, all you must do is:

```
sMySession = new Session()
```

To use a session you must assign a *session* property for those objects (database and query) that are to be affected by that specific session, and the *session* property must be assigned before the object's *active* property is set to *true*.

For example:

```
sMySession   = new Session()
dMyDatabase = new Database()
dMyDatabase.databaseName  := "MyAlias"
dMyDatabase.session        := sMySession
dMyDatabase.active         := true

qMyQuery = new Query()
qMyQuery.database  := dMyDatabase
qMyQuery.session   := sMySession
qMyQuery.sql       := "select * from MyTable"
qMyQuery.active    := true

qMyQuery2 = new Query()
qMyQuery2.database  := dMyDatabase
qMyQuery2.session   := sMySession
qMyQuery2.sql       := "select * from MyTable2"
qMyQuery2.active    := true
```

If you wish, with a session, you may use a User BDE Alias (new to dBASE Plus 2.7), instead of using a database object (as shown above). The code could be defined in a fashion similar to:

```
sMySession   = new Session()
sMySession.addAlias( "MyAlias", "DBASE", "Path:C:\PathToDatabase" )
```

```
dMyDatabase = new Database()
dMyDatabase.session       := sMySession
dMyDatabase.databaseName  := "MyAlias"
dMyDatabase.active        := true

// define your query or queries as shown above ...
```

The advantage to using the *addAlias()* method is that you do not have to use the BDE Administrator which under current versions of Windows may cause some difficulties. If your User BDE Alias was created in the application's .INI file (as discussed elsewhere in this book), you do not need to use the *addAlias()* method.

If you no longer need the User BDE Alias, you can delete it with the session object's *deleteAlias()* method.

The Default Session

Note, there is always a default session, which is accessible through the application object's default database object:

```
? _app.databases[1].session.access()
      // or
? _app.session.access()
```

If you want to use sessions in your application, you should consider setting them on your datamodules, forms or reports (depending on your application design). The session object will be discussed a bit more *(in a later chapter)* when we get to multi-user applications.

As with the previous discussion, the default session object can be used to create a User BDE Alias with the *addAlias()* method. The syntax would be the same as above.

Creating and Coding Stored Procedure Objects

If you are working with local tables, then the STOREDPROC object is useless to you. However, if you work with SQL Server (or "backend server") databases, then this object may be quite useful.

The following is from the online help:

"Use a StoredProc object to call a stored procedure in a database. Most stored procedures take one or more parameters as input and may return one or more values as output. Parameters are passed to and from the stored procedure through the StoredProc object's params property, which points to an associative array of Parameter Objects.

"Some stored procedures return a rowset. In that case, the StoredProc object is similar to a Query object; but instead of executing an SQL statement that describes the data to retrieve, you name a stored procedure, pass parameters to it, and execute it. The resulting rowset is accessed through the StoredProc object's rowset property, just like in a Query object.

"Because stored procedures are SQL-server-based, you must create and activate a Database object and assign that object to the StoredProc object's database property. Standard tables do not support stored procedures.

"Next, the procedureName property must be set to the name of the stored procedure. For most SQL servers, the BDE can get the names and types of the parameters for the stored procedure. On some servers, no information is available; in that case you must include the parameter names in the procedureName property as well."

There is more information in online help and the dBASE Knowledgebase *(and also at least one article in dBulletin)* if you need more assistance in using these. I am not familiar with them, but understand that they can give you some extra power and flexibility in your applications.

The TableDef Object

The TableDef object is an interesting and useful object that doesn't get used as often as it might. It is a read-only object used to allow a programmer to obtain information about a table (**Table Def**inition). This object can be used to determine information about a table, such as the table level, and more; about indexes (including index names, expressions, etc.); fields (fieldnames, types, lengths, etc.); and so on.

It is being mentioned here even though it is not directly related to the many objects discussed earlier in this chapter. Using code, a programmer can easily find out details about a table without accidentally modifying anything.

The following couple of examples are just to give you some idea what can be done with the TableDef object to find out information about a table. If you were following along with some of the sample code from earlier, use "MyFish", if not, you may not want to run some of the code – it modifies table structures.

List Field Information
You can get a listing of the fieldnames, field types, and more, using the tableDef object:

```
d = new Database()
d.databaseName := "DBASESAMPLES"
d.active := true
t = new TableDef()
// assign a database reference
t.database := d
t.tableName := "MyFish"
t.load()
for i = 1 to t.fields.size
    ? t.fields[ i ].fieldName
    ?? t.fields[ i ].length
    ?? t.fields[ i ].decimalLength
next
release object t
t = null
```

Now, that example doesn't look all that useful, but what if you wanted to see if a new field has been added to a table? You could check to see if it existed and if not, add the new field using the Local SQL ALTER TABLE command:

```
d = new Database()
d.databaseName := "DBASESAMPLES"
d.active := true
t = new TableDef()
// assign a database reference
t.database := d
t.tableName := "MyFish"
t.load()
```

```
bFound = false
for i = 1 to t.fields.size
    if t.fields[i].fieldName.toUpperCase() == "MYTESTFIELD"
        bFound := true
    endif
next
release object t
t = null
// if it wasn't found:
if not bFound
    // use ALTER TABLE to add the field to the table:
    alter table :DBASESAMPLES:Fish add MyTestField char(10)
endif
```

List Index Information

You can do similar things with Indexes, to list the indexes in a table, or to see if an index exists in the table:

```
d = new Database()
d.databaseName := "DBASESAMPLES"
d.active := true
t = new TableDef()
// assign a database reference
t.database := d
t.tableName := "MyFish"
t.load()
for i = 1 to t.indexes.size
    ? t.indexes[ i ].indexName+"  "+;
        t.indexes[ i ].expression+"  "+;
        t.indexes[ i ].descending
next
release object t
t = null
```

> **NOTE**
> In the code shown above you will see a command (beginning with the ? character) that is displayed across multiple lines. The use of the semicolon (;) allows this – if placed at the end of a command, dBASE knows that the command is continued on the next line.

And you could do something similar as the code given above with fields to see if a specific index exists in the table, and so on.

This should give you *some* ideas what this can be used for. You may never need it in your own applications, but it does have its uses.

The UpdateSet Object

The UpdateSet object was created to allow a developer to do some relatively complex tasks with only a small amount of code.

It can be used to copy tables, it can be used to append data from one table to another, to update data in one table from another and a lot more. This object will be discussed in some detail in a later chapter of the book and is included here in the interests of being complete.

Summary

As you can see, there are quite a few data objects in dBASE and there is a lot that can be done with them. Can you master all the options in a short time? No – can you create powerful, flexible and easy to use applications with them without a lot of effort? Yes! We will take a more detailed look at some of what can be done with these objects in the next chapter.

Part IV: Data Objects and the Language

The next thing to start looking at is how it comes together – OOP, OODML, XDML, dBL – the works. The following chapters will discuss these topics in depth.

Chapter 8: OODML, SQL, and XDML

This chapter is going to delve deeply into dBASE coding techniques, comparing the Object Oriented Data Manipulation Language (OODML), SQL and XBASE Data Manipulation Language (XDML) syntax, to show how various things may be done, using different coding techniques. You will find that in some cases, a mix of these different techniques may be the best, or even in some cases, the only way to complete a task. It is good to be familiar with a variety of techniques as a developer.

The primary focus of this chapter will be on the OODML, using the data objects in dBASE to complete a task, but a comparison will be made to other techniques wherever possible. Note that the language, whether we are using OODML, XDML or SQL, is still the dBASE Language (dBL).

As with the previous chapter, while one of the important things to learn is proper OOP, the main focus of this chapter is learning how to get the dBASE Objects to work for you. In later chapters we will combine what we learned in previous chapters and what we're learning now.

How to Do Things You May Have Done Before

If you have programmed in older versions of dBASE, you may be familiar with many of the following topics and you will want to know how to do the same types of code using the data objects in dBASE.

If you haven't done these sorts of things before, you should read this anyway, as you can learn a lot about the power of the data objects in dBASE.

Finding Data

As you might imagine, there are many ways to find data in a table in dBASE and when we get to the data objects, there are perhaps more than you might expect. Below is a discussion of various means of locating data, again looking at the older XDML command, and then the newer OODML version.

Seek

In XDML, the command "SEEK" is used to find data that matches a string (or numeric, etc.) value in an index tag. This will return the first row that matches.

Using the database objects, the version of this you want to look at is the rowset's *findKey()* and *findKeyNearest()* methods.

findKey() is the equivalent of SEEK, in that it will search in an index and return the first row that matches the value passed. This will only work if you have set the *indexName* property of the rowset (which is discussed elsewhere in this book). It will return a true or false value depending on whether or not a value was found. If the value was found, then this method will move to the matching row in the table – if it is not found, then the rowset pointer is left where it was *(however, navigation occurs and the rowset pointer appears to be moved back to where it was)*. The following example uses the samples table called "FISH":

```
d = new database()
d.databaseName := "DBASESAMPLES"
d.active := true
q = new query()
```

```
q.database := d
q.sql := "select * from fish"
q.active := true
q.rowset.indexName := "name"
if q.rowset.findKey( "Nurse Shark" )
   ? "Nurse Shark found"
else
   ? q.rowset.fields["name"].value
endif
q.active := false
d.active := false
```

This should display the words "Nurse Shark found" in the output pane of the Command Window.

findKeyNearest() is similar to SEEK, but it moves to the nearest row if the value you ask for is not found. Unlike the *findKey()* method, *findKeyNearest()* will navigate in the table to the row that is the closest match to the value you are searching for. In the example below, rather than leaving us at the top of the rowset, the search for "Some Fish" will place us at the row containing "Spotted Eagle Ray". If you examine the data, this is the only row that has a fish name that begins with the letter "S", so dBASE halts at this one, not finding any row that contains a value closer to the string we are looking for. If there is nothing even close to what is being looked for, *findKeyNearest()* will navigate to the rowset's *endOfSet*.

```
d = new database()
d.databaseName := "DBASESAMPLES"
d.active := true
q = new query()
q.database := d
q.sql := "select * from fish"
q.active := true
q.rowset.indexName := "name"
q.rowset.findKeyNearest( "Some Fish" )
? q.rowset.fields["name"].value
q.active := false
d.active := false
```

While the online help states that *findKeyNearest()* returns a *false* value if the exact match is not found, this is not the way the software actually works. This method will *always* return *true* and will, as noted, navigate in the table to the nearest match or to the rowset's *endOfSet* if no match is found. This may cause some difficulties in your code. If using *findKeyNearest()*, you may want to also check for the rowset's *endOfSet*:

```
q.rowset.findKeyNearest( "Some Fish" )
if not q.rowset.endOfSet // not at the endOfSet
   ? q.rowset.fields["name"].value
else
   ? "No match found"
endif
```

It is important to note that when using character values, *findKey()* and *findKeyNearest()* are case sensitive.

Locate
The XDML LOCATE command is useful and there is a version of it that works in the object model for dBASE. Basically LOCATE works similar to SEEK, but it doesn't require an index be

active and it can use an expression to find the value being looked for. This includes the ability to locate data using a "string in a string" type search (using the "$" operator).

```
open database dbasesamples
set database to dbasesamples
use fish
locate for name = "Yellowtail Snapper"
? found()
use
close database
```

The code shown above will open the FISH table and find the first row that contains "Yellowtail Snapper" in the name field, then through the use of the *found()* function display either a true or false.

The rowset's *applyLocate()* method is a little different. It uses a subset of local SQL – it's not a complete subset, which means that the "string in a string" type search is not possible using the *applyLocate()* method. Performing a locate using OODML has some interesting possibilities, however.

The simplest version of this is to tell it to look for a fieldname being equal to a value. If a value is found, navigation will occur to that row, and the *applyLocate()* method will return a value of *true.* If not found, it will return a value of *false* and navigation will move to the end of the rowset (setting the rowset's *endOfSet* property to true). The following is a simple example of *applyLocate()* using the FISH table again:

```
d = new database()
d.databaseName := "DBASESAMPLES"
d.active := true
q = new query()
q.database := d
q.sql := "select * from fish"
q.active := true
? q.rowset.applyLocate( "name = 'Redband Parrotfish'" )
q.active := false
d.active := false
```

Note the quotes – the *applyLocate()* method, when working with a string, requires that the string be in single quotes. We could make this easier to read using the string delimiter of the square brackets:

```
? q.rowset.applyLocate( [name = 'Redband Parrotfish'] )
```

This kind of thing is a style issue for programmers, but it is easier to read than the earlier command.

However, this is the simplest form of the locate using the OODML. It is possible to set options using the rowset property *locateOptions*. This property defaults to "0 - Match Length and Case" which means that the character string being looked for must be an exact match in size and the case (upper and lower case characters) must match.

There are options for this that make it more flexible. These are discussed in more detail in the help for dBASE, but briefly, the options are:

Value	Effect
0	Match length and case
1	Match partial length
2	Ignore case
3	Match partial length and ignore case

This table is copied out of the help for *locateOptions*. If you change the *locateOptions* property of the rowset, any call to the *applyLocate()* method will respect the current value of the property.

This is useful if we want to search for a value that might have been obtained by a user and could be in upper, lower or mixed case that doesn't match what is actually in the table, or if the string starts with a value that the user entered, but they didn't type the whole value. For example:

```
d = new database()
d.databaseName := "DBASESAMPLES"
d.active := true
q = new query()
q.database := d
q.sql := "select * from fish"
q.active := true
q.rowset.locateOptions := 3 // Match partial length, ignore case
? q.rowset.applyLocate( [name = 'redband'] )
q.active := false
d.active := false
```

This should return a *true* value, even though the string isn't an exact match in length or in case.

We can perform a more complex search in a couple of ways. The first is to build a more complex search string for the *applyLocate()* method to execute, the other is to use the *beginLocate()* method, which will be discussed below. The first option might look something like:

```
d = new database()
d.databaseName := "DBASESAMPLES"
d.active := true
q = new query()
q.database := d
q.sql := "select * from fish"
q.active := true
q.rowset.locateOptions := 3 // Match partial length, ignore case
? q.rowset.applyLocate( [name = 'redband' and;
                        :length cm: < 100] )
? q.rowset.fields["name"].value // Display result
q.active := false
d.active := false
```

With this technique, we can use the keywords "and" or "or" to combine conditions – these will be discussed in greater depth in a later chapter. Also note that unlike the option using the *beginLocate()* method (discussed below), we <u>can</u> use the less than and/or greater than operators (< and >).

It is possible to perform a more complex search using the *applyLocate()* method, by using the *beginLocate()* method. If we wanted to search for values in more than one field, we could do so using something like the following:

```
d = new database()
d.databaseName := "DBASESAMPLES"
d.active := true
q = new query()
q.database := d
q.sql := "select * from fish"
q.active := true
q.rowset.locateOptions := 3 // Match partial length, ignore case
q.rowset.beginLocate()
q.rowset.fields["name"].value = "redband"
q.rowset.fields["length cm"].value = 28
q.rowset.applyLocate()
? q.rowset.fields["name"].value // Display result
q.active := false
d.active := false
```

There are a couple of things to note here: The fields must be "equal" to the values given – you cannot use < or > (less than or equal than) in the comparison; and **very importantly** this performs an "and" type operation (in other words, both conditions must be true).

The main purpose of the *beginLocate()* method is really for use with forms where you can create a nice looking form that allows the user to search in a table based on values that are datalinked to a table – this is called "Locate by Form". When we get into working with Forms and Data, we will take another look at this (a later chapter of this book).

Finally, there is one more method associated with *applyLocate()* that you should be aware of. This method is *locateNext()*. This can be used in a case where you are sure you have more than one row that might be the matching row for the value(s) supplied. While *applyLocate()* finds the FIRST match, *locateNext()* works like the XDML CONTINUE command. It uses the criteria specified with the *applyLocate()* but finds the next possible match. This method will navigate to the end of the rowset (setting the rowset's *endOfSet* property to true) if a match is not found. It is possible to tell dBASE, when using the *locateNext()* method how many matches to move ahead – by default the next row matching the criteria given will be found. If you use a numeric value as a parameter, you can skip to the 'nth' matching row and you can even go backward using a negative value (-1, -3, etc.).

String Contained In a Field
In XDML, it is easy to use the "contained in" operator, or "$" symbol with, for example, the LOCATE command. It's not as easy to use this with OODML code. The difficulty is that dBASE's data objects are all based on SQL, and SQL doesn't have a "string contained in a string" operator. When we get to filtering data *(later in this chapter)* we will take a look at some possibilities using the rowset's *canGetRow()* event, and the SQL WHERE clause.

KeyMatch
The XDML function KeyMatch() is used to check the contents of an index expression to see if a value is contained in that expression. There is no direct equivalent of this in OODML, but Gary White *(a member of the dBASE community)* created some code that can emulate this functionality:

```
function keyExists( cTableName, cIndexName, cIndexKey )
   local q, lFound
   q=new query()
   q.sql=[select * from ']+cTableName+[']
   q.active = true
   q.rowset.indexName = cIndexName
   lFound = q.rowset.findKey( cIndexKey )
   q.active = false
   release object q
   q=null
return lFound
```

This function opens a table and searches for the expression, using the data objects, and returns a logical value if the key is found. To use it, you call the function like:

```
? keyExists( "MyTable", "IndexTagName", "KeyValueToLookFor" )
```

You might want to expand on the function if the table is contained in a database. There is an enhanced version of this function in the dUFLP *(see the appendices for details)*.

Filtering Data

Filtering data allows you to limit the data shown in a table to just the rows that match a specific condition or set of conditions. To an extent filtering data is similar to finding data, but when using the options shown above to find data all you are doing is displaying a single row that matches some criteria. Navigating will move to the next row even if that row does not meet the criteria used to find the previously displayed row. When you filter the data, you literally limit the data displayed and that the user can see/interact with to just the rows that match the criteria. When navigating, the only rows the user will see (until a filter is cleared or the condition is changed) are those that meet the criteria given.

The Filter Property

The XDML version of this is the SET FILTER command, which works along these lines:

```
open database dbasesamples
set database to dbasesamples
use fish
set filter to name="Blue Angelfish"
go top
? recno(), name
skip
? eof()
use
close database
```

The rowset has a *filter* property, which can be set directly by a programmer, or through the use of methods set in other ways (discussed below). This property can be queried, modified, etc., through code. The *filter* property of the rowset uses a subset of SQL commands. This subset is fairly limited, which means that there are quite a few things you can do with SQL that you cannot do with the *filter* property.

The simplest use of the *filter* property is to check the value of a field against a value to see if any rows match:

```
d = new database()
d.databaseName := "DBASESAMPLES"
```

```
d.active := true
q = new query()
q.database := d
q.sql := "select * from fish"
q.active := true
q.rowset.filter := [name = 'Blue Angelfish']
? q.rowset.endOfSet
? q.rowset.count()
q.active := false
d.active := false
```

Note that this particular example would show in the output pane of the Command Window first the value *false* (meaning that we are *not* at the rowset's *endOfSet*), and then a number 1, showing that one row meets the condition. This is because there is only one row in the table that contains "Blue Angelfish" in the name field.

We could change the condition used in the filter to look at, say, the "length cm" field, which is a numeric value, and look for a value that is less than or equal to 100:

```
d = new database()
d.databaseName := "DBASESAMPLES"
d.active := true
q = new query()
q.database := d
q.sql := "select * from fish"
q.active := true
q.rowset.filter := [:length cm: <= 100]
? q.rowset.endOfSet
? q.rowset.count()
q.active := false
d.active := false
```

Note that since the "length cm" field has a space in the fieldname, we need to use the ":" character as a delimiter. This should show in the output pane of the Command Window *false*, meaning that we are not at the *endOfSet*, and then the number 5, meaning that five rows in the table meet the filter condition.

We could expand the code a little and have it display for us some values:

```
d = new database()
d.databaseName := "DBASESAMPLES"
d.active := true
q = new query()
q.database := d
q.sql := "select * from fish"
q.active := true
q.rowset.filter := [:length cm: <= 100]
q.rowset.first() // first row
// loop until we get to the endOfSet
do while not q.rowset.endOfSet
   ? q.rowset.fields["name"].value.rightTrim(),+;
       q.rowset.fields["length cm"].value
   q.rowset.next()
enddo
q.active := false
d.active := false
```

> **NOTE**
>
> When displaying output as shown above inside the do/enddo loop, the comma can be used to separate values by a space if "SET SPACE" is "ON", which is the default in dBASE PLUS. When you use the plus sign without a comma to separate the items, the two values will be concatenated without a space, which may be disconcerting. You can of course bypass this issue completely by replacing the comma with +" " which would concatenate the first value with a space and then the second value.
>
> As with the *applyLocate()* method, you can modify how a filter works by changing the value assigned to the rowset's *filterOptions* property. This has the same options as the *locateOptions* property, and has the same effects on the way a filter works.

This code would display the value of the name and length cm fields for each row that meets the criteria given in the output pane of the Command Window.

applyFilter()

You can use the rowset's *applyFilter()* method in the same way that the *applyLocate()* method works. You can assign a filter using *applyFilter()*, you can use the *beginFilter()* method to start "filter mode", and then use the *applyFilter()* method and the *filterOptions* property of the rowset affects these methods as well as the evaluation of the *filter* property.

In addition, once *applyFilter()* is executed, you can view the rowset's *filter* property, which can be useful in seeing how the method works.

Using *beginFilter()* and *applyFilter()*, we can create a "Filter by Form" type form, similar to the "Locate by Form" as discussed earlier. We will take another look at this in a later chapter when discussing working with data and forms.

Clearing Out a Filter

There are two ways to clear out a filter that is set for a rowset. The first is to use the *clearFilter()* method of the rowset. This quite literally removes any filter that is set. The other is in some ways perhaps even more obvious after the discussion of the *filter* property above – simply assign a blank or null value to the rowset's *filter* property:

```
q.rowset.filter := null
```

Filtering on Substrings and Complex Filters

While flexible and fairly powerful, eventually you will find that there are times when you need to filter the data in ways that are not possible, or are very difficult to do using the *filter* property and/or *beginFilter()* and *applyFilter()* methods.

One example is filtering data on a substring – in other words, trying to find a string that is contained in a field, but not necessarily at the beginning of the field. In XDML we were able to set a filter using the "$" operator – which is used to represent the concept of a string "contained in" another string. As it turns out, you can do this kind of thing by using the *canGetRow()* event of the rowset.

The *canGetRow()* event is fired *(if an event handler is assigned to it)* each time navigation occurs in a rowset, to see if the row being navigated to can be returned based on what the event handler is coded for.

For the moment, let's stick with the concept of the substring. Let's say we want to filter the data to display only rows in the fish table that contain the value 'Blue' anywhere in the name field. If we used the *filter* property, we could only find this word at the beginning of the name. However, by using the *canGetRow()* event, combined with the "$" operator, we can actually find the value *anywhere* in the string:

```
d = new database()
d.databaseName := "DBASESAMPLES"
d.active := true
q = new query()
q.database := d
q.sql := "select * from fish"
q.active := true
q.rowset.canGetRow := {|| 'blue' $ ;
                           this.fields["name"].value.toLowerCase()}
q.rowset.first() // first row
// loop until we get to the endOfSet
do while not q.rowset.endOfSet
   ? q.rowset.fields["name"].value.rightTrim(),+;
       q.rowset.fields["length cm"].value
   q.rowset.next()
enddo
q.active := false
d.active := false
```

When reading the code, it should be noted that "this" refers to the *rowset*, because the event is a rowset event. Also note that the "$" operator returns a *true* or *false* value, so this is what tells dBASE if a row can be displayed.

In this example, as it turns out, only two fish have the word "Blue" in the name field, and both of those start with that word, but the concept is there. In this example, we used a codeblock, because the filter was fairly simple. However, what if we needed to do something more complex? We can assign a function as the event handler, and then determine if a row can be returned that way.

```
d = new database()
d.databaseName := "DBASESAMPLES"
d.active := true
q = new query()
q.database := d
q.sql := "select * from fish"
q.active := true
q.rowset.canGetRow := FilterMyData
q.rowset.first() // first row
// loop until we get to the endOfSet
do while not q.rowset.endOfSet
   ? q.rowset.fields["name"].value.rightTrim(),+;
       q.rowset.fields["length cm"].value
   q.rowset.next()
enddo
q.active := false
d.active := false

function FilterMyData
   local bReturn
   bReturn = "blue" $ this.fields["name"].value.toLowerCase() and;
```

```
                    this.fields["length cm"].value < 100
    return bReturn
```

In this example, in the function "FilterMyData", the keyword "this" refers to the rowset object, as that is the object that is active and calling the function. From an OOP design perspective, pointing to functions that are outside a proper class hierarchy might be considered wrong, but this is a simple example, designed to show some basic techniques. We will be coming back to this kind of thing with datamodules and with forms in later chapters.

The great thing about *canGetRow()* is that you can do any sort of check that you might need to here, from the examples given, to more complex, relatively simple, etc. It should be noted however that in some cases the use of *canGetRow()* can substantially slow a process down. The question for the developer then becomes "Is the speed difference more important than the flexibility afforded by this method?" With the speed of computers constantly getting faster, in most cases the answer is often "no" and the developer should use this method except for a large rowset (on which the SQL equivalent may be dramatically faster).

One thing that is rather useful to a programmer is that you could create two (or more) different "FilterMyData" functions, and based on what is happening in your code, change the *canGetRow()* event handler, something like:

```
    q.rowset.canGetRow := FilterMyData1
    // do some code
    q.rowset.canGetRow := FilterMyData2
```

This can add even more flexibility to your applications.

SQL SELECT/WHERE
In addition to other ways of filter data, the local SQL command SELECT has a filter clause that can be used with your query object(s). The SQL WHERE clause has a slightly different format than some of what you may be used to with dBASE filtering, so we will briefly discuss some of that.

You need to understand that using the SQL WHERE clause in a query object filters the data from the moment that the query is activated, rather than the more flexible methods shown earlier in this chapter that can be used to set and clear filters easily.

However, the SQL WHERE clause has a lot of power and flexibility, including the ability to use "wildcard" characters in a filter, and more. We are going to look at a few options, but not all – you would want to use a good SQL reference to find all the possibilities.

In XDML, the "$" operator can be used to see if a string is contained in a list of strings. In SQL, this can be done with the "IN" clause combined with the WHERE clause:

```
    SELECT * FROM customer WHERE customer."state id" IN ("CA", "NY" )
```

You can also use what are called "wildcard" characters in a WHERE clause to filter the data, which will get you a substring search, however the resulting rowset may be read-only.

The two wildcard characters are "%" and "_" (percent and underscore).

The percent sign refers to anything on that side of the character string (see example below), the underscore refers to a single character. If you are familiar with DOS wildcards for filenames, the percent sign is similar to the asterisk (*) and the underscore works identically to the question mark (?).

It's important to note that SQL is case sensitive when performing searches, just like the commands used above, but SQL also has UPPER() and LOWER() functions, used to do a temporary conversion of the data to lower case. If they are not used, then you will only get rows that match the exact case as given. So we could try something like:

```
SELECT * FROM fish WHERE LOWER(name) LIKE "blue%"
```

This would return a result set that had the word "blue" at the beginning of the name field, followed by any character value.

```
SELECT * FROM fish WHERE LOWER(name) LIKE "%blue%"
```

Which would return a result set that had the word "blue" anywhere in the name field.

```
SELECT * FROM fish WHERE LOWER(name) LIKE "%fish"
```

This would return any row where the name field ends in the word "fish".

```
SELECT * FROM fish WHERE LOWER(name) LIKE "__ue%"
```

This filter would limit the data to anything that started with any two characters (two underscores), the letters "ue", and then any characters after it.

It is important to note that like the *canGetRow()* event handler above, you can change the SQL Select statement of a query object on the fly, adding a lot of flexibility to your application.

```
nVar = 6
q.sql := "select * from fish where id="+nVar
// do some code
nVar = 2
q.sql := "select * from fish where id="+nVar
```

It is also important to note that in code like that of the example given above, you must restate the query object's *sql* property, because the value of the variable nVar will not be reevaluated automatically in the query's *sql* property by dBASE.

Romain Strieff, a member of the dBASE developer community and former dBVIPS pointed out, after some testing, that if you need speed in your application, that the SQL WHERE clause with local tables is generally slower than the use of the *filter* property of the rowset. He notes that for the fastest filtering the following appears to make a difference (again, with local tables):

1. A simple index on all involved fields
2. Turn the index off (set the rowset's *indexName* property to a blank or null value), just prior to filtering and set it back on (reset the value of the *indexName* property) afterward.

SQL SELECT/WHERE and Parameters

In addition to just using the WHERE clause, you can enhance this with the ability to define parameters for the query object. The advantage to this is that you might want to call a form or report with some specific values and assign the values before the form or report is displayed. This would handle it automatically for you. One way to do this is using the *params* property of the query object, which is an object reference to an associative array (discussed in detail in a later chapter). The *params* property is used to store references to the values you wish to pass to the WHERE clause and the WHERE clause uses the colon to tell it that the information shown is a parameter:

```
d = new database()
d.databaseName := "DBASESAMPLES"
d.active        := true

q = new query()
q.database := d
q.sql       := [select * from fish where fish."length cm" < :nSize]
q.params["nSize"] = 100
q.active   := true
q.rowset.first()
do while not q.rowset.endOfSet
    ? q.rowset.fields["name"].value, q.rowset.fields["length cm"].value
    q.rowset.next()
enddo
```

This code will open the fish table and show only the fish that have a "length cm" value less than 100. To change this in your code however, you would have to change the value of the parameter and then tell dBASE to requery the table. This is done like:

```
q.params["nSize"] = 80
q.requery()
```

Note that you can add more parameters to the *params* associative array, you are not limited to a single parameter.

The second way to do this is to simply use memory variables:

```
nSize = 100
```

And the code shown above would be the same, but you would leave out the code assigning the value to the params array (q.params...). The same limits apply, however – you must call the *requery()* method to apply a change in the value used for the parameters.

It should be noted that the *params* property *must* be set before the query's *active* property is set to true.

SET KEY TO ...

In XDML there is another way of filtering data, using the SET KEY command, which works with the active index of a table. This allows you to set a range if you wish, and so on.

```
open database dbasesamples
set database to dbasesamples
use fish order id
set key to range 4,7
scan
```

```
    ? id, name
endscan
use
close database
```

In OODML we have the rowset's *setRange()* and *clearRange()* methods. This does not have quite as many options as the SET KEY command, but it allows you to set a beginning and ending range to filter the data on.

Let's say we want to filter the fish table on rows that have an ID that is between 4 and 7. To do that we would use the *setRange()* method:

```
d = new database()
d.databaseName := "DBASESAMPLES"
d.active := true
q = new query()
q.database := d
q.sql := "select * from fish"
q.active := true
q.rowset.indexName := "ID"
q.rowset.setRange( 4, 7 )
q.rowset.first() // first row
// loop until we get to the endOfSet
do while not q.rowset.endOfSet
   ? q.rowset.fields["ID"].value+;
      q.rowset.fields["name"].value
   q.rowset.next()
enddo
q.active := false
d.active := false
```

If you wanted to limit the data to an ID that was greater or equal to 4, but not have an upper limit, you can just leave the second parameter off:

```
q.rowset.setRange( 4, null )
```

If you wanted to limit the data to IDs that were less than or equal to 7, but not have a *lower* limit, you would have to put a 'null' value in:

```
q.rowset.setRange( null, 7 )
```

Finally, if you wanted to limit the data to just those rows that were an exact match for an ID of 4:

```
q.rowset.setRange( 4 )
```

To clear out a range once it has been set, simply call the rowset's *clearRange()* method:

```
q.rowset.clearRange()
```

Performing Lookups in Other Tables

One thing that the XDML programming techniques really lacked was a good way to do a lookup in another table. You could do it, but it took a lot of code.

Using lookupSQL

Using the data objects in dBASE PLUS, this becomes pretty easy. The field object has a *lookupSQL* property, which can be set to a SQL statement to return a value that matches the value contained in the field.

A simple example of this might be in an address table, rather than storing the full name of the states in the U.S. (or if you are writing an "international" application perhaps the full names of countries), you could store the standard abbreviations in the address table. However, you might want your users to see the full names, even if you were only storing the abbreviations.

So, if you had a table called "STATES" that contained two fields – "CODE" and "StateName", with the first being the two-letter abbreviations used in the United States (i.e., "CA" is the abbreviation for the state of California), and the "StateName" field containing the full name. Once you have set up your query, you can then set up the lookup along these lines (this assumes that the link field in the address table is named "StateId"):

```
q.rowset.fields["STATEPROV"].lookupSQL := "select * from STATEPROV"
```

If the "STATES" table had more fields you might want to limit the fields to just the two that are required. Also, if for some reason in the design of the table the "StateID" field is not the first field, you would want to use this syntax as well:

```
q.rowset.fields["STATEPROV"].lookupSQL := "select Code, StateProv from STATEPROV"
```

It is very important that the field you are linking to is the first one in the table or the first in the result set from the SELECT statement; it is also very important that the value you wish to display is the second field.

If you are working with a lookup in a form, you might want to set the display order for the SELECT statement of the lookup table using the ORDER BY clause:

```
q.rowset.fields["STATEPROV"].lookupSQL := ;
        "select * from STATEPROV order by StateProv"
```

This would allow the display to be in alphabetical sequence on the name of the state. The best thing about using the *lookupRowset* or *lookupSQL* properties, is that you do not have to write *any* code that does the lookup, or stores the appropriate value in your table it is all handled automatically for you.

One concern that comes up once in a while is accessing the actual value stored in the field, not displaying the looked-up value. This can be a little tricky, but your application may need to obtain that information. In the example shown here, if you had looked up "CA" and were displaying "California", the question would then be returning "CA" for use in some other part of your application.

One method of doing this is to traverse the object model carefully. There are other options (such as removing the lookupSQL, finding the value in the field and then returning the lookupSQL – this can get a bit odd). The following will return the value actually contained in the field:

```
q.rowset.fields["STATEPROV"].lookupRowset.fields[1].value
```

lookupRowset Instead of lookupSQL

It is also possible to use a rowset that is already defined for a lookup, using the *lookupRowset* property of the rowset object. This must follow the requirements given above, but rather than assigning a SQL statement to a property, you are assigning an object reference to the rowset. This might be done along these lines:

```
qState = new query()
qState.sql := "select Code, StateProv from StateProv"
qState.active := true
q = new query()
q.sql := "select * from AddressBook"
q.active := true
q.rowset.fields["StateProv"].lookupRowset := qState.rowset
```

The advantage to this is if you have more than one field that you need to do the same lookup – it would take less memory than having multiple assignments of the SELECT statement, which opens the table for each SELECT statement.

Shortening References

One of the frustrating issues for many developers is the long syntax used with the data objects to reference objects and properties, events and methods of objects.

As it turns out, dBASE allows you to shorten these long references to something more manageable, and in the process, because dBASE itself is not having to parse these references out each time it sees them, you can theoretically speed up a process *(I don't have figures available that verifies this, but I have been told by reliable sources that this is indeed the case)*.

Let's say you are working with the sample FISH table, and you intend to do some fairly complex processing on the rowset and fields of that table. You can do something along these lines:

```
d = new database()
d.databaseName := "DBASESAMPLES"
d.active := true
qFish = new query()
qFish.database := d
qFish.sql := "select * from fish"
qFish.active := true
// Short reference to rowset
rFish = qFish.rowset
// Short reference to fields array
fFish = rFish.fields
```

> **REMINDER**
> In an earlier chapter it was mentioned that you can store the object reference to variables, a property of another object, or in an array. In this example the object references qFish, rFish and fFish are being stored to variables with references to a query object, a rowset object and a fields array object.

Once you have done this, your code doesn't have to look like:

```
do while not qFish.rowset.endOfSet
   ? qFish.rowset.fields["name"].value
   qFish.rowset.next()
enddo
```

Instead it can look like:

```
do while not rFish.endOfSet
   ? fFish["name"].value
   rFish.next()
enddo
```

The second version is a bit easier to read and a lot easier to type. This can get to be even more useful in reports, where if you are writing code in, say, a text control's *canRender* event, you might need to write something like:

```
if this.parent.parent.rowset.fields["Name"].value == " something"
```

If you instead do:

```
fFields = this.parent.parent.rowset.fields
if fFields["Name"].value == "something"
```

You still have readable code, but if that *canRender* event is fairly complex, it's much easier to type and create references to the fields array.

Relating Tables

There are a couple of things that can cause some difficulties in code (in your forms as well), when developing applications that work with parent/child tables. The first is adding a parent row to a parent/child relationship if the child row is constrained in such a way that only parent rows that have a child row are displayed (sound convoluted? It is). The other is if you delete a parent row and want to remove the associated child rows in a child rowset. This is called a "cascading delete".

Setting a Relationship between Parent and Child Tables

Before looking at anything else, we must take a look at setting relationships between tables in the first place. There are two ways to relate tables, one that is designed for local tables and uses indexes; the other is for SQL Server tables and does not use indexes.

Local Tables, Using Indexes

This is the one most dBASE developers need to be concerned with. The rowset objects have two properties that are specific to setting relationships: *masterRowset* and *masterFields*. These two properties are set for the *child* rowset. The first is a pointer to the parent rowset and the second is a pointer to the field that is the linking field. The name of the *masterFields* property is a bit misleading, as DBF tables can only have one linking field. The following example is based on one in the online help:

```
qEmp = new Query( )
qEmp.sql := "select * from EMPLOYEE"
qEmp.active := true
qPos = new Query( )
qPos.sql := "select * from POSITION"
```

```
qPos.active := true
qPos.rowset.indexName := "EMP_ID"
qPos.rowset.masterRowset := qEmp.rowset    // Identify master rowset
qPos.rowset.masterFields := "EMP_ID"       // Field matches index order
```

SQL Server Tables, No Indexes

If you need to work with SQL Server tables, many of the SQL server databases do not allow the creation of indexes. In those cases the rowset's *masterRowset* and *masterFields* properties cannot be used. The query object has a property called *masterSource* that is used for this purpose. The example below is again based on an example in the online help:

```
qCust = new Query( )
qCust.sql := "select * from CUST"
qCust.active := true
qOrder := new Query( )
qOrder.sql := ;
    "select * from ORDERS where CUST_ID = :CUST_ID order by ORDER_DATE"
qOrder.masterSource := qCust.rowset
qCust.active := true
```

The online help notes that the parameter "CUST_ID" is automatically filled in with the "CUST_ID" field value in the Cust table. *(In this case, while a little confusing, the fieldname "CUST_ID" is the same in both tables – this is by design.)*

While it is possible to use this syntax with local DBF tables, you will find you have more control and ease of coding with local tables if you use the rowset's *masterRowset* and *masterFields* properties.

Set Skip

In XDML, the SET SKIP command is used to tell dBASE where navigation is when you have a relationship set between two tables (using SET RELATION).

If you want the navigation to be in the parent rowset, you would issue your SET RELATION statement, and then issue a command like:

```
SET SKIP TO parenttable
```

If you want the navigation to be in the child rowset, then as you might imagine, the command would be:

```
SET SKIP TO childtable
```

(In both cases, you would substitute the words "parenttable" or "childtable" with the name of the table.)

In the OODML form, the command SET RELATION is not used. Instead, if you are using local tables (.DBFs, etc.), you would use the rowset's *masterRowset* and *masterFields* properties to set the relationship between the tables. If you are using SQL Server tables, you would instead define the query object's *masterSource* property. Then you would set either *navigateByMaster* to navigate in the parent table, or *navigateMaster* to navigate in the child table.

navigateMaster, when set to true, if navigation in the child rowset reaches the last row, it will then move to the next parent rowset and navigation will then begin again in the child rowset. For example, let's assume you have a pair of tables showing customers (parent) and orders (child) and the child rowset's *navigateMaster* is set to true. If you call the child rowset's *next()* method, it will move to the next order associated with the customer. If you reach the last order that is linked to the current customer and call the child rowset's *next()* method again, rather than stopping navigation, dBASE will move to the next parent row (the next customer) and show the first order for that customer. The next call to the child rowset's *next()* method would now move to the next order for the new customer, and so on.

navigateByMaster works just the opposite of the *navigateMaster* property. This causes the child rowset to navigate as you navigate in the parent rowset. If using a pair of tables showing customers (parent) and orders (child), when navigating in the customer table (using the rowset's *next()* method), the orders table would change to show the orders associated with the currently selected customer (there is a lot more very detailed information in the online help).

The important thing to note is that these properties allow navigation to occur as if the two tables in question were a single table, but depending on which property is set will affect the actual sequence of navigation.

The following code can be used to create a couple of tables that will help us see the difference between *navigateMaster* and *navigateByMaster*. If you wish to use it, it should be in a folder that you are doing testing in … create a program (as we have done before), call it something like "MakeParentChild.prg" (this is XDML style code because it's short and easy to type):

```
// close any open databases and tables
close database
// if tables by these names exist, delete them:
if file( "ParentTest.dbf" )
   drop table ParentTest
endif
if file( "ChildTest.dbf" )
   drop table ChildTest
endif

// create the parent table, and add some rows:
create table ParentTest (;
          LinkField autoinc,;
          ParentData char(10) )
use ParentTest
append blank
replace ParentData with "Parent 1"
append blank
replace ParentData with "Parent 2"
append blank
replace ParentData with "Parent 3"
append blank
replace ParentData with "Parent 4"
use // close table

// create the child table, and add some rows
create table ChildTest (;
          LinkField integer,;
          ChildData char(20) )
create index LinkField on ChildTest (LinkField)
use ChildTest
append blank
```

```
// child data is not 100% "in sequence" intentionally
replace LinkField with 1, ChildData with "Parent 1, Child 1"
append blank
replace LinkField with 1, ChildData with "Parent 1, Child 3"
append blank
replace LinkField with 1, ChildData with "Parent 1, Child 2"
append blank
replace LinkField with 2, ChildData with "Parent 2, Child 1"
append blank
replace LinkField with 3, ChildData with "Parent 3, Child 2"
append blank
replace LinkField with 3, ChildData with "Parent 3, Child 1"
append blank
replace LinkField with 4, ChildData with "Parent 4, Child 1"
append blank
replace LinkField with 4, ChildData with "Parent 4, Child 5"
append blank
replace LinkField with 4, ChildData with "Parent 4, Child 3"
append blank
replace LinkField with 4, ChildData with "Parent 4, Child 2"
append blank
replace LinkField with 4, ChildData with "Parent 4, Child 4"
use // close table

? "Done"
```

This looks like a lot, but it will give us some data to work with and see what is happening with the data.

The following code will show the way that *navigateMaster* affects a parent/child relationship, as we navigate through the CHILD table:

```
// navigateMaster example:
clear
// Parent table:
qParent = new query()
qParent.sql := "select * from ParentTest"
qParent.active := true
// short references:
rParent = qParent.rowset
fParent = rParent.fields

// Child table:
qChild = new query()
qChild.sql := "select * from ChildTest"
qChild.active := true
// short references:
rChild = qChild.rowset
fChild = rChild.fields
// set the index:
rChild.indexName := "LinkField"
// set the masterRowset/masterFields:
rChild.masterRowset := rParent
rChild.masterFields := "LINKFIELD"
// the navigateMaster property is not set,
// and is the default: false
? "navigateMaster = false"
```

```
// navigate through the master table, and show the linked data:
rChild.first()
do while not rChild.endOfSet
   ? fParent["ParentData"].value+" "+;
     fChild["ChildData"].value
   rChild.next()
enddo

// now set the navigateMaster to true:
rChild.navigateMaster := true
?
? "navigateMaster = true"
// navigate through the child table, and show the linked data:
rChild.first()
do while not rChild.endOfSet
   ? fParent["ParentData"].value+" "+;
     fChild["ChildData"].value
   rChild.next()
enddo
```

The code as shown should show that navigating through the child rowset is constrained to just the rows associated with the current parent table. When the loop completes, it shows just the child rows for that table. When *navigateMaster* is set to true, when we get to the last row of the child table that is associated with the current parent row, we navigate to the next parent row, and then loop through each child row.

The following code shows the way that *navigateByMaster* affects a parent/child relationship, as we navigate through the PARENT table. If you use this code with the tables created above, you will see that the first loop through the parent table shows only one child row for each parent row, but in the second loop we treat the two tables as if they were one table:

```
// navigateByMaster example:
clear
// Parent table:
qParent = new query()
qParent.sql := "select * from ParentTest"
qParent.active := true
// short references:
rParent = qParent.rowset
fParent = rParent.fields

// Child table:
qChild = new query()
qChild.sql := "select * from ChildTest"
qChild.active := true
// short references:
rChild = qChild.rowset
fChild = rChild.fields
// set the index:
rChild.indexName := "LinkField"
// set the masterRowset/masterFields:
rChild.masterRowset := rParent
rChild.masterFields := "LINKFIELD"
// the navigateByMaster property is not set,
// and is the default: false
? "navigateByMaster = false"
```

```
// navigate through the master table, and show the linked data:
rParent.first()
do while not rParent.endOfSet
   ? fParent["ParentData"].value+" "+;
     fChild["ChildData"].value
   rParent.next()
enddo

// now set the navigateByMaster to true:
rChild.navigateByMaster := true
?
? "navigateByMaster = true"
// navigate through the master table, and show the linked data:
rParent.first()
do while not rParent.endOfSet
   ? fParent["ParentData"].value+" "+;
     fChild["ChildData"].value
   rParent.next()
enddo
```

Referential Integrity – Adding a Parent to Parent/Child

One problem that you might see if you use a *masterFields/masterRowset* setup for parent/child tables, is that if you add a row to a parent table, you may see it disappear immediately in your form. This is due to default constraints in the rowset objects. By default a parent row <u>must</u> have a child row. The rowset property that affects this is *masterChild*, which defaults to *0 - Constrained* – if you need the behavior shown, you should leave this property set to the default (in the child rowset). If you do not need the requirement that every parent row has a child row, then you should change this property for the child rowset to *1 - Unconstrained.* (This property is ignored unless the rowset's *masterRowset* and *masterFields* properties have been set.)

So, how do you ensure that you *have* a child row? When I worked at Borland with the R&D team, I sweated over this one when I first started tinkering with dBASE's data objects *(as I had an application that required this – each parent must have a child row)* and spent some time working with both the developers and one of the folk in the docs team, and came up with the following solution. If you are using datamodules, you should set this code in the datamodule.

First, you need to use the parent rowset's *canSave()* event, which will set the following custom property *(this event will fire before the actually save of the parent row, which is very important as we have to know the rowset's state before the save – we don't want to do the associated code if the user was editing or viewing the parent row)*:

```
function rowset_canSave
   this.parentAppend = ( this.state == 3 ) // append
return true
```

The next part is to use the parent rowset's *onSave()* event – this fires after the code associated with the *save()* method fires:

```
function rowset_onSave
   if this.parentAppend
      // change "childquery" to the name of the
      // query object for the child rowset
      r = this.parent.parent.childquery.rowset
```

```
       // now we add a child row:
       r.beginAppend()
       //set the key field value:
       r.fields["keyfield"].value :=  this.fields["keyfield"].value
       // this is a good place to set any
       // default values you may need as well.
       // Now we save the child row so that it
       // exists:
       r.save()
     endif
     // reset this value:
     this.parentAppend = false
     // and save the parent row - this happens
     // automatically, so no code is required!
   return true // must return true!
```

After all that, you may want to add some code in your form that forces the user to the child rowset and the new (effectively blank) row, so that they can add whatever is necessary to the child row (put them into edit mode for the child row with *beginEdit()* for example).

Another note on this – if you set defaults for the child rowset, you will want to add an *onAppend()* event for the child that sets the defaults there as well, since this method only gets called when the parent is being appended to.

Referential Integrity –Cascading Deletes

When you work with the parent/child or master/detail relationship, as noted in the section above on adding a parent record, there is another issue to be concerned with – that is deleting a parent row and having the child rows left behind (this is called "orphaning" the child rows).

If you delete the parent, you have no reference to the child rows, they are not available to do anything with *(this is once again due to the constraint in the masterRowset/masterFields settings)*. You could create a routine that deleted all your orphaned rows, but this is not necessary if you do the following.

You need to use an event in the parent row – this one would be *canDelete()*. The reason to use *canDelete()* is the same reason you would want to use *canSave()* in the code in the previous section of this chapter – it fires before the *delete()* method of the parent.

```
   function rowset_canDelete
      r = rChild.rowset

      // loop until we get to the end of the child rowset -
      // don't panic - the child rowset is constrained
      // by the key field in the parent rowset, and only
      // the child rows that match the current parent
      // are seen here:
      do while not r.endOfSet
         // delete it:
         r.delete()
      enddo
      // that's it - the child rows are deleted, when
      // this method is done, the next event to fire
      // is the delete on the parent, and then if you
      // had an onDelete call, that would fire ...
   return true
```

It's really that simple. *(Most of the 'code' above is really comments which are not executable code ...)*

Referential Integrity –Cascading Updates

Cascading Updates are a different matter in an application. Once you have set up a relationship between two tables, the database engine actually protects the linked fields from being modified. While this is, in normal circumstances a good thing, there may be a point where you need to change the primary key value. If that is the case, changing the primary key in the parent table would orphan (or abandon) the matching records in the child table.

This example is a lot more complicated than a cascading delete, because of the nature of working with related tables.

First you would need to use the parent rowset's *canEdit()* event handler to save the value of the primary key:

```
function rowset_canEdit
    this.PrimaryKey = this.fields["LINKFIELD"].value
    return true
```

Why *canEdit()*, rather than the *canSave()* event handler? The reason is that the value contained in the record buffer will be the modified value in the *canSave()* event handler. We need to get the previous value *before* we attempt to save the rowset.

In the *canSave()* event handler for the parent rowset, you would then need to a) compare the current value in the primary key against the saved value and b) if they are different, perform the cascade update in the child table.

This gets very difficult at this point. See note to the left – there is a program that shows how to do this, but it is complicated enough that I am not placing the code in the book. And of course, as noted, it is a bad idea to change the primary key in the first place.

Child Table Sorted Differently?

One request for help that appears in the newsgroups on a regular basis is the need to index the data in the child rowset on the foreign key field (the one used to link to the parent table), but *also* view the data in a sequence other than that of the linking field by itself *(especially useful in a grid, for example)*. The difficulty most users see is when the linking field is numeric, but in the child table you want to sort the data by a character (or other non-numeric) field. This takes a couple of parts to make work.

First, you have to create a calculated field for the parent table using the rowset's *canGetRow()* event. This calculated field simply converts the numeric value of the primary key to a character string. This assumes a form is being used:

```
function parenttest1_onOpen
    f = new field()
    f.fieldName = "CharLink"
    f.beforeGetValue = {||str(this.parent["LinkField"].value)}
    this.rowset.fields.add(f)
    return
```

You would need to create a compound index on the Child table – the index expression might be:

```
index on str( LinkField ) + ChildData tag Link2
```

(This is the XDML method, but you could do this with the DBFIndex class ...)

Finally, you need to set the index and links for the Child Table:

```
with (this.CHILDTEST1.rowset)
    indexName = "LINK2"
    masterRowset = form.parenttest1.rowset
    masterFields = "CharLink"
    navigateByMaster = true
endwith
```

If you then set a grid on the form and set the appropriate properties of the form and grid, you could view the data and it might something like:

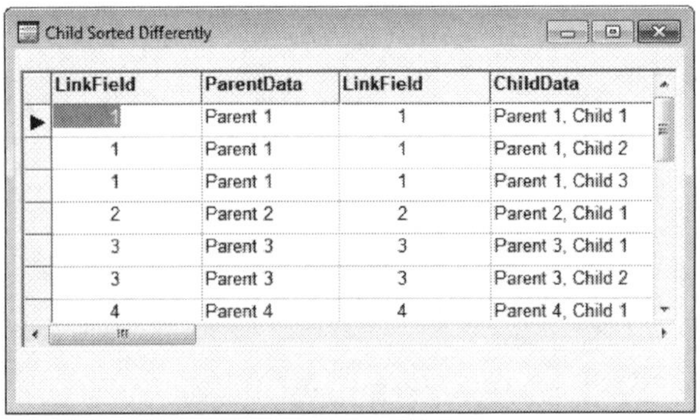

LinkField	ParentData	LinkField	ChildData
	Parent 1	1	Parent 1, Child 1
1	Parent 1	1	Parent 1, Child 2
1	Parent 1	1	Parent 1, Child 3
2	Parent 2	2	Parent 2, Child 1
3	Parent 3	3	Parent 3, Child 1
3	Parent 3	3	Parent 3, Child 2
4	Parent 4	4	Parent 4, Child 1

Figure 8-1

At first glance this doesn't appear to be a big deal, but if you examine the program used to generate the tables and populate them with data, the child data is not in the same sequence that it was added to the child table.

Other Parent/Child Concerns

When you lock a parent record for editing or other purposes, the child records are automatically locked. This has been the default since these objects were created and in most cases is desirable. If you have a situation where you do not wish to lock the child records, you couldn't set this up – until release 2.61 of dBASE. The developers added a property to the rowset class called *autoLockChildRows*. This property defaults to a value of *true*, which is the same behavior that currently exists. If, however, you wish to be able to edit the parent without locking the child rows, on the parent rowset, you would set the *autoLockChildRows* property to false *(using the sample object references in this chapter)*:

```
rParent.autoLockChildRows := false
```

Calculated Fields

Calculated fields are rather important in a lot of applications. These are simply fields that display a calculation or a value not in the table for the user (some folk think of a calculated field as specifically being aimed at math, but combining two fields into one is considered to be a calculated field and getting a value from a *lookupRowset* is a calculated field). The user cannot directly interact with them, because they are, by their nature, read-only – they are not directly datalinked to a field in a table. (The user can actually edit the value of a calculated field unless you set the *readOnly* property on the field, but it won't make a difference to the table itself.)

To create a calculated field, you must create an instance of a field object, set some properties (as discussed below) and then add the field to the *fields* array for the rowset. If set properly, as the user navigates through the table, this field will be calculated (using the *beforeGetValue()* event) and the results will be displayed on the form (or report).

The following is a simple example of creating a calculated field to display a "full name" from first and last name fields in a table. Keep in mind that any valid dBASE expression will work. This example assumes that the field object is being added in a query's *canOpen()* or *onOpen()* event:

```
// instantiate the field object
f = new Field()
f.fieldName := "Full Name"
// "this" in the following statement refers to the
// field object (important information)
f.beforeGetValue := {|| trim( this.parent["first name"].value )+;
                     " "+this.parent["last name"].value }
// "this" in the following statement refers to the query:
this.rowset.fields.add( f )
```

It is very important that you use the *beforeGetValue()* event to actually perform the calculation, or the value will not update as you navigate through your table. If you assign the *value* property instead, it will display the value assigned for the first row seen and not update as you navigate.

You can have multiple calculated fields for a rowset, you just want to make sure that each has a unique value in the *fieldName* property.

You can use options for a SQL select statement, as shown in other chapters of this book to create a similar calculated field to that shown above.

Morphing Data

Morphing is a means of changing the value of a field for the purpose of display and editing, but storing something different in a table.

This is particularly useful if you want to use a SQL Server table and you want to use checkboxes for logical values. The problem is that many SQL Server tables do not actually have a boolean or logical field type. Instead, you need to use, for example, a one digit wide numeric or integer (not all SQL Servers have "numeric" fields either) field that you store either 0 or 1 in *(in reality, this is pretty close to what dBASE does internally with .DBF type tables)*.

There are of course other uses for field morphing, but this one is a pretty clear cut example.

To morph a field there are two events of the field object that you need to work with – *beforeGetValue()* and *canChange()*. You use *beforeGetValue()* to return the value you wish to actually use/display, and you use *canChange()* to determine what is to be stored back in the table.

If you want to follow along, then go to the Command Window in dBASE PLUS, and type the following:

```
create table TestMorph ( MyLogical numeric(1) )
```

This will create a small table with a logical field. Now to add a couple of rows of data, type the following commands in the Command Window:

```
use TestMorph
append blank
replace MyLogical with 1
append blank
replace MyLogical with 0
append blank
replace MyLogical with 1
use
```

This series of XDML commands opened the TestMorph table, added three rows, placing values of 1, 0 and 1 in them, then closed the table. This was quicker than using OODML (creating objects, and such) for a simple test.

For the rest of the test, however, we need to create a small program for test purposes that will create a query object and therefore a rowset object with a fields array. You could type all this in the Command Window, but it will be easier to do it as a small program that can be modified as needed. So, in the Command Window, type:

```
create command TestMorph
```

Enter the following in the main window:

```
q = new query()
q.sql := "select * from TestMorph"
q.active := true
// create some shortcuts to the rowset and field array objects:
r = q.rowset
f = r.fields
r.first()
// show the value before morphing
? f["MyLogical"].value
// tell dBASE to morph the value to a logical:
f["MyLogical"].beforeGetValue = {; return iif( this.value==1, true, false ) }
// show the value after morphing
? f["MyLogical"].value
// cleanup
q.active := false
release object q
```

When run this will create a query and the associated rowset, fields array and field object(s). Then it will display the value of the field in the first row, before we morphed it, it will set the code that performs the morphing of the data and then it will display it again. Finally it simply deactivates the query and releases it from memory – a nice little bit of cleanup.

What we have done is to change the value to a logical value for the purpose of checking the *value* of the field. Rather than returning a 1 or a 0, we will get *true* or *false*.

To run this program save and exit (Ctrl+W) the Source Code Editor then in the Command Window type:

```
do TestMorph
```

You should see, in the output pane of the Command Window:

```
        1
true
```

We can do more complex morphing – the example in the online help performs a lookup in another table.

If we want to be able to change the value of the field and treat it like a logical value (let's say we want to change a true to a false, for example), then what needs to be stored back in the table is the new value, but the field is actually a numeric field – we can't store *true* or *false* in a numeric field. So we need to morph this back to the correct type.

This is done in the field object's *canChange()* event which allows us to change the value before it can be stored, as it fires at the time you assign a new value to the field. So if we tried to save *true* or *false* to the field, the *canChange()* event would fire any handler assigned to it. You could then morph the data back in the event handler.

To see this, let's modify the program we created before by going to the Command Window and typing:

```
modify command TestMorph
```

Change or add the lines that are in bold below:

```
q = new query()
q.sql := "select * from TestMorph"
q.active := true
// create some shortcuts to the rowset and field array objects:
r = q.rowset
f = r.fields
r.first()
// show the value before morphing
? f["MyLogical"].value
// tell dBASE to morph the value to a logical:
f["MyLogical"].beforeGetValue := ;
        {; return iif( this.value==1, true, false ) }
// tell dBASE how to morph the value back to numeric:
f["MyLogical"].canChange := ;
        {|bValue|; this.value=iif(bValue, 1, 0); return false}
// show the value after morphing
? f["MyLogical"].value
// assign a new value
f["MyLogical"].value := false
// attempt to save it:
r.save()
// turn off the morphing so we can see the actual value:
f["MyLogical"].beforeGetValue := null
// show the actual value in the field:
? f["MyLogical"].value
// cleanup
q.active := false
release object q
```

The tricky part of this code to understand is the *canChange()* event handler. Since we're using a codeblock, and we need to pass the current value that is being assigned to the field to the event handler, we are using the codeblock parameter option (the part that looks like: |bValue|). Then we are assigning to the value of the field a 1 or a 0 depending on the value that was assigned to the field (a bit confusing, but ...). The reason we return a value of *false* in the "return" statement, has to do with the way the record buffer works. If we returned a value of *true*, because of the way the field morphing works, we would end up with what is called a "data type mismatch" – an attempt to assign the wrong type of data to the field. This is a bit confusing, but once you start working with it, you will find you can do a lot with it.

Rather than codeblocks, we could have used separate functions like we have done in some of the earlier code shown here. This gives us more flexibility, because you can do a lot more in a function than in a codeblock, and generally the code in a function is easier to read.

To see the program work, press `Ctrl`+`W` (save and exit in the Source Code Editor), and in the Command Window, type:

```
do TestMorph
```

Note that in the output pane of the Command Window, you should now see:

```
          1
true
          0
```

Record Numbers?

When the OODML was created for dBASE, the old .DBF record numbers became an obsolete feature. What do I mean by that?

The data objects in dBASE do not understand the record number as it is stored in a .DBF. This is because the data objects were designed to work with many types of tables and the .DBF is the *only* table type that has this feature. In dBASE for DOS applications this was useful to keep track of navigation and such. Some developers treated it as a Primary Key. The problem with doing this is that deleting a record caused dBASE to renumber the records. A primary key should not be changed – especially if you are using it as a link to another table. It gets worse if the software makes the change for you! In addition, the rowset object does not know what the record number of a record is, there is no "recno()" in the data objects.

Some developers have found that there is a method of the rowset object called *rowNo()*. The difficulty with *rowNo()* is that it works great with most database tables, but not with the local .DBF. Why, you may ask? This method relies on what is called a *logical row number*.

> "rowNo( ) returns the current logical row number in the rowset, if known. The logical row number is the relative row number, using the rowset's current index and filter conditions. The first row is row number 1 and the last row is equal to the number of rows in the current rowset." – The dBASE OLH

With a local .DBF, the *rowNo()* method will work fine until you use an index or an *Order By* in the SQL statement in a query object. As soon as you do that, the *rowNo()* method returns -1. Always. No matter what row you are on. This is because the rowset is no longer returning *logical row numbers*.

Why is this important? I want to make sure that a developer does not attempt to rely on the use of the *rowNo()* method of the rowset if they use the local .DBF table. For any other table type this should work perfectly.

Keep in mind however, that if your SQL statement in your query returns a subset of the data in the table (through the use of a WHERE clause, or what have you), or if the data is sorted (using ORDER BY, or you use an index), the values returned by *rowNo()* are not always going to point to the same record in the table each time. The logical row number is based on the records currently selected, not on the overall records in the table. This can be confusing.

Instead, if you need a primary key field, there are other ways to do this. One is to use an *autoincrement* field type. This is by definition unique and it is automatically generated. Some developers feel that reliance on this field type is not a good idea, but as long as a developer is careful, they can do this. I have successfully used these in several applications. There is more discussion on this field type in other places in this book.

If you do not wish to use the autoincrement field type, you will need to have some method of generating your primary key fields.

More on Data Object Events

There are an awful lot of events associated with the query and rowset objects and sometimes it can be confusing. You might look at them and ask yourself "Why would I ever need that?"

We're going to take a quick look at a few events with the idea of helping you see possibilities. This book cannot cover every single event in huge detail, so we're going to take a look at three in particular.

Query Object - canOpen()

The query object has events such as *canOpen()*, which seem a bit odd – why would you want to not open a query? You might want to check for specific conditions to see if they evaluate to *true* or *false*, and only allow a query to be opened if the conditions evaluated to *true*.

The *canOpen()* event fires when the query object's *active* property is set to true and it evaluates the return value which must be either *true* or *false*.

However, you can also do just about *anything* you want to in the rowset's *canOpen()* event, such as add a filter condition to a table's SQL statement based on a value. You might try something like:

```
d = new database()
d.databaseName := "DBASESAMPLES"
d.active := true

q = new query()
q.sql := "select * from fish"
// assign an event handler in a function:
q.canOpen := CanItOpen
nMaxLength = 70
q.active := true
```

```
? "Fish: "+q.rowset.fields["name"].value
? "Length CM: "+q.rowset.fields["length cm"].value
function CanItOpen
    if type( "nMaxLength" ) == "N"
        this.sql += [ where fish."length cm" <= ]+nMaxLength
    endif
return true
```

This is just one example, and perhaps not the best, but it should give you some ideas.

Rowset Object – onAppend()

You may remember the discussion about events with special names in earlier chapters, where events that begin with the word "can" occur <u>before</u> the method of that name (i.e., *canAppend()* fires before the *append()* method and must return a *true* or *false* value) and events that begin with the word "on" occur <u>after</u> the method of that name (i.e., *onAppend()* fires <u>after</u> the *append()* method).

In this case, the *onAppend()* event fires after the user is placed into append mode with the *append()* method is executed. Why would you need to do anything with this? Well, way back in Chapter 3, we discussed custom properties, which included default values for fields and that using the custom properties of fields (created in the Table Designer) may not be the best way to deal with defaults.

You could set in the rowset object's *onAppend()* event handler the default values for any fields that might require them. If you were using a form, and the fields were datalinked to controls on the form, then the values would appear when the user went into append mode. This is a rather handy use of the *onAppend()* event.

You could use code along the following to set default values in a table (this is just a sample that is not associated with any actual table – don't try it "as is"):

```
q = new query()
q.sql := "select * from MyTable"
q.active := true
q.rowset.onAppend := SetDefaults
// other code

function SetDefaults
    local f
    f = q.rowset.fields
    f["MyNumericField"].value := 0
    f["MyBooleanField"].value := true
    f["MyCharField"].value := "Some Text"
return
```

Rowset Object – canSave()

The rowset object's *canSave()* event is sort of the opposite of the rowset object's *onAppend()* event. It fires just before the *save()* method of the rowset – and must return a boolean or logical value (*true* or *false*). If this event returns a value of *false*, the rowset cannot be saved. If the event returns a value of *true*, the rowset can be saved. Then if there is code associated with the rowset's *onSave()* event, that code is fired.

The question is, what good is this? One purpose that comes immediately to mind is performing validation of data that the user may have entered. You will find that there are often requirements for fields – a numeric value must fall in a specific range, a date field must be after some date or before the current date, for example.

There are many ways to do validation of fields, one of them is the whole rowset at a time. You could do something like these lines to perform some validation (as above, this is a sample, and not associated with any table – don't try it "as is"):

```
q = new query()
q.sql := "select * from MyTable"
q.active := true
q.rowset.canSave := ValidateRow
// other code, includes obtaining data from the user,
// calling the save method ...

function ValidateRow
   local f
   f = q.rowset.fields
   // check for numeric field value:
   if f["MyNumericField"].value < 10
      msgbox( "MyNumericField must be 10 or greater!", "Invalid Value")
      return false
   endif

   // check for date — must be <= today's date
   if f["MyDateField"].value > date()
      msgbox( "MyDateField must be less than or equal to today's date!",;
                 "Invalid Value")
      return false
   endif
return true
```

The purpose of discussing these three events is to give you a feel for some of what can be done. Hopefully this will help you have an understanding for some of what is possible as you are working on your own applications.

UpdateSet

A rather interesting and useful feature of dBASE that a lot of folk don't understand well is the updateSet class.

This particular object allows you to copy tables, append from tables, update from tables, a combination of append and update and then handle errors generated if the table you are updating has a primary key.

You must always have a *source* and a *destination*. The *changedTableName*, *keyViolationTableName* and *problemTableName* properties are optional, although very useful in some circumstances. The *indexName* is needed for most of the methods, but not all.

Copying a Table or Rowset
Let's take a look at some examples. The first is copying one rowset or table to another. To do this, we must have a table or rowset that is the source – i.e., what we are copying, and we must name a table or rowset as the destination, or the new table.

At its simplest, we can do:

```
open database dbasesamples
u = new UpdateSet()
u.source        := ":DBASESAMPLES:FISH.DBF"
u.destination := ":DBASESAMPLES:COPYFISH.DBF"
u.copy()
close database
```

This will copy the rows in the "FISH" table in the samples directory to "COPYFISH", creating a new table, but without the indexes that might be associated with the source table. Note that you must use the extension for local tables – ".DBF" or ".DB", or you will get an error.

This is not very exciting and we could do this as well as including the index tags with the local SQL command:

```
open database dbasesamples
set database to dbasesamples
copy table fish to copyfish with production
close database
```

So, what's the big deal? Among other things, we can create tables of different types. If you were using a local table and wanted to copy that table to a database alias for a SQL server database, you could:

```
open database dbasesamples
open database myalis
u = new UpdateSet()
u.source        := ":DBASESAMPLES:FISH.DBF"
u.destination := ":myalias:Fish"
u.copy()
close database
```

This should create a new table in "myalias" (as it is defined in the data engine), then convert the table to that appropriate type. This is one way to get your table into an Interbase database, for example.

Another and potentially even more useful thing to note is that we can create a rowset from a query and copy just the rows that match whatever conditions we need. The example here assumes we might want to copy just those rows that have a "length cm" of less than 100 from the FISH table:

```
d = new database()
d.databaseName      := "DBASESAMPLES"
d.active            := true
q = new query()
q.database          := d
q.sql               := "select * from FISH"
q.active            := true
q.rowset.filter     := [:length cm: < 100]
q.rowset.indexName  := "Name"

u = new UpdateSet()
u.source            := q.rowset
u.destination       := "SMALLFISH.DBF"
u.copy()
```

```
// cleanup
q.active              := false
d.active              := false
```

In this example, the new table will be created "locally" — i.e. wherever you were currently working as opposed to in the DBASESAMPLES database. If you wanted to copy this to the DBASESAMPLES database, you would have set the destination as ":DBASESAMPLES:SMALLFISH.DBF".

> **NOTE**
> You can use a query object's rowset for either or both of the source and destination rowsets. i.e.,
>
> ```
>        q1 = new query()
>        q1.sql = "select * from fish"
>        q1.active = true
>
>        q2. = new query()
>        q2.sql = "select * from copyfish"
>        q2.active = true
>
>        u = new updateSet()
>        u.source := q1.rowset
>        u.destination := q2.rowset
>        u.copy()
> ```

You must usually give a table extension if the table is a local (.DBF or .DB) table type when using a database alias, otherwise an error will occur. It is probably a good idea to always set the extension for your destination table if you are using local tables.

One thing you need to be aware of when using the various methods of the updateSet object: the source table, if not at the first row, will start from wherever the row pointer is currently. You may (unless this is intentional) wish to make sure you issue a call to the source rowset's *first()* method before issuing the call to the updateSet object's *copy()*,*append()*, etc., methods.

In the case of the copy method, you cannot create a *rowset* that does not exist, i.e.:

```
q2 = new query()
q2.sql = "select * from sometable"

[...skipped code...]
u.destination := q2.rowset
```

If this rowset does not exist, you will get an invalid reference error. What this means is that if you want to create a new table, you must reference it differently – using a call to a non-existent rowset will not work as shown above, but as shown earlier, giving the name of the *table* in the *destination* property will create a new table.

> **NOTE**
> Using the copy method of this class will NOT copy the index tags of the original table. This is a serious drawback, and while I believe it is working "as designed", is a bit annoying. If you want to copy a table using the database objects in dBASE, use the database *copyTable()* method, or you can use the local SQL COPY TABLE command.

Using *copy()* with Calculated Fields

There are two ways to get calculated fields in your queries in dBASE, unfortunately, the UpdateSet object only recognizes one of them. Note the following:

```
d = new database()
d.databaseName        := "DBASESAMPLES"
d.active              := true
q = new query()
q.database            := d
q.sql                 := "select * from fish"
q.active              := true

// add calculated field:
f = new field()
f.fieldName           := "doubleLen"
f.beforeGetValue := {|| this.parent["length cm"].value * 2 }
q.rowset.fields.add( f )

// the calculated field shown above does not get
// copied.
u = new updateSet()
u.source = q.rowset
u.destination = "test.dbf"
u.copy()
```

The UpdateSet object does not recognize a field object when added in this way. However, if you use the ability to create a calculated field in the SQL Select statement you can copy the calculated field *(more details can be found in the local SQL online help reference that ships with the BDE)*. The syntax is a bit more complex, but it does work. Note that in the following we are assuming all fields (and the calculated field) – if you wanted to limit the number of fields copied you could do that here as well:

```
d = new database()
d.databaseName        := "DBASESAMPLES"
d.active              := true
q = new query()
q.database            := d
q.sql                 := "select id, name, species, fish.'length cm',"+;
                         "fish.'description',fish.'fish image',"+;
                         "fish.'length cm'*2 as doubleLen from fish"
q.active = true
// the calculated field "doubleLen" shown above does get
// copied:
u = new updateSet()
u.source = q.rowset
u.destination = "test.dbf"
u.copy()
```

Appending Rows From Another Table

The *append()* method of the updateSet class is useful because it allows you to add rows with matching structures from one table to another. The syntax will be similar to above, with the added ability to use a *keyViolationTable* – if your table has a primary key, and a row in the table you are adding from (the source) has the same value as a row in the table, you can have the updateSet copy that table from the source to a new table named in the *keyViolationTable* property.

The *append()* and *appendUpdate()* methods assume that the structures of both tables are the same. If they are not, you will not receive an error, but you may receive some interesting results *(as soon as a field does not match, the append will stop for that row – so only the matching fields will be appended).*

> **NOTE**
> A Key Violation will not occur if the primary key is an autoincrement field. Instead, the autoincrement will do what it is supposed to, and new rows will be appended.

The sample below is based on the FISH sample in the samples tables, rather than the customer table – see note above about key violations, since part of the reason I am doing this is to show you that ability.

The Fish table has the name field set as the primary key. For the example I am using, I have made a copy of the fish table locally, deleted some rows and added a couple. In addition, I have also copied the FISH table itself locally for testing. The first example does not set a *keyViolationTableName*, the second does.

```
d = new database()
d.databaseName      := "DBASESAMPLES"
d.active            := true

q = new query()
q.database          := d
q.sql               := "select * from FISH"
q.active            := true

u = new UpdateSet()
u.source            := "FISHCOPY"
u.destination       := q.rowset
u.indexName         := "PrimaryName"

u.append()
```

When this is completed, the rows that might cause a keyViolation simply do not go anywhere — they are not added to the Fish table as they would have caused a violation. No error will occur, which may be a problem for your users.

However, if the same code is executed with the addition of a *keyViolationTableName* property which points to a table (it does not have to exist – it will be created if necessary), it should contain any rows that cause a violation.

```
u = new UpdateSet()
u.source               := "FISHCOPY"
u.destination          := q.rowset
u.indexName            := "PrimaryName"
u.keyViolationTableName := "COPYERROR"
u.append()
```

NOTE

The *keyViolationTable* does work when using local tables if a database alias is used, but you have to do it differently. The following code has been shown to work:

```
d = new Database()
d.databaseName := "DBASESAMPLES"
d.active        := true

u = new updateSet()
u.destination := ":DBASESAMPLES:FISH.DBF"
u.source        := "FISHCOPY.DBF"
u.indexName    := "PrimaryName"
u.keyViolationTableName := "COPYERROR.DBF"
u.append()

d.active := false
release object u
```

In this example, "FISHCOPY" is a local table and the keyViolationTable will be created in the folder referenced by the database alias! What is happening is that the keyViolationTable is created in the same folder (directory) as the destination table. This is probably working as designed.

Updating Rows From Another Rowset

The update method allows you to update a table from another table with the same structure. What this does is look for a match between the two tables, and if a row matches (this requires that either a primary key be used, or that the field(s) used in the index expression not be changed) but has been modified in the second table, changes will be made in the main table.

This has the added capability of copying any rows that have been changed to a "changedTable" before the update actually occurs. This may be very useful in the case of errors.

For the following example, we will use the fish table as used in the last append examples, which assumes that I have changed the data in a couple of records.

```
d = new database()
d.databaseName     := "DBASESAMPLES"
d.active           := true
q = new query()
q.database         := d
q.sql              := "select * from FISH"
q.active           := true

u = new UpdateSet()
u.source           := "FISHCOPY"
u.destination      := q.rowset
u.indexName        := "PrimaryName"

u.update()
```

 NOTE

It is necessary to use the updateSet's *indexName* property for this to work properly and the *indexName* must exist in the destination table/rowset.

The changes get made to the rows that match, but since we did not use the *changedTableName* property, the data was not saved before the update was made. In addition, any new rows are not copied over (see below).

```
d = new database()
d.databaseName     := "DBASESAMPLES"
d.active           := true

q = new query()
q.database         := d
q.sql              := "select * from FISH"
q.active           := true

u = new UpdateSet()
u.source           := "FISHCOPY"
u.destination      := q.rowset
u.changedTableName := "OLDROWS"
u.indexName        := "PrimaryName"

u.update()
```

Interestingly, it appears that any row in the destination table (the one we are updating) that matches any row in the source table (the one we update from) will be copied to the OLDROWS table, even if no update actually occurs.

Updating Rows and Adding NEW Rows

The big deal here is that if you use the *update()* method, any new rows in the source table are not added to the destination table. You can use the *appendUpdate()* method and this will work exactly like update, with the added feature that any new rows will be appended. While we could add a *keyViolation* table to this, it would be pointless, as any primary key matches should be caught automatically in the update process. Only rows that do not match the index expression will be appended to the destination rowset.

```
d = new database()
d.databaseName     := "DBASESAMPLES"
d.active           := true
q = new query()
q.database         := d
q.sql              := "select * from FISH"
q.active           := true

u = new UpdateSet()
u.source           := "FISHCOPY"
u.destination      := q.rowset
u.indexName        := "PrimaryName"
u.changedTableName := "OLDROWS"
u.appendUpdate()
```

Deleting Rows

Finally, you can take any rows that have the same structure as the main table and delete any rows that match. The match will be on the expression used for the index.

> **NOTE**
>
> It is necessary to use the updateSet's *indexName* property for this to work properly and the *indexName* must exist in the destination table/rowset.

```
d = new database()
d.databaseName      := "DBASESAMPLES"
d.active            := true
q = new query()
q.database          := d
q.sql               := "select * from FISH"
q.active            := true

u = new UpdateSet()
u.source            := "FISHCOPY"
u.destination       := q.rowset
u.indexName         := "PrimaryName"

u. delete()
```

Any rows that match in the *source* will be deleted in the *destination*. (There is no method to copy out the actually deleted rows to another table. However, if you need to preserve a copy, you may wish to create a routine yourself to find matches between the two and copy the matching rows to another table before you run an updateSet delete.)

Summary

As you can see, dBASE's object oriented programming is quite powerful and the data classes give you a lot of ability and flexibility. It should be noted that not everything can be done easily using the data objects, but once you get used to working with them, you will find that the extra flexibility and control you gain over the older XDML syntax is worth the effort.

Chapter 9: Creating and Working With Datamodules

What Is a Datamodule, and Why Should You Care?

The Datamodule in dBASE is a very important part of any good object-oriented database program. It allows you to set up your database aliases and tables, including creating relationships between tables, referential integrity rules, data validation and any other code that you might need, then allows you to re-use that setup anywhere in your application. This is part of the heart of good object-oriented program design and the Datamodule is a prime example of re-usable code.

A Datamodule is an object class that is a container for data objects. It allows you to place any database aliases you need, create settings for them into a container. From there you can setup tables, indexes for those tables and set relationships between tables as required.

dBASE ships with a design tool called *dQuery* that allows you to do all this visually. dQuery is a very robust design surface and a whole book could be written to discuss ways of using it. For our purposes we are going to focus specifically on working with Datamodules – creating and modifying them and the basic tools built in for the purpose of setting up tables. If you spend a bit of time looking at the menus and options you will see there is *much* more than could be covered here.

Starting dQuery

If you have not made any changes to your environment in dBASE PLUS, dQuery will start when you start dBASE itself. As noted in Chapter 1 of this book, I prefer working with the Navigator and Command Window in dBASE and only use dQuery when I need to, so after installing dBASE, one of the first things I do is turn off the "auto start" feature for dQuery.

If you have either turned off the auto start feature for dQuery, or if you have closed it down for any reason, there are many ways to start dQuery in dBASE PLUS:

With the Navigator window in dBASE selected, click on the "Datamodules" tab. In that tab, you will see two icons with the word "(Untitled)" by them – Datamodule and Custom Datamodule (yellow icon). The simplest way to start dQuery is by using one of the following options:

- Select the File menu, New and Datamodule (or Custom Datamodule)
- Double-click the (Untitled) icon for Datamodule
- Right-click on the (Untitled) icon for Datamodule and select "New Datamodule"
- Click on the (Untitled) icon for Datamodule and press Shift + F2
- Click on the (Untitled) icon for Datamodule and click on the "Open" button in the toolbar
- Click on the (Untitled) icon for Datamodule, press the space bar, and select "New Datamodule" from the popup that appears (it will be the only option).
- In the Command Window, type:

```
CREATE DATAMODULE
```

- Select the "File" menu, and then "dQuery".

Once you have started dQuery, the screen should look something like:

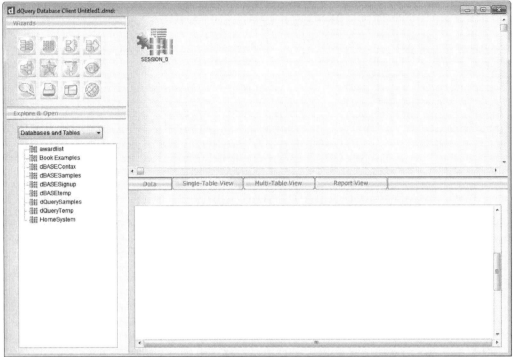

Figure 9-1

As with the other design surfaces in dBASE *(these will be discussed in a later chapter of this book)*, the toolbar and menu change along with the main screen.

dQuery is a complex tool and there are many options and parts to the screen. In the upper left you will see a set of buttons, with a "heading" that says "Wizards". If you move the mouse over these, you will see what each of these buttons will call. For example, the first one says "Create a database connection or add one to this dataModule". If you were to click that button, you would start a "Wizard" (a program with a front end to guide you through a process) that would help you do just that.

Below the Wizards is a section that says "Explore and Open". By default you see a listing of all Database Aliases that are defined in the BDE. To see the tables in any alias, you can double-click on the alias and the list will open showing all the tables in that alias. However, doing so will also place a database object on the dQuery design surface.

The main window is the top/right part of the screen. This is the dQuery design surface and it is used to define the different data objects that will be a part of your datamodule. The bottom half of the screen provides a view of the currently selected table or is used to view to view reports.

Using dQuery to Create and Modify Datamodules

Now that we've taken a short look at dQuery, let's actually step through the process of creating a simple datamodule. If you wish to follow along, you will be creating a datamodule that uses one of the sample tables that comes with dBASE itself which includes a single table.

The first thing you need to do is to open the appropriate database alias. In this case, the alias should be in the listing on the left under "Explore and Open". The one we want is "dBASESamples". Double-click this, and two things will occur:

1. A database object will be placed on the main design surface.
2. A list of tables that are in the database alias will be listed.

Your screen should look something like:

Figure 9-2

To place a table on the design surface, you can either double-click it, or you can drag it from the list to the design surface. For our example, we'll use the "Fish" table. I suggest simply double-clicking the table. Your screen should now look like:

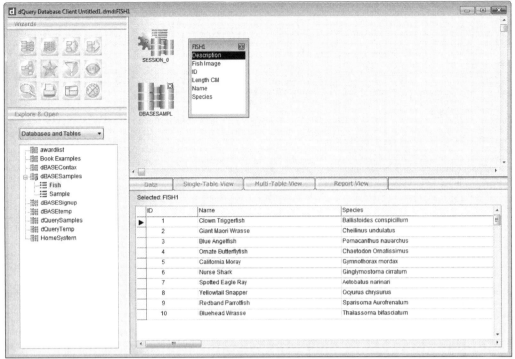

Figure 9-3

Not only is the table shown as well as the names of the fields in the table, but in the grid at the bottom of the screen is the actual data. It is important to understand that this is what is called "live" data – if you change something in the grid, the change will be saved unless you abandon the change. You can scroll through the data, examine different columns, change column widths and even move the columns around in the grid. You can add rows, delete rows, and more.

I often change the widths of the columns, so that I can see more data. For example, notice that while the "Name" column is quite large, you aren't really using all of it. You can see a bit more if you shorten the width (by clicking on the right of the column header of the "Name" column in the grid and dragging it to the left). If you do the same for the "Species" column, you will see more and so on. Eventually you will see all of the columns of the table.

You will want to save your datamodule at some point and now is as good a time as any. Press +⑤ or select the "File" menu, and select the word "Save" from the menu. Alternatively, use the toolbutton that shows "Save datamodule" when the mouse hovers over it. Once clicked, dQuery will display a dialog asking for a name to be entered … call the datamodule "Fish".

At this point, there are lots of things we *could* do. We are not going to get into all of the possibilities, because as noted earlier, this is a complex program and there are too many options for us to cover here. We are looking specifically at things that a programmer or application developer might find useful.

We could change the index so that the data is sorted by fish name, for example.

> 📋 **NOTE**
> It is necessary to use the updateSet's *indexName* property for this to work properly and the *indexName* must exist in the destination table/rowset.

To change the index, click on the "Tables" menu. When you do this you will see quite a few options, we want to use "Set Indexes (Keys) ...". This will open a dialog form for us.

Figure 9-4

You can select any particular index tag you wish, but for our purposes, select (if it is not already selected) "PRIMARYNAME" and click "Set Order".

Notice that the data in the grid is now in the correct sequence, sorting by name.

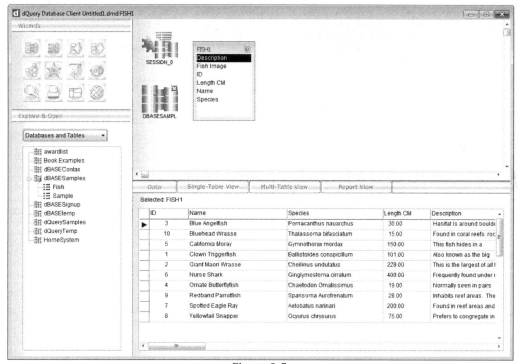

Figure 9-5

If you save this, dQuery will save the setting for the index tag as part of the datamodule so that the next time dQuery opens this datamodule, or if you were to use it for a form or report, the data would automatically be sorted. This can be a real time saver if you always wanted to see the data sorted.

We could set filters, by using the filter options and do a lot more. However, this is a simple query, and we don't really need to delve into all the options right away. For the moment, save the datamodule (⌨Ctrl+⌨S) and then exit dQuery by using the 'x' in the titlebar, or selecting the "File" menu and then "Close".

Opening an Existing Datamodule

Once you have saved a datamodule, some things will be saved and some won't. This can be seen by opening the datamodule we just created in dQuery.

As with starting a new datamodule, there are many ways to open an existing one. The simplest is to go to the "Datamodules" tab of the Navigator window and you should now see "Fish.dmd". If you double-click this, the datamodule will be opened in dQuery.

The first thing to notice is that the column widths have not been restored. Also notice that the bottom part of the left side of the screen is different. Rather than showing the "Database and Tables" we saw in the previous example, it now shows the "Object Tree" and lists the objects in the datamodule. We could go back to "Database and Tables", but for the moment we can leave this as it is.

The main idea here was to show that you can reopen the datamodule in the designer. Notice that the data is sorted, the way it was when we saved the datamodule and closed dQuery. That aspect alone will be very important as we move on.

The question now is, why can we not open and close the datamodule and have various settings restored to the way they were when we exited? Because the dBASE and dQuery design surfaces are what are called "Two Way Tools" – you can modify the datamodule, and then can re-open it in dQuery. You can also modify the source code in the Source Editor and then open the datamodule in dQuery. The changes you made will be respected by dQuery!

Examining the Source Code

If you close dQuery ("File" menu, "Close"; or use the 'x' in the titlebar), we can take a different look at the datamodule.

A datamodule in dBASE PLUS is simply source code. In this case, it is a definition of a datamodule class, which is a container of data objects. To see this, in the Navigator window, make sure that the "Datamodules" tab is selected and right click on "Fish.dmd". Notice that one option is "Open in Source Editor". Select this option (we could also have pressed the ⌨F12 key) and the Fish datamodule will open in the Source Code Editor of dBASE PLUS. The code itself will look like:

```
** END HEADER — do not remove this line
//
// Generated on 01/29/2007
//
class FishDATAMODULE of DATAMODULE
   with (this)
      left = -1.0
      top = -1.0
   endwith

   this.DBASESAMPLES1 = new DATABASE()
   this.DBASESAMPLES1.parent = this
   with (this.DBASESAMPLES1)
      left = 19.0
      top = 135.0
```

```
            databaseName = "dBASESamples"
            active = true
        endwith

        this.FISH1 = new QUERY()
        this.FISH1.parent = this
        with (this.FISH1)
            left = 125.0
            top = 45.0
            width = 114.0
            height = 127.0
            database = form.dbasesamples1
            sql = 'Select * from "Fish"'
            active = true
        endwith

        with (this.FISH1.rowset)
            indexName = "PRIMARYNAME"
        endwith

    endclass
```

This should look very similar to code we have worked with in earlier chapters (examining the object oriented data language of dBASE, or OODML). The big difference is that the database and query class definitions are contained by the datamodule class definition.

Also notice that there are *top* and *left* properties for the objects and *height* and *width* properties for the query object. These properties are not normally part of the data objects, but we have a visual representation in dQuery, so these are listed in the datamodule definition so that they open where they were in on the design surface in dQuery each time.

A simple example of making a change in the source code that is reflected in dQuery the next time we open the datamodule, is to change the *indexName* property to point to a different index tag. The table has several index tags, and if you change "PRIMARYNAME" to "SPECIES" in this code below:

```
        with (this.FISH1.rowset)
            indexName = "PRIMARYNAME"
        endwith
```

so that it now reads:

```
        with (this.FISH1.rowset)
            indexName = "SPECIES"
        endwith
```

Then save the changes and exit the Source Code Editor (Ctrl+W). We can open the datamodule in dQuery and see that the sequence of the data has changed.

Double-click on the datamodule and note when you bring this up in dQuery that the rows are now sorted by the "Species" column rather than the "Name" column.

Filtering Data with Conditional Statements

One of the useful things that you can do in a datamodule is to set filter conditions. These might be used for a report or a form that uses the datamodule as the source of the data.

Filters can be set in the Source Code the same way we modified the *indexName* property of the rowset, but we can also do it in dQuery. One of the best aspects of dQuery is that you can try things out such as setting filters and see the results right there.

For this quick overview we will look at one of several methods of filtering data that are available in dQuery. Assuming that you still have the Fish datamodule open, notice there is a menu option called "Filter". If you click on that you will see a drop-down menu listing multiple selections. If you select "Standard Filter", a dialog will appear like:

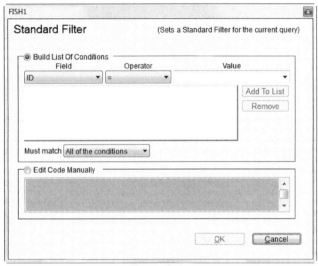

Figure 9-6

Notice that the radiobuttons show "Build List Of Conditions" and "Edit Code Manually" of which the first is selected. If you were to click "OK", we would display all rows in the table.

Click on "Build List Of Conditions" and notice that the comboboxes are now active and editable.

- Select for the "Field", the "Name" field.
- Select for the "Operator","<- Within".
- Enter in the "Value" list the word "Blue".

The "Within" operator allows us to do a string search as we discussed in the previous chapter to see if a string is contained in another – in this case we are telling dBASE to filter the data for rows where the string on the right is contained within the string on the left.

Next, click the "Add To List" button. Notice that you now have a condition listed and in the bottom of the screen you can see the actual dBASE code that is generated.

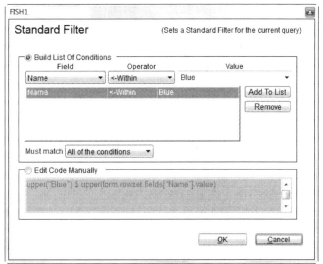

Figure 9-7

You could add more conditions at this point if you wished, or you could remove the current condition to create another, and so on. If you wanted to, you could go in and edit the code (that is what the section at the bottom is for).

To test the filter, click the "OK" button. You should see something like:

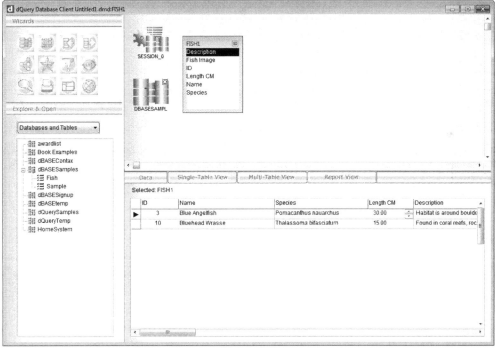

Figure 9-8

If you don't wish to use the filter, you can go to the "Filter" menu and select "Clear All Filters" – at this point, it is probably a good idea. But if this filter did what you needed for an application, saving your datamodule at this point would save the filter condition as part of the datamodule.

If you've been following along, select the "Filter" menu and then select "Clear All Filters".

It should be noted that there are quite a few filtering options available in dQuery and the one we just used is pretty basic, although pretty powerful as well.

Adding Calculated Fields

One of the most common requests in the dBASE newsgroups with respect to dQuery and a datamodule is "how do I add a calculated field to my datamodule?" Calculated fields, as discussed in earlier chapters of this book, are very useful and you can do a lot with them. At this time, dQuery does not have a "calculated field" Wizard or dialog, to help you do this, but the process is similar to what we did earlier in the book.

Click on the FISH1 table on the design surface of dQuery *(the list of fields, not the grid at the bottom of the screen)* and right click with the mouse. This will bring up a popup menu, with several options.

Click on the "Table and Query Properties" option. This will bring the Inspector to the top and it will be pointing to the query object (form.fish1).

Click on the "Events" tab on the Inspector, then click on the tool button next to the word *onOpen*. This will open the Source Code Editor. The Editor, add the code needed to create a calculated field, and tell dBASE what to calculate, etc.

```
function fish1_onOpen
   local oField
   oField = new Field()
   oField.fieldName := "LengthDoubled"
   // this = query:
   this.rowset.fields.add( oField )
   // this.parent = the fields array
   oField.beforeGetValue := {|| this.parent["Length CM"].value * 2 }
return
```

This will create a field called "LengthDoubled" and it will return a value of the "Length CM" field times 2. The calculated field will be created in the query's *onOpen* event and will display the next time you open this datamodule in dQuery. If you close this datamodule in dQuery then open it again in dQuery, you will see the new field, which will display in the grid, as well as the field list.

A More Complex Calculated Field?

Of course, it is possible that you may want to do something more complex than the simple calculation shown here. In such a case, what you may want to do is to add most of the code as shown above, except for the line that begins with "oField.beforeGetValue :=". You would want to save the datamodule and close it. This ensures that all changes are saved. Reopening it in dQuery will add the field, but no value will be assigned to it.

Then you can go back to the Inspector and add the code for the *beforeGetValue()* event by clicking on the tool button by that event for that field. You should keep in mind that in this case, the keyword "this" will refer to the field object, as opposed to the code above, where it referred to the query object.

Using Multiple-Table Queries

It is possible and often desirable to place more than one table on the design surface of dQuery. This allows you to have multiple tables open, which you may need for reports, forms, etc. It is also possible to create parent/child links for tables and in dQuery you can do this in a nice, visual fashion.

If you did the follow-along exercises in Chapter 8, you will have created a couple of tables somewhere called "ParentTest.dbf" and "ChildTest.dbf". In Chapter 8, we did not use a database alias and these tables were placed whereever you had dBASE pointed at the time.

If you wish to do the follow-along parts of the following, we need to create a new database alias using the Borland Database Engine Administrator, so we can work with the parent/child table examples (dQuery requires that we work with database aliases, which is a good thing for the most part).

If you have dBASE open, you should close it as any changes in the BDE will not be recognized until dBASE has been re-started. Then start the BDE Administrator *(on Windows Vista or later, you will want to do this by right clicking the icon for the BDE Administrator program, and selecting "Run as Administrator")*.

I am going to give a series of quick steps to do this:

- Click on the "Databases" tab if it is not selected
- Press `Ctrl`+`N` (for "New" or select "Object" followed by "New" from the menu)
- When the dialog appears the default Database Driver Name is set to "Standard" … Click "OK".
- In the left hand pane select "Standard1" and change the name to "Book Examples"
- On the right side of the screen (the definition pane):
  - Change "DEFAULT DRIVER" to "dBASE"
  - Click the ellipsis button "..." for the "PATH" entry. In the dialog that appears, navigate to the folder that has the "ParentTest.dbf" and "ChildTest.dbf" tables.
  - Click "OK"
- Press `Ctrl`+`A` (for "Apply" or click the "Apply" button on the toolbar)
- Click "OK" and if told to restart any applications that require the BDE, click "OK".
- Close the BDE Administrator

Now you will want to restart dBASE and then start dQuery.

With dQuery starts you should see in the list on the left, your new database alias "BookExamples".

If you do not see this database, you may wish to, instead, close dQuery, and try the following in the Command Window:

```
_app.session.addAlias( "BookExamples", "DBASE", "PATH:C:\PathToYourTables" )
```

Then restart dQuery by double-clicking on the first "untitled" query object in the Navigator.

Double-click the database "BookExamples" and you should then see any tables that are in that folder. In addition dQuery will place a database object on the design surface.

If you drag "ParentTest" to the design surface and do the same for "ChildTest", you should see something like:

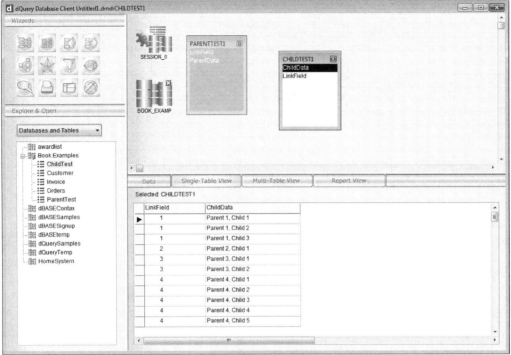

Figure 9-9

This may not look all that fancy, but we're just getting started. If you click on the ParentTest table, you will see the contents of the grid change.

Understanding Relationships among Different Tables

In dQuery, we can create a parent/child relationship by simply dragging from one table to another. In this case, if you click on the ParentTest table and drag to the ChildTest table, dQuer will display a new dialog which is meant to help you set things up properly. This is the Parent-Child Wizard. In this case, the child table is not indexed, but in reality it should be – what this means is that we did not turn *on* the index, to tell dBASE to use it. This Wizard will allow us to do that.

If you click on "Indexed Link", you will see a single field listed – that is the index tag for the ChildTest table. We only had one. But if we had more than one, you would see multiple items in the list. If you click on the "Key" tab on the notebook control, you will see details.

For our purposes, this index tag is all we need, so if you click "OK", you will see a small change in dQuery – there is now an arrow going from the parent table to the child table. This does not show if the link is really working properly. To get a better idea if the link works, click on the ChildTest table. Note the display in the grid, it should only show the child rows that are associated with the currently selected row in the ParentTest table.

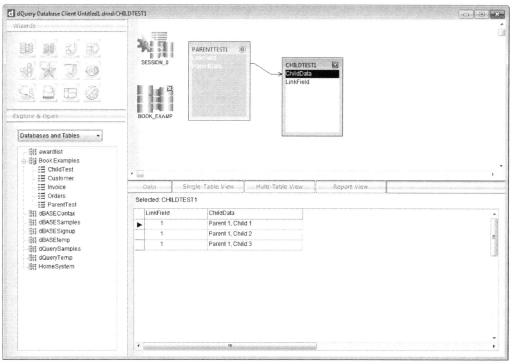

Figure 9-10

There is a lot more that can be done with parent/child tables in dQuery. I am just trying to get you used to the concept and the ideas involved.

For example, if you had a complex application, you could conceivably have 20 or 30 tables (or more – I've heard of applications with nearly 100 tables in a datamodule) on the design surface and you could have parent/child links between tables, some tables may not be related, and so on.

Using Multiple Database Queries

It might be necessary for you to have a datamodule that works with more than one database alias. One example that comes to mind is that in a corporate environment, the primary customer database might be stored in say, an Oracle database. However, you may have a collection of local data in .DBF tables that you need to use at the same time.

One of the more powerful and useful aspects of dBASE and dQuery is that you can work with these in the same datamodule. All you would need to do is to open the appropriate databases in the left part of the screen, the table lists appear and you can then place the tables you need on the design surface.

It is even possible to create parent/child table links between different types of data (say a Customer and Invoice link where the Customer table was in Oracle and the Invoice table was a .DBF table).

Cleanup

You might want to do this in the Command Window to ensure your databases are closed:

```
close database
```

Summary

This chapter discussed the purpose of Datamodules, why they are very important for a good object-oriented design and the basics of working with dQuery to create them. We also examined the code in a Datamodule, to be sure that if needed, you can modify it by hand-coding and noted that as with much of what goes on in dBASE, the Datamodule is simply dBL code at its core. Due to the complex nature of dQuery, this chapter really only discusses some basic functionality and does not get into such things as the Star Filter, or the ability to create One-Click Windows & Web Applications *(we will look at this briefly in a later chapter)*. Luckily, dQuery itself has a pretty good help file, you should be able to look things up if you cannot figure them out intuitively.

Chapter 10: Working in a Shared Environment

dBASE has always been able to handle a networked or shared environment, but many developers have not spent much time delving into this aspect of the software, unless absolutely necessary. In some environments, their programs may be installed on single-user machines; they may be focused on internet based applications, etc. a lot depends on the needs of the end user.

Sharing data is important and in order to do that, there's an extra layer of complexity that comes into play. This is not *really* as bad as it sounds and you will see that you can do a lot with this in dBL.

The biggest problem a developer will encounter is when two users attempt to edit the same row of a table. In some applications, what ends up happening is that the last person who edited the data wins, because their changes overwrite whatever the first person had done.

dBASE provides some safeguards for this kind of thing, with implicit and explicit locking. Basically if you attempt to edit a row an implicit lock occurs. This will not allow another user to edit the row while you are editing it. You can also code explicit locks to give your application greater control. With that greater control comes more coding.

It should be noted that a Windows application is by definition "multi-user" if any of the following is true:

- The application may be opened more than once on the same computer.

 NOTE
While this is not discussed in any depth in this book, you may want to avoid a user being able to open an application more than once. In the freeware library of code called the dUFLP *(discussed in the appendices of this book)*, is a custom class called AppFlag.cc that can be used to disable the ability to open the application multiple times.

- A form within the application may be opened more than once *(this is discussed later in this chapter)*.
- If the application accesses the same table in different forms or datamodules.

While this may be obvious to some, it's not always as obvious as it might seem.

Programming for a Shared Environment

In order for an application to use shared data on a network, you must make sure that the BDE Administrator has the *localshare* setting set to true. To do this, go to the BDE Administrator (Use the Windows "Start" Menu, select "dBASE PLUS", and then select "BDE Administrator" – in Windows Vista or later, you should right click the icon for the BDE Administrator, and select "Run as Administrator").

When the BDE Administrator comes up, select the "Configuration" tab. If there is a plus sign (+) next to the word "Configuration" in the window below the tabs, click on it. This will open up the Configuration options, showing "Drivers" and "System".

- Click on the plus sign (+) next to "System" which will open up the options. You should see 2 options: "Init" and "Formats", click on "Init".
- On the right you should see a list of options, find "LOCAL SHARE". If this says "FALSE", change it to "TRUE", by selecting the combobox down arrow ...
- Select the "Object" menu, and "Apply" (or press ⌨Ctrl+⌨A) then close and exit the BDE Administrator.

Once you have done that which should be done for any computer that is using an application (or just dBASE PLUS) that shares data on your network, you should be in good shape.

Opening a Table for Exclusive Use

There are commands that require that a table be opened for exclusive use, some of which are older XDML commands that have no OODML equivalent. In most cases, these commands are ones that do major changes to a table, such as altering the table structure, adding an index tag, removing deleted records, etc.

In XDML you could use a command like:

```
use MyTableName exclusive
```

to ensure that the table was opened exclusively. In older versions of dBASE, an error occurs if you attempt to do this and the table is in use.

One confusing issue in versions of dBASE from Visual dBASE 7.01 to the present, is that due to some internal changes in the BDE, if a table is being used by another user, no error will occur and the table will be opened. However, it will not be opened exclusively and no warning or error message will be given. This can cause some consternation to a developer who is writing code that relies on the need to open a table for exclusive use.

Is it possible to check to see if a table can be opened for specific commands in dBASE PLUS? Well yes, although this is not built in. There is a small function that was written some time ago, placed on the newsgroups used by the developer community, and reproduced here:

This code relies on some error handling code that will be discussed in depth in a later chapter of this book:

```
function IsExclusive( cTable )
   use (cTable) exclusive
   bSuccess = false
   try
      drop index DUMMY
      // this will throw an error,
      // we're interested in one in
      // particular
   catch( exception e )
      if e.code == 53 // Tag not found
        bSuccess := true
      endif
   endtry
   use // close table for OODML,
       // if doing xDML comment this line out
   return bSuccess
```

This is a relatively simple version of this kind of test. There are more complex versions that deal with more thorough testing, but this will do the trick for most cases.

 NOTE

There is a version of this in the freeware library of code called the dUFLP, discussed in the appendices of this book, that is more complex (called "UseExclusive.prg"), that handles some situations a bit more completely.

It should also be noted that there is the unlikely possibility that between the USE command in the function shown, and an attempt to open the table in OODML, a user might be able to access the table and therefore cause the same conflict you are trying to avoid. It might be necessary to create a "lockout flag", but that gets into more complex code than we are covering in this book.

To use it, you would save the above in a .PRG file named IsExclusive.prg, then in your own program (or even at the Command Window) you would use a command like:

```
if IsExclusive( "MyTableName" )
   // do whatever you need to do
else
   // let the user know that the table is
   // not available at this time for this
   // operation
endif
```

What commands in dBL require exclusive use of a table? The following chart gives the basics:

XDML	OODML	Explanation
CONVERT	No OODML Equivalent	Adds _dBASELOCK field to a table.
DELETE TAG	database.dropIndex()	Deletes an index tag or an index from a table *(depending on the table type)*.
INDEX ON	database.createIndex()	Creates an index tag or index on a table.
INSERT	No OODML Equivalent	Adds a row to a table (in older versions of dBASE, this occurs at the current position in the table, in dBL this appends to the end.)
MODIFY STRUCTURE	No OODML Equivalent	This brings up the Table Designer in dBASE.
PACK	database.packTable()	Removes any deleted rows in a .DBF, this is not useful for other table types.
REINDEX	database.reindex()	Rebuilds index tags from the description in the table header.
ZAP	database.emptyTable()	Probably the most dangerous command in dBASE, this removes all rows in a table.

These are the most common commands that require exclusive use of a table. There are likely others that are not discussed here.

Opening a Table for Read-Only (RO) Access

There are times you may wish to open a table for read-only access by a user. There are many ways that this can be done. In XDML you can open a table with the NOUPDATE option, such as:

```
use MyTable noupdate
```

And the user can view the data, but not edit it.

In OODML, the query object allows you to set a property called *requestLive* to false. If this property is set to *true* which is the default, the rowset is editable. If the property is set to *false*, the rowset is not editable. Note that this should be set *before* you set the query's *active* property:

```
q = new query()
q.sql := "select * from MyTable"
q.requestLive := false
q.active := true
```

If you would like to have a "conditional" setting for the table, so that it can be edited in some cases, but not others, the rowset has the *autoEdit* property. Like the query object's *requestLive* property, *autoEdit* defaults to *true*. If you set it to *false*, any code that attempts to change a value will not be able to and any controls on a form that are datalinked to fields in the table will be disabled. A call to the rowset's *beginEdit()* method will place a row in edit mode and to add a new row, the rowset's *append()* method can be called. Unless one of those two methods is used, the rowset is not editable by the user.

There are other ways to set a rowset to not be editable (the rowset's *canEdit()* or *canGetRow()* events can be set to return a *false* value, for example, but that seems like a bit of overkill).

Locking Data

Locking data, as mentioned earlier in this chapter, can be done through *implicit* locks or *explicit* locks. The advantage to implicit locks is that the programmer does not have to do any extra coding to handle locking rows. If a row is being modified and another user attempts to edit it, dBASE returns a dialog that states that the row is locked and attempts to obtain a lock itself. If the first user releases the row (save, abandon ...), then the row that was locked is now available and if the second user just left the dialog on screen, they could eventually be allowed to edit the row.

Implicit Locks

Implicit locks are set by specific actions and are done automatically. An implicit lock is specifically caused when a user starts to edit a row – pressing a key that changes a value in any field in a row causes an implicit lock on that row.

An implicit lock is released by one of the following, all assume changes have been made to the row, causing the lock in the first place:

- The user saves changes to the current row by an explicit call to the *save()* method of the rowset;

- The user navigates away from the current row – an implicit call to the *save()* method of the rowset;
- The user abandons changes to the record (through an explicit call to the *abandon()* method of the rowset).

How do you create an implicit call to the *abandon()* method of the rowset? By placing the rowset into specific modes: *beginAppend()*, *applyFilter()*, *applyLocate()*. If the user was editing and somehow one of these three methods are called, the row buffer is disassociated with the row it was buffering and the user is placed in the appropriate mode. This will lose any changes made to the row by the user. As a programmer, you may want to make sure that the user is asked before abandoning (use the rowset's *canAbandon()* event, for example).

How do you create an implicit call to the *save()* method of the rowset? Generally through navigation – any method that causes the rowset to navigate, such as the rowset's *next()*, *applyFilter()*, *applyLocate()*, *findKey()*, *findKeyNearest()*, *goto()*, *first()*, *last()*, and *refresh()* methods, or setting the *filter* property.

Explicit Locks

Explicit locks are ones that are set by the programmer in code and they must be released by the programmer in code. This allows the programmer to, for example, display a custom dialog for the end user. The most important thing about explicit locks is that you have to explicitly unlock them. If you do not explicitly unlock them, the row is locked forever (or until the query is deactivated/closed).

Explicit locks can be set on a row or a table. The rowset object has two methods for this: *lockRow()* and *lockSet()*. The first locks the current row and the second locks the whole rowset.

In addition to the methods to create the locks, the rowset object has methods to check to see if the row or rowset are locked – but be warned – this only works within the current session and does *not* work to see if another user has obtained a lock (if user 1 has a row locked, then user 2 checks with one of the following methods, the value returned is not useful).

These methods are *isRowLocked()* and *isSetLocked()*. They return a boolean (logical) value of either *true* or *false*. The purpose of these two methods is to assist a developer in checking to see if their locks worked. They should not be relied upon in an application.

If you wish to see *if* you can lock a row or rowset you will need to test it with the *lockRow()* or *lockSet()* methods, which also return a boolean value of *true* or *false*, depending on whether the lock was successful or not.

So for example, you could try:

```
if queryname.rowset.lockRow()
   // success - we got a lock!
   queryname.rowset.beginEdit()
else
   // tell the user ...
   msgbox( "The row is locked, try again later!",;
           "Cannot lock row." )
endif
```

The problem with the code as shown, is that there are other factors that affect the message that is displayed. If you recall from earlier in this chapter, I mentioned that there is a default message that displays. This dialog will stay on screen until either the user clicks "Cancel", closes the table, or is able to obtain a lock on the row. The sample code shown above says "tell the user", but in this case they are already being told, so if you display another message, the user will be told that they cannot lock the row twice.

How do you get around this? You have to take a look at the Session Object, which we briefly discussed in earlier chapters.

Control of Locked Rows

In build 2.61.5 *(April, 2008)*, the developers of dBASE added a new property to the rowset, *lockType*. The purpose is to control explicit locks (setting the rowset's *lockRow()*). By default, when a call is made to the rowset's *save()* or *abandon()* methods, locks are released. The *lockType* property allows the developer to specify that locks are retained (if needed). The *lockType* property uses these values:

- 0 – Automatic: row locks obtained by calling rowset.*lockRow()* are released by calls to rowset.*save()* or rowset.*abandon()*. This is the default behavior.
- 1 – Explicit: row locks obtained by calling rowset.*lockRow()* are **NOT** released by calls to rowset.*save()* or rowset.*abandon()*.

The default for *lockType* is 0, unless an overriding setting is put into the Plus.ini or application's .INI file. To change the default, modify the .INI file by adding:

```
[Rowset]
LockType = 1
```

Using the Session Object to Modify Lock Behavior

The session object is used to create sessions. If you are familiar with Visual dBASE 5.x, the best way to deal with multi-user situations was to use the CREATE SESSION command, although it was not a perfect implementation (it had some problems). The session object is the OODML version of that and because of the nature of the session object, it resolves some of the problems in earlier versions of dBASE. If you want to test multi-user access in a single session of dBASE, you can use a session object. In addition, there is *always* a session object in effect in dBASE PLUS (and applications built in dBASE PLUS), which is accessed from the application object: _app.session.

If two users, or two *sessions* in a dBASE application attempt to lock a row in a rowset, the following dialog appears on the screen:

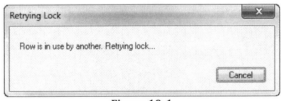

Figure 10-1

This error will stay on the screen until an attempt to lock the record is successful in the second session (or by the second user), or the user clicks the "Cancel" button.

The session object has two properties that affect record locking: *lockRetryInterval*, and *lockRetryCount*.

The first, *lockRetryInterval* tells dBASE how long in between attempts to lock the row to wait. If set at the default value of zero, it will continually attempt to lock the row *(leaving the message shown in Figure 10-1 on screen)*. If you change it, the number is the number of seconds between each attempt to lock the row.

The second property, *lockRetryCount* tells dBASE how many times to try to retry the lock. If it is set to the default of zero, it will try forever (or until the user clicks "Cancel" on the dialog as shown above, etc.) *see Figure 10-1*. If the value is set to a higher value, then dBASE will continue to attempt to lock the row until that number of attempts has been made.

For our purposes the simplest thing to do is use _app.session's *lockRetryInterval* property and set it to any value greater than zero. This needs to be done *before* you set the *active* property to *true* for any query you are concerned with locking the rows. You can change the value of that property after a query is opened, but it has no effect. It should be noted that unless you create your own session object, a query object when instantiated assumes the _app.session as the associated session object. What this means is that we do not need to create a session object, nor do we need to assign the session object reference to the query's *session* property. The following code will not work properly if testing with dBASE as a single user, unless either you either open a second instance of dBASE (something I do as needed), or you use the session object.

So we could do something like:

```
_app.session.lockRetryInterval := 1 // one second between attempts
q = new query()
q.sql := "select * from mytable"
q.active := true

if q.rowset.lockRow()
   // success - we got a lock!
   q.rowset.beginEdit()
else
   // tell the user ...
   msgbox( "The row is locked, try again later!",;
           "Cannot lock row." )
endif
```

The code could be modified so that it worked for a single user by testing the rowset's *isRowLocked()* method – this method only works in the case of a single-user. To do that, you would modify the code shown above so it looked like:

```
_app.session.lockRetryInterval := 1 // one second between attempts
q = new query()
q.sql := "select * from mytable"
q.active := true

if q.rowset.isRowLocked() // locked in default session
   msgbox( "You have locked the row somewhere else, "+;
           "try again later!",;
           "Cannot edit row.")
else
   if q.rowset.lockRow()
      // success - we got a lock!
      q.rowset.beginEdit()
```

```
        else
            // tell the user ...
            msgbox( "The row is locked, try again later!",;
                    "Cannot lock row." )
        endif
    endif
```

> **NOTE**
> The _app.session's *(or any session object's)* properties must be set before you set the
> *active* property of any query you wish affected to *true*. Otherwise you will see no effect.

If the row is locked, the user cannot edit it and the message we want to display will appear
on the screen. Otherwise, the user is able to lock the row and we place them in edit mode.
The default message does *not* display.

As noted elsewhere, you *must* unlock the row when the user saves or abandons changes to
that row. If you do not, then the row will remain locked until your code sets the query
object's *active* property to false, or the user shuts down your application (which effectively
closes the table).

How do you unlock a row? The rowset has a method called *unlock()*. This has the effect of
unlocking all locked rows, or if the rowset was locked, unlocking the rowset. I would
recommend that if you do an explicit lock, that you use the rowset's *onSave()* event and call
the rowset's *unlock()* method. In addition, if you allow the user to abandon changes, that
you use the rowset's *onAbandon()* method to call the *unlock()* method.

Locking the Rowset

Why would you want to lock a whole rowset? You may have some specific code that loops
through many rows in a table and if you don't wish for there to be lock contention issues,
then you may want to lock the whole rowset. If you *do* need to lock the rowset, there is the
method of the rowset object called *lockSet()*. As before, you would want to be sure that you
explicitly called the rowset's *unlock()* method, because otherwise the whole rowset will be
locked until deactivated or the application is closed.

The _DBASELOCK Field

This has only briefly been discussed elsewhere in the book. Since we are dealing with row
locking and such, this is really the place to discuss it.

The _DBASELOCK field is very specific to the .DBF table and cannot be used for other table
types. If you may be planning on upsizing your data to a SQL server, then you should not
use it or any code that relies on it.

That said, this is kind of a nifty feature of the dBASE table format. The _DBASELOCK field is
the only field that can begin with an underscore (_) character and it is created specifically
by the CONVERT command. You cannot create this field in the Table Designer or with the
ALTER TABLE command.

The CONVERT command is an XDML command, and there is no OODML equivalent (at this
time). There is a lot of information about the command in the online help, so we're only
going to touch on the basics here.

The _DBASELOCK field must always be the last field in a table. This can be a bit frustrating
if you write code that adds fields (such as the ALTER TABLE command) to a table

programmatically or even try to add fields in the table designer. If you are writing code to add a field to a table that you have previously added a _DBASELOCK field to, you may want to drop the _DBASELOCK field, then issue a CONVERT command after you have added any/all fields to the table you need to. This will ensure that the field is the last one in the table structure.

The _DBASELOCK field is read-only – dBASE itself can change the values stored in the field, but a user or a programmer cannot. This is all done internally. The fact that this field is read-only can cause some problems for a developer who has code that loops through fields in a table and works with them. A special check has to be made on the *fieldName* property of the field for the name _DBASELOCK (all in capital letters). For example:

```
for i = 1 to q.rowset.fields.size
   if q.rowset.fields[ i ].fieldName == "_DBASELOCK"
      loop
   endif
   // do whatever
next
```

If this field exists in a .DBF table, record locking adds a new dimension, as you can query the date and time a lock was applied to a row and the user on the network who did so. In XDML this was achieved through the use of the LKSYS() function. By passing it a numeric value from 0 to 5 you could get the various information such as the date, time and name of the user who locked the row, and the previous date, time and name of the user who locked it.

In OODML, there is a special field class called the *lockfield class*. If you have a _DBASELOCK field in a table, the lockfield class is automatically created and added to the fields array of the rowset object. The lockfield class allows you to display information for a user. Using similar code to what we had before, if we have a _DBASELOCK field in the table, we can change the msgbox that is displayed when a lock occurs to display very specific information for the user attempting to lock the row:

```
if queryname.rowset.lockRow()
   // success - we got a lock!
   queryname.rowset.beginEdit()
else
   // tell the user ...
   cUser = queryname.rowset.fields["_DBASELOCK"].user
   cDateTime = queryname.rowset.fields["_DBASELOCK"].lock
   msgbox( "The row is locked by '"+cUser+"' who locked "+;
           "it at: "+cDateTime+"! Try again later!",;
           "Cannot lock row." )
endif
```

Note that the _DBASELOCK field is *not* necessary for network applications using DBF tables *(many people think it is, but it is not required)*. It may be a good idea, but it is certainly not required.

Maximum Locks

The database engine (BDE) that ships with dBASE has a maximum number of locks that can be set for local tables:

dBF 100 Locks maximum

DB (Paradox) 255 Locks maximum

What this means is that if you use explicit locks, you have to remember to unlock the rows. This will also be discussed when we look at transaction processing later in this chapter.

Using Session Objects

The session object in dBASE is sort of ignored by most dBASE developers. The reason? There is a default session object (referenced from the application object as *_app.session*). For most dBASE developers that is all that is needed.

However, if you are working in a multi-user situation, or even more, in a situation where a single user may need to open a form more than once and you want record locking to work properly (as noted earlier in this chapter), you should seriously consider using session objects in your datamodules and/or forms. When a datamodule or form is instantiated, a new session is created. This allows easier testing of locking locally and it allows for situations as noted where an application may allow the same form to be opened multiple times and a user might be editing a row in one form and attempt to do so again in another instance of the form.

Assuming some of the earlier examples, you could set up your application to use individual session objects in a fashion along the lines of:

```
s = new session()
s.lockRetryInterval := 1 // one second between attempts
q = new query()
q.session := s // add the session object
q.sql := "select * from mytable"
q.active := true
```

Session Objects and User BDE Aliases

User BDE Aliases, if defined in the application's .INI file (or PLUS.INI), belong only to the default session (_app.session) and are not accessible if you create a new session. In other words, with current versions of dBASE Plus running on current versions of Windows if you attempted to access the database that ships with dBASE called DBASESAMPLES using a session object with code similar to:

```
s = new session()
d = new database()
d.session     := s
d.databaseName := "DBASESAMPLES"
d.active      := true
```

You would receive an error on the last statement shown above stating:

```
Error: Unknown databasename: DBASESAMPLES
```

If you use the session object's *addAlias()* method to add the same database alias to that session object, it should work *(this has been tested)*:

```
// get path to the Samples folder, this will be used
// in a temporary database alias as shown below:
cPath = _app.currentUserPath
cPath = left( cPath, len( cPath ) - 4 )+"\SAMPLES"
```

```
// create session and database objects
s = new Session()
s.addAlias( "DBASESAMPLES", "DBASE", "Path: "+cPath )
d = new database()
d.session      := s
d.databaseName := "DBASESAMPLES"
d.active       := true
```

If you do not have the path hard-coded somewhere in your application, but the .INI file has the information you have a couple of options for obtaining it. The first is to try to read the .INI file itself. However, the folk at dBASE have come up with another method, using a custom class that ships with dBASE:

```
set procedure to :NonVisual:qBDEMgr.cc
oBDE = new qBDEManager()
oDbDesc = oBDE.GetAliasDesc( "DBASESAMPLES" )
cPath = oDBDesc.szPhyName()
```

From here you have the items you need for many User BDE Aliases, it might be possible to get other items such as login info, if the database needs it, but for the DBASESAMPLES database, this is what we need. Then your User BDE Alias could added to a session object in the following way:

```
s = new session()
s.addAlias( "DBASESAMPLES", "DBASE", "Path: "+cPath )
// and continue from here.
```

This custom class (qBDEMgr.cc) will be discussed in later chapters a bit more.

Adding a Session Object in the Form Designer

For a form you can drag a session object from the Component Palette in the Form Designer. If no database objects or tables are already on the form, you can then drag them onto it and the Form Designer will assume that they use that session object and set the session property properly. If however, you already have database object(s) or query object(s) on the form, you will need to do this in a specific sequence:

- set the *active* property to *false*
- set the *session* property to the session object (not "DEFAULT")
- set the *active* property to *true*

This gets trickier if you have a database object as well as query objects, as when you set the *active* property to *false* for the database object, it is automatically set to *false* for the query objects that reference that database. You will need to set the *session* property for those query objects and then set the *active* property back to *true*. However, the biggest difficulty is that once you set a query object's *active* property to *false*, all datalinks are removed. In other words, the *dataLink* property for any objects that had them set have now been set to blank values.

In the long run it will be easier to decide if you wish or need to use a session object *before* you start designing the form. You could add the session object in the Source Code Editor and add the appropriate settings of the *session* property for the objects needed. The only difficulty is remembering to get every object that needs it.

Adding a Session Object to a DataModule

For a datamodule, since dQuery does not appear to have a way to add a session object to a datamodule (it assumes you will want to use the default _app.session), you have to manually add a session object into the source code of the datamodule. I recommend doing this with dQuery closed, so there is no confusion by the software and open the .DMD file in the Source Code Editor. Then add a new session object before any data objects that may be there (it must be instantiated before the data objects that use it):

```
this.SESSION1 = new SESSION()
this.SESSION1.parent = this
with (this.SESSION1)
   left = 126.0
   top = 24.0
   width = 115.0
   height = 112.0
   lockRetryInterval = 1 // if you wish to use lockRetryInterval
endwith
```

If your datamodule has database or query objects, you may want to manually add a line such as the following to the constructor code for these objects while you are in the source code editor:

```
session = form.session1
```

Note that this should be done before a database object's *active* property is set to *true*. The code might look something like:

```
this.DBASETEST1 = new DATABASE()
this.DBASETEST1.parent = this
with (this.DBASETEST1)
   left = 23.0
   top = 106.0
   width = 115.0
   height = 112.0
   databaseName = "dBASETest"
   session = form.session1
   active = true
endwith
```

And in a query object you would want to add the statement shown before setting the database property, so the code might look like:

```
this.TESTPARENT1 = new QUERY()
this.TESTPARENT1.parent = this
with (this.TESTPARENT1)
   left = 119.0
   top = 99.0
   width = 114.0
   height = 123.0
   session = form.session1
   database = form.dbasetest1
   sql = 'Select * from "TestParent"'
   active = true
endwith
```

dQuery also handles things differently than the Form Designer if you want to start with a session object *(you would still need to add it manually as noted above)*. You will see the session object on the dQuery design surface, but if you add a database or query object, the *session* property is not set automatically for you. You would need to set the *active* property to false, set the *session* property and then set the *active* property back to true again for each data object (database or query) you add to the datamodule that you wish to be affected by the specific session object.

It should be noted that using Session objects using the designers is covered in more detail in Chapter 13.

The Session Object and Encrypted Tables
This is discussed in the next chapter, but if you wish to work with encrypted tables – ones that require a userid and a password (and sometimes a group), the Session Object is often a good idea.

Temporary Database?
Does your application need a temporary database? Under older versions of dBASE you could create database aliases using special calls to the BDE's API (Application Programming Interface). This is a bit trickier with current versions of dBASE and Windows, due to the nature of the UAC. However, the developers at dBASE have given us a new feature of the session object, a method called *addAlias()*, which allows us to add a database.

If you are not using your own session object, there is a default session in use, referenced from the _app (application) object. To add a temporary database alias for use, perhaps with temporary tables, or even a specific user's preferences, or whatever you may need, you would call the *addAlias()* method to create a new (temporary) alias:

```
_app.session.addAlias( "MyAlias", "DBASE", "PATH:C:\SomePath" )
```

From here the database reference should be able to be accessed as normal. There is more detail on this in Chapter 5.

Locking Related Tables

When you work with tables that are related, such as a parent/child relationship, there may be times when it is important to be able to lock the child rows when editing a parent, or vice versa – lock a parent when editing a child row. As a matter of fact, it is generally a good idea to do this.

One of the best things about dBASE when it comes to this sort of thing is that this kind of locking is done automatically for you, both with XDML and OODML. If you edit or lock a parent row, the child rows are automatically locked. When you save/abandon, navigate or otherwise unlock the parent row, the child rows are automatically unlocked. It should be noted that in dBASE Plus release 2.61 a new property was added to the rowset object: *autoLockChildRows*. The default for this property is *true*, changing this to *false* will allow you to lock the parent row without locking the child rows.

If you lock a child row, however, you do not lock the parent row. If you need the parent row to be locked, you would have to force a lock (using the rowset's *lockRow()* method for the parent rowset). Of course, as noted elsewhere, when you need to unlock it, you would have to call the rowset's *unlock()* method, or the parent row will remain locked (which would lock all the child rows associated with it).

Processing Transactions

Having only ever written applications for the PC world, I tend to think of transaction processing as belonging to the mainframe computer world. However, there may easily be reasons for needing transaction processing with your own applications.

So, what exactly *is* transaction processing? It is processing multiple records at once, storing them in a buffer and not committing the changes in the buffer until the user specifies, or a specific time.

An example of this is the way banks used to handle transactions. If you do any sort of transaction, it is usually not posted until late that day, or the next day of business (if you withdraw cash from an Automated Teller Machine on a Saturday, the transaction will most likely not be posted until the end of business on Monday, unless Monday is a holiday). This is because there are multiple transactions actually going on in many cases – if you buy something with an ATM card, money has to be debited from your account and credited to the store you made the purchase at. It is easier for the bank to track all of this by doing it at once. Another reason for this is that reindexing the many indexes that are likely on the data, for hundreds of millions of records, would be a slow process – doing this at night when no one is modifying the data makes more sense, rather than causing the computer to appear locked up during the daytime as users access their data.

In XDML there are some functions for this: BEGINTRANS() starts a transaction – it effectively creates the buffer area where any changes to records will be stored. COMMIT() saves the changes. ROLLBACK() abandons the changes.

In OODML, this is done through the use of the database object, which has methods that perform pretty much the same exact tasks: *beginTrans()*, *commit()*, and *rollback()*. A database object may have only one transaction set at a time and you cannot nest transactions.

Very importantly, any locks on rows made between the time the database object's *beginTrans()*, method is called and either the *commit()* or *rollback()* methods are called, will be honored, to ensure that no data corruption occurs.

Drawbacks to Using Transactions

Due to the very nature of transaction processing, there are some issues that may cause difficulties. The most obvious one is that all transactions that occur until either *commit()* is processed are not stored to the table(s) in use. This means that if a power failure or crash of any sort occurs, the changes are lost.

AutoIncrement Fields

In addition to the above, if your application uses autoIncrement fields to link tables – the autoIncrement value is not created in the parent table until the row is saved to the table, which means that the value that is set for child table's link field will be blank when the *commit()* occurs! There are ways to resolve this – mostly you would have to avoid using autoIncrement fields and create an autoincrementing value yourself that was incremented for the parent and stored there and saved to the child table appropriately.

Maximum Number of Locks

The other drawback to using Transactions, is the issue of the maximum number of locks you can have on a table. The database engine that is used by default with dBASE (the BDE) has a maximum number of locks (100 per table), as noted earlier in this chapter. If your transaction allows the number of edits to reach this maximum, the next edit will return an error about the number of locks being exceeded. Once you issue a *commit()* or *rollback()* the locks will be released.

There are two ways I can think of to avoid this. The first is that to use a counter of some sort for every row you edit – this counter will allow you to determine if you are at the maximum number of locks. If you reach that point you can then commit (or rollback) all changes so far. This may not be optimal, however.

The other solution, which also has problems, is to issue right after you start the transaction (database.beginTrans()) a call to the rowset's *lockSet()* method. This will lock the whole rowset and you will have only one lock on the table, no matter how many changes are made. The drawback? No one else can edit the table until either a *commit()* or *rollback()* occurs.

For more details on transaction processing, see the online help.

CacheUpdates

The database object has a property called *cacheUpdates*, which by default is set to *false*. This is because normally you want your row buffer changes to be saved to disk as the user works with the data. The primary reason for using this property of the database object in a network situation that has a lot of traffic can slow processing when constantly reading and writing to the network. To commit any cached changes, you would use the *applyUpdates()* method of the database object and to abandon them, you would use the *abandonUpdates()* method of the database object.

However, like Transactions, similar issues (see Drawbacks, above) will occur if this is used with your application. In addition to the drawbacks mentioned above is the issue that other users attempting to access the data will not see changes in the transaction until the cache has been updated (using the *applyUpdates()* method of the database object). For more details on using *cacheUpdates*, see the online help.

Using UNC Paths on a Network

UNC Paths ("Universal Naming Convention") to reference folders on a network can be a bit tricky, but can also work just fine. The basic structure for this is:

```
\\ComputerName\drive name\path\to\files
```

These can be used to define a path to a database, to reference the path to a file, and so on. The difficulty is that commands in dBASE that are used to verify if a file exists (the *file()* function, etc.) have difficulties with the UNC path structure and return *FALSE* when searching, even if a file exists.

Working with Non-dBASE Tables

With the exception of the discussion on the _DBASELOCK field, dBASE treats tables from other database servers pretty much the same as it does .DBF tables.

Transaction Processing

The database object's *isolationLevel* property affects the level of "isolation" involved in a transaction. *(Details are in the online help.)*

Issues When Deploying an Application

Application deployment (getting the application to your customers, in the proper way) is an important final part of application development. Chapter 28 is all about that.

One thing you need to be aware of is a file that is used by the BDE called PDOXUSRS.NET. There is a lot of concern by a few users who have run into issues with the location of this file. This is discussed a little in Chapter 28, and you may want to scan the dBASE newsgroups for this topic. Some users have had few problems with it, others have had a lot. I bring it up here just so that you are aware of it.

Summary

As you can see, there is a bit more to know about multi-user systems than you may have thought. However, as a dBASE developer, it is not as complex as it might be in some other applications. dBASE handles a lot of things automatically, unless you, the programmer, need to modify the behavior.

In addition I would like to thank Frank Polan who, having recently spent some time working through the issues covered in this chapter, was happy to look this over and help make sure that I covered the topic more completely and made sure it was accurate.

And one more thank you to Andrew Shimmin who has spent a lot of time working with some of changes in dBASE Plus 2.7 and later, and helped me get a grip on the Session object / User BDE Alias issue mentioned in this chapter.

Chapter 11: Security

dBASE has the ability to put passwords on local tables, which will protect them from being accessed from outside of your application. There are some issues involved with this and you should seriously consider whether or not you wish to do this. Once a table has been "protected", if you do not make sure that the password is securely stored somewhere, you can cause some serious havoc for the users of your application. What happens if you are no longer available to work on the project? Suddenly no one can access the tables.

That said, this chapter will take a look at the security that can be provided for local tables. Note that security is provided for SQL Server tables through their own interface. Most SQL Servers require that you login to the database. If you are using a SQL Server for your data, you will need to see the documentation for that software to create your own passwords, user lists, etc.

The PROTECT Command

The PROTECT command is the way that the database administrator creates users and passwords, and encrypt tables. This command can be used to encrypt and password protect a single dBASE table (.DBF), or you can force users to enter a userid/password when they start dBASE or your application.

The online help for this command is very useful and anything not covered here is discussed in the help.

> ⚠ **WARNING**
> The Borland Database Engine, which handles a good portion of the encryption of tables, is 32-bit. This means there may be problems if your application is going to run on 64-bit versions of Windows. In addition, there are sometimes issues that users have found with encrypted tables on current operating systems due to requirements of the UAC in Windows for permissions on folders and files. Encryption via dBASE has been problematic over the years, and while it is discussed here, this author does not recommend using it.

One very important thing to note: The first time that PROTECT is executed, an administrator password will be created. You should keep a hardcopy (on paper) of this password somewhere safe, because you cannot retrieve this password from anywhere.

Once you enter the administrator password, the database engine (BDE) creates a file called DBSYSTEM.DB, by default in the BIN folder for dBASE (see below). You can change where this file is saved/used by modifying the Plus.ini file (or the.ini file for your application), in the [CommandSettings] section. If you are using an older version of Windows, or dBASE Plus, then the path will be:

```
DBSYSTEM=C:\Program Files\dBASE\Plus\BIN
```

If you are using Windows Vista or later, and dBASE Plus 2.7 or later, the path will be:

```
DBSYSTEM=C:\ProgramData\dBASE\Plus\BIN
```

This file (DBSYSTEM.DB) is an encrypted file, meaning that you cannot open it in dBASE to view the contents. You should, like the administrator password, keep a hardcopy of all information stored in this file, because if you cannot remember it, there is no way to retrieve it.

For your application the path becomes very important. When you deploy the application if the DBSYSTEM.DB file is placed somewhere that is not modifiable, you may run into problems. This is why the entry for the application's .INI file mentioned above is so important.

If there is no entry in the application's .INI file (dBASE itself, or your own application), the software will look in the same folder as the executable. If it finds a file named DBSYSTEM.DB, it will initiate the login process. If it is not there, it will look in the path shown above (C:\ProgramData ...).

> ⚠ **WARNING**
> If you encrypt a table that contains data, dBASE (or the BDE) sometimes causes the data in the table to be corrupted. You should normally copy the table structure, encrypt the new table, then copy data into the encrypted copy of the table. The table shown in the examples for this chapter appears to work okay, but in general it is a bad idea to encrypt a table that contains data.

If you wish to follow along, you should make a copy of the FISH table and call it FISHPROTECTED. To do this, type the following in the Command Window of dBASE PLUS:

```
use :DBASESAMPLES:FISH
COPY STRUCTURE to FISHPROTECTED
use
```

If you type PROTECT in the Command Window, you will see the following dialog:

Figure 11-1

You will need to enter the administrator password. Make sure you write it down! *(For the following exercise, I simply used the word "Test" all the way through – making it easy to remember ...)*

Once you have entered the administrator password, and clicked "OK" (and confirmed the password – meaning you have to enter it twice) you should see the following (multi-page) dialog:

Figure 11-2

For security to work, you must define groups and users. Groups are 'groups' of users – you could create "ReadOnly" groups and so on.

If you click the "New" button on this page, you will see:

Figure 11-3

You can add as many users as you want. For the purposes of a demonstration, a single test user will be created:

Figure 11-4

This is pretty basic, I really just put "TEST" in for everything. When you click "OK" you will see:

Figure 11-5

With a new user added, you can then select a table to modify and encrypt (as an example). To do this, you now need to click on the "Tables" tab of the dialog. This tab will display a list of tables you can encrypt.

Figure 11-6

We have a test table called FISHPROTECTED.DBF. Selecting that table, then the "Modify Table ..." button, we see this dialog:

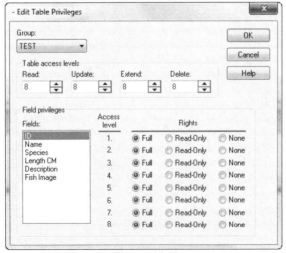

Figure 11-7

This allows us to set the access level for the table as well as for individual fields. To find out more about this dialog, click on the HELP button. The access levels are used to limit who can access the table at what level. This can get fairly complex and as noted earlier it is a good idea to write down any changes you make. If we leave everything as it is, the user group "TEST", which contains one user – "TEST", will have full access to the table, but we could limit them to read only, etc. We could even limit what fields they had access to.

To encrypt this table, click the "OK" button. Finally, we want to specify the security enforcement. (Click the "Enforcement" tab.)

Figure 11-8

If you leave it at the default "Opening an encrypted table", then the user will only be asked for group, userid and password if they attempt to open this table. If instead the "Loading dBASE PLUS" radiobutton is selected, then every time someone loads dBASE they will have to "log in". Make sure you actually click the radiobutton, because for some reason the default is ignored, clicking "Close" will change this to "Loading dBASE PLUS", even though it doesn't look like it.

Leaving things "as is", click the "Close" button.

When you close the dialog, any encryptions needed will be performed and the DBSYSTEM.DB file will be created/updated appropriately.

To open the table that's been encrypted, find the table in the Navigator and double-click it. You will see:

Figure 11-9

Note that the user has to enter the Group, Userid and Password. Clicking "OK" will open the table. At this point the table will be empty, so if you wanted to copy the data from the original into it:

```
use FishProtected
append from :DBASESAMPLES:Fish
use
```

If you need to decrypt a table, there is no "one-step" to decryption. See the section of this chapter on SET ENCRYPTION.

IMPORTANT
If you have created the DBSYSTEM.DB file and do not require encryption, or security, you can delete it, but you should be careful. If you encrypted a table and need the data contained in that table, you will want to decrypt it first, or you will never be able to open that table again. If you have been following along, you may want to simply delete the FISHPROTECTED table and then go to the folder that contains the DBSYSTEM.DB file and delete that.

SET ENCRYPTION

This setting in dBASE tells the software what to do when copying a table that has been encrypted. By default encryption is set ON, which means that when you create a copy of an encrypted table, the copy is also encrypted.

What this means is tables that are created from an encrypted table, using commands such as COPY TABLE, JOIN, and TOTAL (and their OODML/SQL equivalents) will be encrypted.

If you wish to copy a table in a non-encrypted form, then you should make sure that this command is issued first:

```
SET ENCRYPTION OFF
```

This command, combined with COPY TABLE and other commands, is the only way to decrypt an encrypted table.

LOGOUT

This command forces a user to be logged out and a new login window to appear. This is only useful when you have encrypted tables, or set dBASE to require a login for a session. The LOGOUT command closes all open tables, program files, etc.

Security and Paradox Tables

So far, everything we've talked about has involved the dBASE (.DBF) table format. Paradox tables (.DB) have their own form of security. It may even be possible to use the Paradox table security and then use .DBF tables for the rest of an application if you are not comfortable with using the .DBF security.

The only way I can find to get to the Paradox security (ability to encrypt, password protect, etc.) is while in the Table Designer. While you have a Paradox table in the Table Designer, select the "File" menu, and the "Database Administration ..." menu option.

This will bring up a dialog:

Figure 11-10

Note that this dialog defaults to "DBASE" – if you change this to "PARADOX", and click "Security ...", you will see:

Figure 11-11

For our purposes, we have only the one Paradox table, so if you click "Modify Table ...", you will see:

Figure 11-12

Here you must enter a master password before you can do anything else. Enter the password you choose (write it down!) in both entryfields, and click the "Set" button.

This will set the password and you will then want to close the other dialogs as needed. The next time you open the table, you will need to enter the password that you created.

To remove the password, you need to go back to the designer and go through the various options as before, but rather than using the "Set" button, use the "Delete" button.

Interestingly enough, the Paradox table security system does *not* use the DBSYSTEM.DB table, so there is no concern with that. Instead this information is stored in the Paradox table. You could have different Paradox tables using different passwords if you needed to.

Security and SQL Server Tables

Security issues involving SQL Server tables must be dealt with through the SQL Server engine and any front-ends used there. While you can login to a SQL Server database through the OODML objects, creating and modifying security options (user groups, userids, passwords, etc.) must all be handled through that database. For more information you will want to see the documentation for the software you are using.

MSSQL and Oracle (and others) implement "Common User Login" methodologies in that when the user logs into Windows, their active directory profile provides access levels to the SQL server. In addition, these servers provide access and encryption to everything from the database right down through the tables, views, triggers and procedures to the individual fields.

The Session Object

The session object provides a way to handle logging into an application, or opening an encrypted file. One nice feature is that you can open an encrypted table with the session object, without the user having to enter group, userid and password. This can be done through the use of the *login()* method:

```
s = new session()
s.login( "TEST", "TEST", "test" )
q = new query()
q.sql := "select * from FISHPROTECTED"
q.active := true
```

Without the session object, the user would have to login, typing the group, userid and password correctly, etc. This allows a developer to have an encrypted table in an application, without the user ever having to know.

The Database Object

In release 2.61 of dBASE Plus, a new property was added to the database object: *loginDBAlias*. The purpose of this property is to allow a second database connection to a database using the credentials (userid and password) already in use. See the online help for more details on this new functionality.

Application Security

With what you have gotten so far in this chapter, you have several ways of handling security. For example, the first part of this chapter that deals with the PROTECT command will allow you to require a login for an application. You can take that one step further and as shown, password protects the tables, but as noted, this can have some serious drawbacks/side effects.

There are of course other ways to provide security that involve creating your own login forms and possibly a userid/password table and so on. There are various examples around, including a fairly extensive one in the freeware dBASE library called the dUFLP (referenced in the appendices of this book).

The one difficulty with storing passwords in a table is that you either need to password protect that table, or you need to encrypt the passwords somehow. Again, there is code to assist with encryption and decryption in the dUFLP, it is fairly lengthy code so duplicating it here is not useful.

You may instead require the use of your LAN administrator's security capabilities. It is possible through your local area network to require logins and such for applications, to access data, etc.

Summary

While the functionality to protect/encrypt tables exists in dBASE, you may find that it's not worth the trouble. However, if you *do* need to do it you now have some idea what is involved. Reminder, if you use this functionality, back up your DBSYSTEM.DB file regularly and make sure you write down passwords and store them in a safe place. Also remember that it is a bad idea to encrypt a table that contains data, as it may become corrupted in the process.

NOTES:

Part V: Designing the User Interface

The User Interface is how the user communicates with your application. It includes the main window of the application, the menus, toolbars, forms, reports, dialogs, and so on. The next few chapters of this book will be dealing with the user interface: creating it, modifying it, using the design tools of dBASE to help you do the job and creating custom controls to make your applications easier to create, modify and update.

Chapter 12: Working With the Designers

It is important that a developer be somewhat familiar with the design surfaces, and some of the options available, and that is what this chapter is about. Note that this chapter is just an overview of the various Designers in dBASE, the actual details of using the Designers will be gotten into in later chapters of this book.

A Warning

One caveat that should be noted is most of these designers generate standard dBASE code. This is great and wonderful, because you are provided with "two-way tools" that allow you to modify the source code and have it recognized by the designers.

There is however one aspect of the way these tools work that while working as designed, can be frustrating for a developer. If you add code in a form, report, etc. in the constructor *(the code that defines the class)* that might be variable – such as defining a file path, or something of that nature – the designer will stream out the evaluated version. For example – you might have a form that uses a query object. The query object's *sql* property is one that you want to be flexible for the form, so that you can pass a value such as a data folder based on the individual user. So you might open the form file in the Source Code Editor and modify the source code so that it looks like:

```
this.FISH1 = new QUERY()
this.FISH1.parent = this
with (this.FISH1)
   left = 5.2857
   top = 9.3636
   sql = 'select * from "&datafolder\fish.dbf"'
   active = true
endwith
```

The problem is that if you then open the form in the Form Designer, this value will be evaluated when it is opened and the evaluated version will be streamed out, so you might end up with:

```
sql = 'select * from "C:\Program Files\dBASE\Plus\Samples\fish.dbf"'
```

If you need this kind of functionality, your best bet is to override the form's *open()* and/or *readModal()* methods and then this will be evaluated before the form opens. *(This is for any code that needs to be evaluated. If it is in the constructor, it will be evaluated in the Designer and saved back out that way.)*

The Form Designer

The basic form "visual" editing utility is the Form Designer.
With the Navigator window in dBASE selected, click on the "Forms" tab. In that tab, you will see several icons, with the word "(Untitled)" by them. There are four: Form, Custom Form (yellow), Menu, and Popup Menu. You can design a new form in one of several ways:

- Select the File menu, New, then Form
- Double-click the (Untitled) icon for Forms
- Right-click on the (Untitled) icon for Forms, and select "New Form"
- Click on the (Untitled) icon for Forms and press ⌨Ctrl⌨+⌨F2⌨
- Click on the (Untitled) icon for Forms and click on the "Open" button in the toolbar
- Click on the (Untitled) icon for Forms, press the space bar, and select "New Form" from the popup that appears (it will be the only option).
- In the Command Window, type:

CREATE FORM

When installed, dBASE creates various settings for you, one of which is the option to ask about using the Form Wizard when you create a new form. The window that appears looks like:

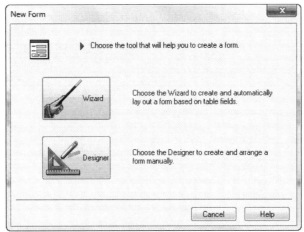

Figure 12-1

The Form Wizard can be useful, as it allows you to create a form quickly, by answering a few questions and making a few selections, but it is limited as to what it can do. It also sets up themes for color schemes. We will not be spending time with the Form Wizard, because as a programmer we need the control provided by the Form Designer *(if you want themes, when we get to the custom forms and custom controls chapter, you can do this easily)*.

Click on the button that says "Designer" and we will move on.

 NOTE

I am one of those developers who *never* uses the Wizards. You can go to the Properties menu in dBASE and select the "Desktop Properties" option. Select the "Application" tab and you will see a set of checkboxes with the heading "Prompt for Wizard". If you uncheck specific options, when you create a new form, report, etc., you will not be prompted for the Wizard and will be placed directly in the designer instead. This is a preference issue, but for me it is an important one.

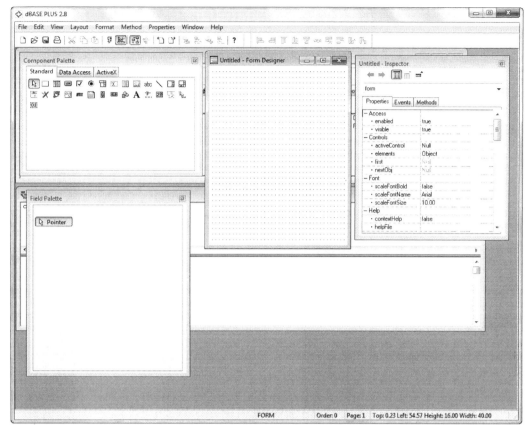

Figure 12-2

As you can see, there are several windows to work with.

In the center (or close to the center) is the new form surface. This is effectively a blank palette, in that you can do pretty much anything you want to with it. At the top of the screen you will see that the menus have changed a little and that the dBASE toolbar has changed as well. As we work with the Form Designer we will take a look at these options.

Below the toolbar (the position, size, and shape of this window may be different) is the Component Palette – this is where we can select controls and objects to be placed on a form. To the lower left is the Field Palette – if we have a table on a form (we will get to that later), then we can drag fields directly from this palette to the design surface.

To the right is one of the most important tools in the designer – the Inspector. The inspector is used to view and modify properties, events and even methods for a form (or as we will see later, reports, datamodules, etc.) and the controls contained by the form.

We need to get familiar with these tools, which is the next step ...

Form Designer Properties

There is one aspect of the designer that we need to look at and that is the "properties" dialog, which affects such things as whether or not to display a ruler on the form design surface, a grid, and so on.

To see this dialog, you can open it when in the Form Designer by right clicking on the design surface, and selecting "Form Designer Properties" in the popup.

221

Figure 12-3

I find that "Snap to grid" *(which by default is checked)*, is frustrating to me, so I tend to turn this off (uncheck it).

You will find a similar dialog for the Report Designer, with some different options that are appropriate to working with reports.

The Menu Designer

The Menu Designer can be used to create either standard menus (like you see at the top of most software, menus that when you click on them, a new menu may appear below it, etc.); and it is also used to create popup menus (right click style menus).

You can start the Menu Designer in the same ways as the form designer, just using either the Menu icon or the Popup icon. Depending on which icon you select, you will get the appropriate version of the designer. Note that there are no palettes for components or fields. There are no real properties to discuss for the Menu/Popup Designer as far as things we might want to change.

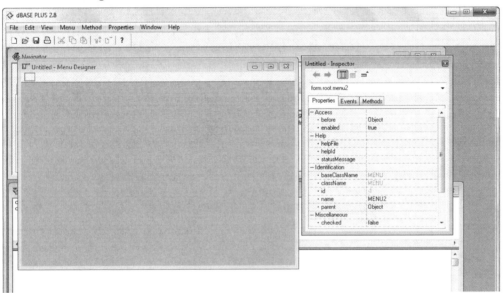

Figure 12-4

We will discuss this designer in more detail when we actually get to the chapter on creating menus.

The Report/Label Designer

The Report Designer is used for both Reports and for Labels. As with the Form Designer, there are many ways to start it and it can be used for Custom Reports, Reports, and to create Labels (sheets of labels, based on your specifications). The Report Designer can be used with a Wizard, as with the Form Designer, but we will not be looking at that.

The Report Designer, by default, looks something like the following:

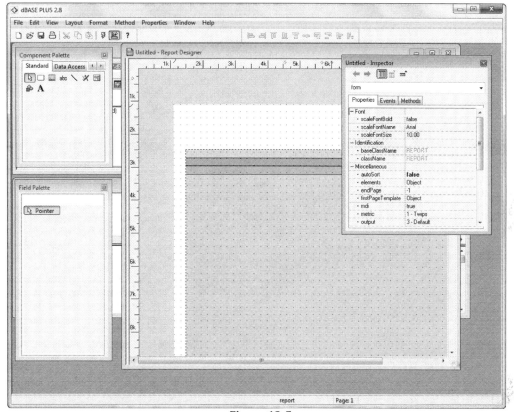

Figure 12-5

As with the Form Designer, there is a Component Palette, a Field Palette, and the Inspector.

If you right click on the Report Designer surface, you will see that there is an option to bring up the Report Designer Properties dialog, which looks like:

Figure 12-6

Notice that I have turned off "Snap to grid" again because I find that functionality frustrating when designing my reports.

As with the other designers discussed here, we will get into this in more depth and detail when we start looking at creating reports and labels.

The Table Designer

The Table Designer is used, as it sounds, to create and modify table structures. This is a fairly complex tool, as you can not only add or modify fields to a table, you can add or modify indexes.

You can start the Table Designer much like with the other Designers in dBASE as well as a Wizard you can use to create tables.

When you start the Table Designer (without the Wizard), you see a screen like:

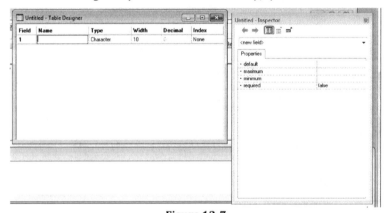

Figure 12-7

There are no "Property" dialogs for the Table Designer.

If you notice, the Inspector appears by default on the first field. If you click on the Table Designer surface (not on a field), you will see properties of the table in the Inspector.

The SQL Designer

The SQL Designer can be used to create SQL files (they will have an extension of .SQL) that can be used with forms, reports and datamodules. However, in my experience, except for some basics for designing a SQL statement, the SQL designer has a lot of problems – this is because it was actually created for another software package at Borland when they were creating Visual dBASE 7.0. This tool was modified to work in dBASE, but because of the fact that it was put together for a different purpose, it has never worked as well in dBASE as it could and sometimes yields difficulties with the .SQL files that are generated. It is recommended that you don't use this much and not to rely on it for your applications.

The Data Module Designer

This is *dQuery*, which was discussed in an earlier chapter of this book. There is no need to go into detail about it again here.

Designer Common Tools

The various designers use many common tools and we will be taking a quick look at each of them to get you more familiar with the various tools that are available to you.

The Inspector

The Inspector is the most commonly used component in the design surfaces, as it is used to set properties, events and methods for the various objects. We have used this in previous chapters of this book. It is a very important tool.

Figure 12-8

Tabs
The Inspector has three tabs, one each for Properties, Events and Methods. If an object being inspected does not have accessible Properties, Events or Methods, then that (tab) page will be blank.

There are five buttons at the top of the inspector. The first two are arrow buttons. These will move to the previous or next object you have inspected. An example of this might be if you were inspecting a form and clicked on "rowset", then clicked on the "I" (Inspect) button. This moves you down one level in the object hierarchy.

To go back up in the hierarchy, in the case of some objects, you could click on a parent property, and then the "Inspect" button. Some objects do not have a parent property and therefore no obvious way of moving back up except through the combobox (more on this in a bit). You could close the inspector and start over, but it's easier than that. Use the "Previous" button (which is now enabled). This will take you to the previous object that you inspected.

The "Next" button works the same way, if you have been going up and down the hierarchy ...

Next to this are three buttons that affect the layout of the inspector. The first is a toggle button, it is either up or it is down. If it is "down" (which is the default), you are in "Category" view, which means that you see the properties grouped by categories. Some objects have categories, some do not. Most of the UI objects (Forms, objects that can be used on Forms, and the same for Reports, as well as most of the data objects). However, you may be more comfortable with looking at the properties in an alphabetical listing. Click on this button and it moves to the "up" state, which is an alphabetical view.

If the Inspector is in a Category view, the two buttons to the right can be used to expand or collapse all of the categories in the inspector. If the Inspector is in an alphabetic view, these buttons are disabled.

Below the buttons is a combobox. This will be available in the design surfaces (but not if you use the inspector outside of the design surfaces) – it is used to find objects that can be inspected and bring them to the inspector. It can be a very useful way to see the object hierarchy on a form or report as well ...

Selecting/Modifying Properties, Events and/or Methods
When you use the inspector it is possible to view, as well as to modify, properties events and methods of an object.

Viewing is pretty straightforward, but if you wish to change an object's property, you have to click on it. Then you may either enter a new value, or in some cases, you may click on a button or a series of buttons.

Properties
Click on the "Expand all categories" button, so you see all of the properties.

- Logical values: these can be set by one of several means. The first is to double-click on the property (on either the left or the right of the vertical line that separates the properties and their values). The second is to use the combobox that appears if you click on the value and select the opposite of what is currently selected. The last is to simply type the value you wish to change this to – if it is an invalid value, when you press ⌷Enter⌷ (which is required for the inspector to accept the new value), it will change the value to *false*. For example, if you click on the *enabled* property and type "1" and press ⌷Enter⌷ you should see the *enabled* property's value change to *false*.

- Numeric values: if you click on a numeric property, the value part will turn into a spinbox. You may change the value by using the spinbox control, or by typing a new value and pressing ⌷Enter⌷. If the value is invalid, usually you will be told so (sometimes the inspector may let you enter an invalid value and not warn you about it).

  Some numeric values have text associated with them as well. An example of this might be the metric property of the form. If you move down in the inspector until you see this, you will see something like "0 - Chars". If you click on this, a combobox will appear with a listing of the options. However, if you were to programmatically change the value, or even do so at the command window, you would enter the numeric value — entering the character value would not be accepted!

- Character values: There are a lot of things that can happen with Character values. Most character values, if you click on the value or the property, the inspector will display an entryfield with a "Tool" button (a button with a wrench on it). If you wish, you may enter a value directly by typing it in (and pressing ⌨Enter when done).

   You may, however, decide to use the "tool" button, which will bring up a dialog. In some cases, the dialog is a pre-designed dialog either from Windows or dBASE itself.

   Try this: click on the *scaleFontName* property, and then the tool button. You will get a "getFont()" dialog. (Click the "Cancel" button.)

   Try this: click on the *helpFile* property and then on the tool button. You will get a "getFile()" dialog (Click the "Cancel" button.)

   Try this: click on the *statusMessage* property and then on the tool button. You will get a "String Builder" dialog, which was designed for dBASE. The other two are either Windows dialogs or ones that were designed for dBASE to act like standard Windows dialogs.

- Object references: Some of the properties will display a value of "Null" or "Object". These are pointers to objects. If we had placed a query object onto the form, the form's *rowset* property might show something completely different than "Null".

   If the object reference shows anything other than "Null", it is possible to select the "I" (Inspect) button, and actually inspect that object (remember the bit about the object hierarchy?). At that point in time, the properties, events and methods will be those of the new object, not the form.

Note that any time the value part of a property or event is yellow, it means that you are changing it - if you leave this property or event without pressing the ⌨Enter or the Up/Down arrow keys, you have abandoned those changes!! In other words – if you want the change to "stick", make sure you press ⌨Enter or up/down.

Events
Events can have code attached to them (event handlers, as discussed in earlier chapters). For example, a form has *onGotFocus* – when the form gains focus, this event will fire.

Methods
Methods are code that is already written. These can be called by the developer in their own code (possibly in an event) and sometimes these methods can be overwritten. In most cases you do not want to do this, but there are times you might.

Other Options
If you right click on the inspector, you will see a Popup Menu appear. This menu has the following options:

- Undo – standard Windows "Undo" from a copy, cut or paste operation
- Cut – Cuts the value out of the current property
- Copy – Copies whatever is in the current property to the clipboard
- Paste – Pastes the clipboard's contents to the current property. These first four options can be handy for copying properties.
- Revert property to default – exactly what it says.
- Go backward – This matches the button at the top of the inspector
- Go forward – same
- Category View – same

- Expand all Categories – same
- Collapse all Categories – same
- Customize Tool Windows – This allows you to customize the inspector and other components. We'll look at this momentarily.
- Always on Top – what it says. This can be a bit annoying and in the designers actually defaults to *false*. However, some developers prefer the inspector to always be on top, and you can toggle it - if it is set to be on top, a checkmark will appear by it, otherwise it will not.

The "Customize Tool Windows" menu option mentioned above defaults to whatever tool or component you were using when you selected it, although you can move to other components.

Figure 12-9

There are only three options in this dialog for the Inspector: Category View, Always on Top and Dockable. The "Dockable" option is only selectable if the Inspector is set to "Always on Top". What it means is that if you want the inspector to always be on top, you may want the inspector to be docked to the top, bottom, left or right of the screen. It will stay there unless you "tear" it off by clicking on the top and dragging it. Most developers don't particularly like this option, but it is there in case.

We will learn more about the Inspector as we go. The more you use it, the more you will see how useful and important it is.

The Component Palette

The Component Palette is used in the Form and Report designers, to provide a simple way for the developer to visually select components to place onto the design surface.

This palette may have several tabs, depending on what you are doing, and whether or not you have any custom components available.

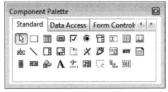

Figure 12-10

If this palette is not on screen, you can bring it up by right clicking on the design surface and selecting it. You can also turn it off in the same way.

In the Form Designer, the Component Palette will display "Standard", "Data Access" and maybe some other tabs, depending on what custom components may be loaded when you start dBASE. In the Report Designer you will see different tabs, depending again on what custom components may be loaded, etc.

Each page of this component has an "Arrow" icon, which sets you back to the pointer. The reason for this is that while in the designer you can click on an object and then click on the design surface. This will place an instance of that object on the surface. There is an option (again, below) to "Revert to Pointer" which is set to "True". If this is changed to "False", what it means is that if you click on the surface a second time, you will get another instance of the same object, unless you go back to the component palette and click on the arrow ...

Options

Like the Inspector, if you right click on the component palette, you will get a popup menu. The options here are:

- Set Up Custom Components ... – this option brings up a dialog for setting up custom component files (.CC files) so that any controls defined in them are available on the Custom tab. PROBLEM: this information gets written into the .INI file and every time you load dBASE from that point on these .CC files will be loaded in memory. While this can be useful, it can a) slow down the load time of dBASE and b) open files you may not want available for all of your applications.

  There are ways around this. At the command window you could type:

  ```
  set procedure to mycc.cc
  ```

  and any controls contained in that .CC file will be available in the designers until you exit dBASE, or close the procedure file. This is the simplest.

- Set Up ActiveX Components ... – this is related to the above. It makes ActiveX controls available to your application. If you select this option you will see more than what may have been shipped with dBASE as being available, but if you do not have permission to distribute them, don't (some don't work well with dBASE)!

- Customize Tool Windows ... – the same option as the Inspector, but this defaults to the Component Palette. The options available here are:

  Display: "Text", "Image", "Image with text below", or "Image with text to the right". The default is "Image". If you have a lot of custom controls, you may want to experiment so you find the layout that works best for you.

  Show Tabs – unchecking this will turn off the tabs in the palette and jumble everything together on one page. This is probably not a good idea, but if you'd rather not use tabs ...

  Revert Cursor to Pointer – this was discussed above — it means that when you drag an object from this palette to the design surface, you want the mouse to revert back to a pointer. Otherwise, the next time you click on the design surface, you may get another instance of the object you just placed on the surface.

  Always on Top – as it says. If this is true, it allows the developer to set the "Dockable" option.

  Dockable – as with the inspector, you may wish the component palette to be "docked" at the side of the screen ... most developers don't.

- Always on Top – you can set this option here, as well as in the Customize Tool Windows menu.

The Field Palette

This tool is used to display the fields available for the developer to place onto the form or report (or label).If there is no table open, and no query object or data module object available, this palette is empty.

Figure 12-11

If you have a query object or data module object on the form (or report), you will see something like this:

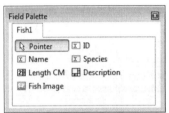

Figure 12-12

You can drag fields directly from here to the design surface. However, if you read later chapters in this book, you will see that this is not a good idea (I highly recommend that you use custom controls).

If there is only one table open or rowset available in the designer, there will be a single tab with the fields available listed.

If there are multiple tables available, there will be a tab for each, with the fields for each table listed on the appropriate page of the palette.

Options

Right clicking on the palette will bring up a short menu:

- Associate Component Types – the default associations for various field types may not be what you want. For example, when you install dBASE the default association for numeric and date fields is a spinbox. You may prefer entryfields. If you right click on the field palette and select this option, you can change the default, so when you drag a numeric or date field to the design surface you will get an entryfield instead of a spinbox.

- Customize Tool Windows –selecting this defaults to this palette. The options for this palette are:

    Display – options are "Text", "Image with text below" and "Image with text to the right". The default is "Image with text to the right".

    Add field label – options are "Above field", "Left of field" and "None". What this means is that when you drag a field from the palette, a descriptive text control (or a "heading") can be placed on the form or report, either above or to the left of the control. This is a nice feature, but if you have a need to do things in a different way it can be annoying, so you can turn it off (set the option to "None").

Always on top – as previous tools

Dockable – as previous tools

● Always on Top – what it says.

The Format Toolbar

This toolbar or floating palette is used to allow the developer to format text using HTML tags. Text controls on forms and reports or labels are all able to evaluate a sub-set of HTML 3. In addition the editor control is able to evaluate the same set of HTML 3, but be warned – once you embed HTML tags into a memo field, you may not be able to remove them. *(This toolbar is available from mdi forms when using an editor control, there are ways to turn it on/off.)*

This is only active in the designers when text controls are the current controls and it defaults to not being available. You can turn it on by right clicking on the design surface and selecting it from the menu. When a form is running you have some options to turn this on or off for editor controls.

There are quite a few options here that can be used to modify your text.

Figure 12-13

You have some styles (Paragraph and Heading) – this is the first combobox at the top of the palette. You can select a font from the combobox under that, which is kind of nice – selecting the font will change the *fontName* property of the text control, unless you choose to only change the font for part of the text (highlight it and select a new font – only that text will get that value) – in which case the text gets HTML tags.

You can change the size of selected text within the control, the color of the text or selected text, set bold, italic or underline (and again if it is selected text, HTML tags will be inserted).

If you have a large text object you can set list styles, you can set indentation, and alignment of text.

This is rather spiffy, but the problem is that the HTML interpreter for the text control adds a lot of overhead to a form.

Options
Note that right clicking this, there is only one menu option, and that is the "Customize Tool Windows" option. If you select that, there is no setting for the Format Toolbar.

231

Summary

There are many options available to a developer for working with the various design surfaces in dBASE. Some of them are available in some designers, some in others and some are available to all design surfaces (such as the Inspector). You should be familiar with these, as you will be using them when you use the designers. There are other tools such as the Toolbars, which change depending on what you are doing in dBASE and there are options specific to individual designers in the menus. As you learn how to work with the specific designers, you will see some options discussed in this book.

Chapter 13: Creating Forms

Forms are the standard means of communicating with users of your applications. A dialog box is a form; a screen used to display data for editing, or adding, viewing data – is a form. Forms have many uses in dBASE applications, we will be looking at forms themselves and the controls that are placed on forms to allow the user to communicate with your application.

What is a Form?

A form is a container for visual controls (objects) that are used to interact with the user in the Microsoft Windows environment. Any place where a user can interact with or get information about an application is done through a form / window.

A form may be used to interact with data, to query a user for specific options for a report, to obtain information about what to name a file, or to simply display the status of a long operation. If you need a way to interact with the user, you will most likely use a form to do so.

As a developer, you will spend a lot of time in the form designer and this chapter is aimed at helping you out. If you are new to dBASE, you are in for a treat — this development environment is pretty amazing. If you are coming to dBASE from earlier versions of dBASE (dBASE/DOS or Visual dBASE 5.x) you may have some things to learn or even un-learn. The main thrust of this chapter is to get you, the developer, familiar with the Form Designer and a lot of the concepts involved in designing forms.

Design Concepts

One of the more interesting concepts of application development is that of "MDI" or "SDI" applications. What does all that mean?

SDI is "Single Document Interface" – this is a way of creating an application such that each window is handled by Windows' "window manager" separately from other windows. Typically each window has its own menu or toolbar (or both). The application may use (if a dBASE app) the framewindow for dBASE or not. An SDI application that uses the framewindow does not restrain the child windows to the edges of the framewindow.

MDI is a "Multiple Document Interface" – one parent window which typically contains other "child" windows. The parent window typically is the one with the menu or toolbar. An example would be dBASE itself – as you work with the Navigator and Command Windows, as well as the various design surfaces, the menu and toolbar tend to be on the framewindow. An MDI application typically restrains the child windows – they must be inside the framewindow.

There are also some applications that are sort of hybrids – a combination of MDI and SDI. We won't spend much time on those, but you may see why you might want to develop something like that as we go.

First let's compare MDI and SDI applications and highlight a few comparisons that may help. Hopefully, as we work our way through this chapter some of it will make more sense as there are advantages and disadvantages to each:

Feature	MDI	SDI
Contained in application frame (_app.framewin)?	Yes	No
Menubar Window on each form?	No	Yes
Menubar Window on application frame?	Yes	No
Toolbar Window on each form?	No	Yes
Toolbar Window on application frame?	Yes	No
Window Menu Applicable?	Yes	No
Forms appear in taskbar?	No	Yes
Minimize/Maximize forms affects all open forms?	Yes	No
Each form treated separately when minimizing/maximizing?	No	Yes
Windows always offers resize, minimize and maximize?	Yes	No

Types of Forms

There are three main "types" of forms:

- **Data Forms** – these are ones that interact with the data. They can have datamodules, databases, queries, rowsets etc. and objects that are designed specifically to interact with the rowset and field objects. There are many, many ways to design data forms, but these are the ones that you see the most in any application as they are the most important for the application. These forms may be modal or modeless (opened with the *readModal()* or *open()* methods of the form).

  Data forms should use the *rowset* property of the form if you are using the OODML (if you are migrating forms from earlier versions of dBASE, then you will be using the *view* and/or *designView* properties). The reason to use the *rowset* property is that it is much easier to work with an object reference of:

  ```
  form.rowset.next()
  ```

  than one that looks like the following:

  ```
  form.query1.rowset.next()
     // or:
  form.datamodref1.query1.rowset.next()
  ```

  There are some tricks to using this discussed in this chapter.

- **Dialog Forms** – these are forms that interact with the user to get specific information. These may or may not interact with the data (rowset/field objects). In most cases dialog forms are modal (opened with the *readmodal()* method of the form).

  dBASE has many built-in dialogs, which allow you to hook into quite a few of these for your own use as a developer. Here are the ones I can think of off the top of my head — use online help for each of these dialogs for more details:

- MsgBox() –allows you to ask the user questions or let them know something (warning, error, information, etc.). The code then reacts based on what button the user clicks on.
- GetFont() – allows the user to select a font and font attributes. For the most part this is not really useful in most applications, but as a developer it might come in handy to obtain information about a specific font.
- GetColor() – allows the user to select a color and returns the hexidecimal value. *(You need to usually translate this as the GetColor() dialog returns values in a different value than is used by the color properties of forms and form controls.)*
- GetDir() – allows the user to select a directory/folder.
- GetFile() – allows the user to select a file to open.
- PutFile() – allows the user to select a file to save to.
- ChoosePrinter() – allows the user to select the printer to print to and set properties for a report (or for the whole application – not necessarily a good idea). You may want to use this from the report object's printer object:
  reportName.printer.choosePrinter(), rather than using it from the application object: _app.choosePrinter(). Using it from the application object will set the default printer for your application, using it from the report's printer object will set the printer for that one report.
- **Message/Information Forms** – these forms usually are not designed for the user to directly interact with, but to let them know that a process is occurring and often what stage in the processing the program is currently at. This lets the user realize something is really happening and that their computer is not just "frozen". These forms must be opened using the *open()* method of the form, rather than the *readModal()* method because if they were modal, your application would stop while the form was open, defeating the whole purpose.

Creating a Form

We discussed working in the designers a little in the previous chapter, but now we need to get specific. We're going to take a look at creating a simple form in the form designer. We will slowly build this up through the rest of the chapter and see some of what can be done with forms. We will not be discussing every single property, event or method of the form because there are many and they are covered in detail in the online help and articles in the Knowledgebase for dBASE PLUS. Of course, as we go, we will examine the properties, events and methods that we use for any samples. One could write an entire book that dealt with creating forms and still not feel that every single aspect of what can be done with them in dBASE was properly discussed.

In addition to the discussion here there are design issues to consider such as "What Makes a Good User Interface". Appendix 7 will discuss this a little, with some pointers to a couple of books/websites on what makes a good design. This book is really aimed at getting you used to working with the controls, so you can work out what makes good design for yourself, although we try to steer you away from some really bad ideas.

One of the most important concepts of the form is that it is a container. What is meant by this is that it is an object that can contain other objects. We discussed this concept in earlier chapters, but with the form we get a visual representation of what is meant by object containership by the very nature of the form object itself. There are many controls that may be placed on a form and we will examine most of them to some extent in this and later chapters.

Now, all of that said, to create a form visually *(we could do it all in code, but that is very difficult)*, we need to start the Form Designer. In the previous chapter we mentioned ways to open the Form Designer for a new form. The simplest way is to go to the Navigator window and double-click on the first icon that says "(Untitled)". If you have left dBASE's defaults for properties, the first thing that will happen is that you will be asked if you want to use the Form Wizard, or go straight to the Designer. We want to use the designer, so click on that button. *(If you turned off the "Prompt for Wizards", you will not see this dialog.)*

This will place you in the designer and you should see something like the following (Figure 13-1), although the exact location of the individual tools will vary based on whether you have used them before, moved them, resized them, etc.

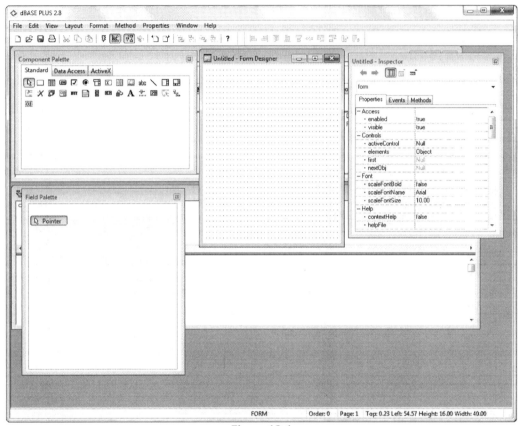

Figure 13-1

Notice that the form title has the name "Untitled" in it. This is because the form has not been saved, or because we did not name it when we created it. If we had typed in the Command Window:

```
create form MyForm
```

The designer would have automatically named this "MyForm.wfm".

Form Metrics

One aspect of the form that should be discussed early is that of the form's metrics. By default, when the form designer creates a new form, the metrics are set to "characters". What is meant by that? It's kind of hard to explain without going back to the old DOS days. In DOS, all characters used the same width for any character size. What this means is that the letter "i", which uses a tiny amount of width, always used the same amount of space as, say, the letter "W", which as you can see looking at it here, takes up quite a bit more space than the letter "i". This is called "monospaced" – each character uses the same amount of space on a line. The problem is that unless you actually use a monospaced font (such as "Courier") for your forms, the concept of a character when defining how big something is, is useless.

Windows itself tends to define everything by pixels. A monitor has a very large number of dots (pixels) to represent what you see on the screen. Based on the screen resolution, Windows regroups these dots in clusters. A pixel is each of these clusters of "screen dots". There are other metric options available in the form designer, but since Windows uses pixels, it may be a good idea to do that with your forms. It allows great control in placing each of the components on a form exactly where you want them and is "the Windows way".

To set the form's metrics, go to the Inspector and scroll down to find the category "Miscellaneous", there you will see *metric*. On the right you should see "0 - Chars". Select that, notice there is a combobox (drop down list – indicated by the down-arrow button). If you select the button for the combobox a list will appear. Select "6 - Pixels", that is all there is to it. Unfortunately, there is no way to tell dBASE to always use pixels in the form designer at this time, although when we look at custom forms in a later chapter we will see there are ways to do almost anything. This means that for now, you have to try to remember to set this property for any new form you create.

WARNING: it is a bad idea to modify the *metric* property outside of the form designer for a form you have already created. If you go to the Source Code Editor and change the value of the metric property, then bring the form into the designer, you will find that your controls are sized very oddly and it will be difficult to fix everything. It is best to only change this property in the designer, as the designer will handle the conversion for you.

Add a Text Control

To see how to use the designer, we will start by placing a text control on the design surface. A text control is a read-only control – the user cannot normally directly interact with it *(caveat, which we will examine later – using specific events the user might be able to click on a text control with the mouse and fire an event ... but this is not the primary purpose of a text control).*

For now, if you wish to follow along, click on the icon in the Component Palette that looks like a letter "A", and drag this to the design surface. You should see something like (Figure 13-2):

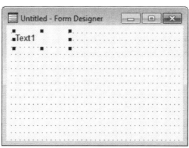

Figure 13-2

The text control defaults to showing the name that was automatically created for it, as the text. We can change the text in one of a couple of ways. The first and simplest is to click on the text control and start typing.

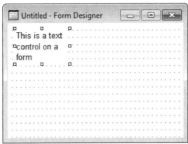

Figure 13-3

Note that as you click on the text, the handles (the small black boxes) turn to white, which is to give a visual cue as to what is happening. You can delete the text that is there and enter whatever you want. As you type, note that the width of the text control does not change, but if you type enough text, the height will. This is automatic. If you want the width to change, you will have to do that yourself (you can drag the handle to the right, or use the Inspector and change the *width* property).

When you are done typing, click on the design surface, or if there are other controls on the form you can click on one of those and focus will be removed from the text control. If you click on it once again, it gains focus, if you click on it when it has focus, you will be able to modify the text again.

With the handles being black (the control has focus, but is not in "type text mode"), you can move the text control, resize it, and so on. For example, to move the control up, click on it so it has focus, and then drag it up (hold the left mouse button down and move it up). To change the width, select the handle on the right and drag it to the right. Notice that the height of the control does not automatically get smaller as the control gets wider. You can change that by clicking on the bottom handle and dragging that up.

Saving the Form

It is a good idea to save your work often. The simplest way is to press [Ctrl]+[S] (Save), but you could use the "File" menu and select "Save" from there. The first time you save a form, a dialog will appear asking for the name. If you are following along, type "MyForm". Note that you do not need to add the file extension, it will be added for you. Once the form is saved, the name of the form is shown in the titlebar.

Modifying Properties of the Text Control

You can modify properties of the text control by using the Inspector. What properties can you modify? Nearly all of them (a few are read-only, such as *baseClassName*, *className*, and the *hWnd* properties, which can be queried but not changed). Any property that is not grey in the Inspector (a visual sign to distinguish disabled properties) can be modified.

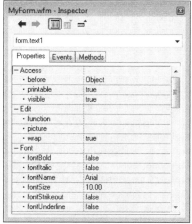

Figure 13-4

If you look at the combobox, it says "form.text1". That is because the name of the text control is "text1". One of the properties that can be changed is the name. (It is not shown on the screen in Figure 13-4.) We can change the appearance of the text by changing the properties such as the *fontName*, *fontSize* and more. We can change the text color (both foreground and background), set a border on the text control and a lot more. To see all of the possibilities for a text control, the best place is to either look at one in the inspector (as we are doing now), or to go to the online help and use the keywords "class text" to look it up.

For now let's keep things simple, set the *fontBold* property to *true* and change the *fontSize* to 12. To do this, select the *fontBold* property and either double click on the word *false* or select *true* in the combobox that appears. Notice that the text is bold *immediately* – there is no waiting, this is a very interactive environment. Now to change the *fontSize* – you can either type in the number 12, or use the spinbox (up/down arrows) that will appear when you click on this in the inspector. If you type the value, you must press the Enter key (or use the up or down arrow keys) or the value will not be stored. Again notice that the change is immediate.

Add a Pushbutton

Why a pushbutton? Because it is a very common control, many or all forms have them and it is interactive. The user can interact with a pushbutton, where in normal circumstances they cannot interact with a text control *(it is possible through the use of certain events, such as* onLeftMouseDown(), *to add code that will execute if the user interacts with a text control, but for the most part it is not standard Windows behavior)*.

Click on the pushbutton icon in the Component Palette and drag it to the design surface. You will note that the text for the button is "Pushbutton 1", which is the same behavior noted with the text control. To change the text, unlike the text control, we will have to go to the inspector. Find the *text* property in the inspector. You can type new text in, change the type to numeric (you might want to do that for some very specific purpose) by using the "T" button in the inspector, you can change the text by bringing up the "Build String" dialog by clicking on the "Tool" button (the one with the wrench on it). In any case, simply change the text to "My Button".

You should have something that looks like:

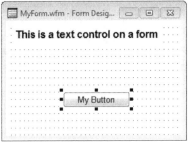

Figure 13-5

Before doing anything else, save your work with ⌨Ctrl⌨+⌨S⌨.

Run the Form

To learn how things work, we now need to learn how to run a form. There are many ways to run a form – for the moment we will just look at one, but we need to come back to this topic later.

When you are in the form designer, there is a toolbar at the top of the screen. There is one about 1/3 of the way across the toolbar that has a lightning bolt on it. If you hold your mouse over it, a speedTip will appear that says "Run Form".

Figure 13-6

Click this button. The form designer will shut down, and the form will be executed.

This is the form that we created in the form designer. There is the text at the top, and the pushbutton. Notice that the text for the pushbutton has a small box around it – this is the Windows method of showing the button has focus.

Try clicking the button with the mouse. Notice that it goes down and up, but – nothing actually *happens*. When you click on a pushbutton, you are firing the pushbutton's *onClick()* event. However, in this case there is no event handler assigned to that event, so when you click on it nothing happens.

> **NOTE**
> There are several mouse events that could be used. You should try to understand the difference in these events:
>
> - *onClick()* – The left mouse button is clicked down and let go to complete a "click" event.
> - *onLeftMouseDown()* – The left mouse button is in a down position.
> - *onLeftMouseUp()* – The left mouse button is in an up position, released from a down position. If you use this you are effectively using the same event as an *onClick()* event, except that this can be used with drag and drop operations (discussed in another chapter).
> - *onLeftDblClick()* – Literally two *onClick()* events quickly one after the other with the left mouse button. Windows determines the difference between two *onClick()* events and one *onLeftDblClick()* event.
>
> Most of the time when working with a pushbutton you need to deal with the *onClick()* event. It can be confusing to use more than one of these events for a pushbutton.

To add an event handler for the pushbutton's *onClick()* event, we need to go back to the designer. We can return to design mode by clicking on the toolbutton in the dBASE toolbar next to the "Run Form" button that says *(when you place the mouse over it – in the speedtip)* "Design Form". This will close the running form and open it back in the form designer.

Add an Event Handler
To add an event handler for the pushbutton, give it focus by clicking on it. In the Inspector you should see properties of the pushbutton. We want to look at events, so click on the "Events" tab.

Notice that the second event is *onClick()* and that the right side of the inspector says "Null" for this event (it should show that for each event displayed). There are many ways we add code to the event, for now we are going to simply tell dBASE that when the user clicks on the pushbutton, the form will close.

To do that, we need to call the form's *close()* method, from the event handler for the pushbutton, using a codeblock. Click on the word "Null" in the inspector next to the *onClick()* event, and type:

```
{; form.close()}
```

Then press the Enter key. Remember, if we do not press the Enter key, the code we entered may disappear.

If we run the form to test it again and click the button, the form will close. To test this, run the form by clicking on the "Run Form" button in the toolbar, when your form appears in run mode, click the button with your mouse. Notice that the form closes.

Modifying .WFM files
Now that you have worked with this form in the designer, let us take a brief look at what is happening "behind the scenes".

A .WFM file is a "windows form" – this name is used because when dBASE 5.0 was created there was a DOS version and a Windows version and the file extensions were created to differentiate the versions (a dBASE 5.0 for DOS form used .DFM for the file extension).

In reality, a form *really* is simply very specific code. It is code that defines a form class. This code could have an extension of .PRG (program), the only difficulty being that the form designer would not understand it because it looks for the .wfm file extension.

If you look at the Navigator window in dBASE, you should see a form *(assuming that you have clicked on the "Forms" tab)* named "MyForm.wfm" which is the form we have been working with. If you right click on this form, you should see several options, including "Run Form" and "Design Form".

There is one option we want to use right now, that is the option to "Open in Source Editor".

If you select that option, the form will be opened in the Source Code Editor of dBASE. You should see something like:

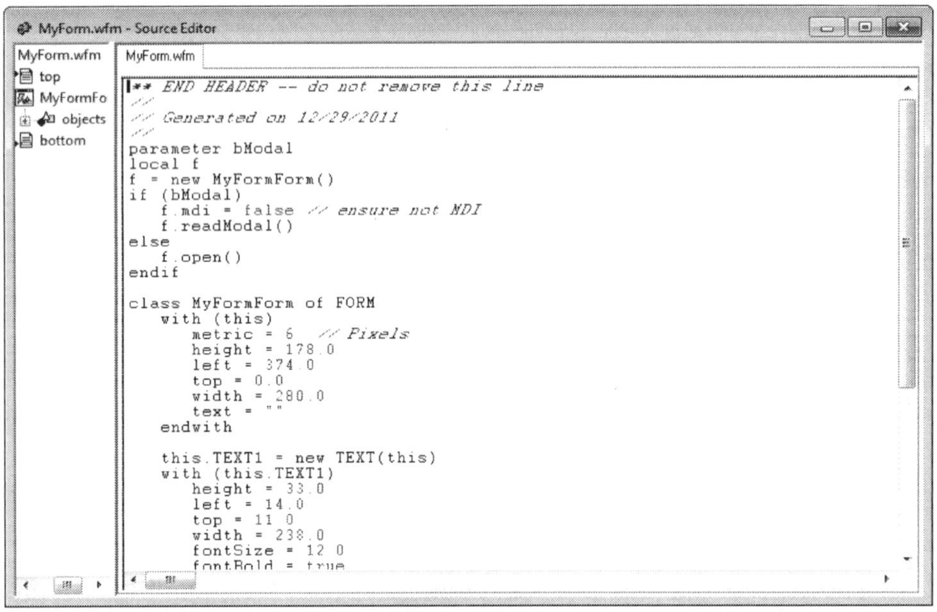

Figure 13-7

On the left in the source code editor is what is called a *treeView*, and on the right is the source code. The treeView offers a way to go straight to individual controls or code – the more complex your form is, the more useful this can be.

A brief look at what we are seeing shows that there are some comments at the top – comments are placed in code either by designers or developers and are ignored when dBASE runs the program. Their sole purpose is to assist the developer (or in some cases the designer) understand the code.

You should always leave the "*** END HEADER ..." comment as the Form Designer looks for that. It is a sort of place marker so it knows where to put its own information. We can place code before that comment if we want, but that's a more advanced feature than what we want to look at now.

The first block of code, which looks like this:

```
parameter bModal
local f
f = new MyFormForm()
if (bModal)
   f.mdi = false // ensure not MDI
   f.readModal()
else
   f.open()
endif
```

is what is called the "bootstrap" code. This is code that is used to run a form when it is double-clicked, or if you run the form by typing ...

```
do MyForm.wfm
```

... in the Command Window (or a program).

A form can be opened either with the form's *open()* or *readModal()* methods. A form run in what is called "modal" mode, using *readModal()* – is very much like the way an old DOS editing screen worked (if you are familiar with dBASE for DOS). Basically it creates a form that *must* be interacted with and nothing else can be done in an application until this form is closed. A form opened with the *open()* method *allows* for multiple forms to be running as well as the ability to switch between them if needed.

You could run your form as a modal form, by typing the following in the Command Window:

```
do MyForm.wfm with true
```

It now acts as a dBASE for DOS screen or as a Windows dialog. In some cases this may be desirable and in others it may not.

Why does the above command work? The "with" operator for programs, forms and reports in dBASE allows you to pass parameters *(we will discuss these in more depth in a later chapter)* to the program (remember a form is just a program in dBASE) and the program can then decide what to do with the parameter.

In this case, the bootstrap code creates an instance of the form, looks for a parameter and if passed to the form it is called "bModal". If it is not passed, dBASE assumes a value of *false* for the parameter. So, we are telling dBASE that if the parameter is *true*, we want to change the form's *mdi* property to *false* and then open the form with the *readModal()* method. Otherwise, we want to call the form's *open()* method.

This is a simple explanation of what the bootstrap code is doing, as you learn more about dBASE programming techniques (in later chapters), this will be more clear.

Note that even if you change the bootstrap code in the source code editor, the form designer will re-write it exactly as shown the next time you open this form in the designer and save it. This is because this particular code is expected to always be there.

The rest of the code in the Source Code Editor, is the class description. The class describes the form and any controls that are contained by the form, as well as any event handlers, and so on.

Two-Way Tools

One of the best things about the way the dBASE Form Designer and other design tools work, is that the source code is saved in a file that can be edited (either in dBASE or a third party text editor if you so desire) and the design surfaces will recognize those changes. This is called a "two-way tool". Some software design tools only write the code out, but do not recognize changes not made in the designer.

This particular feature can make your life much easier. There may be times when you want to make a very quick change to something and it is often easier to just open the source code in the editor, than to open the form in the designer to make changes. When you next run the form, the changes will be there and when you next open the form in the form designer, they will also be there. You may decide you just want to work in the Source Code Editor after you have designed the interface, so you can open the form there and work on code that you need for your application.

For an example of this, if you look at this code:

```
class MyFormForm of FORM
   with (this)
      metric = 6    // Pixels
      height = 352.0
      left = 326.0
      top = 118.0
      width = 280.0
      text = ""
   endwith
```

notice that the *text* property of the form is blank. If we change this to:

```
text = "This is My Form"
```

And run the form, we will see the text (look at the titlebar) has changed. To run the form from the source code editor, click on the toolbar button that says "Run" when you hold the mouse over it – it is the one with the lightning bolt and the paper.

You should see something like:

Figure 13-8

Unlike running code from the designer, the Source Code Editor does not shut down first but continues to run in the background.

Click on the pushbutton and the form will close. You can close the Source Code Editor by using Ctrl + W, or clicking the "x" in the titlebar on the right.

If you opened this form in the Form Designer and scrolled down to the *text* property for the form (in the Inspector), you would see that the change we made is still there. This is a great feature of dBASE and one that I am sure you will use a lot.

> ⚠ **WARNING**
>
> Most developers discover that while the Two-Way Tools aspect of the designers is very useful, there are some places that this does not work as "expected" – at least not until they have spent some time with it.
>
> Inserting code, comments, etc. inside the constructor code of a form or Report or Data Module will cause problems. The designers are set to stream out *just* the necessary code to create the form (etc.). What does this mean? If you add comments to explain why you did something, or you add code that is not part of the constructor, then open the form in the designer, saving the form streams out *just* the controls and their properties. This gets more tricky, because if you have custom code (event handlers and that sort of thing) after the constructor parts of the code, they work fine and are ignored by the designers.
>
> Inserting code right after the CLASS statement referring to custom class or other procedure files can be a problem if the custom class or procedure file is not referenced by the code in the constructor part of the form. For example, a custom class definition for your entryfields – this would be left in the form by the designer because the controls are being subclassed from that file. However, if you have a non-visual custom class file and reference it in the constructor, the designer does not see a need for it and will not stream that out.
>
> After a bit of experience with the designers, you will get a better feel for what this is about.

OODML and Forms

Now that we have looked at the basics, let's start looking at one of the really important purposes of a form – working with data.

In order to work with data and a form, you have to create what are called *datalinks* to controls. For our first form with data, we will do this simply.

We are going to use the Fish table that is installed in the samples for dBASE. To do that, before we go to the designer, click on the "Tables" tab of the Navigator window. Select the "Look In:" combobox, then select the combobox (click on the down arrow). Click the database icon for "DBASESAMPLES". You should now see "Fish.dbf" and "Samples.dbf" showing in the Navigator.

> **NOTE**
>
> For this example we will be using the *DBASESAMPLES* database alias, but in later chapters using the same table we will create a custom database alias using *User BDE Aliases*. This chapter is aimed at learning about how to do forms. But to deploy an application you need to do more than what we're doing here. More details when we get into Chapters 26 and 28 ...

Click on the "Forms" tab. Double-click on the first "Untitled" icon, which will create a new form in the form designer. Set the form's *metric* property to pixels by going to the inspector, finding the *metric* property and selecting "6 - Pixels" from the drop down list.

Next, click on the Navigator window, which should be in the background behind the new form. Select the "Tables" tab again and drag the "Fish.dbf" table to the design surface of the form.

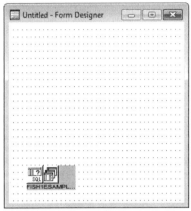

Figure 13-9

You should see two icons, although they tend to overlap. The first one is a Query icon (it says "SQL" and has a question mark (?) on it). The second is the Database icon. These are visual representations of non-visual controls – the query icon represents the query object that is used to work with the Fish table. The database icon represents the database object that is used to work with tables associated with the database alias named "DBASESAMPLES". You can drag these to wherever you want to on the form. I tend to drag them out of the area I want to work and often move them many times. However, you should not delete them if you wish to work with the data objects that they represent – deleting the icons will remove the objects from the form. Indeed, you may wish to do something such as change the *indexName* property for the rowset associated with the query object, for example – you can do that here by clicking on the query, and going to the *rowset*, and then to the *indexName* property. We will look at that later.

In addition to placing these icons on the design surface, the form's *rowset* property has been set to point to the rowset object that is associated with the Fish query. Also note that the Fields Palette now lists the fields in the Fish table.

Put Some Fields on the Form
We are going to use the Field Palette to drag fields from the table to the form. If you are developing a real-world application, you may not wish to do this *(see the chapter on Custom Controls – we will discuss why and why not there)*.

The Field Palette contains a list of the fields in your table and by default shows icons for each, the icons indicate the type of control that will be placed on the form (entryfields, etc.).

Drag the ID field to the design surface. Notice that a text control is placed on the form, as well as an entryfield. Do the same for the other fields – drag them to the design surface. You may want to (at least for now) drag the SQL and Database icons to the upper right corner of the form.

You should set the *enabled* property for the ID field to *false* (in the Inspector). The reason for this is that the field cannot be modified by the user – this is an AutoIncrement field and the value is assigned when a new row is added to a table. Setting the *enabled* property will avoid the user being frustrated by trying to modify the value. This will show the entryfield with text in a light grey color, which is the Windows standard for a disabled control.

You should see something *like* the following – where your controls ended up will depend on where you dragged them to on the form.

Figure 13-10

Before we go very far, let's line things up so that they look a bit better. This will also familiarize you with part of the toolbar used with the Form Designer.

We want to line up all of the controls that are not text (the entryfields, spinbox, editor and image) on the left and then line up the text controls on the right.

Let's start with the text controls. Select the one that says "ID", then hold the ⌨Ctrl key down and click on each of the others ("Name", "Species", "Length CM", "Description", and "Fish Image"). In the toolbar on the right, you will see a set of images that show controls lined up in certain ways. If you hold the mouse over them, a speedtip will show you what they do. Hold the mouse over them and move it until you find the one that says "Align Right". Click on that button.

Notice that the text controls all line up on the right now. Use the left arrow key to move the selected controls (all of them) to the left just a bit, so that the longest one ("Description") is still on the form, but is as far to the left as you can go and still see it.

Next, we're going to select all of the other controls and rearrange them. Click on the first entryfield then hold ⌨Ctrl and click on the other entryfields, spinbox, editor and image controls. Next find the toolbutton that says "Align Left" when you hold the mouse over it and click that. This will line up all of these controls on the left side. Use the RIGHT arrow key to move these over so that the text shows for all of the controls. You can do more moving around of controls and you might want to resize the form a little so that the entryfields fit properly. Resize some of the controls if you feel it to be necessary by dragging the handles as discussed earlier in this chapter.

Eventually you should end up with something *like* the following:

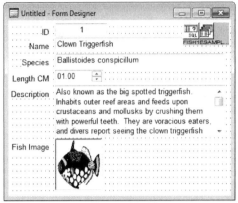

Figure 13-11

I would suggest one more minor cosmetic change and that is to set the *alignment* property of the image control used to display the image at the bottom of the screen. By default this is set to *stretch* which tells dBASE to make it fit the dimensions given. This can distort the image. Click on the image control, and in the Inspector, find the *alignment* property. Set this to read: "3 - Keep Aspect Stretch". What this means is that when the image control's *height* or *width* property is modified, to keep the same ratio for the other dimension, which means the image will not be distorted. You may then want to make the image a bit wider – this should now look similar to:

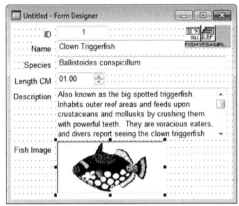

Figure 13-12

You should save your form by pressing Ctrl + S, when asked for a filename enter: FishSample.

An important property that is used for all "datalinked" controls (controls that are linked to data in the rowset) is the *dataLink* property. To see this, click on one of the entryfield objects and in the inspector click on the *dataLink* property (this is under the "Data Linkage" category). You will see something like:

```
form.fish1.rowset.fields["ID"]
```

This was done for you by dragging the object from the Field Palette to the form's surface. You can also do this by hand, or by dragging an Entryfield from the Component Palette and then setting the *datalink* property in the inspector yourself.

Interacting With the Data

Now that this is all here, how do we interact with the data? Well, basically, if you simply run the form you can now use it. You could consider it done *(although for this exercise we won't)*.

To see this, run the form – you can do this by clicking on the "Run Form" button in the toolbar at the top of the screen.

With the form running, the toolbar at the top of the screen changes and you will see some navigation buttons. You can also put the cursor in an entryfield and change the data. There are other buttons in the toolbar that will change if you change the data, there's an "Add" button to add a row (record) to the table and so on.

However, what we want is to be able to do this kind of stuff ourselves. In a real application, you may not want the user to see the IDE (Interactive Development Environment).

To go back to development mode, click on the "Design Form" button next to the "Run Form" button.

Putting Buttons on the Form

Why pushbuttons? These are the standard Windows method of navigating through a table. We will create a series of buttons here that will have event handlers for the *onClick()* event that will control the form and the table on the form.

These buttons can be done in quite a few ways, but we're going to do simple text, no images. If you want to do more you can spend a bit of time tinkering. For our purposes we want to keep it as simple as possible, as we are concentrating on getting these objects communicating with the rowset. We're not as concerned with esthetics, although we'll take another look at some of the properties you might want to modify later.

Before delving into the pushbuttons in a lot of detail as follows, a brief mention of a change in the software starting with dBASE Plus 2.6 is necessary. When this version was released it started using the default Windows Theme for the appearance of pushbuttons (and to different degrees other controls). In the first edition of this book, dBASE Plus 2.5 was new, but this change in the software had not been effected yet. The first edition of the book therefore showed pushbuttons in the old squared off style that was the default in Windows for many years. With Windows XP and later versions of Windows, pushbuttons actually by default take on the appearance defined by the active Windows Theme as displayed in the examples in this book will use this. There is some functionality that goes away, however. For example, the *colorNormal* property of a pushbutton is pointless, unless you choose to ignore the Theme. You can use the new property *systemTheme* (set the property to *false*) for a pushbutton and it will ignore the Windows XP Theme. More detail on this will be discussed in later chapters of this book.

Navigation Buttons

We'll start with navigation buttons. What are the standard navigation buttons? You need to be able to step through a table row by row, so you need "Next" and "Previous" buttons. You probably want to be able to go to the top of the table and to the end of the table (first row/last row). So we need four pushbuttons. *(We could get fancy and have buttons that moved either direction by 10 rows, or something, but let's not be greedy!)*

We'll start with the "first" button. Set aside some space on your form for buttons *(move the objects around, make the form wider)* so you have room for a few different buttons. In the example, we will place them down the right side of the form *(there are many ways to do this)*.

You should see a "Component Palette" on the screen in the design mode. If not, right click on the form's surface and select this ("Component Palette") – it should now appear.

The "First" Button

On the "Standard" page of this palette, you will see a variety of controls. If you are not sure what one is, place the mouse over it and a speedtip will appear, telling you what the object is. We want a pushbutton – click on the pushbutton object and drag it to the form's surface. You can move it around to wherever you need it to be.

The text of this button defaults to the name of the object, which is "Pushbutton1" – we are going to change the name of the button as well as the text, because if you have a lot of pushbuttons, it gets confusing working with them if they are simply "Pushbutton1", "Pushbutton23", etc.

So, with the pushbutton having focus (if it doesn't, click on it), go to the inspector and find the property *name* — it will be under the category "Identification". Click on the property, and on the right side, type "FirstButton" and press the Enter key.

Next, find the *text* property, which will be under the "Miscellaneous" category. Click on "text" and enter "First" and press the Enter key. You should see the text on the pushbutton change to "First" on the form.

Now, at this point, the pushbutton will not do anything when the user clicks on it as there is no event handler associated with the *onClick()* event. We must add some code to the button. The code for this button will be pretty simple. The question is, where do we assign the code?

Look at the inspector – you should see an "Events" tab – click on this. When you do, you should see a set of events – you can assign an event handler to any of these events. It just so happens, with pushbuttons, that the second event listed is the one we want to use to assign code when the user clicks the button with their mouse.

Click on the *onClick()* event. Where it says "Null" you should also see two small buttons, one shows the end of a wrench, the other shows a "T" for "Type". We want to use the wrench (or tool). Click on this and you will see the dBASE source editor window, with the following:

```
function FIRSTBUTTON_onClick

   return
```

Any code you want to be executed when the user clicks on the button goes after the "function" statement and before the "return" statement.

The code we want is quite simple. We want to go to the first row in the rowset when the user clicks on this button. To do this, we have to execute a method of the rowset, called *first()*. To do this, we type the code:

```
form.rowset.first()
```

What this does is it goes to the form object and looks at the rowset property – if no rowset is assigned to this property, this code will not work. However, we did that when we placed the table reference (the query object) on the form earlier. Assuming that a form's *rowset* property is assigned, it then executes the *first()* method (the parentheses are necessary to execute the code).

That's all there is to it. So you should see now in the editor window:

```
function FIRSTBUTTON_onClick
    form.rowset.first()
    return
```

To test this out, we need to run the form. So click on the lightning button. With the form running, we need to move to a different row (we start at the first one by default). Use the navigation buttons at the top of the screen in the toolbar, to move a few records into the rowset (use the "next" button). Now, rather than using the button in the toolbar, use the button we just created on our form – click on it and you should find yourself back at the first row in the table.

Now that we have created one pushbutton, the steps should be easier for doing more.

The "Next" Button

We need to add the "Next" button, so do the following steps:

- Drag a pushbutton from the Component Palette to the form and place it near the "First" button
- Change the name of the pushbutton to "NextButton"
  - Click on the "Properties" tab in the inspector,
  - Find the "Name" property and click on it
  - Type "NEXTBUTTON" and press the Enter key
- Change the text of the pushbutton to "Next"
  - Find the *text* property and click on it
  - Type "Next" and press the Enter key
- Find the *onClick()* event
  - Click on the "Events" tab in the inspector
  - Click on "onClick"
  - Click on the "Tool" button

Now we get to the more interesting part of this. The code can be very simple, as we will do the simple version first.

Enter the code:

```
form.rowset.next()
```

In the editor, so that your onClick event code looks like:

```
function NEXTBUTTON_onClick
    form.rowset.next()
    return
```

Like before, let's test this. Run the form (click on the "Run Form" button), and use the "Next" button to go to the next row. Keep doing this until you get to the end of the table – you'll know when it happens as you'll get a blank row!!

What happened here? You are pointing to the "end of rowset" pointer, and all the fields went blank. You don't really want your users to do that – they might think this is a valid row, and try to enter data. This won't do at ALL!

So, how do we deal with it? How do we, rather than display the "end of rowset", display an error message for the user?

Obviously, we need to modify the code, so go back to design mode (the button in the toolbar next to the "Run Form" button).

The *next()* method of the rowset object returns a logical value (true or false) – if *next()* is successful, the method returns the value *true*, if it wasn't dBASE returns the value *false*. We can check for that in our code – if we get a *false* value, which indicates *endOfSet* (we'll look at this later), we don't want to be at the end of rowset, so we tell the user that they cannot continue and display a message.

What we want to do is to try to navigate using the *next()* method of the rowset and if the method returns "false", we hit the "end of rowset". So we need to back up one row or go to the last row in the rowset (we can do this using the *next()* method with the optional parameter for the number of rows to navigate, or we could use the *last()* method). We will then display a message to the user that says we can't do this. The code is actually fairly simple:

```
if ( not form.rowset.next() )
   form.rowset.last()
   msgbox( "At end of rowset", "Can't Navigate", 64 )
endif
```

To do the above, change the code for the "NextButton" by clicking on the button in the inspector, click on the "Events" tab, click on the *onClick()* event and then the Tool button. Change the code in the editor so it looks like the following:

```
function NEXTBUTTON_onClick
   if ( not form.rowset.next() )
      form.rowset.last()
      msgbox( "At end of rowset", "Can't Navigate", 64 )
   endif
   return
```

For details on the use of the msgbox() function, see online help – it gives a lot of information.

Now to test this, run the form again and try navigating past the last row. You should get the error message we created and we will not see the end of rowset.

The "Previous" Button
We need to add the "Previous" button, so do the following steps:

- Drag a pushbutton from the Component Palette to the form and place it near the "Next" button
- Change the name of the pushbutton to "PreviousButton"
  - Click on the "Properties" tab in the inspector,
  - Find the "Name" property and click on it

- Type "PREVIOUSBUTTON" and press the Enter key
- Change the text of the pushbutton to "Previous"
  - Find the *text* property and click on it
  - Type "Previous" and press the Enter key
- Find the *onClick()* event
  - Click on the "Events" tab in the inspector
  - Click on "onClick"
  - Click on the "Tool" button

Enter code like the following:

```
function PREVIOUSBUTTON_onClick
   if ( not form.rowset.next(-1) )
      form.rowset.first()
      msgbox( "At beginning of rowset", "Can't Navigate", 64 )
   endif
   return
```

Note that this code is almost, but not quite, identical to that used for the "Next" button. It works very much the same, except we are going in the opposite direction. The "if" statement checks to see if we can navigate "backward" (if you will) through the table, and so on.

You can test this by running the form, clicking on it, and seeing the error message, navigating with the "next" button and then the "previous" button ... and so on. Then come back to the designer.

The "Last" Button

We need to add the "Last" button, so do the following steps:

- Drag a pushbutton from the Component Palette to the form and place it near the "Previous" button
- Change the name of the pushbutton to "LastButton"
  - Click on the "Properties" tab in the inspector,
  - Find the "Name" property and click on it
  - Type "LASTBUTTON" and press the Enter key
- Change the text of the pushbutton to "Last"
  - Find the *text* property and click on it
  - Type "Last" and press the Enter key
- Find the *onClick()* event
  - Click on the "Events" tab in the inspector
  - Click on "onClick"
  - Click on the "Tool" button

Enter code like the following:

```
function LASTBUTTON_onClick
   form.rowset.last()
   return
```

One more time, you can test this by running the form, then clicking on the button – it should take you to the last row in the rowset ... when done bring the form back to the designer.

Your form should look something like this:

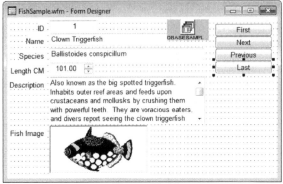

Figure 13-13

Editing Buttons

Now that we can navigate through the table, we need to have some pushbuttons that allow us to edit rows, add rows, delete rows, save changes, and abandon changes. Sound like a tall order? Well, not that tall, but there are a variety of new things to learn.

The first thing we need to note is that by default, a rowset is in "edit" mode – meaning that when a user clicks on a field and types something, they are editing the data. This could mean that a user might accidentally change something that they didn't want to. At the same time, they are creating a lock on that row, which means another user in a networked application cannot edit the row if they need to.

What's worse is that if they close the form at this point, the changes made to the row will be saved. If they click on a navigation button, the changes will be saved. *(See discussion in an earlier chapter on implicit saves.)* So, what can we do?

There is a property of the rowset object called *autoEdit* – this defaults to *true*. It means that the row is automatically in edit mode. If you want to keep the user from automatically editing the row, the simple solution is to set this property to *false*.

To change this property, we need to modify it in the inspector, but to get there we must go through the query object. Click on the query object (the "SQL" icon on the form) and then go to the inspector. Click on the *rowset* property (it will say "Object"), and then click on the "I" button ("I" is for "Inspect"). This technique is called "Drilling Down" to an object that is contained by another object. You should see the *autoEdit* property (under the "Miscellaneous" category) and it should show as *true*. Double-click on it and it will change to *false*.

To see if it works, run the form again. Click on one of the entryfields, and try to type something – note that you cannot. This is because of the *autoEdit* property being set to *false*.

Of course, we will want to allow the user to edit a row – otherwise what's the point of the form *(well, okay, you might want or need a readonly form, but for our purposes right now)*? However, we'll start with a button to allow the user to add a new row to the table.

Add Row Button

We need to add the "Add Row" button, so do the following steps:

- Drag a pushbutton from the Component Palette to the form and place it near the "Last" button
- Change the name of the pushbutton to "AddRowButton"
  - Click on the "Properties" tab in the inspector,
  - Find the "Name" property and click on it
  - Type "ADDROWBUTTON" and press the Enter key
- Change the text of the pushbutton to "Add Row"
  - Find the *text* property and click on it
  - Type "Add Row" and press the Enter key
- Find the *onClick()* event
  - Click on the "Events" tab in the inspector
  - Click on "onClick"
  - Click on the "Tool" button

Enter code like the following:

```
function ADDROWBUTTON_onClick
    form.rowset.beginAppend()
    return
```

Note that when your user clicks this button, the form will clear – all objects that are "datalinked" will suddenly be empty, so that the user can add new data to a new row.

What the user has done at this point is created a blank row – it is not real, until the user saves the row. Until they save it, the new row is in what is called a "buffer". The buffer is important, both here and in editing mode. The user can save the row by using a "save" button (that calls the *save()* method of the rowset), or by navigating in the rowset (using the buttons we created earlier) – either way, the row will be saved.

Another effect of the user clicking on the "Add Row" button is that there is a property of the rowset called *state* that gets changed, based on what the rowset's *state* happens to be. We will take a look at the *state* property later.

We can test it right now, but let's move on and add the other editing buttons first, and then we can test the series.

Edit Row Button
We need to add the "Edit Row" button, so do the following steps:

- Drag a pushbutton from the Component Palette to the form and place it near the "Add Row" button
- Change the name of the pushbutton to "EditRowButton"
  - Click on the "Properties" tab in the inspector,
  - Find the "Name" property and click on it
  - Type "EDITROWBUTTON" and press the Enter key
- Change the text of the pushbutton to "Edit Row"
  - Find the *text* property and click on it
  - Type "Edit Row" and press the Enter key
- Find the *onClick()* event
  - Click on the "Events" tab in the inspector
  - Click on "onClick"
  - Click on the "Tool" button

Enter code like the following:

```
function EDITROWBUTTON_onClick
   form.rowset.beginEdit()
   return
```

The *beginEdit()* method of the rowset allows the user to modify the copy of the row – the user is not editing the actual data – as soon as the row is saved, the copy in the buffer is written back to the actual row making the changes in the table. This is important, because there is an *abandon()* method (which we will see soon) that allows the user to abandon their changes to the row.

Like with the "Add Row" button, clicking this button (or running the code) sets the rowset into a special *state* (again we'll look at the state property later). In addition, if the user changes the row in any way, we set a property of the rowset called *modified* to *true* (it defaults to *false*). This property can be quite useful, and we'll come back to it later.

Delete Row Button

We need to add the "Delete Row" button, so do the following steps:

- Drag a pushbutton from the Component Palette to the form and place it near the "Edit Row" button
- Change the name of the pushbutton to "DeleteRowButton"
  - Click on the "Properties" tab in the inspector,
  - Find the "Name" property and click on it
  - Type "DELETEROWBUTTON" and press the Enter key
- Change the text of the pushbutton to "Delete Row"
  - Find the *text* property and click on it
  - Type "Delete Row" and press the Enter key
- Find the *onClick()* event
  - Click on the "Events" tab in the inspector
  - Click on "onClick"
  - Click on the "Tool" button

The problem with deleting a row in a table in dBASE, using the OODML (as we are doing here) is that the row is not easily recoverable. To all intents and purposes, it is completely gone. You may want to ask the user if they really want to delete the row by adding a quick dialog box that asks. If the user clicks the "Yes" pushbutton, then go ahead and delete the row.

There are two ways this can be written – the first is a bit more wordy, but is easier to read:

```
function DELETEROWBUTTON_onClick
   local nAnswer
   // nAnswer is the returned value of the messagebox:
   nAnswer = msgbox( "Delete this row?", "Delete Row?", 32+4 )
   // now check to see what button the user clicked:
   if nAnswer == 6 // Yes
      form.rowset.delete()
   endif
   return
```

A more compact form of this would look like:

```
function DELETEROWBUTTON_onClick
   if msgbox( "Delete this row?", "Delete Row?", 36 ) == 6
      form.rowset.delete()
```

```
      endif
      return
```

Save Row Button

We need to add the "Save Row" button, so do the following steps:

- Drag a pushbutton from the Component Palette to the form and place it near the "Delete Row" button
- Change the name of the pushbutton to "SaveRowButton"
  - Click on the "Properties" tab in the inspector,
  - Find the "Name" property and click on it
  - Type "SAVEROWBUTTON" and press the Enter key
- Change the text of the pushbutton to "Save Row"
  - Find the *text* property and click on it
  - Type "Save Row" and press the Enter key
- Find the *onClick()* event
  - Click on the "Events" tab in the inspector
  - Click on "onClick"
  - Click on the "Tool" button

Enter code like the following:

```
function SAVEROWBUTTON_onClick
    form.rowset.save()
    return
```

Abandon Changes Button

We need to add the "Abandon Changes" button, so do the following steps:

- Drag a pushbutton from the Component Palette to the form and place it near the "Save Row" button
- Change the name of the pushbutton to "AbandonRowButton"
  - Click on the "Properties" tab in the inspector,
  - Find the "Name" property and click on it
  - Type "ABANDONROWBUTTON" and press the Enter key
- Change the text of the pushbutton to "Abandon Row"
  - Find the *text* property and click on it
  - Type "Abandon Row" and press the Enter key
- Find the *onClick()* event
  - Click on the "Events" tab in the inspector
  - Click on "onClick"
  - Click on the "Tool" button

When abandoning changes, you may want to ask the user first. If adding a new row, abandoning would release the new row in the buffer – erasing any data that the user had entered. If editing a row, abandoning changes the copy of the row in the buffer back to what the row looked like before editing the row. A person may have done some real work to get all the data just right and accidentally hitting the abandon button could wipe all that out.

Enter code like the following:

```
function ABANDONBUTTON_onClick
    if msgbox( "Abandon changes to this row?", "Abandon changes?", 36 ) == 6
        form.rowset.abandon()
```

```
    endif
    return
```

At this point, your form should look similar to:

Figure 13-14

The Modified and State Properties of the Rowset

These two properties of the rowset have been mentioned elsewhere in this chapter; let's take another look at them.

The *modified* property is used when a row is placed into edit or append mode to determine if the row's buffer has been actually modified by the user. You can easily check the value of this property in your code by simply using:

```
if form.rowset.modified
    // do something
endif
```

This can be quite useful in some situations. For example, what if the user hits a navigation button after modifying a row? Do you want to just assume that the user wants to save the changes made? Wouldn't it be better to ask? You can do that by adding code to your navigation buttons to check for this. *(We won't do it for the example here, but it is a good idea.)*

In addition, if you have code that modifies the data when a user does some task your code does not automatically set the *modified* property to *true*. Therefore, you may need to set this property to have the rest of your form's code work properly. This is done by simply assigning a value:

```
form.rowset.modified := true // or false if you need it to be false
```

The *state* property is one that is constantly changed, based on what state the rowset is currently in. There are six different possible states: closed, browse, edit, append, filter and locate. By default, your rowset is in browse mode, but if your user modifies the data, the rowset is now in edit mode, if they are adding a new row, the rowset is in append mode and so on. "Closed" means that the query object's *active* property is *false*.

What does this mean? Well, it means that like the *modified* property, you can query it. However, the different modes are determined by numbers, starting at the number 0, and going to 5. So, the modes are:

0	Closed
1	Browse
2	Edit
3	Append
4	Filter
5	Locate

One of the problems with the way the form works when it is running is that it is difficult to tell what "state" the rowset is in. You might want to add a text object to the form that shows the *state*, or you might want to use a calculated field that updates an entryfield to show the *state*. The advantage to using a calculated field is that this is automatically updated, where a text field would need to be updated by your own code. The following is a simplified version of this, based on work by Gary White, a former dBVIPS. The steps are provided to make it as easy to create as possible.

- Drag an entryfield object onto the form surface from the Component Palette (above the buttons, line it up a bit …)
- Click on the *name* property and type: ROWSTATE and press the Enter key
- Click on the *value* property and type: State and press the Enter key
- Find the *borderStyle* property and set it to "1 - Raised" (Raised Border)
- Set the *colorNormal* property to "Maroon/BtnFace" (maroon is the text color, "BtnFace" is the default Form/Button color)
- Set the *fontBold* and *fontItalic* properties to true.
- Select the "Events" tab, and do the following:
    - Click on the *when* event, and enter the following exactly:

        ```
        {;return false}
        ```

        and press the Enter key (this keeps the control from getting focus, and the user from changing the value)
    - Click on the onOpen event, then click on the tool button (the wrench) – in the editor, enter the following code:

        ```
        // if we haven't already defined the calc field
        if type('form.rowset.fields["Rowstate"]') # "O"
           // do it here
           local f
           f = new field()        // create it
            f.states = new array()   // build an array with the
                                    // possible states
           f.states.add("Closed")
           f.states.add("Browse")
           f.states.add("Edit")
           f.states.add("Append")
           f.states.add("Filter")
           f.states.add("Locate")
           f.fieldName      := "Rowstate"
           f.beforegetvalue := ;
              {;return this.states[ this.parent.parent.state + 1 ]}
           form.rowset.fields.add( f )
        endif
        this.datalink = form.rowset.fields["Rowstate"]
        ```

Now, after all that, try running the form, note that this control shows "Browse". Click the "Add Row" button, and the word "Browse" should change to "Append".

Click the "Abandon" button (select "Yes" to abandon). Click the "Edit Row" button, note that the rowstate control shows "Edit". This is pretty spiffy and it allows your users to know what they are doing in case they got sidetracked. Click the "Abandon" button again and select "Yes" again.

Filter by Form

It is possible to allow the user to filter data based on criteria. One method of doing this is to use the "filter by form" technique – this can be done by putting a button on a form and using the rowset's *beginFilter()* method – this method will clear out the datalinked controls on the form, allowing the user to specify what to filter the data on. For example, they could type a specific name that they wanted to look for in the name field (if you have one).

Once the criteria is entered, the user would need to then apply the filter, which could be done either with the same pushbutton, or with another. This would tell dBASE to find all rows that match the condition(s) specified and only display those in the form – the user could move through the table looking at those.

Finally, you would to have a method of clearing the filter condition.

The following is based on code that is much more complicated in the dBASE Users' Function Library Project (dUFLP) – this code was compiled from several sources and has had various developers put their touch on it. I am simplifying it for this example. All of the following is for a single pushbutton. The code (which is more complex than anything we've looked at to now) performs object morphing or *polymorphism* – the object changes what it does based on specific conditions.

Filter Button

We need to add the "Filter" button, so do the following steps:

- Drag a pushbutton from the Component Palette to the form and place it near the "Abandon Row" button
- Change the name of the pushbutton to "FilterButton"
    - Click on the "Properties" tab in the inspector,
    - Find the "Name" property and click on it
    - Type "FILTERBUTTON" and press the Enter key
- Change the text of the pushbutton to "Filter"
    - Find the *text* property and click on it
    - Type "Filter" and press the Enter key
- Find the *onClick()* event
    - Click on the "Events" tab in the inspector
    - Click on "onClick"
    - Click on the "Tool" button

Enter the following code. Be careful and look out for typos!

```
function FILTERBUTTON_onClick
   do case
      // we are in "beginFilter" mode:
      case this.text == "Filter"
            // change Text
            this.text := "Run Filter"
            // save current bookMark so we can return
            // to it:
            form.bookMark = form.rowset.bookMark()
```

```
              // set form to "filter" mode
              form.rowset.beginFilter()

          // we are in "Run" mode (applyFilter() )
          case this.text == "Run Filter"
              // don't update the controls until told otherwise
              form.rowset.notifyControls := false
              // try the filter — if we don't find a match
              // we'll clear it out ...
              try // catch error about memo:
                  if not form.rowset.applyFilter()
                      // reset the text back to "Filter"
                      this.text := "Filter"
                      // clear the filter
                      form.rowset.clearFilter()
                      try
                          //attempt to go back to the 'bookMark'
                          // if we can't, we go to the first row
                          // in the table
                          form.rowset.goto( form.bookMark )
                      catch ( exception e )
                          form.rowset.first()
                      endtry
                      // let the user know that no match was found
                      msgbox( "No match found", "Filter error", 48 )
                  else
                      // otherwise the filter worked,
                      // so now we want to change the image to
                      // a "clear Filter" ...
                      this.text := "Clear Filter"
                  endif
              catch ( dbexception e )
                  msgbox( "Can't filter on a memo field", "Filter error", 48 )
                  form.rowset.goto( form.bookmark )
                  this.text := "Filter"
              endtry

              // turn this back on
              form.rowset.notifyControls := true
              // and actually refresh to show the first row
              // that matches the filter
              form.rowset.refreshControls()

          // clearFilter()
          case this.text == "Clear Filter"
              // reset text
              this.text := "Filter"
              // clear out the current filter ...
              form.rowset.clearFilter()
      endcase
      return
```

Before testing this, we need to do one more thing, which is to set the rowset's *filterOptions* property to allow as much flexibility as possible. To do this, click on the query icon on the form, in the inspector click on the *rowset* object, then the "I" button. For the rowset object, then click on *filterOptions* and select "3 - Match Partial and Ignore Case". If you do not do this, then the default for the filter is to match both the length and case, so the filter may not find a match easily.

Now that this is done, try it out. Try filtering on something you know exists, on something you know doesn't exist, etc. It works pretty well. Note that the Rowstate control automatically updates.

It should be noted that "Filter by Form" tends to be slow, as dBASE has to look at each field that is datalinked on the form. In addition, the condition that is created by dBASE is an "AND" condition only – if the user enters a value in two fields, the condition will always be "field1 = whatever was entered AND field2 = whatever was entered". You cannot use "OR" conditions. Other limitations include the fact that you can only have one condition per field. You might limit the use of this to forms where the user might enter a last name or postal code to find all possible matches.

While it seems like it should be useful, in real-world applications with hundreds of thousands of records, it may be worthwhile to put the effort into creating your own filter forms and using other methods to filter the data.

Locate by Form
The ability to locate a row in a table by form is similar to the way the filter-by-form works, but is also slightly different. A filter limits you to just the rows that match whereas locate finds the first row that matches, but no filter is applied to the data. This allows you to see data around the row that was found.

Just like the filter button shown above, the code is a bit complex, but this is still simplified quite a bit from the code in the dUFLP custom code.

Locate Button
We need to add the "Locate" button, so do the following steps:

- Drag a pushbutton from the Component Palette to the form and place it near the "Filter" button
- Change the name of the pushbutton to "LocateButton"
  - Click on the "Properties" tab in the inspector,
  - Find the "Name" property and click on it
  - Type "LOCATEBUTTON" and press the Enter key
- Change the text of the pushbutton to "Locate"
  - Find the *text* property and click on it
  - Type "Locate" and press the Enter key
- Find the *onClick()* event
  - Click on the "Events" tab in the inspector
  - Click on "onClick"
  - Click on the "Tool" button

Enter this code after the Function statement:

```
// here's where all the work starts:
do case
   // we're now in "locate by form" mode:
   case this.text == "Locate"
        this.text := "Run Locate"
        form.bookmark = form.rowset.bookmark()
        form.rowset.beginLocate()
```

```
        // we're in "Run" mode ...
   case this.text == "Run Locate"
        // if user hit 'run' but didn't
        // change anything on the form:
        if not form.rowset.modified
           this.text := "Locate"
           form.rowset.abandon()
           return
        endif

        // problem with doing a locate on
        // memo fields:
        try // the first 'try'
            // here's the search:
           form.rowset.notifyControls := false
           if not form.rowset.applyLocate()
               this.text := "Locate"
               try // second/nested try
                  form.rowset.goto( form.bookMark )
               catch ( exception e )
                  form.rowset.first()
               endtry
             msgbox( "No rows match the condition", "Locate error", 48 )
           else
               // we found a match ...
               // "Continue" text:
               this.text := "Continue Locate"
               // save *this* bookmark ...
               form.bookmark = form.rowset.bookmark()
           endif
        catch ( exception e )
           msgbox( "Cannot search in memo", "Locate error", 48 )
           form.rowset.goto( form.bookmark )
           this.text := "Locate"
        endtry // end of catch for memo

        form.rowset.notifyControls := true
        form.rowset.refreshControls()

    // we're "searching again"
    case this.text == "Continue Locate"
        // look for the next match:
        if not form.rowset.locateNext()
           form.rowset.goto( form.bookmark )
           msgbox( "No more rows match the condition", "Locate error",48)
           this.text := "Locate"
        else
           form.bookmark = form.rowset.bookmark()
        endif
   endcase
```

Just like with the filter, the *locateOptions* property of the rowset will affect your ability to find a matching row or rows in the rowset. And, just like the *filterOptions* property, setting the *locateOptions* property for the rowset to "3 - Match Partial and Ignore Case" will solve this and make it possible to find most matches.

The locate option is rather handy, but it has similar limitations to what were mentioned above with filters – if you need a more complex "locate" you would have to write your own code.

It should be noted that like "Filter by Form", "Locate by Form" tends to be slow and again in a real-world application you may want to find another means for doing this sort of thing.

After all that, hopefully you're starting to get a feel for how all this works.

One More Button – To Close the Form

There's only one more button needed, and that is a "close" button – it's not really necessary, but it can be useful. The user can close a form from the "x" button on the titlebar of your form. However, we'll throw this one in to be complete.

Close Button

We need to add the "Close" button, so do the following steps:

- Drag a pushbutton from the Component Palette to the form and place it near the "Locate" button
- Change the name of the pushbutton to "CloseFormButton"
  - Click on the "Properties" tab in the inspector,
  - Find the "Name" property and click on it
  - Type "CLOSEFORMBUTTON" and press the Enter key
- Change the text of the pushbutton to "Close Form"
  - Find the *text* property and click on it
  - Type "Close Form" and press the Enter key
- Find the *onClick()* event
  - Click on the "Events" tab in the inspector
  - Click on "onClick"
  - Click on the "Tool" button

Add the code shown below, and the form will be close to done.

```
function CLOSEBUTTON_onClick
    form.close()
    return
```

You could check the state of the rowset and if the user is in edit or append mode, ask if they want to save it. There's a lot more that you might want to do. This is just a beginning.

Form Cosmetics

Once you have the controls on your form and everything works pretty much the way you want it to, you should spend some time making the form look professional. You don't want the pushbuttons laying about all willy-nilly, for example. You might want to line them up (using the alignment buttons in the toolbar).

You could start working with colors and coming up with color schemes for your form(s) or think about whether you want to let your application take on the look of whatever theme (Windows XP) your users may be using for the operating system. However, if you are going to start doing that sort of thing, you may seriously want to wait until we get into working with custom forms and custom controls – it will make changes much easier. We'll discuss these in later chapters of the book.

For now, you have a nice form that allows your user to do much of what might be needed. Your form may not look exactly the same as mine (see below), but you get the idea.

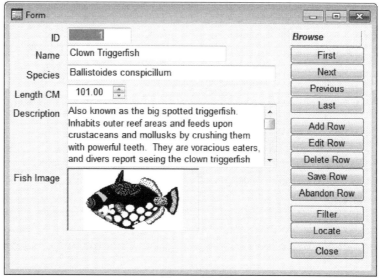

Figure 13-15

We could have set the *text* property of the form and a lot more, but we were focusing more on the OODML side of things. This form is pretty good, pretty flexible. But we will probably want to revisit it. There are some things that we might need that haven't been discussed yet. If you have the FishSample form running or in the Form Designer, you should close it.

Multi-Page Forms

It is possible to create forms that have controls on more than one page. What is a page? So far, we've been working with a single page of a form. A form can have many "pages" – sort of like with a book - there is something different on each page.

If you work with an install program, you will see this kind of behavior. You can go from one page to another, usually with a button that says "Next" and sometimes there is a "Back" or "Previous" button. dBASE has wizards, particularly in dQuery, that do this kind of thing.

For a data form, you might want one page to display a single record (as we just worked on) and a second page to search the data to find a specific record (we will return to this concept in a while). There are lots of reasons you might need a form to have multiple pages.

It sounds like it would be difficult or complex, right? Actually, it's quite simple. The form has a property called *pageno*. By changing the value of this property we will end up on a different page. Objects that can be placed on a form also have a *pageno* property, which is used to show what page they will display on. If you examine the source code for a single-page form, you will see that the controls do not have the *pageno* property streamed out.

However, if you place controls on a page that is not page 1, then the *pageno* property is streamed out to the source code. In other words, if you place a control on page 1, the *pageno* property is not needed, as the default page is 1. If you place a control on page 2, the *pageno* property is streamed out so that both the Form Designer and the internal mechanics of the software understand to place the control on page 2 rather than the default page of 1.

You can also place controls on page "0" – this means that they will appear on *all* pages of the form. This can be useful if you have a text control at the top of the form that you need to appear on all pages, or as we will see below, the Tabbox control.

There are a couple of methods of changing pages when a form is running, and we will look at those.

Changing Pages Using a TabBox Control

The TabBox Control is a dBASE control and is designed to allow you to create and manipulate multi-page forms easily.

> 📝 **NOTE**
> The Tabbox control is not limited to working with multiple page forms. It is possible to have multiple tabbox controls on the same form, with various code associated to do things. dBASE is a powerful language and if you can think of a use for the Tabbox control, use it for that purpose. However, it should be noted that the Tabbox control does not really have the "modern" look and feel to it and you may want to consider using Notebook controls (which are "containers", but more on them in a later chapter).

To see this, create a new form (double-click the first "Untitled" icon in the Navigator under the "Forms" tab). Set the form's *metric* property to "6 - Pixels".

On the "Standard" page of the Component Palette, you will see an icon for the TabBox. If you click on it and drag it to a form, a single-tab tabbox will be placed on the bottom of your form.

Figure 13-16

The TabBox should default to having a *pageno* property of 0. If it does not have this number, please set it in the Inspector now. You can assign a *name* to the TabBox if you want. The default is usually TabBox1, which is fine if you only have one of them on a form.

You need to set the tabs for this yourself. If you look at the *dataSource* property, you should see: ARRAY {"TabBox1"}.

This brings up a topic of interest that we will briefly examine (arrays are covered in more detail in later chapters):

Literal Arrays – The default array type for a TabBox is what is called a Literal Array. This is an array that may be defined with the visual designer. The one thing about it that is a little disconcerting is that it has no name. There is no way to refer to the contents of this array. In most cases, when using a TabBox, this is absolutely fine. However, you don't have to use a literal array if you don't want to. You can use a more standard dBASE Array instead (one with a name) – the only reason I can think of for doing this would be if you needed to know the text of the tab the cursor is currently on, but there could easily be other reasons.

The visual designers allow you to build your array through a really spiffy dialog box. To get to it, click on the tool icon next to the current array definition. You can add and remove and rearrange items quite easily with this dialog and when you're done the "OK" button will place the contents of the array on the form. The number of tabs on your tabbox is the same as the number of elements in the array.

For the purposes of the demonstration, delete "Tabbox1" as a value in this array and add "Page 1" and "Page 2" by following these instructions:

- With "Tabbox1" selected, click the "Delete" button.
- Click on the entryfield for "String", and type: Page 1
- Click the "Add" button
- Click on the entryfield for "String", and type: Page 2
- Click the "Add" button
- Click the "OK" button
- Click "OK" again on the first dialog

Note that the tabbox now shows two tabs, and they have the text we have given it. You can have as many tabs as you need on your form.

To make this example easier to see, we will place an object on each page of the form. By default the form designer places you on Page 1 of a form. So, let's place a text control on the page. Click on the text control so the handles turn white, delete the text there, and type: This is page 1. Your form should look like:

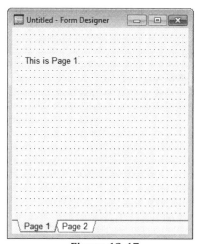

Figure 13-17

How do we get to "Page 2"? Well, in the Form Designer the tabbox is not functional (we have not hooked up code to do anything yet anyway). However, the Form Designer has its own toolbar and if you look there are some buttons specifically for switching pages of a form. If you hold your mouse over the two buttons that look like a piece of paper with arrow heads going left and right, you will see "Previous Form Page" and "Next Form Page". We want to go to the next form page, so click that button. This will place the form designer on page 2 of the form.

Notice that the text control we had placed on page 1 is not visible ... it shouldn't be. Let's drag another text control to page 2 of the form and change the text to say "This is Page 2".

Before we do anything else, you may want to save the form. One interesting "feature" of the Form Designer is that if you save a form, while on a page other than "1", dBASE will stream out the current page number as a property of the form. If we saved it right now, when the form was run it would open on page 2 of the form, which may not be desirable. Instead, you should generally make sure you are on page 1 of a form when you save it. Press ⌨Ctrl+⌨S and type "TabboxSample" for the filename.

The Tabbox's onSelChange Event
In the inspector, if you click on the events page, you should see the *onSelChange()* event. This event fires when the user clicks a tab on the tabbox and is the most important event associated with the Tabbox control.

Click on this event. Click on the tool button in the inspector for this event. The Form Designer will bring up the Source Code Editor, and place a heading for the event handler, and a place to put your own code:

```
function Tabbox1_onSelChange
```

In this event handler you will want to set the form's *pageno* to the current tab number. The current tab number property is *curSel*. The code might look like:

```
function Tabbox1_onSelChange
   form.pageno := this.cursel
   return
```

The reason to put this into its own event handling code is that you may wish to get more fancy (such things as perhaps checking to see which page is now the current one and setting specific values for objects on the form, maybe changing the form's rowset to a new one ... lots of possibilities spring to mind).

Test It
Let's test this form. First, make sure that you are starting on page 1, by going to the toolbar and selecting the "Previous Form Page" button (the last page we looked at was 2), or click on the form design surface (giving it focus) and go to the Inspector. Find the *pageno* property and set it to 1.

Then save (⌨Ctrl+⌨S) and run the form (click the "Run Form" button in the toolbar). Click on the two different tabs, and see that we can switch between pages easily.

Changing Pages Using PushButtons
While TabBoxes are a method of choice for most new applications, there are other methods of changing pages. Another method that can be quite effective is to use PushButtons. This method is commonly used for dialogs that need multiple pages, for example a Wizard style dialog.

If you drop a couple of pushbuttons on a form, you will need to set the *onClick* event handlers to handle changing page numbers. This is simple enough (example below).

One suggestion is to simply create an event for each that handles incrementing and decrementing the page number and then calls another routine to handle anything else that may need to be accomplished when you change pages (such as setting the focus to the appropriate object on the appropriate page).

If you have any forms running, close them and let's create a simple test form for this.

- Double click on the first "Untitled" under the "Forms" tab of the Navigator
- Set the form's *metric* property to "6 - Pixels".
- Drag two pushbuttons to the form, placing them toward the bottom of the page (you may want to resize the form a bit, that's up to you).
- For the first pushbutton,
  - Set the *name* property to "PreviousPageButton"
  - Set the *text* property to "Previous Page"
  - Set the *pageno* property to 0
  - Go to the "Events" tab in the Inspector and select *onClick*
  - Click the "Tool" button and set the code to look like:

```
function PreviousPage_OnClick
   if form.pageno > 1
      form.pageno--   // decrement the page number
   endif
return
```

- For the second pushbutton,
  - Set the *name* property to "NextPageButton"
  - Set the *text* property to "Next Page"
  - Set the *pageno* property to 0
  - Go to the "Events" tab in the Inspector and select *onClick*
  - Click the "Tool" button and set the code to look like:

```
function NextPage_OnClick
   if form.pageno < 3
      form.pageno++   // increment the page number
   endif
return
```

We're going to create a THREE page form, so on each of the three pages place a text control that shows the page number like we did with the Tabbox example.

The code for the event handlers checks to see if we are in the range of the pages – 1 to 3. If we are clicking on the next page button, and the page number is less than 3, we want to go to the next page. If we are clicking on the previous page button, and the page number is greater than 1, we want to go to the previous page. We could get fancier and add code to set the *enabled* property of the pushbuttons and so on.

Once you have the form designed, try running it and switching between pages using the pushbuttons.

Figure 13-18

Potential Problems

It is probably not a good idea to add data in other tables on other pages of a form if a master record on the first page has not been saved. One solution is to prevent users from changing pages until the master record on the first page (or wherever) has been saved by turning off the *enabled* property of a tabbox control (or if using pushbuttons to navigate, the pushbuttons involved) until the record has been saved.

When saving a form that uses multiple pages in the Form Designer, you may find that if you were working on a page other than page 1 when you saved the form that the page number you were working on got streamed out to your source code (the .WFM file). When you run the form the next time, you may not start on Page 1. The fix for this is to ensure that no matter what page you were working on, when the form opens, it starts on page 1. This is best done in an *onOpen()* event for the form (or perhaps an overridden *open()* method for the form):

```
PROCEDURE form_onOpen
    form.Tabbox1.curSel := 1 // this will fire the onSelChange
                             // event of the tabbox
    // any other code you need
return
```

Running Forms

Earlier in this chapter we discussed the "bootstrap" code that the form designer creates. This is one method of running a form, and is quite useful. You can test a form simply by double-clicking it in the Navigator window, or in the Command Window issuing a command such as:

```
do MyForm.wfm
```

However, in an application you will find that there are many times this can cause you some difficulty. How do you access that form in code that is not contained in the .WFM file? How do you communicate with a form, passing information to it? *(We will look at methods of communicating between forms in a bit.)* The problem is that there is no handy name reference that we can use for the form. As we discussed in Chapter 6, all objects have a name *(object reference variable)* that we can use. However, the bootstrap code uses a local object reference variable, which means that it is not available outside of that form's code.

There are better ways to instantiate and run a form, particularly within an application. For a few instances I find that I may still use the syntax given above, but for the most part the best thing to do is something along the following lines:

```
set procedure to MyForm.wfm
fMyForm = new MyFormForm()
fMyForm.open()
```

The "set procedure" statement ensures that the code in the .WFM file is available to be used.

fMyForm is a variable that is used to assign a name to a new instance of your form. As discussed in earlier chapters, this is a pretty standard way of creating an instance of an object and in this case we are creating an instance of your form. The "MyFormForm" bit is because if you create a form in the form designer named "MyForm", dBASE adds to the classname the word "Form", so while the filename may be "MyForm", the classname of the form is "MyFormForm".

The last line opens the form. You could close the form using:

```
fMyForm.close()
```

You could do a lot of other things with this. The important thing to note is that you can now reference the form until it is released from memory.

You can do the same thing with a modal form (dialog style):

```
set procedure to MyForm.wfm additive
fMyForm = new MyFormForm()
fMyForm.mdi := false
fMyForm.readModal()
```

(The form's mdi property <u>must</u> be false for readModal() to function – if it is not you will get an error message.)

ⓘ SUGGESTION

In order to avoid hard-coding a constant value like the last page number in your form directly, is to use a method of the form itself, used to display the highest page number that has any components on it:

```
form.pageCount()
```

To use this in the code for the NextPage button described above, try:

```
if form.pageno < form.pageCount()
```

The advantage to doing this is that if you add pages to the form later (or remove them) you do not have to update the code to handle it.

However, as noted elsewhere, once the call to the form's *readModal()* method is made, no code that may be in a program that is after that statement will be executed until the form is closed.

Communicating Between Forms

As your application(s) get more complicated, more forms get added and it starts to become necessary to pass information between forms, or make information available to more than one form. You may want to call a popup dialog (such as a calendar); or you may want to place a parent table on one form and a child table on another, ensuring the child table only uses the child rows that match the parent; you may need to create a lookup form and so on.

Passing Data to and Returning Data from a Dialog Form

We will take a brief look at this. As you work with dBASE more, you will find many ways to do what you need to do. To see how this works, we will create two forms, a "main" form and a dialog. One could consider these a parent form and a child form, but that can be confusing, particularly if you are using parent/child *data* as well.

For our example, we want to create a form that allows the user to select a row and then click a button to see other information about that specific item in a "popup" type form – a form that popups up at their request.

If you wish to follow along, close any open forms and go to the Navigator. Click the "Forms" tab and double-click the first "Untitled" icon. This will create a new form in the form designer. Set the form's *metric* property to "6 - Pixels". Now set the form's *text* property to "Fish Information" (without the quotes).

We are going to step back and use the Fish table again, but we will do something a little different here. We need to place a few of the fields from the Fish Table on this form, so with the Field Palette drag the "Name", "Species", "Length CM" and "Description" fields to the new form and spending a few minutes making it look nice – line up the controls, etc. Save this (Ctrl + S) as "FishMain.wfm".

You should have something that looks similar to:

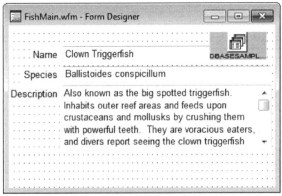

Figure 13-19

The next thing we need is a pushbutton that will call our detail form which is going to display more information. To do this, we need to place a pushbutton control on the form, so drag one from the Component Palette to below the Description of the fish.

Find the *text* property of the pushbutton and change it to read "View Image". Save the form again and exit the designer (⌃Ctrl+W), so we can create the child form. The reason for this is that we need to know certain things, such as the name of the child form before we can create the actual code that communicates between the two forms.

Create another form by using the same method we did before. Set the form's *metric* property to pixels and this time set the form's *mdi* property to false. Find the form's *autoCenter* property and set that to *true.* Find the *text* property of the form and type "Fish Image" (without the quotes).

Drag the Fish table to the design surface from the Navigator as we did before. Set the rowset's *indexName* property to "ID" (click on the FISH1 object, find *rowset* in the inspector, click on the "I" button).

We are going to display some information from the Fish table, in a "read-only" mode, specifically the Name (so the user knows which fish it is we're looking at) and the image of the fish. Normally we would display the name field in an entryfield, but this time we're going to use a text control. Drag a text control to the design surface from the Component Palette. Set the *fontSize* property to 12 and the *fontBold* property to *true.* Find the *alignHorizontal* property and set it to "1 - Center". And finally, change the *text* to say "Fish Name Here". This is a placeholder that will change when the form is actually run.

Next drag the "Fish Image" field to the form, then delete the label that is placed by it – we don't really need it for this form. Find the *alignment* property and set it to "3 - Keep Aspect Stretch", then resize the image, placing it approximately center under the text. Find the *enabled* property and set it to *false.* (The reason for this is that if it is *enabled*, dBASE will try to give it focus and it will look funny. We don't need the user to interact with it so it's better to bypass that now.)

Press ⌃Ctrl+S to save it as "FishImage". It should look something like:

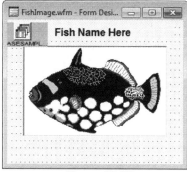

Figure 13-20

The next thing we need is a pushbutton to close the form (making it *very* obvious to the user). I would place it under the image. Change the *text* property of the pushbutton to "Close Form", find the *onClick* event in the Inspector and enter:

```
{; form.close()}
```

(Press the Enter key after you type the above, because if you do not, it may not be saved.)

For appearance' sake, I would shift all the controls up (over the query and database objects – these don't display when the form is run anyway), then reduce the height of the form. You should end up with something that looks like:

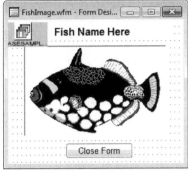

Figure 13-21

The next thing we need to do is to tell dBASE what to do when this form is opened. We are going to do that by overriding the form's *readModal* method. Why this one? We want this form to *always* be a dialog – the user must close it before doing anything with the form that closed it. The child form relies on the main or parent form telling it what the ID is, so that this form can display the information associated with the ID field. You can add code to make sure that this form does not actually open unless a value is passed to it.

In order to do what we need to do, click on the form surface in the Form Designer so that the form has focus. In the Inspector, click on the "Methods" tab, select the *readModal* method and click the tool button. This will place you in the Source Code Editor. Type the following:

```
function form_readModal
   // This code will execute before the form opens:

   // First check to see if the custom property
   // "FishID" exists:
   if type( "form.FishID" ) == "U"
      // if it doesn't, then we inform the user, and
      // don't open the form!
      msgbox( "This form must be called from FishMain.wfm",;
            "Form Error", 16 )
      return
   endif

   // if here, we have a value — for sake of brevity
   // in our code, we are assuming it is a correct TYPE:
   if form.rowset.findKey( form.FishID )
      // assign the value of the name field to the text control
      // for the fish that matches the ID passed ...
      form.Text1.text := form.rowset.fields["Name"].value
   else
      msgbox( "FISHID '"+form.FishID+"' not found!",;
            "Form Error", 16 )
      return
   endif
return FORM::readModal()
```

This code will check if it is opened modally (using the *readModal* method) if the property "form.FishID" was created. If not, it will return an error and then not open the form.

Otherwise, it will try to find the value in the custom property and set the *text* property of the text control to the fish name field. It will automatically update the image because that control is dataLinked to the "Fish Image" field. If no match is found, an error will be displayed and the form will not open.

Now we need to save this form and close it (`Ctrl`+`W`), then open the "FishMain" form again in the Form Designer. (Click on it in the Navigator and right click, selecting "Design Form".)

Click on the pushbutton (that says "View Image") then using the Inspector, find the *onClick* event and click the tool button. We need to add some specific code for this:

```
function PUSHBUTTON1_onClick
   // This code will open the FishImage form,
   // pass the ID field to the custom property
   // FishID of that form, and then open the
   // form:
   local fImage
   set procedure to FishImage.wfm
   fImage = new FishImageForm()
   fImage.FishID = form.rowset.fields["ID"].value
   fImage.readModal()

   // when the user closes the modal dialog:
   fImage.release()
   close procedure FishImage.wfm
return
```

So what does this code do? It opens the FishImage form file with the "set procedure" statement, then assigns an object reference "fImage" to the form. Then we create the custom property "FishID" of the child form, then open the form with the *readModal* method. If you continue looking at the code, you will see we release the form (fImage.release()), then close the procedure file. How can we get away with doing this? Because when we open a form with *readModal()*, no code that is listed after it will execute until the form is closed! So we are including some cleanup by releasing the form and closing the procedure file *when* the form is closed, and not until that time.

Save the changes we've made and then run the form. It should look something like:

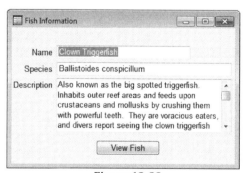

Figure 13-22

Using the toolbar at the top of the dBASE screen, navigate a few rows, then click on the "View Image" button. You should see something like:

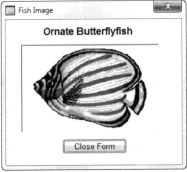

Figure 13-23

When you close this form, you can move on. You should close the main form as well.

It Is Important That You Understand ...

It is important that you understand a few concepts from this exercise.

Executing the Constructor Code

When the pushbutton on "FishMain" is executed, the third command is:

```
fImage = new FishImageForm()
```

This command runs the entire constructor code for the form and at this point *all* of the properties of the form are accessible to you. This is called *instantiating* the form. We could modify a lot of things about the form before it is opened!

You can create new *(custom)* properties (which is what we did) before the form is opened. We could even have done more with this by doing the search in the code in the main form, basically not having any code execute in the lookup form. There are many ways to do things in dBASE and this example is just one.

Creating and Destroying the Form (Object)

The code to create the form object is not the same act as opening the form. The command:

```
fImage = new FishImageForm()
```

creates the form object. But as noted above, it does not actually open the form. The same is true of closing the form – it is still in memory if it is closed. It is just not being displayed at this time. So issuing:

```
form.close()
```

as a command does not release the form from memory – it is still there. We could re-open it. We could close it, change some properties and open it again. When you are really done with the form, in a situation like this – it is a good idea to not only close it, but to release it from memory or "destroy" it:

```
fImage.release()
```

In addition, the procedure file will remain open, so it's probably a good idea to make sure you close the procedure file:

```
close procedure FishImage.wfm
```

What Can This Be Used For?

There are many ways you can use the type of code we looked at in this example. As examples go, it's probably not the most complete; however you could do a wide variety of things with this. You could call a Calendar form from a pushbutton and assign the value returned from the calendar to an entryfield or spinbox that was dataLinked to a date field. You could display a child row (or rows) from a parent/child related set of tables; even allow the user to edit the data in the child row(s). The important things to understand from this exercise are that you can have forms communicate, execute code in another form before the form is opened and pass information back and forth between the two.

Naming Your Controls

As we have only briefly discussed this issue, we ought to discuss it a bit here. Consider this to be advice that you can ignore if you choose.

The more complex your forms become, the more controls you will have on a form. If you have a large table you may have many entryfields or other datalinked controls. If what is streamed out to your form is ENTRYFIELD1, ENTRYFIELD2, etc., which is the default in dBASE, you will find that it may get hard to know which entryfield you need to reference in any code you use.

It is, in general, a good idea to name your controls by changing the *name* property. This allows you to create names such as:

FirstNameEntryfield
LastNameEntryfield
Address1Entry
InvoiceNumberSpinbox

And so on. By using the type of the control as part of the name, you make it easier to know what the object is. This is important because different controls have different properties, events and methods. If you just assume everything is an entryfield, you may be in for a surprise somewhere down the road when writing and testing your code. This also allows you to perhaps have: "FirstNameText" and "FirstNameEntryfield", where if you used "FirstName" and tried to use that for more than one control, you will be in for a rude surprise as dBASE tells you that you cannot have two controls with the same name.

Tab Order of Controls

One thing should be discussed before we complete our look at forms. This is an important topic, often ignored until the end user starts working with a form and wondering why?

The issue at hand is the order in which the user can "tab" from control to control. Some users just use the mouse and click on each item on a form. However, many users like to use the tab and back-tab keys to move back and forth between controls on a form. The question becomes, what sequence is used by dBASE for the tab order?

By default dBASE uses the order in which controls are streamed out to the source code (the .WFM file). How does dBASE determine this order? Normally this is the order in which you placed controls onto the form. What often happens is that you layout your form and then either you or the user realize you needed to add something to the form. So you come back later, add that control, readjust the position of the controls on the form and then move on.

However, the user then finds that when tabbing from one control to another they are not necessarily moving in a logical sequence!

In order to see this, we will do something pretty simple. Let's create a new form (double-click on the first "(Untitled)" icon in the "Forms" page of the Navigator).

- Drag an entryfield control to the top of the form. Set the entryfield's *value* property to "First Control".
- Drag a second entryfield control to the form, about halfway down. Set the *value* property to "Third Control".
- Drag a third entryfield control to the form, and place it between the two controls, and set the *value* property to "Second Control". *(Yes, I had you name these the way I did intentionally!)*
- Widen the controls a bit so that you can see the values.

You should have a form that looks something like:

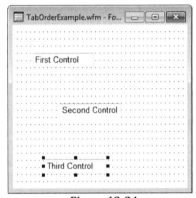

Figure 13-24

Save it (⌨Ctrl+⌨S) and run it (use the "lightning bolt" toolbutton). By default the "First Control" entryfield will have focus. Use the tab key noting that rather than jumping to the obvious "Second Control", you jump to "Third Control". Now use the tab key again and notice you jump from "Third Control" to "Second Control".

As mentioned previously, this is due to the sequence the controls were placed on the form. Bring this back into the designer (using the "Design Form" toolbutton).

So the question is, how do you put the controls in the right sequence? One solution is to simply make sure you have everything in the right order in the first place, which is not always possible. Any developer who has worked in the industry for any length of time knows that either he adds new controls after he thought he was done, or the end-user realizes that something is needed and asks for the new control(s) to be added. There are ways to deal with this.

One way to deal with this is to open the form in the Source Code Editor and literally move blocks of code around to get everything in sequence. However, this is unwieldy and not recommended. dBASE has a nice solution for this built in to the IDE.

With the form in the Form Designer, select the "Layout" menu. At the bottom you will see "Set Component Order ...". Select this and you should see a dialog like:

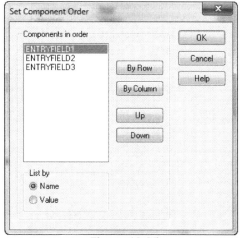

Figure 13-25

If you look at the form itself (move the dialog if needed) you will see that dBASE shows a number by each control on the form. As you move the controls up and down in this dialog, the numbers on the form will change. This is a pretty simple form, as you can see. What we want to do is move "ENTRYFIELD3" above "ENTRYFIELD2". To do this, the simplest way is to click on "ENTRYFIELD3" and drag it up. You can also click on it and click the "Up" button. This should look like:

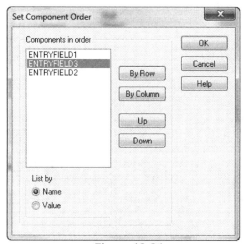

Figure 13-26

When you click the "OK" button, you will have told dBASE that if you save this form, to stream out the controls in the sequence shown, which means that when you run the form again, the Tab order will make more sense to your user(s). You can test this by saving the form and running it. Once you see how this works, go ahead and close the form.

The "Tab Order" is also often called by developers the "Z-Order", which is an oblique reference to the mathematical concept of X, Y and Z to reference dimensions, where "X" is typically the width, "Y" is typically the height, and "Z" is typically the *depth*. In this case, the "depth" is the order in which the user moves through the controls (and the order in which the code is streamed out to the form file).

If you examine the dialog carefully, you can see where naming your controls (changing the *name* property) can start to become very useful when developing an application!

Some Notes on Tab Order

There are some controls and properties of controls that you should be aware of, specifically with regards to the Tab or Z-Order.

Radiobuttons

Radiobuttons rely on the *group* property, as well as the z-order. If any control gets "between" them in the z-order, it can throw off the grouping of the radiobuttons. For example, you might have six radiobuttons on a form and a text control between them, perhaps to explain one of the radiobuttons in more detail. If you placed the first three radiobuttons on the form, then the text control, then finally the last three radiobuttons, dBASE will consider this to be two groups of three, rather than one group of six.

You can solve this by placing the radiobuttons on the form first and then adding the text control later. You can also work with the tab order as noted above, however you will then want to go to all but the first radiobutton and set the *group* property to *false*.

The final solution *only* works in dBASE PLUS 2.5 and later. The radiobutton's *group* property is normally a logical value (*true* or *false*). However, in Plus 2.5 and later releases, you can place a character string there, naming the group. However, you have to change this property for each radiobutton in the group. This is done by changing the *group* property's "Type" to "Character" (in the Inspector, select the "T" button), then change the value of the property to something like "MyRadioButtons". Do the same for each radioButton in the group of radioButtons, and you should be fine. You may want to set the first radiobutton's *value* property to *true*, as well.

Rectangles and Shapes

Rectangle and Shape objects are often used to enhance the appearance of a form. They need to be *behind* controls normally, as they are often used in the background and if they are not *behind* those controls, then you won't see the controls you might need. In addition to the dialog we looked at previously, the "Layout" menu has a really useful set of options above it that can be used to move things back and forth in the z-order, so that they appear as needed. You can overlap controls, but if the z-order is wrong, dBASE will place the rectangle or shape over the top of what you placed on it. In the designer, if you click on "Layout", notice the options "Bring to Front", "Send to Back", "Bring Closer", "Send Farther". The first two deal with moving something to the very front or the very back of a stack of objects. The last two deal with one layer at a time. If you use these objects on your forms, you should experiment with this functionality.

While the menu options mentioned here can be used for all controls, I find that most of the time I never need it unless I am layering controls on a form, which I don't do all that often, except with rectangles or shapes.

The tabStop Property

Interactive controls have a *tabStop* property – this defaults to a value of *true*. You can actually take a control out of the tab order completely by setting the *tabStop* property to *false*.

The enabled Property

If a control has the *enabled* property set to *false*, then it cannot get focus and by definition is out of the tab order.

The when() Event

Rather than using the *enabled* property as noted above, there are times you may want to use the *when()* event, with a codeblock such as {; return false } to disable the control (usually if you want to take over the appearance of the control, rather than letting Windows do it). This will also remove a control from the tab order.

The speedBar Property

Pushbuttons have a *speedBar* property – this takes them out of the tab order, which is useful if you need a pushbutton to leave focus on a control, but do some specific code, such as call a dialog form. The property defaults to *false*, setting this to *true* will take the pushbutton out of the tab order.

Adding Help to Your Forms

As a developer you will want to decide the best way to create help for your applications. There have been many discussions in the dBASE newsgroups over the years on tools to create standard Windows style help.

With build 2.61.4, the developers of dBASE have added a *contextHelp* property to the form object itself. The default for this property is *false*. When set to *true*, a button will display on the titlebar of the form, to the left of the form's close button, showing a question mark (?).

When a user clicks on the question mark button on the titlebar, the mouse pointer changes and the user can then click on a form component. If the component has an *onHelp()* event handler, that event will fire.

Windows Form Control Appearance

In build 2.61.4 the developers of dBASE added a new property called *systemTheme* to the following:

- _app.Framewin
- The Form class
- The Subform class
- All form control classes that have their own window

What does this mean? When the *systemTheme* property is set to *true* (the default setting) and when running on Windows XP, Vista, or Windows 7 provided a manifest file installed that instructs Windows to load the version 6 common controls, windows and their controls are painted using the current Visual Style set in the operating system.

When the *systemTheme* property is *false*, the version 5 common controls are used and painted using the classic Windows appearance.

The best part of this is that as most controls use their own windows, if you prefer the classic appearance for individual controls, you can set this property either on an individual form, or in a custom class definition for that control.

Forms and User BDE Aliases

One issue that might come up with an application that uses forms with the *open()* method and using the new User BDE Aliases is separating your forms from each other. What do I mean by that? If you open a form more than once in the same session, navigating in one instance of the form will navigate in both to the same record.

In a real application this is less than optimal. Your users really would expect that if you navigate in one form, the other form would not navigate until you did so there.

To make this work you would want to create a session object for the form and then hook up the data to the session. However, if your BDE Alias is a User BDE Alias it belongs by definition to the default session of dBASE (_app.session).

This topic is covered in a lot of detail in Chapter 10. If we used the form created earlier in this chapter "FishSample.wfm", we would need the session object, and more. Modifying the source code (enter the following in the Command Window):

```
copy file FishSample.wfm to FishSampleSession.wfm
modify command FishSampleSession.wfm
```

We would need to insert a session object thusly (add the code in bold):

```
class FishSampleSessionForm of FORM
   with (this)
      metric = 6        // Pixels
      height = 339.0
      left = 255.0
      top = 94.0
      width = 512.0
      text = ""
   endwith

   this.SESSION1 = new SESSION()
   this.SESSION1.parent = this
   with (this.SESSION1)
      left = 200
      top = 5
   endwith

   this.DBASESAMPLES1 = new DATABASE()
   this.DBASESAMPLES1.parent = this
   with (this.DBASESAMPLES1)
      open = class::DBASESAMPLES1_OPEN
      left = 304.0
      top = 5.0
      session = form.session1
      databaseName = "DBASESAMPLES"
      active = true
   endwith

   this.FISH1 = new QUERY()
   this.FISH1.parent = this
   with (this.FISH1)
      left = 304.0
      top = 5.0
      session = form.session1
      database = form.dbasesamples1
      sql = "select * from fish.dbf"
      active = true
   endwith

   // after the rest of the constructor code, you need to add
```

```
// the following overridden method of the database object:
function DATABASESAMPLES1_open
    this.parent.session1.addalias( "DBASESAMPLES", "DBASE",;
        "PATH:C:\Users\Ken\AppData\Local\dBASE\PLUS\Samples")
    return DATABASE::open()
```

Currently the designer surfaces (Form Designer, Report Designer, etc.) do not recognize the session object's *addAlias()* method, which is why we are using the database object's Open method to set the User BDE Alias.

⚙ WARNING

The design surfaces in dBASE (Form Designer, Report Designer, etc.) currently are streaming out a *tempPath* property for the session object that can cause some problems with your application. Removing the *tempPath* property from the constructor code for the session object resolves the issue, but it means any time you modify the form *(or other object such as a Report or Query)*, you may have to do this. The R&D team at dBASE knows about this, and have promised to fix it for the next major release of dBASE.

Before Moving On To A New Chapter ...

If you've been following along and doing the exercises associated with the text, you should issue the following command in the Command Window:

```
close database
```

If you do not, then the next time you open dBASE, the DBASESAMPLES database may be open and when you create a new table, you may find it being saved in the wrong place, or if you try to open a table you may not be pointing to the correct folder on your hard drive, causing some confusion.

Summary

We've covered a *lot* of ground in this chapter, but we haven't covered all the possibilities of what can be done with forms in dBASE PLUS. The next chapter will discuss the various stock controls in an "overview" type fashion – in other words without a lot of demonstration going into all of the properties, events and methods for these controls.

We learned the differences between single-document interface (SDI) and multiple document interface (MDI), as well as the basics of using the form designer to create forms, forms that have controls datalinked to a table, multiple page forms and the basics of communicating between forms. Now we will move on and learn more about what can be done with forms.

One method of learning more about forms is simply to work with them, trying various techniques. You can get a lot of help if you are unsure how to do something in the dBASE newsgroups *(see the appendices …)*.

Chapter 14: Stock Form Controls

In the previous chapter we looked at creating forms, and various techniques for using forms. But we only looked at a small fraction of the form controls that are part of dBASE.

In the Form Designer, the Component Palette gives you a listing of what are called the "Stock" controls – these are the controls that are always available, as they are "built in" to dBASE. As we will find in later chapters, there are custom controls which are (usually) built from the stock classes, and so on. For now we are going to concentrate on the Stock Controls.

This chapter is only going to give an overview of the Stock Controls, because there are many properties, events and methods, and many ways to use these controls. I could write a whole book just about working with these. Instead, we are going to spend some time looking at some of the controls briefly, some ideas about ways to use them and some features that are the most useful. In addition, some of the controls that appear on the Component Palette will not be discussed in this chapter – keep in mind that this book is aimed at beginning developers and there are some controls that even advanced developers use seldom, if at all.

After going through this chapter, you may want to do some experimentation with some of the controls you are already using, see what you can do with them and maybe even change some of them to other controls you have learned about here.

Windows Themes and Other Changes

When the first edition of this book was released, dBASE Plus 2.5 was fairly new and some enhancements that were in development at that time were released in a new build of dBASE called 2.6. Some of those enhancements had to deal with the method used by dBASE's visual controls for forms in recognizing and using, by default, the appearance of the Themes built into Windows XP. This is done, among other things, through the automatic inclusion of a "manifest" file, which is used by many Windows applications to tell them to recognize the Windows XP Themes. The developers at dBASE, LLC have been testing dBASE Plus under Windows 7.

What does this mean to you, as a dBASE developer? It means that under Windows XP and probably under Windows Vista, your controls may not look the same (and in the case of some properties may not act the same) as they do under earlier operating systems such as Windows 95, Windows 98, Windows ME ...

You have two choices. The first is the easiest - let your applications use the Windows Themes when run on operating systems such as XP or Vista. The second might mean doing something such as deleting the Manifest file (or not deploying it with your applications), or working around these issues in other ways. For example, the pushbutton class in dBASE Plus 2.6 and later, has a property called *systemTheme* which, if set to *false*, can be used to tell dBASE to ignore the XP Theme.

I am spending so much time on this because it affects the examples in this and later chapters of this book. If you read the first edition of this book, you will find the examples are a little different in places, because frankly I think that using the Theme is a good thing to do - your client may have spent some time customizing the appearance of their Theme and having your application take on the appearance of their Theme will make you look like a superstar - with little or no effort on your part. The controls that currently have the greatest appearance difference are pushbuttons, rectangles, and notebook controls. You will undoubtedly see some minor differences in other controls, but these are the big ones.

You will find a chapter on the dBASE grid class after this one, because this control is very important to a developer. I will attempt to show various techniques and combinations of techniques in that chapter that I couldn't do by simply including the grid in this chapter.

Exercises

As with other chapters in this book, there are plenty of "follow-along" exercises here. As this chapter is concerned with the form controls and part of the functionality of these form controls is the ability to datalink them to fields in a table, you may benefit from creating and running the following program. It will create three tables and populate them with data so that they can be used for the examples. Some of the fields are a bit silly perhaps *(meaning they probably would not be used in a real-world application in this combination)*, but they should let us see how things work.

To create the program, in the Command Window, type:

```
create command MakeChapter14Tables
```

When the Source Code Editor comes up, type the following:

```
/*
   Create tables used in Chapter 14 of Ken's dBASE Programming book
   for the purpose of showing how to use stock form controls in
   dBASE PLUS.
*/

// Check to see if the table exists:
if file( "AddressBook.dbf" )
   // delete it so we can  start over:
   drop table AddressBook
endif

// localSQL create table command:
create table AddressBook (;
            FirstName       char( 15 ),;
            LastName        char( 20 ),;
            Address1        char( 25 ),;
            Address2        char( 25 ),;
            City            char( 30 ),;
            StateProv       char(  3 ),;
            PostalCode      char( 10 ),;
            Country         char(  3 ),;
            Phone           char( 14 ),;
            Business        boolean,;
            Notes           blob( 10, 1 ),;
            Birthday        date,;
            FavoriteFlavor char( 25 );
                       )

// OODML method of creating an index:
local i
i = new DBFIndex()
```

```
i.expression := "upper( LastName )+upper( FirstName )"
i.indexName  := "Name"
_app.databases[1].createIndex( "AddressBook", i )

// XDML is faster for some things:
use AddressBook
// first row:
append blank
replace FirstName       with  "Fred"
replace LastName        with  "Smith"
replace Address1        with  "1234 First Street"
replace City            with  "Testville"
replace StateProv       with  "CA"
replace PostalCode      with  "99999-9999"
replace Country         with  "USA"
replace Phone           with  "(999) 999-9999"
replace Business        with false
// this should be one single line in the program:
replace Notes           with  "Fred is an old family friend, his wife's
name is Judy. No children at this time."
replace Birthday        with {03/31/1963}
replace FavoriteFlavor with  "Chocolate"
// Second row
append blank
replace FirstName       with  "Joe"
replace LastName        with  "Jones"
replace Address1        with  "111 Main St."
replace Address2        with  "Box 5678"
replace City            with  "Somecity"
replace StateProv       with  "OR"
replace PostalCode      with  "88888-8888"
replace Country         with  "USA"
replace Phone           with  "(888) 888-9999"
replace Business        with true
replace Notes           with ;
        "Joe's business needs some help, and he contacted me ..."
replace Birthday        with {07/15/1960}
replace FavoriteFlavor with  "Macadamia Nut"
// close the table
use

// ----- create two lookup tables, without all the data that
//        might normally be in them:

if file( "StateProv.dbf" )
   // delete it so we can  start over :
   drop table StateProv
endif

create table StateProv (;
        Code     char(3),;
        StateProv char( 30 ) )

i = new DBFIndex()
i.expression := "upper( StateProv )"
i.indexName  := "StateProv"
_app.databases[1].createIndex( "StateProv", i )
```

```
use StateProv
append blank
replace Code      with  "CA"
replace StateProv with  "California"
append blank
replace code      with  "OR"
replace StateProv with  "Oregon"
append blank
replace code      with  "WA"
replace StateProv with  "Washington"
use
// normally we would add all 50 states in the US, possibly
// the provinces in Canada, etc. We're keeping it simple

if file( "Country.dbf" )
   // delete it so we can start over :
   drop table Country
endif

create table Country (;
            Code      char(3),,;
            Country   char( 30 ) )

i = new DBFIndex()
i.expression := "upper( Country )"
i.indexName  := "Country"
_app.databases[1].createIndex( "Country", i )

use country
append blank
replace Code     with  "USA"
replace Country with  "United States of America"
append blank
replace Code     with  "CAN"
replace Country with  "Canada"
use
// as with the StateProv table, we're keeping this simple ...
// end of program Chapter14Tables
```

Double-check your work, then save the program by typing ⌨Ctrl+⌨W. Try running it. If you have any errors try to fix them by comparing against the program listing here. If you run this without errors you will end up with three tables, which will be used for many of the examples throughout the rest of this chapter.

Common Properties, Events and Methods

The stock controls have some common properties, events and methods that are available to most or all of these controls. These include such things as the *anchor* property (used to "anchor" a control to a part of a form – top, bottom, left, right, etc.); mouse events such as *onLeftMouseUp()*, etc.. Most of these are pretty easy to decipher, but the best way to see if they are available is to look at the properties, events and methods in the Inspector, or to examine what is listed in the online help for a specific control. You shouldn't assume these will be associated with the control you are using, because they may not be. For example, a line object does not have any of the mouse events or the *hWnd* property because it is not a standard "window".

A Brief Overview of the Stock User-Interface Controls

The rest of this chapter is a brief overview of the various stock controls with an attempt to give some idea what they can be used for, as well as creating an example form that uses most of the controls. Some of the controls have more information because either we have discussed and used some of these controls in earlier chapters and so they don't need as much discussion here, or they are fairly complex and need more discussion.

Text

The Text control is designed to place text on a form for whatever purpose. It can be formatted in several ways, including the standard boldface, underline, etc. The more useful aspect of the Text control is that it can be used with some basic HTML tags *(some tags are not recognized)* so that part of the text can be formatted one way, part of it another. The screen below is an extreme example of some of what can be done with a Text control using HTML tags:

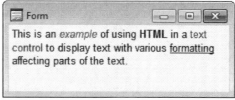

Figure 14-1

The actual *text* property of this control looks like:

```
'This is an <i><font color= red >example</font></i> of using <b>HTML</b>
in a <font color= blue >text control</font> to display text with various
<u>formatting</u> affecting parts of the text.'
```

If you understand HTML, this can be very useful for a Text control. However, because of the HTML interpreter, the Text control has a bit of a memory overhead that can cause some application slow-down if you use a *lot* of text on your forms.

In many cases, as the use of a Text control is used for things such as the name of a field on a form, you may want to consider using the TextLabel control instead, which does not understand HTML – this means that the HTML interpreter is not loaded for each control. The basic formatting that you have with the Text control still exists for a TextLabel, the only real difference is the lack of HTML. So you can change the properties *fontName*, *fontSize*, *fontBold*, and so on for the TextLabel control.

There are some other differences – you can rotate a Text control in 90° increments which you cannot do with a TextLabel control; there are some properties used in reports such as *suppressIfBlank*, not available to TextLabel controls, and so on.

What Do You Use It For?

Text and TextLabel controls (see below) are used to label items on a form, explain to a user what the form does, put titles on forms and so on.

Example

To get started with our examples throughout this chapter, if you created and ran the program given at the beginning of the chapter, you will have some tables. We will use those for many examples here, but before we get to anything dealing with the data in those tables, let's create a sample form.

Go to the Navigator in dBASE PLUS, find the "Forms" tab and click on it, then double-click the first "(Untitled)" icon. This will start the Form Designer.

Set the form's *metric* property to "6 - Pixels", and the form's *text* property to "Chapter 13, Example 1", and then follow along:

- Place a text control on the form, and set the following properties:

Anchor	2 - Top
alignHorizontal	1 - Center
name	TitleText
fontSize	14
borderStyle	1 - Raised
	(If you set the borderStyle property, the border property is set to true automatically)
colorNormal	Blue/BtnFace
height	28
text	Chapter 14, Example 1

- Save the form with `Ctrl`+`S`, and call it "Chapter14Example1".

You have just placed a text control on a form, and set a variety of properties. There are of course many others that you might want to set, this is enough to get you started. You should have a form that looks something like:

Figure 14-2

TextLabel

The TextLabel control is similar to the Text control noted above, but the TextLabel does not have an HTML interpreter in it. If you were to use a TextLabel control and place the same text as shown above in Figure 14-1, in the *text* property you would see the HTML tags displayed in the text.

This control was created because of the HTML interpreter's overhead with standard Text controls. It is recommended when designing forms that rather than using the Text control for field labels, you use the TextLabel control instead. With the exception of the HTML interpreter, these two controls are pretty much the same, although the Text control does have some extra properties that have very specific uses for reports and such.

Example
We will come back to using TextLabels in a moment, so hang in there.

Entryfield

The Entryfield control is the basic interface when working with data and obtaining information from a user. It is what it sounds like, a place to enter data.

Figure 14-3

An Entryfield can be datalinked to a field and it can have some editing options applied to it (using the *picture* and *function* properties).

The *dataLink* property is used to link an entryfield (or other controls with this property) to a field in a table. There are a few things you should be aware of:

- Numeric values are handled differently in dBASE PLUS from version 2.2 on to the current release, than in earlier versions of dBASE. The following should be kept in mind *(these changes affect Spinboxes and the cells of a Grid control as well)*:
- Numeric values now start entering data from the left of the decimal point, much like calculators and a variety of software. If you type the decimal, the cursor jumps to the right of the decimal point and data entry goes to the right.
- Numeric values are left justified in the entryfield (or spinbox) unless you set a *picture*. In older versions of the software numeric values were right justified in the entryfield/spinbox/etc.
- Zero values will appear as '.00' when editing. Null values will show an empty entryfield, although if a decimal point is defined, that will appear. (i.e., if your entryfield is datalinked to a numeric field with decimal values). What is meant by "when editing" is when the user is in either append or edit mode, the entryfield has focus. When the entryfield does not have focus, zero values should appear as '0.00' (unless a picture or function is defined, in which case the picture and/or function will take effect as soon as the cursor exits the entryfield).
- It is a good idea to set the *picture* property (ex. "9999.99", if your numeric field is defined as width of 7 with two decimal places, for example). If you use a picture without any decimals (values to right of the decimal point), i.e., "999" and the value is zero, you will see a zero.
- When you are adding or entering numeric data that has been formatted with the picture and/or function properties these will disappear when the entryfield has focus (while

modifying the data), and once the entryfield loses focus the data will be formatted appropriately.

- The entryfield's *selectAll* property will act like always – if the property is *true* (the default state) then tabbing to an entryfield will highlight everything and if the user types, whatever is contained in the entryfield will be overwritten, and entry will start at the decimal point (numbers will move left) as described above.
- If the *selectAll* property is *false*, tabbing to the entryfield will not highlight what is in the entryfield. The cursor will start at the left of the entryfield, and the user may need to delete numbers in the entryfield.
- If the user clicks on the entryfield with the mouse, the cursor will appear where they clicked, no matter the state of the *selectAll* property.

What Do You Use It For?

Entryfield controls are most commonly used to link to fields in a table, or to obtain input from a user (you might need to ask for a userid, for example), then act upon it. As we saw in earlier chapters of this book, if an entryfield is datalinked to a field in a table, (the *dataLink* property is set to a field), then updates to the data are handled by mechanisms associated with the rowset, and other data controls.

If you do not wish to (or need to) dataLink to a field in a table, then you will need to consider the *value* property.

Example

Coming back to the example form (Chapter 14, Example 1), we can use Entryfields for quite a few of the fields in the Address table we created at the beginning of this chapter. We could do this by using the Field Palette, but once you start looking at working with Custom Controls, you will find you may not want to do that, so we're going to start you in that direction now (start with "good habits").

To actually work with the data in a table, we need to make the table available to the form and the Form Designer. So, the simplest thing if you started the example earlier, is to go to the Navigator window (if you can't see it, click on the "Window" menu and select "Navigator" from the list) and click on the "Tables" tab. Drag the "AddressBook" table to the form.

- In the Inspector, find the *rowset* property of the query object ("ADDRESSBOOK1") and click on the Inspect ("I") button. Change the following:

      indexName   "NAME"

Click on the Form to give it focus, and in the Inspector find the form's *onOpen* event. Click the tool button and enter the code shown between the Function form_onOpen and the Return lines:

```
function form_onOpen
   // start at the first row:
   form.rowset.first()
return
```

This will ensure that when the form runs, you are on the first row to start.

In the past we have dragged fields to the design surface from the Fields Palette. Now we will do it a little differently – the reason? So we have more control over what happens and to get you used to setting specific properties yourself. When you design your forms for your own applications you obviously are free to do as you will.

Follow along with the following:

- Place a TextLabel control on the design surface, and set the following properties:

  text   Name:
  alignHorizontal   2 - Right

- Place an Entryfield control on the design surface to the right of the TextLabel control we just placed there, and set the following properties:

  dataLink   FIRSTNAME field

  (Click on the dataLink property, click the tool button, select the FIRSTNAME field and click "OK" – dBASE will stream out something that looks like:

  form.addressbook1.rowset.fields[firstname])

  name   FNameEntryfield
  width   140
  colorHighlight   WindowText/0x80ffff

  (This will give a yellow background when the control has focus, making it easier to tell where the user is)

- We need to do pretty much the same thing for the last name – place an entryfield on the design surface and change these properties:

  dataLink   LASTNAME field
  name   LNameEntryfield
  width   170
  colorHighlight   WindowText/0x80ffff

- Spend a moment and line these up. Next, repeat for the Address1, Address2, City, StateProv, PostalCode, Country and Phone fields. *(We will come back to the StateProv and PostalCode fields in a bit to take a look at a different approach.)* Set the *dataLink* to an appropriate field, *name* to an appropriate name, set the *colorHighlight* property as shown above, place textlabels for the fields, set the *width* property to an appropriate width and so on. Play with the design a bit – you will most likely need to widen the form a little, and you should come out with something that looks close to:

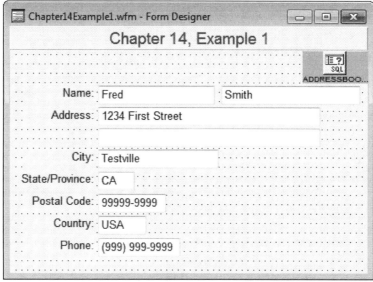

Figure 14-4

- Save your work (Ctrl + S)

Spinbox

The Spinbox control is a special type of entryfield that has two pushbuttons on the right, one with an up arrowhead, the other with a down arrowhead. The purpose of a spinbox is to allow a user to change a value (numeric or date) with the pushbuttons or by typing in a value.

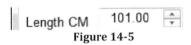

Figure 14-5

For the most part the spinbox control has many or all of the same attributes as an entryfield, but here are a few things you should be aware of that are spinbox specific:

- The *rangeMax*, *rangeMin*, *rangeRequired* properties are used to set a top/lower *value* and to enforce that *value* – i.e., if the *rangeRequired* property is set to *true* the user cannot move past the *rangeMin* or *rangeMax* values or enter a *value* outside that range. If a value is entered that is outside of the range, dBASE will enforce it by changing the value to either the minimum or maximum value. For example, if you set the *rangeMax* to 100, and the *rangeMin* to 5, and typed 105, it would be changed to 100; if you typed 2 the value would be changed to 5.
- In addition, there is the *spinOnly* property – this can be used to enforce the use of the buttons and ONLY the buttons, by the user – they cannot enter a value by typing it if this is set to true.
- The *step* property is used to set the value the pushbuttons increment/decrement the *value* of the spinbox. The default for this is 1, but it can be changed to something else. You might want the user to be able to increment by .05 for example.

What Do You Use It For?

Spinbox controls are most commonly used to link to numeric or date fields in a table, or to obtain input from a user (you might need to ask for a userid, for example), then act upon it.

If you do not wish to (or need to) dataLink to a field in a table, then you will need to consider the *value* property.

To use a spinbox control at its most basic, you would use it like you do an entryfield – place it on a form, and set the *dataLink* property.

Example

We will use the spinbox control for the Birthdate field. The default setting for dBASE for both numeric and date type fields is to use Spinboxes, unless you changed this (discussed in an earlier chapter).

- Drag another TextLabel object to the design surface, and set these properties:
    - text   Birthdate:
    - alignHorizontal   2 - Right
- Place a Spinbox control on the design surface to the right of the TextLabel control we just placed there, and set the following properties:
    - dataLink   Birthdate field
    - name   BirthdateSpinbox
    - colorHighlight   WindowText/0x80ffff
- When you set the *datalink* property, you may see something like "/1963", which is a little disconcerting. I have found that if I close the Form Designer (save and exit –

+W), then open the form back in the Designer again, the Spinbox refreshes properly and displays properly.

> **NOTE**
>
> I personally don't generally use spinbox controls for date fields. The reason is that they don't work the way that they do for other software that uses dates. As an example, if you work with Quicken[tm], for a date, if your cursor is on the month, the spinbox buttons affect only the month, the same for the year. When using a dBASE spinbox associated with a date, the buttons effect the day of the month only. This can be a bit frustrating. We're using the spinbox for this example to give you a feel for them. One solution would be to use a spinbox for the entry of the month, one for the entry of the day, and one for the entry of the year would work, but would take some extra effort on your part *(you would have to split the date into three elements and recombine it before saving the row)*. There are controls in the dBASE Users' Function Library Project (dUFLP) that are already designed to create some of this functionality. See the Appendices (in Vol. II) for details.

Your form should look something like:

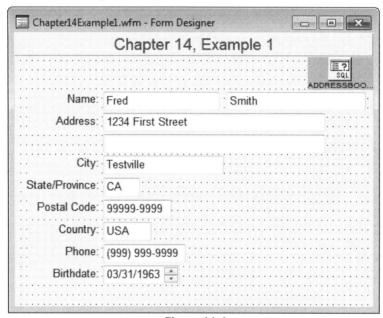

Figure 14-6

Checkbox

The Checkbox control is specifically designed to be used with logical fields. If the *value* of a field that the checkbox is datalinked to is either *null* or *false*, the box will not be checked, if the *value* is true, the box will be checked. You can have *text* associated with a checkbox and you can set the text on the left or the right based on the *textLeft* property. By default the text of a checkbox is on the right side of it, by setting the *textLeft* property to *true*, the text will be on the left side of the checkbox.

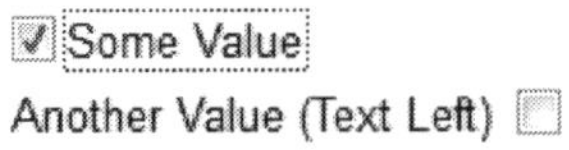

Figure 14-7

What Do You Use It For?

Checkbox controls are most commonly used to link to logical fields in a table.

Once the control is placed on a form, you can simply find the *dataLink* property and set this to the appropriate field. The *text* property will not automatically be set – you will have to set this to read how you need it to.

If you do not wish to (or need to) *dataLink* to a field in a table, then you will need to consider the *value* property.

Example

Working with the example form we are building, there is a logical field in the table called "Business". To use this on the form, follow these steps:

- Place a Checkbox control on the form from the Component Palette, below the "Birthday" field we set up earlier. Change the properties as shown below and modify width/position as necessary to make it line up in a meaningful way with other controls on the form:

dataLink	Business field
name	BusinessCheckbox
text	Business Contact?

- Your form should look something like:

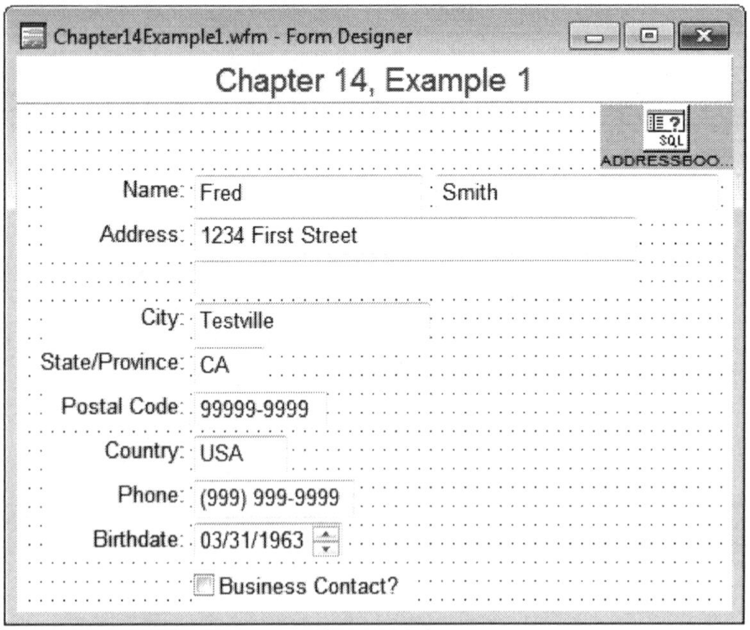

Figure 14-8

- Save your work ([Ctrl]+[S])

Radiobutton

The Radiobutton control is designed to be used with character values and to limit the options that can be selected to those shown by the radiobuttons. For example, you may want to limit a user to three choices of flavors: "Chocolate", "Vanilla" and "Strawberry." By using radiobuttons you can display the three choices on the screen, so that the user may select only one of these.

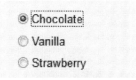

Figure 14-9

First time users of dBASE are often confused by radiobuttons because they have a *value* property that shows a logical value (*true/false*). Because of this and the fact that most *datalinked* controls store the contents of the *value* property to a field, a developer might assume that these should be used with logical fields. The radiobutton actually does something different – it stores the *text* property to a datalinked field and reads the value of the datalinked field to see if it matches the text of one of the radiobuttons in a group. In the example shown here, if the character field the radiobutton was datalinked to contained "Strawberry", you would see the Strawberry radiobutton as selected. If the user then changed to "Chocolate" and the row was saved, then the word "Chocolate" would be saved to the field that the radiobutton is datalinked to.

> **NOTE**
> If you wish to store a different value from the *text* property, you can "morph" the field. This was discussed in an earlier chapter of this book, using the field object's *canChange()* and *beforeGetValue()* event handlers.

The following tip is important for use of radiobuttons on a form:

- Use the *group* property, setting it for the **first** radiobutton in the group ONLY (you can have multiple groups). Make sure that the radiobuttons are placed on the form together and when looking at the "Z-Order" of a form (this is discussed elsewhere), make sure no other controls are between the radiobuttons. If they are all together in the Z-Order and the first radiobutton's *group* property is set to *true*, your radiobuttons should act exactly the way you want. Also, if datalinking these to a field, make sure that **each** radiobutton's *datalink* property is set to the same field in the table.

The R&D engineers at dBASE have changed the radiobutton's *group* property to accept a character value (in dBASE PLUS 2.5 and later releases). For this to work properly, set the *group* property to the same character value for each radiobutton in the group *(NOTE: you will have to change the type of the group property – there is a "T" button in the Inspector – so that it knows it is using Character)* and dBASE should recognize that they are part of the same group, even if the z-order shows controls between the radiobuttons in the group.

What Do You Use It For?

As noted, you can use radioButton controls to link to character fields in a table, for a small list of options. It is not a good idea to use a large number of radioButtons if you have a large number of options – for example, if you have 20 options, that is probably too many. It is suggested that 5-6 are enough – any more than that and the form gets cluttered and confusing for your user and you should consider as mentioned above using either a combobox or listbox control.

Place one radiobutton for each option you wish to supply the user and set the *dataLink* property for each radiobutton to the same (character) field in the table. Make sure that the first radiobutton's *group* property is set to *true* and the *group* property for the other radiobutton controls is set to *false* (or use the character value as noted earlier). Make sure that the radiobuttons are all in the correct "z-order" (tab order) as explained in an earlier chapter of this book. Set the *text* property for each radioButton to the value you wish to be saved to the field.

One way to help you keep your radioButton controls together is to use a container control, as described later in this chapter. The advantage to this is that you can get them all lined up exactly the way you need, then if you find you have to move them, you can move the group of controls by moving the container object and not have to spend time lining up your radioButtons. You can add any other text you may want on the container as well, and keep it all grouped together.

> **📝 NOTE**
> The more you work with controls in dBASE the more times you may find you need to do something that is not described here, or elsewhere. There are many tricks to working with controls and the **radioButton** is one of those that you can use for many things.

For example, using the radioButton *onChange()* event, you can cause your form to do something such as changing the *indexName* property of the rowset of the form. Doing so would change the sort order of the data.

One disadvantage to using the *onChange()* event is that depending on how you define the code, it may fire more than once, which might slow processing down on your form. You may wish to do some experimenting to see what works for you.

Example
For this example we are going to use the "FavoriteFlavor" field, but we want to do something special, because we're going to be working with two ways of working with the flavor field. We will place a Notebook control on the form. This is sort of jumping ahead of the discussion on the Notebook stock control, which is described later in this chapter, but it will prove useful and I prefer to not have to move controls onto the Notebook control after we have them established.

- Place a Notebook control on the form, and change these properties:
  name   FlavorNotebook
  dataSource   ARRAY '{ "Radiobuttons" , "Combobox" }'
  (Click on the dataSource property and select the tool button. In the dialog that appears, click the tool button on the right, then in the new dialog, click "Delete" twice to get rid of the current two tab entries ("First Tab" and Second Tab"). Click on the "String" entryfield and type "Radiobuttons" without the quotes and click the "Add" button, type "Combobox" and click the "Add" button. Click "OK", and then in the first dialog, click "OK".)
- Click on the first tab ("Radiobuttons"), and drag four radiobuttons to the form. Select "Radiobutton1" (the first radiobutton), and set the following properties:
  group   true *// it should default to this*
  dataLink   FavoriteFlavor field
  name   ChocolateRadiobutton

text   Chocolate
- For the second Radiobutton, change these properties:
  dataLink   FavoriteFlavor field
  name   VanillaRadiobutton
  text   Vanilla
- For the third Radiobutton, change these properties:
  dataLink   FavoriteFlavor field
  name   StrawberryRadiobutton
  text   Strawberry
- For the fourth Radiobutton, change these properties:
  dataLink   FavoriteFlavor field
  name   MacadamiaRadiobutton
  text   Macadamia Nut

NOTE
It should be noted that the *dataLink* property is for the **same field** for each of these radioButtons. This is because, as noted earlier, the contents of the *text* property is what is evaluated and stored to the dataLinked field. The *text* property must show exactly what you wish to store in the field.

- Put a little work in lining up the radiobuttons so that they appear in the order given, one below the other, the form should look something like:

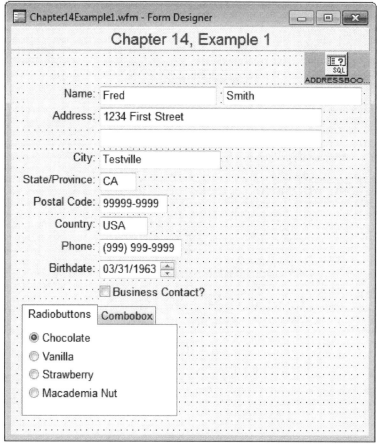

Figure 14-10

- Save your work (Ctrl+S)

Container

The Container object is a very useful tool in dBASE. It allows you to group controls, then on the design surface, move them all at once. In appearance, it looks like a rectangle, without the (default) text property. However, if you place a rectangle on a form, then place some objects inside the rectangle, moving the rectangle does not affect the other objects. If you do the same with a container, moving the container will move the objects. This is particularly useful for designing a form, or designing a custom control that might actually be a series of objects.

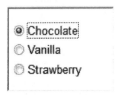

Figure 14-11

What Do You Use It For?

The container object has many options, as you can see from the discussion above. In addition to the suggestion to group controls, it can also be used when designing complex custom classes.

For example, if you go to the chapter that discusses the custom classes that ship with dBASE, there is a calendar class. This class is a combination of text controls, pushbuttons and a container. Rather than having to place each individual control on a form when you want to use the calendar class, you just have to place the container object. I am sure that with a small amount of experimentation you will find that containers can make your life more productive as a dBASE developer.

Another useful feature of the container object is that there may be times when you need to enable or disable a collection of controls on a form based on some condition. If you place those controls directly on the form's surface, you would need to set the *enabled* property for each control. However, if you used a container for those controls, you could simply set the *enabled* property of the container and it would enable or disable all controls that are contained within it – this makes for much simpler and easier to work with code!

Notebook

The notebook control is a specialized form of container – it is a multi-paged container with tabs. Some developers have taken to using Notebook controls more than Tabbox controls to do multi-page forms. Like a container object, if you place objects on the notebook, then move the notebook, all of the objects move with it.

Figure 14-12

The example shown in Figure 14-12 is pretty basic, no controls added to it and no options have been set or modified.

The Notebook control takes on, by default the appearance used by the Windows Theme definitions. The largest effect is that the *colorNormal* property does not work at all. In dBASE Plus release 2.61.2 the developers fixed a minor issue with the background of the parent container for a Notebook and the color to the right of the tabs – it now uses that background color rather than its own.

What Do You Use It For?

Notebook controls are another way of working with multiple pages of information on a form. You see them all the time these days, in dialogs and on forms (for example, see the "Properties" menu, and "Desktop Properties" dialog in dBASE itself). I have forms that use a combination of Tabbox (multi-page form) as well as Notebooks, to allow me to organize the data in ways that make sense for those particular forms.

Users of dBASE have requested for some abilities with the Notebook not currently available, including the ability to place images on the notebook tabs, to have different color tabs for different pages and to have the page and tab match colors, and more. Currently these options are not possible with the built-in Notebook control.

Example

We used a Notebook control already on the example form we've been building and we will add more to it in a bit.

Editor

The Editor control is designed to be used with large amounts of text. You can set the *dataLink* property to a character field (which can be useful for longer fields), a memo field or even a text file.

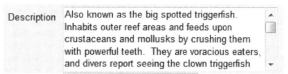

Figure 14-13

There are some properties you should be aware of:

● The *modify* property allows or disallows the user's ability to edit the contents of the editor object's *value* property. You might wonder why this exists, when there is also an *enabled* property. The reason is that the *enabled* property, if set to *false*, also disables the scrollbars of an editor control. If you want the user to be able to view a large amount of text, which would most likely require the use of the scrollbars, rather than use the *enabled* property, set the *modify* property to false. The user will be able to scroll the contents of the editor control up and down (or side to side) but not be able to modify the text.

- The *popupEnable* property allows a special popup for memos to appear on a right mouse click. It includes some useful things, like a find dialog to find text and more. The last item in the popup "Show Format Toolbar" can be interesting. It allows the user to insert HTML into the editor (see *evalTags* below). The problem is, once the HTML is inserted, there is no way to remove it and it becomes part of the text – even if you set the *evalTags* property to *false*, it's pretty much impossible to remove the HTML from a memo field. If the form is opened with the *open()* method, this toolbar is available; if the form is opened with *readModal()* the toolbar is NOT available. You can use the form's *showFormatBar()* method to close this particular toolbar.

- The *evalTags* property is used to evaluate HTML tags in the editor. If it is set to *false* (the default is *true*), then rather than evaluating them, you should see the tags.

What Do You Use It For?

As noted earlier, editor controls can work with large quantities of text from a variety of sources. Most often this is used for memo fields in a table, as they are effectively unlimited in size which an entryfield cannot handle.

A couple of suggestions – if you wish to use HTML to format the contents of a memo field, leave the *evalTags* property set to *true*, then set the *popupEnable* property to *true*. You can even make sure that the HTML format toolbar appears when the editor control gains focus, by using code like (in the editor control's *onGotFocus()* event):

```
function EDITOR1_onGotFocus
   // turn on the formatBar:
   form.showFormatBar( true )
return
```

You would most likely want to turn this off when the editor loses focus (use the editor control's *onLostFocus()* event):

```
function EDITOR1_onLostFocus
   // turn off the formatBar:
   form.showFormatBar( false )
return
```

Then when you tab or click on the editor the toolbar appears, likewise when the editor loses focus the toolbar disappears.

You should be warned that there are some difficulties with the formatting – once you insert HTML formatting into a memo control it will affect the memo and there is no way to stop it. Most of the time, I do not recommend using HTML with the editor and dBASE memo fields.

That said, I also have some situations where I allow HTML tags to be inserted into memos, but set the editor control's *evalTags* property to *false*, which allows me to edit the tags, then output them to an HTML document. A lot depends on what you need to do, and what your users need to do.

Example

We have a memo field that we can use for our example, so let's do some basic work with that. Follow along:

- Drag a TextLabel control to the form, to the right of the Notebook control, and set the following properties:
  text   Notes:
  alignHorizontal 2 - Right
- Drag an Editor control to the form to the right of the TextLabel that you just put on the form and set the following properties:
  name   NotesEditor
  dataLink   Notes field
  popupEnable   false
  colorHighlight WindowText/0x80ffff
  evalTags   false
- You should have a form that looks something like:

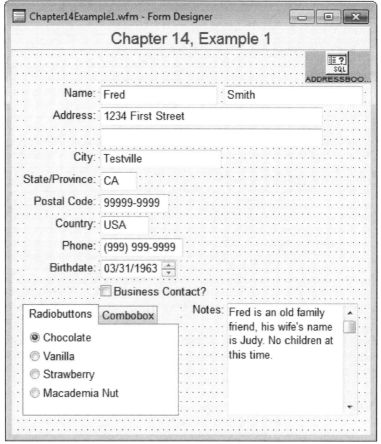

Figure 14-14

- Save your work ([Ctrl]+[S])

Combobox

The Combobox may seem like it is related to the listbox, but it is really related more to the entryfield. It is an entryfield object with a pushbutton used to "drop down" a list of selections (from the *dataSource*).

Figure 14-15

The combobox control is designed to be used when you have large quantities of options for the user *(however, it should be noted that a combobox with 1000 entries is going to take a long time to load, use a lot of memory, which may not be a good idea – in such a case you may want to consider creating a lookup form for your user to find what they are looking for)*. If you have a small number, you might want to use the radiobutton control (mentioned earlier – one radiobutton per option). However comboboxes can be quite useful for a lot of different situations and can be automatically used if you set up a field in a table with the *lookupSQL* property.

- The field object's *lookupSQL* property can be handy (this was discussed in an earlier chapter). It gives you the ability to do an automatic lookup on another table. Briefly, you can set this as a custom property of the field you wish to lookup in another table, or you can set it in the Data Module or Query object in the query's *onOpen()* (or *canOpen()*) event.

  More details on this can be found in online help.

 NOTE
If you use a combobox with your *lookupSQL* field do NOT set the *dataSource* property – the *dataSource* is created automatically for you, anything you do will be overridden by dBASE.

- The *style* property is used to define which style combobox to use. The default is "1 - DropDown", which means that the user must click the button to cause the list to drop. You can set it to:
  - "0 - Simple" which means that the drop down list appears automatically, OR
  - "2 - DropDownList" which means that a) the user must click the button to see the list (unless the *autoDrop* property is set to true), and b) the user cannot enter a value into the entryfield portion of the combobox which they can do with styles of zero and one.
- You may find that you need to change the *height* of a combobox by just a bit. Due to the way that they display, you often need to provide a little more room, so that the descenders on some characters will appear. When using pixels for the metric of a form, I tend to add just one or two pixels to the *height* of a combobox.

In dBASE Plus 2.61.2, a lot of work has been done on the Combobox class. There have been numerous fixes to the Combobox class, many bugs were addressed. In addition, the following new events (to which you can hook your own event handlers) were created - these will be discussed in the online help in depth, I am listing them here so that you are aware of them. There are a huge number of bug fixes as well.

- *beforeDropDown()* - Fires before the dropdown list opens for style 1 or style 2 comboboxes.
- *beforeCloseUp()* - Fires just before the dropdown list is closed for a style 1 or style 2 combobox.
- *onChangeCommitted()* - Fires when the user takes an action indicating that they are choosing a value. (This includes mouse clicks, pressing enter on a highlighted item, and more - see the OLH for details.)

- *onChangeCancel()* - Fires if user takes an action that closes the list without choosing an item.
- *beforeEditPaint()* - In a style 0 or 1 combobox - fires for each keystroke that modifies the value of a combobox.
- *onEditPaint()* - In a style 0 or 1 combobox - fires for each keystroke that modifies the value of the combobox.

In addition, in dBASE Plus 2.61.3, the combobox added two new properties:

- *selectAll* – this property defaults to *true*, but allows a developer to set it to *false* similar to the entryfield control.
- *autoTrim* – will automatically remove spaces at the end of a selection, which is useful in your code – it means you do not have to trim the value yourself if you need it to search, or do other things. This defaults to *false*, setting it to *true* will trim the results.

Example
We're going to use the Combobox in two ways for this example and use three actual comboboxes. The first is actually the more simple one to do.

- Click on the Notebook, and then the "Combobox" tab.
- Drag a combobox to the Notebook control on the blank page of the Notebook, and set the following properties:
  dataLink   FavoriteFlavor field
  dataSource   array {"Chocolate","Vanilla","Strawberry", "Macadamia Nut"}
  (This is similar to what we did with the Notebook control: click the tool button, in the dialog that appears, click the tool button on the right. In the new dialog, in the "String" entryfield, type "Chocolate" without the quotes, then click "Add". Do the same for "Vanilla", "Strawberry", and "Macadamia Nut"; click "OK", then on the first dialog click "OK" again.)
  name   FlavorCombobox
  style   2 - DropDownList
  (This forces the user to select from the list ... when you select this, the currently selected value may appear as blank, but when the form runs all will be well.)
- We will run the form later to see this working, but now we want to do something a little different. The entryfields that are set for the State/Province and Country fields are not really adequate. The problem with them is that your user could just enter whatever they wanted here, which may not be acceptable. What if we wanted to allow them to select from values stored in another table? Even better, rather than using codes, why not display text that is associated with those codes, so that they make more sense to the user (in other words, rather than "CA", why not display the word "California"?)
- The first thing we need to do is to remove the "StateProvince" entryfield. Click on that, ensuring sure it has focus, then press the DEL key on your keyboard. This will remove that control completely.
- Next is actually going to require modifying the description of the field itself. To do this, click on the ADDRESSBOOK1 query object on the form. In the Inspector:
  - Find the *rowset* object and click the Inspect button.
  - Find the *fields* object and click the Inspect button.
  - Find the StateProv *field* and click the Inspect button.
  - Find the *lookupSQL* property, and enter:

```
select * from StateProv order by StateProv
```

This sets the *lookupSQL* property for this field to perform a lookup in the StateProv table. This table has two fields – Code and StateProv. The code field matches the StateProv field in the AddressBook table by type (Character) and field width/size (3). This is quite important.

- Drag a Combobox to the place that the entryfield used to be and set the following properties:

    dataLink   StateProv field

    name   StateProvCombobox

    colorHighlight WindowText/0x80ffff

    style   2 - DropDownList

    Why did we not set a *dataSource?* Because dBASE understands when we set the *lookupSQL* property for this field that the data will come from the StateProv table. If we were to set the *dataSource* property we would be confusing the software. When the *lookupSQL* property set for a field, there is no need to select a *dataSource*.

- Work with the layout a little. Notice that because we set the *style* property after we set the *dataLink* property, the value disappears. That is okay – when the form runs, it should be fine.

- Do the same thing for the Country field: delete the entryfield currently on the form for the Country. Then do similar steps to what are shown above, including setting the lookupSQL property, but this time the select statement should read:

```
select * from country order by country
```

- You should have a form that looks something like this:

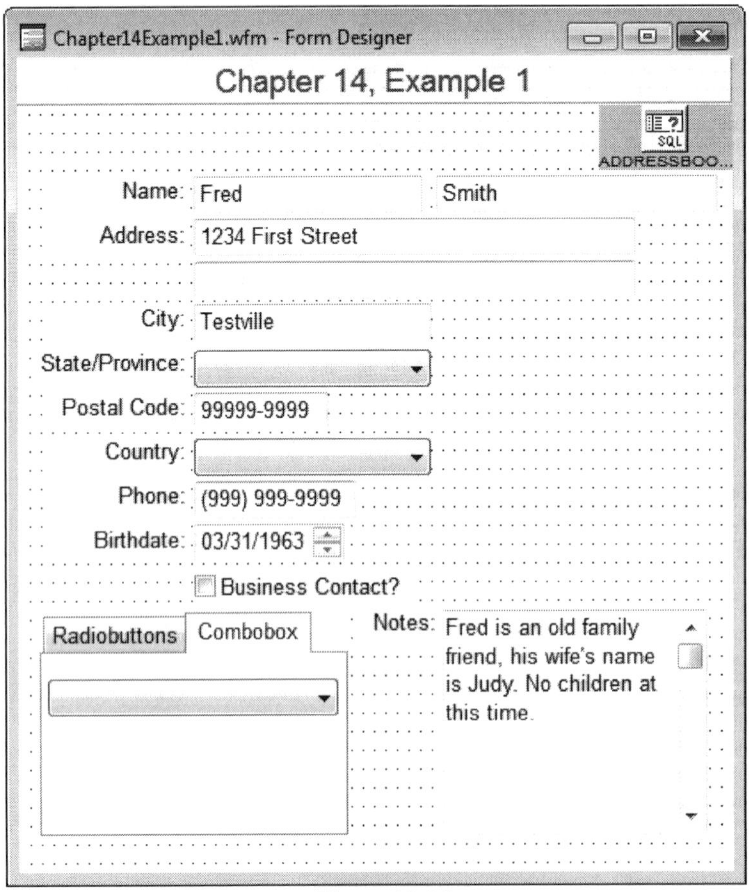

Figure 14-16

- Save your work (⌈Ctrl⌉+⌈S⌉).

Listbox

The Listbox control is one way to allow a user to access a lot of options for a character field in a table. The difficulty is that the Listbox control does not have a *dataLink* property. To provide this sort of functionality, you have to add your own code that checked when the rowset navigated what the current value of the field is, changing the value in the field when the currently selected item in the Listbox changed.

You do have to consider the *dataSource* for a listbox – where is the data coming from? It can be from an array, or the contents of a field in another table. You can set the *dataSource* to a field in the table that is currently active, but this has an effect that may not be desirable as selecting a value in the list will actually navigate in the table to that row. For some situations (a read-only form, for example) this may be acceptable, but if the user is editing a row, you probably do not want them navigating like that.

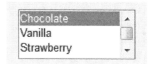

Figure 14-17

- The *dataSource* property has several options here. The *dataSource* is the source of information for the items listed.
  - Array – If you are using an array, you must include the word "Array" (case is not important), followed either by a literal array (i.e., {"Item 1", "Item 2", etc.}) or the name of the array object (i.e., form.listbox1.myarray or aMyArray).
  - Field – you can display the contents of a field from a table. If this is the "current" table (i.e., the one that other controls are set to "edit"), selecting an element in the listbox will actually move the record pointer – this may not be what you wanted to have happen.
  - File – must have a filename skeleton – it is possible to list all files in a directory (*.*) or files of a specific type (*.TXT) and so on.
  - Structure – this creates a listing of all the fields in the active table – the table that is the "active" one for the form. Note: Currently this only works if you are using XDML syntax to access tables.
  - Tables – creates a listing all the tables in the current database (if using local tables, *.DBF, *.DB). Note: this option does not currently appear to work in the 32-bit version of dBASE. To populate the *dataSource* with a list of local tables you would need to write code to get the table names.

As you can see, the *dataSource* can open up the possibilities for use of the listbox rather widely.

Tip: If you (or the user) make any changes to the *dataSource*, those changes are not automatically reflected. The *dataSource* is read when the form is instantiated and is not re-read unless you specifically tell it to do so. You can accomplish this by simply issuing the following command (using the name of your listbox):

```
form.listbox1.dataSource += ""
```

This causes the listbox to re-evaluate the *dataSource* property. Note that this would be called in the *onChange()* event of the control that changed the *dataSource* of the listbox.

- The *curSel* property is a numeric reference to the currently selected item. If you want to show the prompt, use the *value* property (unless you are using the *multiple* property and *selected* method – see above).
- The *value* property shows the currently highlighted item (even if not selected in the case of the *multiple* property being set to *true*).

Example
There isn't really a good use for a listbox on this form. As noted at the beginning of the discussion, we could try to emulate a *dataLink* but that's not really something we need to get into here.

Grid

The Grid is just what it sounds like – a means of displaying the contents of a table in rows and columns. You can limit the rows you want the user to view, you can set colors for specific columns and a lot more. This is a logical way of displaying large amounts of data in a table and is one that most people are familiar with. This chapter will only briefly discuss the grid, the next chapter will provide a more detailed look at this particularly database oriented control.

The grid itself is an object and it has objects associated with it. The following is a brief description of the object model.

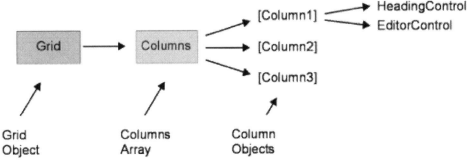

Figure 14-17
(Image by Michael Nuwer, used with permission)

The grid has many properties, events and methods associated with it, a lot of these are discussed in the next chapter.

When using a grid, at the simplest, you can place a grid on a form and set the grid's *dataLink* property to the rowset you wish to display in the grid. However, doing so does not allow you to have the fine control over the display that you might wish, such as setting column colors, or font changes, etc.. The *only* way to have that kind of control is if you add columns to the *columns* array of the grid.

The following are instructions which explain how to add grid columns using the designer. Each grid *column* object which is contained in the grid's *columns* array, contains an *editorControl* and a *headingControl*.

Getting Started With a Grid
Grids have rows (corresponding to the rows of a table), and columns (corresponding to the columns or fields of a table) and cells (where the rows and columns intersect).

When designing a form that uses the Grid control in dBASE, if you wish programmatic control over the grid, here are some steps you must follow [this assumes you have your query/queries or datamodule(s) on the form]:

1. Place the grid on the form
2. Set the *dataLink* property to the rowset you wish to display
3. *(And most important)* while the grid should be displaying all columns from your rowset, you do not have real control yet – in the Inspector click on the *columns* property. Note that it shows the word "object" in boldfaced text, and should display two buttons – a tool (wrench) and the letter "I" in a small graphic. Click on the tool button. Select the columns you wish to display, in the order you wish to display them, and then click the OK button.

At this point, you have a lot of control over your grid. That's the absolute basics, but to get a better understanding of the grid and some idea what you can do with it, read on.

The Grid Columns

Grid columns, which are accessed through the *columns* array, have an *editorControl* defined by the *editorType* property. These are how we define the grid. The *editorType* may be one of the following:

1. Entryfield *(the default)* (Works for all field types)
2. Spinbox (Numeric and Date field types)
3. Checkbox (Logical field types)
4. Combobox (Character field types)
5. Editor (Memo and Character field types) – this is only available in more recent versions of dBASE.

Note that dBASE will check which type you select against the type of field, if it is not valid, you will not be able to set the column's *editorType* to that value.

Each column also has a *headingControl*, in which you can set the text for the column header, color, font properties and so on.

ID	Name	Species	Length CM	Description	Fish Image
1	Clown Triggerfish	Ballistoides conspicillum	101.00	Also known as the big	
2	Giant Maori Wrasse	Cheilinus undulatus	228.00	This is the largest of all	
3	Blue Angelfish	Pomacanthus nauarchus	30.00	Habitat is around	
4	Ornate Butterflyfish	Chaetodon Ornatissimus	19.00	Normally seen in pairs	
5	California Moray	Gymnothorax mordax	150.00	This fish hides in a	
6	Nurse Shark	Ginglymostoma cirratum	400.00	Frequently found under	
7	Spotted Eagle Ray	Aetobatus narinari	200.00	Found in reef areas and	
8	Yellowtail Snapper	Ocyurus chrysurus	75.00	Prefers to congregate in	
9	Redband Parrotfish	Sparisoma Aurofrenatum	28.00	Inhabits reef areas. The	

Figure 14-19

There is a lot more that could be said about the grid, indeed, one of the papers in the dBASE Knowledgebase is dedicated to the grid. The folk in R&D at dBASE, LLC. have been working hard, for example in dBASE PLUS release 2.5 they added the ability to set properties *(such as colorNormal, fontSize, etc.)* of individual cells. More will come, I am sure.

Example

We're going to add a grid to this form, but the main page is getting a little cluttered. How to deal with it? Well, if you will recall in an earlier chapter we discussed multi-page forms. We can add a grid to this form without cluttering up the main page *(when we get to the discussion of the Tabbox control below, we'll add one to this form to allow for navigation between pages ...).*

To get to the second page of the form, in the toolbar while in the Form Designer you should see a toolbutton that if you hold the mouse over it will show a speedTip that says "Next Form Page". Click on that button and you will see a completely blank slate – a new page of the form.

Where did the Title go? Well, most controls on a form have, by default, a *pageNo* property of 1 – or whatever page they were dropped onto the form. If you want a control to appear on all pages of a form, set the *pageNo* property to 0. Let's go back to the first page and go to the TitleText control at the top of the form. (Use the toolbutton in the toolbar that goes the other direction "Previous Form Page".) Click on the title text, then in the Inspector find the *pageNo* property. Change the value to 0. Now click on the "Next Form Page" toolbutton.

Next, drag a grid control to the design surface. Set the following properties:

> dataLink   addressbook1
> columns   Set the columns to display
> *(Click the tool button in the Inspector by the columns object, and the FirstName, LastName, StateProv, and Country fields.)*
> rowSelect   true
> colorRowSelect   WindowText/0x80ffff

The next step is to set some properties for the columns. One way to do this is to double-click on a column, but that can be a little tricky – sometimes dBASE assumes you are clicking on the whole grid, other times the column. You can use the Inspector to get to individual columns just as easily and perhaps more accurately. You should now see an "I" (Inspect) button next to the tool button in the Inspector by the *columns* object. Click on the Inspect button. This will give a list of each column.

- Click on "COLUMN1", click the Inspect button and change the *width* property to 100.
- Click on the *headingControl* object, click the Inspect button.
- Find the *value* property and insert a space between "First" and "Name", so that rather than "FirstName" it appears as "First Name".
- Repeat for the second column, setting the headingControl's *value* property to "Last Name".
- Repeat for the third column, setting the width to 150 (pixels) and the headingControl's *value* property to "State/Province".
- Repeat for the fourth column, setting the width to 150, and leave the headingControl's *value* property as it is.

> **📝 NOTE**
> When you set the *dataLink* property you may find only one row displays. However, if you are working with dBASE PLUS 2.5 or later, the scrollbar is active and you can click on it above the "thumb" (the sliding part) and it will show you both the rows in this small table. This is useful both for vertical and horizontal scrollbars.

- Modify the width of the form to accommodate the grid, modify the grid so that all the columns show and set the height to a good portion of the height of the form. This will allow the user to see more than a couple of rows (although in our example there are only two rows).
- The form should look something like:

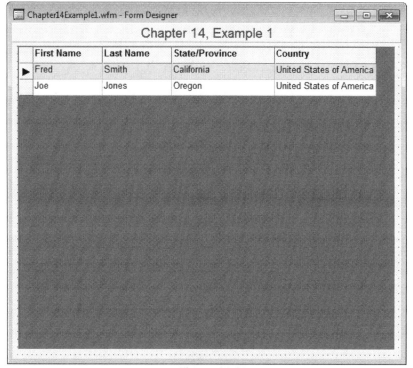

Figure 14-20

- We could set a lot more properties of the grid, but for now let's leave it as is.
- Save your form (Ctrl+S).

As noted earlier, there is a *much* more detailed discussion of the grid in Chapter 15 of this book.

Tabbox

The primary purpose of the Tabbox control is to allow a form to work with multiple pages in a nice, easy to understand fashion (this was discussed in an earlier chapter of this book). However, the Tabbox control can be used for other purposes as well.

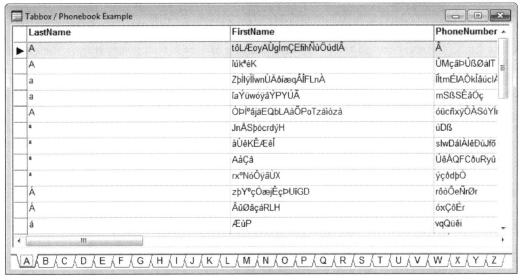

Figure 14-21

The image above (Figure 14-21) shows a Tabbox that is used as a means of searching an index quickly, finding the first item that begins with the letter you click on in the Tabbox. This takes a bit more code than I want to show in this chapter, but it is a good example of some of what can be done with this control. *(The data shown was created using an XDML command in dBASE called GENERATE, which can be used to create random data for testing an application.)*

Example
Finishing up the first example form for this chapter, which has been awhile in building, we need a way to switch between pages of the form. We'll use a Tabbox control for this.

- Drag a Tabbox control from the Component Palette to the form. Notice that by default it appears at the bottom of the form (the *anchor* property is set to "1 - Bottom") and that the *pageno* property is set to 0 (all pages of the form).

  You will probably have to make the form a little bit taller (change the *height* of the form, either by dragging the bottom down or using the Inspector) to make room for the Tabbox control. Set the following properties:

  dataSource   array { "Individual", "Find Record"}
  (This works the same way we set the dataSource for comboboxes and the notebook control earlier.)
  name   FormPageTabbox
  colorNormal   Navy *(this is the background of the Tabbox control)*
  colorHighlight Blue/BtnFace *(this is the currently selected tab)*
  onSelChange *(event)* Click the tool button and enter:

```
function FORMPAGETABBOX_onSelChange
   form.pageNo := this. curSel
return
```

- You should have a form that looks something like:

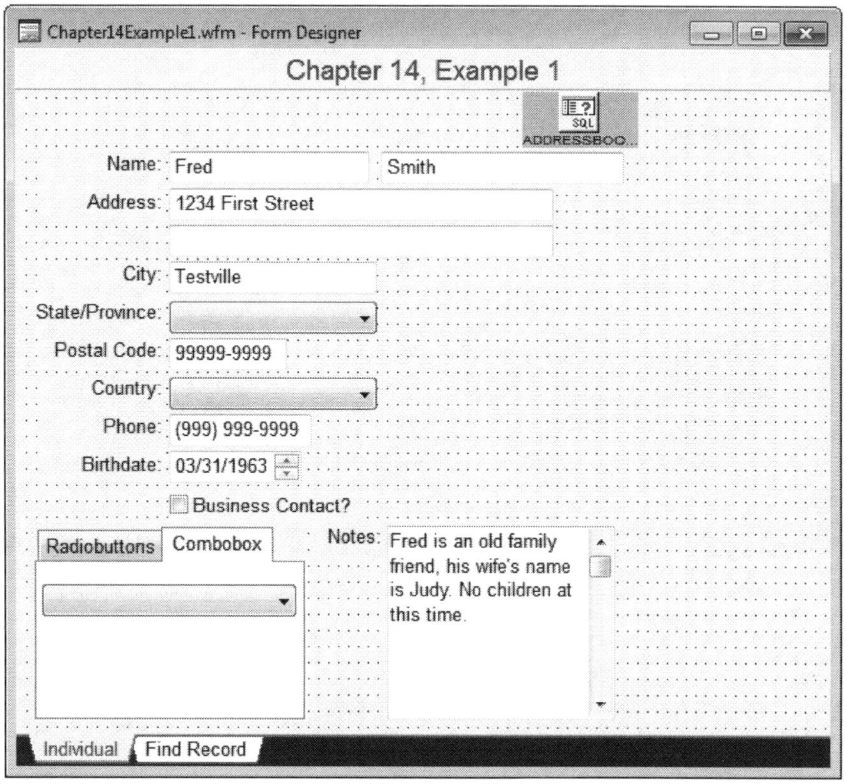

Figure 14-22

- Save the form (⎡Ctrl⎤+⎡S⎤).

Testing the Example

Up until now we haven't actually tested the example form. We've just been assembling it a little at a time. It's probably time to test drive this. As you do notice when you tab through controls that the tab sequence is a little bit odd. That's because we removed some controls and added others in their place. Remember in the previous chapter the discussion about z-order? I would suggest you bring this back into the Form Designer and modify the layout so that the z-order works properly. Notice what happens as you navigate through the form (all two rows), and tab from control to control and notice the color change as some controls get focus.

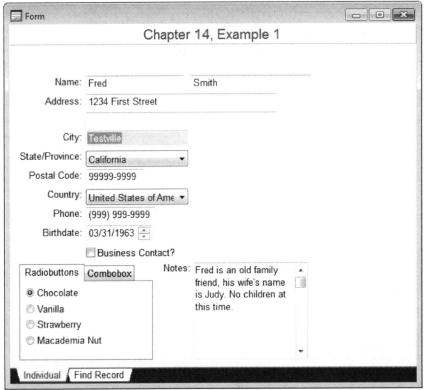

Figure 14-23

Pushbutton

The Pushbutton is one of the more useful controls and is seen all over the place. If you open a dialog there will (almost) always be at least one button that closes the form when done; most forms have more than one pushbutton. They are used in many ways to do many things.

As such, you should spend some time working with pushbutton objects.

Windows XP and Later Versions, Themes, and Pushbuttons

As mentioned in Chapter 1, there are some things that have changed, fairly dramatically, between dBASE Plus 2.5 and dBASE Plus 2.6 and following versions. The Pushbutton object is one that has changed in appearance fairly heavily.

By default, if you are using Windows XP or Windows Vista *(and later operating systems, one assumes)*, the use of the Windows Theme might throw off the appearance of your application. If you want your application to be uniform in appearance across Windows 95, Windows 98, Windows NT, as well as Windows XP and Windows Vista, you will find that the defaults are different in the later operating systems. To an extent, the pushbutton behaves differently as well, under these later operating systems, in that to use the themes that are built into the operating system, the appearance must change and some properties may not work the way you expect.

The *colorNormal* property of the pushbutton class behaves differently under Windows XP and Windows Vista/7 than earlier operating systems, which is the primary difference, besides general appearance. When using XP, setting the colorNormal property has no effect at all. When using Windows Vista (and later versions of Windows), the foreground color of the *colorNormal* property is recognized.

Otherwise, except as noted (and shown in the example below) with the appearance issues, the pushbutton object should work fine across all platforms.

If you do not wish your pushbuttons to use the Windows Themes, then you can under Windows XP delete the manifest file (plus.exe.manifest) in the dBASE\Plus\BIN folder (the full path may vary, but it's the folder that "Plus.exe" is in); or (in dBASE Plus 2.6 and later versions) you can use the new *systemTheme* property, which defaults to *true*. If it is set to *false* for each pushbutton you modify, the appearance will default to the older appearance and the behavior will revert to the older behavior (meaning the *colorNormal* property will function properly).

Figure 14-24, below, shows pushbuttons in both variations and using some of the special properties of pushbuttons that can define where images are displayed, etc..

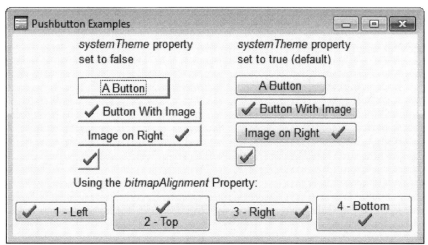

Figure 14-24

Here are a few properties, events and/or methods you should be aware of with the Pushbutton:

- *onClick()* – this is the event most used with a pushbutton – it is how you tell dBASE what to do when the user clicks on the pushbutton *(or when the button has focus, presses the Enter key)*.
- *text* – the text displayed on the pushbutton.
- *disabledBitmap*, *downBitmap*, *focusBitmap* and *upBitmap* properties are used to set images for each of the states shown. The most often used is *upBitmap*.

> **NOTE**
> A fairly thorough discussion of the images used for pushbuttons (and other controls) is in the appendices (Vol. II), including any details I could get from the R&D team at dBASE, LLC.

- *textLeft* – this property can be used to display an image on the right side of the text, as opposed to the default, where the image is on the right.
- The *speedBar* property is used to set a pushbutton that cannot get focus (like a set of toolbar buttons) which means you cannot tab to it.

- The *bitmapAlignment* property is used to set the placement of an image on a pushbutton, with five options: Default (same as Left), Left, Right, Top and Bottom. This property is new to dBASE Plus 2.6.

There are of course many more properties, events and methods. Again, as we work through with actual applications we will start to see the use of these.

What Do You Use It For?

Pushbuttons are one of the more common controls used on forms. They are used for many purposes, ranging from opening new forms, to closing the current form, to navigating in the data and a lot more. With a little thought you can probably find many things where you might need to pushbuttons for *(earlier chapters of this book and some later chapters use pushbuttons extensively)*.

Line

The Line object is one of the more unusual objects in dBASE because it does not have an *hWnd* property. It is quite simply, a line. You can draw lines from one point to another on a form. Most often they are used to separate parts of a form from other parts, giving a visual cue to the user of the form.

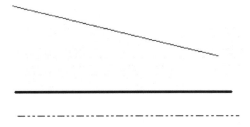

Figure 14-25

What Do You Use It For?

Lines are useful to separate parts of a form from each other. You may wish to group some data, or perhaps have a section of read-only data separate from the interactive parts of the form. Lines can provide a useful visual cue to what is happening on a form. A line can be used under a menubar or toolbar on a form to add a bit of separation from the rest of the form as well.

Rectangle

The Rectangle object is similar to the line object – it is a visual control that can be used to add some interest to a page. It can be used, for example, to group some objects together that are related. By default a rectangle object has text in the upper left, but if you set the *text* property to a blank value, the text goes away.

Figure 14-26

It should be noted that the Rectangle was modified to default to using the Windows XP (and later) Themes, so in the example above, the first rectangle has slightly rounded corners and the color of both the line and the text match what is defined for the theme. As with the pushbutton, under Windows XP you could remove the manifest file and the image would revert to the old style rectangle *(or you could set the systemTheme property to false)*.

What Do You Use It For?

A rectangle object is most often used to visually group objects on a form together. The one drawback to using a rectangle is that if you move the rectangle, the controls that appear within it do not move, so you have to move them as well. However, the rectangle object does have text, unlike the container object (discussed earlier in this chapter).

If you have placed controls on your form and then decide to add a rectangle to make it look nicer, the problem will be that the rectangle will appear on *top* of the controls. You can solve this by using the "Layout" menu, "Send to Back" – this will place it below the controls.

Image

This object is used to display an image on a form. The image can come from a field in a table or from some other file such as a .DLL, a .BMP or other file type. There are some limitations, but not many, to the type of image that can be displayed.

Figure 14-27

- The *alignment* property is important here, as it controls whether or not dBASE will attempt to force the image to fit within the size of the image object. The setting I use the most for image controls is "3=Keep aspect stretch" – which literally means that when the image is resized, the control ensures that the ratio of height and width match the original image (meaning that the image will not be distorted).

What Do You Use It For?

As shown in the example above, you can datalink to an image field in a table. However, you can use image objects for many purposes, including a company logo. Some folk have used them for other purposes such as replacements for pushbuttons, where the image object's *onLeftMouseUp()* event is used as if it were the pushbutton's *onClick()* event.

Shape

You can use the Shape object to create some nice displays on a form, putting a shape down and then text over the shape, for example, to create a simple logo. The shape object's *shapeStyle* property determines the actual shape to be displayed.

Figure 14-28

What Do You Use It For?

The shape object can be used to make your form stand out a bit more. They can be used to make logos for forms by placing text over the top of them and so on.

TreeView and TreeItem

The TreeView object will be somewhat familiar to you in that it is used in the Source Code Editor, as well as the Windows Explorer. It presents data in an outline format that may be expanded or contracted by the user. What may be confusing to a developer new to the TreeView object is that the TreeView is really a container for TreeItem objects. You add items to the TreeView object by creating a new TreeItem object. Individual TreeItem objects are containers for more TreeItem objects.

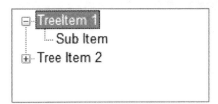

Figure 14-29

The basics for working with a TreeView are to place one on a form. It doesn't look like much – just a white box with no text, no visual cues, etc. To get started, once you have a TreeView on a form, if you right click on the control, you can add a TreeItem. Once you have done that, you can change the text. If you right click on that TreeItem, you can add a TreeItem that is contained by the TreeItem. If you right click on the main TreeView control, you add a TreeItem that is contained by the TreeView.

You can also add TreeItems programmatically, perhaps in the form's *onOpen* event, the TreeView's *onOpen* event.

 NOTE

It is not a good idea to mix how you add TreeItems to the TreeView control – either add them programmatically or add them in the designer. If you add top level treeItems in the designer, then then add lower – level items programmatically, you may find that the plus sign (used to denote children TreeItems) will not appear for the top level items – which means you have to double click on them to show the next level of TreeItem. *(Discovered by Gary White)*

What Do You Use It For?

The TreeView (and TreeItem) is not really designed to interact with data. There are folk who have worked with these and created versions that will read data from a table, which allow the user to modify the data and save them back. But the TreeView and TreeItem controls do not have *dataLink* properties, so you have to do a lot of work to use them for this.

You could create your own dialog box to deal with file folders and files, using a TreeView and TreeItems. I have a form that I use in one application where the user can select a region (first level of TreeItem), then select a more specific region (town/city) within that first level (a second level of TreeItem) and then generate a report based on the selected results.

Note that you can change the graphics used for the TreeItems for selected, non-selected, checked, unchecked, both for the TreeView as a whole and for individual TreeItems. This is a complex control, that will take some work to truly understand it.

Example

As the TreeView and TreeItem objects are not *really* designed to be datalinked to fields in a table, the amount of work involved is fairly extensive, I thought perhaps we would go in a different direction. This is pretty basic and one might ask "Why?", but it is really just to give you a feel for these objects. We are going to create a simple dialog that shows two icons – one for programs, another for forms. When you click on an icon, the TreeItem "opens" and will show a listing of the files that are of the appropriate type.

- Create a new form, set the following properties:

metric	6 - Pixels
text	Chapter 13, Example 2
mdi	false
autoCenter	true

- Drag a TreeView object to the design surface. Widen it so that it mostly fills the form (at least for now). As noted, the TreeView when first placed on the form appears as a white box, and doesn't give any indicator of what it does. Change the following properties:

  name FileTreeView

  There are a lot of properties that we could set, such as the default images, but since we are using different images for each of our options, we won't do that. Settings of this sort for the TreeView mean that the default for TreeItems contained by the TreeView do not need to be set unless you wish them to be different.

- We need some code that will be used later, that will store the text of the currently selected TreeItem into a custom property of the form. This code is called from the TreeView's *onChange()* event handler. In the Inspector click on the "Events" tab, find *onChange* and click the toolbar. In the Source Code Editor, enter:

```
function FILETREEVIEW_onChange
   // Change the form's custom property SelectedItem,
   // to empty if level 1, or to the text of the
   // item, if level 2:
   local cSelected
   cSelected = form.FileTreeView.selected.text

   if form.FileTreeView.selected.level == 2
      form.SelectedItem := cSelected
```

```
else
    form.SelectedItem := ""
endif
return
```

- Back on the design surface, right click on the TreeView object, and select "New Item".
- Click on the item that says TREEITEM1, and change these properties:

name   ProgramFiles
image   resource #18
(Click the tool button. In the Icon Property Builder dialog, select "Resource" for "Location:" and click the tool button to the right of the "Icon:" entryfield. Select #18, which shows a couple of gears, click "OK", and then click "OK" on the first dialog.)
selectedImage   resource #18
text   Program Files

- Click on a blank part of the TreeView object, then right click on the TreeView object, and select "New Item".
- Click on the item that says "TREEITEM2" and change these properties:

name   FormFiles
image   resource #17
selectedImage   resource #17
text   Form Files

- The tricky part of this is that we want to now add TreeItems that are sub-items for the first level items. The way we are going to do this is in the form's overridden *open()* and *readModal()* methods, so that the code we wish to execute is performed *before* the form actually opens. (This avoids the form updating after it opens.) To do this, click on the form surface (outside of the TreeView) and go to the Inspector. In the Inspector, click on the "Methods" tab, then the *open* method. Click the tool button, and enter:

```
function form_open
    class::Init()
return FORM::open()
```

Do the same for the *readModal* method so that you see:

```
function form_readModal
    class::Init()
return FORM::readModal()
```

Next, type the following into the Source Code Editor (watch for typos) – this code will actually create the TreeItems needed:

```
function Init
    /*
        Overridden methods Open and ReadModal for the form
        call this method, to load the treeview with the
        entries from the current folder.
    */
    local aTemp, cFileName, cItem
    private cCmd

    // Start with the ProgramFiles:
    aTemp = new array()
```

```
aTemp.dir( "*.prg" )
aTemp.sort()
for i = 1 to aTemp.size/5
    cFileName = aTemp[i,1]
    // name of the item:
    cItem = ;
        "form.FileTreeView.ProgramFiles.ProgramItem"+i
    // when programmatically creating this, we need
    // to use a special technique called macro
    // substitution:
    cCmd = cItem+ "= ;
        new TreeItem( form.FileTreeView.ProgramFiles )"
    &cCmd.
    // do it again to change the text:
    cCmd = cItem+[.text = ']+cFileName+[']
    &cCmd.
    // and again for the image properties:
    cCmd = cItem+[.image = 'resource #18']
    &cCmd.
    cCmd = cItem+[.selectedImage = 'resource #18']
    &cCmd.
next

// Repeat for FormFiles:
aTemp = new array()
aTemp.dir( "*.wfm" )
aTemp.sort()
for i = 1 to aTemp.size/5
    cFileName = aTemp[i,1]
    // name of the item:
    cItem  = "form.FileTreeView.FormFiles.FormItem"+i
    // when programmatically creating this, we need
    // to use a special technique called macro
    // substitution:
    cCmd = cItem+ ;
        "= new TreeItem( form.FileTreeView.FormFiles )"
    &cCmd.
    // do it again to change the text:
    cCmd = cItem+[.text = ']+cFileName+[']
    &cCmd.
    // and again for the image properties:
    cCmd = cItem+[.image = 'resource #17']
    &cCmd.
    cCmd = cItem+[.selectedImage = 'resource #17']
    &cCmd.
next

// before we're done, set a custom property
// for the form, to show what item (if any)
// has been selected -- set to empty to start:
form.SelectedItem = ""
return
```

- Next place a Pushbutton under the TreeView, and set these properties:

name	CloseFormButton
text	Close Form
onClick *(event)*	{; form.close() }

- Resize the form as needed rearranging the controls to make things look "good" to your eye.
- You should have a form that looks something like the following:

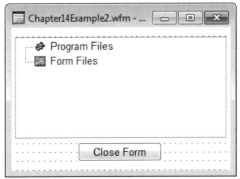

Figure 14-30

- Save your form (`Ctrl`+`S`).
- Run the form. Notice that if there are no .prg or .wfm files, the form TreeView will look similar to what is shown above. If, however, there are either .PRG or .WFM files in the folder, you should see a + image by the TreeItems. If you click on that, it will open, and you will see a list of files. This should look something like:

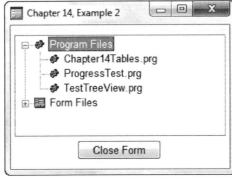

Figure 14-31

If you were to close the form, nothing really happens. We didn't tell dBASE to actually do anything with the files in the TreeView. Rather than just *running* the form, we might want to create some code that runs the form and after it is closed, examines properties of the TreeView object. Something like the following might be more useful – to create this, go to the Command Window and type:

```
modify command TestTreeView
```

Type the following in the Source Code Editor:

```
// Run the form Chapter13Example2.wfm, but be able to
// show the name of the file selected (if any) when
// the form was closed:
set procedure to Chapter13Example2.wfm additive
local fCE
fCE = new Chapter13Example2Form()
fCE.readModal()
// no code will execute after the readModal()
// statement above, until the form is closed.
```

```
// This code will only work if the TreeView's onChange
// code was entered, as described in the book, and
// the appropriate code to create the custom property
// form.SelectedItem is in the Init method of the form:
if not empty( fCE.SelectedItem )
   ? "Selected File: "+fCE.SelectedItem
else
   ? "No file selected"
endif
// release the form file:
fCE.release()
```

Save this code (after checking for typos), and try running it. The form will appear, but depending on what you select (or didn't select) when you close the form, the output in the Command Window will vary. You might use something along these lines in an application to select specific files and manipulate them.

Progress

The Progress control is useful when you want your user(s) to know how far along in a process that a program is. It is a nice visual control for that purpose.

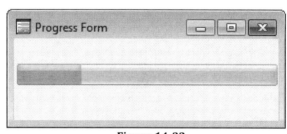

Figure 14-32

An example of the use of the Progress control is to show the progress through a table in a long process. For example, if you had code that needed to work with a large table and extract information, perhaps storing it in another table, you would want to use the progress bar on a form that showed the progress.

In order to work with the Progress control, you need to set three properties: *rangeMin*, *rangeMax* and the *value* property. In addition, inside any loop in your code that you wish to show the results, you would want to update the *value* property of the progress bar.

Example
We will create a simple form that can be used, then some code to show progress in a table:
- Go to the Navigator in dBASE PLUS, and click on the "Forms" tab (if you haven't already). Double-click the first "(Untitled)" icon, and create a new form. Set the following properties for the form itself:

  text   Progress Form
  metric   6 - Pixels
  autoCenter true

- Place a progress control on the form and set the width to almost the width of the form. Change the height of the form so that it is smaller, and then save it (Ctrl+S) as "ProgressForm".

- Close the Form Designer, as we need to create a simple program. This program is going to do several things; first we will create a small table and add some data using a special command to create random data. Then we will open the progress form we just created, loop through the table, updating the progress bar, then close the form and clean up after ourselves (deleting the test table).
- In the Command Window type:

```
modify command ProgressTest
```

In the Source Code Editor, enter:

```
// A program to show how to use a Progress Bar with a table:
// As a side note, this program uses local SQL (create table),
// XDML (USE, GENERATE), and OODML to accomplish the task
// needed.

// Create a test table:
if file( "TestProgress.dbf" )
   drop table  TestProgress
endif

create table TestProgress ( ;
            TestOne    char(10),;
            TestTwo    char(10),;
            TestThree char(10) )

// we will open the table using XDML for
// a moment, generate some data, and then
// close the table:
use TestProgress
generate 200
use

// Now we have data, we're going back to OODML:
q          = new query()
q.sql     := "select * from TestProgress"
q.active := true

// we need to open the form:
set procedure to ProgressForm.wfm additive
f = new ProgressFormForm()
// the lower end of the progress bar's range:
f.Progress1.rangeMin := 1
// the upper end, in this case the number of
// rows in the table:
f.Progress1.rangeMax := q.rowset.count()
// the current value of the progress bar:
f.Progress1.value     := 1
// open the form:
f.open()

// create a simple counter:
n = 0

// loop through the table:
do while not q.rowset.endOfSet
   // increment the counter:
```

```
   n++

   // update the progress bar:
   f.Progress1.value := n

   // do something with the data in the table, in this
   // case we're going to copy the value in field
   // TestOne to field TestTwo:
   q.rowset.fields["TestTwo"].value := ;
   q.rowset.fields["TestOne"].value
   // because this is fast, let's tell the computer
   // to wait just a moment:
   inkey( .01 )

   // next row in the rowset:
   q.rowset.next()
enddo

// cleanup:
q.active := false
release object q
f.close()
f.release()
close procedure ProgressForm.wfm
drop table TestProgress
```

Once you have done this, check for typos, then try running the program. If all works properly the ProgressForm should open and as the program goes through the table, it will increment and close the form so you know the process is done. This is a fairly simple example, but it should give you some idea of how useful this control can be.

Note that you can of course add text controls to the progress form, update the values for those controls and you can do a lot more – this example was primarily designed to focus on the Progress control.

Slider

A slider is a way to let the user control "values" – it is very visual which can be appealing to many users. There are many examples of their use in Windows and Microsoft Office, in dialogs used for a variety of things.

Figure 14-33

The form shown above is a silly example as it is a Slider control that changes the values of a Progress control. By dragging the Slider, the Progress bar moves. When this control was first shown by the developers at Borland in dBASE 5.0 for Windows it "wowed" us, but really this is not the most efficient use of a slider.

To properly use the slider you would need some numeric value that you wanted the user to have an optional method of changing.

Example

We will create a simple form that can be used:

- Go to the Navigator in dBASE PLUS, and click on the "Forms" tab (if you haven't already). Double-click the first "(Untitled)" icon, and create a new form. Set the following properties for the form itself:

text	Slider Form
metric	6 - Pixels
autoCenter	true

- Place a textLabel control on the form and set the following properties:

fontBold	true
text	How Old Are You?

- Widen the control as needed to show all the text.
- Place a spinbox control on the form to the right of the textLabel you just added, and set the following properties:

name	AgeSpinbox
value	25

- Change the height of the form so that it is smaller, and then save it (⌈Ctrl⌋+⌊S⌋) as "SliderForm".
- Place a slider control under the two other controls on the form. Widen it so it takes up about as much room left-to-right as the two controls above it (see Figure 14-34 below). Set the following properties:

name	AgeSlider
rangeMax	100
value	25

- Modify the *onChange* event to the following codeblock:
  ```
  onChange {; form.AgeSpinbox.value := this.value}
  ```
- Click on the AgeSpinbox and modify the *onChange* event to the following codeblock:
  ```
  onChange {; form.AgeSlider.value := this.value}
  ```

Once you have done this, try running the form. If all works, changing the value in the Spinbox will move the slider, and vice-versa.

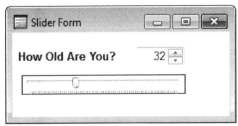

Figure 14-34

This is still a fairly simple method of working with the slider, but it can get you started. The slider has quite a few properties that can be used to alter its appearance, you can make the slider vertical instead of horizontal and much more.

ActiveX

This allows you to make use of the thousands of visual controls available on the internet and in commercial software packages, in your own dBASE applications. ActiveX controls use the .OCX file extension. You don't need to know where they are installed on your computer as dBASE will find them using the Windows Registry. It should be noted that some ActiveX controls do not work with dBASE, although the developers at dBASE, LLC are working on compatibility. Some ActiveX controls are older or have very specific uses that may not work with dBASE itself.

Example
An example of using an ActiveX control might be to use Internet Explorer on a form, allowing your users to view web pages directly through your own application. *(Note, Internet Explorer must be installed on your computer, but it is unusual to find a computer that does not have it installed anymore, so this may be a moot point.)*

- Create a new form in the Form Designer, then follow along here (if you wish). Set the form's *metric* property to "6 - Pixels", and the *text* to "ActiveX Example".
- Drag an ActiveX control from the Component Palette. This should look similar to:

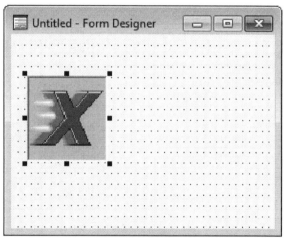

Figure 14-33

- In the Inspector, find the *classID* property and click on the tool button. A dialog that looks similar to the following will appear (the list of available ActiveX controls will vary depending on what is installed on your computer):

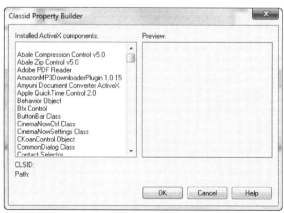

Figure 14-34

- Find in the dialog "Microsoft Web Browser" and click on it. You should see something along these lines:

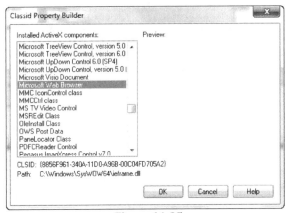

Figure 14-35

- Click "OK". Your form will drastically change appearance:

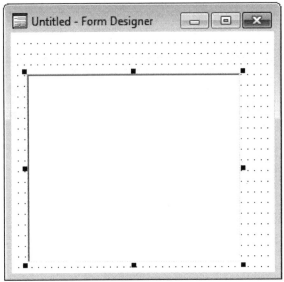

Figure 14-36

- I suggest moving the ActiveX control down a bit, modify the form a little so that it is larger, likewise the ActiveX control so it is also larger *(most web pages are not designed to be displayed on a tiny area like the default form size)*.
- Place a textLabel control at the top and change the *text* property to "URL:", and resize it so that it is smaller in width.
- Place an Entryfield control next to the textLabel and change these properties:

    maxLength   250 // characters
    name   URLEntry
    value   "" (empty)
    width   527 // pixels

- Finally, place a pushbutton to the right of the entryfield and set the following properties:

    name   GotoURLButton
    ext   "" (empty)
    upBitMap   RESOURCE #7030

(Select the property, click the toolbutton, select "Resource" in the combobox, click the tool button to the right, find image 7030 – a green arrow pointing to the right, and click "OK", then click "OK" again ...)
width 23

- For the pushbutton, we are going to tell dBASE to pass along the value in the entryfield to the ActiveX control. To do that, find the pushbutton's *onClick* event in the Inspector, and click the tool button. Enter the following:

```
function GOTOURLBUTTON_onClick
   form.ActiveX1.nativeObject.navigate( form.URLEntry.value )
return
```

- You may wish to change the z-order of the controls (use the "Layout" menu, select the "Set Component Order" option and move the ActiveX control to the bottom of the list ...) so that the Entryfield gets focus when the form is run.
- This is a quick sample and there are many things we could do here. To try this, run the form. If you are connected to the internet, enter a URL that you know is valid, such as my own website:

```
http://www.goldenstag.net/GSP
```

Click on the pushbutton, and you should get the website to appear in the ActiveX window.

- A problem that will occur – if you need to widen the form, or make it taller, the browser window we have now does not resize to match. How can you deal with that? By using the form's *onSize* event, changing the *height* and *width* properties of the ActiveX control. Something like the following:

```
function form_onSize(nSizeType, nWidth, nHeight)
   // Update the size of the ActiveX control:
   this.ActiveX1.width := nWidth - 2
   this.ActiveX1.height := nHeight - this.ActiveX1.top
return
```

This is rather simple code, but notice that the height change takes into account the top of the ActiveX control – otherwise the control would be taller than could fit on the form (the *top* property is not at zero – the top of the form). You have to try to take these things into account. You could add traps so that it doesn't get too small, or even too big.

I've noticed that if you resize the ActiveX control, sometimes things do not display properly now. You may want to add to the code shown above:

```
this.ActiveX1.nativeObject.refresh()
```

Now if you run this and enter a valid URL, you can resize the form. Using the URL for my own website, you should see something like (depending on whether or not I have changed this site between the time I wrote this and the book is published):

Figure 14-37

- One thing we might want to do is to use a method of the ActiveX control to change the title that appears at the top of the form, to show the title associated with the web page. To do this, bring the form back into the form designer.

Click on the ActiveX control (now appearing as a big white space on the form) and select in the Inspector the "Properties" tab. Find *nativeObject*, and click on the Inspect button ("I").

We need to use the *titleChange* event of the ActiveX control to do this, so first click on the "Events" tab, and then find *titleChange*. Now click on the tool button, and enter:

```
function Microsoft_Web_Browser_Control_TitleChange(Text)
   form.text := text
return
```

It is important to note that there appears to be a bug in the Form Designer – the text "Microsoft Web Browser Control" is streamed out with spaces, instead of underscores. You need to manually change this in the statement shown above, but also you need to scroll up in the code and change this line:

```
with (this.ACTIVEX1.nativeObject)
   TitleChange = class::MICROSOFT WEB BROWSER CONTROL_TITLECHANGE
```

```
endwith
```

So that it looks like (note addition of underscores below):

```
with (this.ACTIVEX1.nativeObject)
   TitleChange = class::MICROSOFT_WEB_BROWSER_CONTROL_TITLECHANGE
endwith
```

Now when you run the form, bringing up a web page will change the form's text property to the title that is normally displayed in the titlebar of your web browser when you examine the web page.

This is a simple form and with some work you can probably enhance it quite a bit – but this should give you some ideas.

Five problems with ActiveX controls (from J.P. Martel's article on working with ActiveX controls)

1. Some ActiveX controls are not compatible with dBASE. The best way to know is to drop one of them on a dBASE form and try to access its properties from the Inspector. Even if they appear, there are many cases where the ActiveX will be useless for dBASE developers because the controls need parts of the Visual Basic environment to do their job *(Jørgen Feder, personal conversation)*.

2. ActiveX controls have to be registered in Windows' Registry. Therefore, it is not enough to copy an OCX file from one computer to another. That means that if you plan to use any ActiveX beside those which are part of standard Windows applets, you will have to install it on each of the computers that will use it. If it is a shareware ActiveX control, it usually comes with a setup program (otherwise it is useless).

3. Further, if you rely (as I did) on a Windows' applet installed on every computer, there is no guarantee that your code will be universal under Windows. For example, some components come in different versions depending on the version of Windows. You have to rely on the lowest common denominators or make different versions of your application for different operating systems.

4. In the help files, the examples of the code needed to make an ActiveX work are usually written in Visual Basic. But, even if the ActiveX was made with Visual Basic, once dBASE creates an instance of it on a form, it becomes a pure dBASE control. You will have to translate the examples in the dBASE language. This translation is quite simple even if you never used VB.

5. Another problem with ActiveX controls is the copyright issue. If you are a valid user of a software component and if you use its ActiveX to make a dBASE application for your own personal use, there is no problem. But if you make money using an ActiveX you didn't create, even if you are a legal user of the software with which this ActiveX came and if all your clients will buy a copy of this software, that doesn't mean that the way you are using this ActiveX control is an authorized use of this software. Maybe the software company wants all its users to see its splash screen and receive credit for it. Maybe it wants its user to look once in a while for an upgrade on its Web site: how could they, now that the "engine" of the software is hidden under the hood of your own application? So it would be prudent to read carefully the software license before building a dBASE application based on an ActiveX control. The only "safe" ActiveX are the ones sold as such for the purpose of being used in applications.

There is another problem with ActiveX controls that sometimes comes up and that is a license issue when you try to run them from a compiled application. In some cases it is possible to work around these by deleting the license string in the source code of the form, in others the problem occurs due to a bug or multiple bugs in dBASE when working with

ActiveX controls. The R&D team at dBASE, LLC has been working to find these issues and fix them over the years.

ReportViewer

The ReportViewer class is designed specifically to read and display on a form, the contents of a dBL report (this does not work with third-party report designers). It allows you to display a report on a form in a way that the user can interact with it (page through it, etc.), and view the report without having to print it.

The ReportViewer class requires that the *fileName* property be set to the name of the report file, or the *ref* property be set to an object reference for a report, either in a form or when the form is run (the concept of setting a form's properties from code has been discussed elsewhere in this book). Other than that, it does not take much because this is object-oriented code, your report should be encapsulated and so passing the report to the ReportViewer most of the time will take little, if any effort.

Example
To see how this works, we will take a look at creating a ReportViewer that is designed to use an existing report in the Samples folder.

- Create a new form, as usual set the *metric* property to "6 - Pixels" and change the form's *text* property to "Report Viewer".
- We're going to start with some pushbuttons, then come back and add the ReportViewer.
- Place several pushbuttons at the top of the form (it's easier than putting them at the bottom – trust me), to navigate in the report (first page, previous page, next page) and one to print the report. So that means we need four. Place them next to each other, then change the properties:

First button:
```
    name      FirstPageButton
    text      "" (blank)
    upBitmap  RESOURCE TS_RFIRST
```
(Find the upBitmap property, click the tool button, select "Resource" in the combobox, then select the tool button next to the entryfield. Find "TS_RFIRST" – which stands for "Toolbar Small, Report First Page", and click "OK", then "OK" again ...)
```
    width     24
```

Second button:
```
    name      PreviousPageButton
    text      "" (blank)
    upBitmap  RESOURCE TS_RPREV
    width     24
```

Third button:
```
    name      NextPageButton
    text      "" (blank)
    upBitmap  RESOURCE TS_RNEXT
    width     24
```

Fourth button:
```
    name      PrintReportButton
    text      "" (blank)
    upBitmap  RESOURCE TS_PRINT
```

width   24

Rearrange the buttons so that the first three are next to each other, then a small gap between them and the fourth button.

We'll come back and add code in to the *onClick* event for these in a bit.

- Next we want to add a ReportViewer control to the form. Once you have done that, set the following properties:

filename   :SAMPLES:FISH.REP
left   0

- Click on the form surface, and select the form's *onSize* event. Click the tool button, and add this code:

```
function form_onSize(nSizeType, nWidth, nHeight)
   form.ReportViewer1.height := nHeight - form.ReportViewer.top
   form.ReportViewer1.width  := nWidth
return
```

This code will re-set the size of the reportViewer based on the *height* of the form if the form's size is changed.

- Next we need to go back to the pushbuttons and add code for the *onClick* event for each. This code will handle navigating in the report, and printing the contents of the report.

Click on the FirstPageButton and find the *onClick* event in the Inspector. Enter the following:

```
function FIRSTPAGEBUTTON_onClick
   form.ReportViewer1.ref.startPage := 1
   form.ReportViewer1.ref.endPage   := 1
   form.ReportViewer1.ref.render()
return
```

Notice the use of the ReportViewer's *ref* property *(form.ReportViewer1.ref)*? This is an object reference to the report that is being displayed, and allows you access to the properties, events and methods of that report.

Click on the PreviousPageButton, and set the *onClick* event handler to the following code:

```
function PREVIOUSPAGEBUTTON_onClick
   // get the current page:
   nPage = form.ReportViewer1.ref.startPage
   // decrement it:
   nPage--
   // check to see if by doing so we end up at a page number
   // less than 1:
   if nPage < 1
      nPage := 1
   endif
   // set the values
   form.ReportViewer1.ref.startPage := nPage
   form.ReportViewer1.ref.endPage   := nPage
   form.ReportViewer1.ref.render()
return
```

Next we need to set code for the NextPageButton's *onClick* event handler:

```
function NEXTPAGEBUTTON_onClick
    // get the current page:
    nPage = form.ReportViewer1.ref.startPage
    // increment it:
    nPage++
    // set the values
    form.ReportViewer1.ref.startPage := nPage
    form.ReportViewer1.ref.endPage   := nPage
    form.ReportViewer1.ref.render()
return
```

Note that we are not checking to see if we are going beyond the last page of the report, because the code for that is a bit more complex and we're trying to keep this simple.

The last button to send the report to the printer would need code like:

```
function PRINTBUTTON_onClick
    local bPrint, nPage
    // ask the user what printer to send this to:
    bPrint = form.ReportViewer1.ref.printer.choosePrinter()
    // if they didn't hit the Escape key, or click the Cancel
    // button:
    if bPrint
        // save current page number
        nPage = form.ReportViewer1.ref.startPage
        // Change start/end page values:
        form.ReportViewer1.ref.startPage := 1
        form.ReportViewer1.ref.endPage   := -1 // last page
        // change output:
        form.ReportViewer1.ref.output := 1 // Printer
        // generate report
        form.ReportViewer1.ref.render()
        // now we're done, reset:
        form.ReportViewer1.ref.output := 3 // Default
        form.ReportViewer1.ref.startPage := nPage
        form.ReportViewer1.ref.endPage   := nPage
    endif
return
```

- Now save and run this form, and you should see something like:

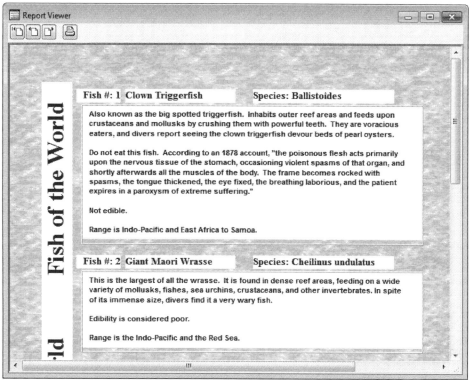

Figure 14-38

Clicking the buttons to navigate will move you around in the report, clicking the print button should print the report if you select a printer, etc.

You could of course enhance this to require that the user either open the form with a report name as a parameter, or to ask the user to select a report name in the form's *onOpen* event, and do even more with it.

SubForm

What exactly is a subform? Simply put, it is a form contained within another form. It is a type of container that can be used in your forms and acts mostly like a regular dBASE form. However – while this is being discussed in the chapter of this book on Stock Form Controls, a subform is not *really* a form control – it is a subclass of a form, subclassed from the stock form class in dBASE.

For all intents and purposes, a subform has all the properties, methods and events of a standard form, except as noted below – the following information is from dBASE's R&D team:

- Subforms do not have the following properties:
    - appSpeedBar
    - designView
    - scaleFontName
    - scaleFontSize
    - scaleFontBold
    - MDI
    - menuFile

- Subforms do not have a *readModal()* method.
- Subforms have a *parent* property, which the form object does not have. The *parent* property is read-only once the subform is instantiated – when you create a subform the property is set at that time, therefore you cannot set the *parent* property by code after it is open. If you need to change the *parent*, close the subform, then reinstantiate it with the new parent form.
- Subforms still have the *inDesign* property, even though you cannot at this time bring the subform into the designer – this is for compatibility with custom controls that need to check the *parent.inDesign* property.
- Subforms behave as if MDI=false and are parented to another form or subform.
- Parenting the subform to a form (or another subform) restricts the subform to be displayed within the client area of the parent form. It also allows the parent form to close the subform when it is being closed.
- Subforms are not form components.
- Subforms should be able to have their own popup menu.
- Subforms are able to have their own toolbar, however, the toolbar appears *on the subform* not the _app.framewin.
- All form components should be able to work properly on a subform as they do on a form.
- A form containing one or more subforms internally tracks which subform (if any) is currently active. When a subform is active, the subform has the focus. When a form component is given focus, the active subform loses focus and is set to inactive. Clicking anywhere on a subform or subform component should activate the subform and set focus to a control on the subform. (This can be seen by the status/color of the titlebar of your subforms.)
- A form's *canClose* will call the *canClose* for any child subforms. If a subform's *canClose* returns *false*, the form's *canClose* will return *false* (and the parent form will not close).
- Subforms can be parents of other subforms.

How Do I Use a Subform?

Programmatically it's as simple as:

```
fMain = new Form()
fSub  = new SubForm( fMain ) // 'fMain' here is the PARENT form
fMain.open()
fSub.open()
```

The code shown above would produce the following:

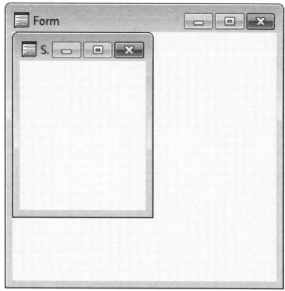

Figure 14-39

Notice that the subform default text is "Subform" and that we did nothing to create that text.

Note also, that there is an optional parameter after the *parent* reference. The optional parameter is the text that appears in the titlebar of the subform. You can either set this when you create an instance of the subform or you can set the subform's *text* property.

```
fMain = new Form()
fSub  = new SubForm( fMain,  My Subform  )
   // 'fMain' here is the PARENT form
   // and the text  My Subform  is the titlebar text
fMain.open()
fSub.open()
```

As a developer there are a few things that are useful to know:

- Opening a parent form does not open any subforms that may be associated with it – you have to open those individually (if you want a subform open when the parent form opens, use an overrridden *open()* method of the form to open your subform(s)).
- If you attempt to release a parent form that has at least one subform, references to the parent will still exist – you have to release the subforms to remove the references to the parent form. (Use the *release()* method of the subform.)
- You can create a subform with no titlebar, no border, etc. by setting the following properties:
  - sizeable = false
  - moveable = false
  - sysMenu = false
  - maximize = false
  - minimize = false

  If you set a *colorNormal* property for the subform you will get just that colored subform. If you set the *clientEdge* property to *true* you will get a border on the subform.
- Objects with *transparent* set to *true* on a subform will show the background of the subform, not the parent form.
- If you wish to use the *title* parameter to pass title text to the subform, make sure that the *text* property of the subform is not included in the constructor code (the form

designer defaults to setting the property to an empty string) – the subform's text property will override the parameter passed to the subform.

You can use a form's *onOpen()* event to open subforms, or use a pushbutton's *onClick()* event – you have a lot of power and flexibility here.

Using the Designers to Create Subforms

The Form Designer does not, at this time, directly support the creation or modification of subforms. However, if you create a form, you can make it a subform by changing the following statement:

```
class TestFormForm of FORM
    // Change to:
class TestFormForm( oParent, cTitle ) of SUBFORM( oParent, cTitle )
```

Note that when you make this change, the subform cannot be modified in the Form Designer unless you change that statement back.

What Do You Use It For?

SubForms were created in dBASE to allow you to create a form that literally belongs to, or is a child of, another form. Indeed, you can have subforms of subforms, if you really wished to. I have not personally started using these in my own applications, so I went out and asked other developers what they were using them for, and got back the following ideas:

- "I am in the process of developing an application that in its look and feel is going to be fairly similar to Outlook^tm. In other words, it is all SDI with various areas of the screen "opening" to different functions as needed. For that, since I don't want the regular borders of a form, I use subforms." – Jan Hoerterling
- "Floating palettes. Very handy." – J.P. Martel
- "A search form, which would search for info in a given area of an application. Open a client form, then you want to find info on that client. Create a search form. [There is] nothing more frustrating than having your search forms all over the desktop, especially if you have other forms open. I find that it can become confusing. Subforms just narrows and tightens this up." – Robert Bravery

This is a sampling of what can be done with subforms. Another example, although it is not apparent, is in dQuery – each query object (that lists fields) is really a subform of the main dQuery window (dQuery itself is written entirely in dBL).

Other Controls

dBASE ships with several other controls that I will only briefly discuss because they are of limited use. Some developers might find ways to incorporate some of these into their applications, but most developers don't.

Paintbox

The Paintbox control is an interesting one, as it allows a developer familiar with the Windows API (see a later chapter in this book) the ability to draw their own controls in Windows. The main reason this is not being discussed here is that it is a very complex control and way beyond the scope of a "beginning" book on dBASE. I mention it here for completeness – it is a stock control in dBASE used on forms. If you need to know more, you should see details in the OLH.

Scrollbars

Scrollbars can be either horizontal or vertical. Forms have them built in, and most controls (listboxes, subforms, etc.) that might need a scrollbar have them as an option that can be turned on and off, or set to "auto" – meaning that they will appear if needed. Once again, these are being mentioned here for completeness' sake, not that the average developer is likely to need these for anything. You could add your own scrollbars to a container control, for example. It would probably take some serious effort to make controls contained by the container to shift with the scrollbar, however.

OLE

The OLE control is meant to work with OLE fields in a table. If you have a table with an OLE field, this control can interact with it, allowing you to add a file to the field, view the contents, etc. Most dBASE developers do not really use OLE fields much. If you need this, see the OLH for details.

Browse

The Browse control is a legacy control left in dBASE so that developers moving applications from Visual dBASE 5.x (and dBASE 5.0 for Windows) to dBASE Plus have a browse control. It is superseded by the Grid in dBASE Plus, and frankly is not recommended – the abilities of the Browse control are quite limited.

Summary

As you can see, there are a huge number of controls available to you, as a developer, with a huge amount of power and flexibility available. The difficulty when designing an interface is deciding what to use and how to make your interface useful to the end user. It is possible to be caught up in trying to use all kinds of nifty gadgets, and end up making an interface that is confusing for the user. If your user is confused, they will not want to use the application, and ... they will not pay for it!

NOTES:

Chapter 15: Working With the Grid

In Chapter 14 of this book we discussed the various visual stock classes that are built in to dBASE to interact with the data in an application. We even discussed the grid a little, but we did not really delve into this complex and extremely important control, because I felt it important enough to dedicate an entire chapter to.

The grid object in dBASE Plus is complex, that many developers (myself included) do not use it to its fullest capability. This chapter is an attempt to explain what you can do with the grid in your own applications, by exploring in some detail the properties, events and methods of the grid and the grid's objects.

In the previous chapter we saw this image:

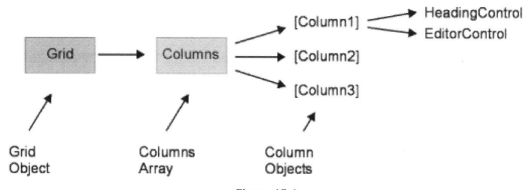

Figure 15-1
(Created by and used with permission of Michael Nuwer)

The image shows the basic object model for the grid. As was noted in the previous chapter, the grid can be used at the basic level by simply using the *dataLink* property of the grid and perhaps working with some colors. However, in order to have access to the columns, which includes the ability to manipulate the column widths, set the *picture* property, change the heading text for individual columns, and a lot more, we must define the columns array.

Getting Started

To get started with the grid, we will create a few forms with examples to highlight some of the abilities of the grid. Of course you may just wish to read about these and look at the examples without actually doing them ... it's up to you. The first part of this will be similar to what we have done in the previous chapter and then we'll start looking at options.

Create a new form by going to the Navigator in dBASE Plus and selecting the "Forms" tab. Double-click the first "Untitled" icon to create a form. When it comes up in the Form Designer, set the *metric* property to 6 ("Pixels").

We need a table and for the moment we'll use the "Fish" table in the dBASE Samples database. Click on the Navigator window and select the "Tables" tab. If you do not see "DBASESAMPLES" in the "Look in" combobox, click on the down arrow, select "DBASESAMPLES", then select the "Fish" table and drag that to the form surface.

Save the form as "GridExample1.wfm" ($\boxed{\text{Ctrl}}+\boxed{\text{S}}$), so that we don't forget. Click on the grid, go to the Inspector, find the *dataLink* property and set it to "FISH1" (select the down arrow for the combobox). The grid is now at its most basic setting. You can use it as is, run the form, interact with the data, etc., however we want to have more control.

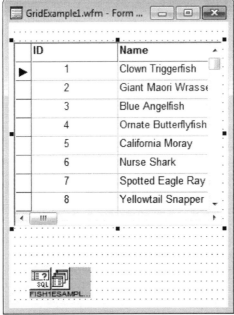

Figure 15-2

The Columns Array

As mentioned in the previous chapter, this control comes from setting the Columns Array for the grid. This is done by going to the Inspector, finding the *columns* object, then click on the tool button. This will bring up the Columns Property Builder dialog:

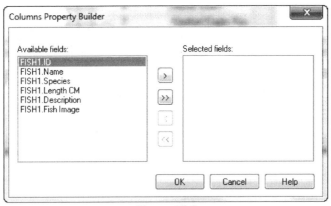

Figure 15-3

This is a very useful tool, in that it allows you to select the field or fields you wish to display in the grid, in any sequence you wish them displayed. For now we want all of the fields in the default sequence. We will come back to this later in this chapter for another example and examine the ability to use fields in different sequences than the table structure defines them and more. For now, to select all of the fields, click the button that shows ">>". This selects all, and moves them to the right side of the dialog:

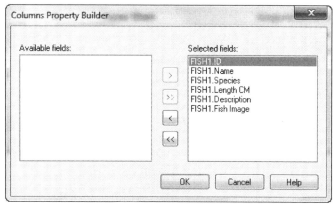

Figure 15-4

Click "OK" and the grid will look exactly like it did before. Why is that? We didn't actually change the appearance, since we are using the default columns in the default sequence, it currently looks like it did before.

Now that we've done this, what we gained was access to the individual columns, with their *editorControl* and *headingControl* objects and all of the properties, methods and events associated with them. For most of the rest of this chapter we will be working with these to allow access to a variety of capabilities of the grid that we didn't have before.

Let's make the form and the grid a bit larger, so we have something more useful – as it is, you can probably only see three columns, not all of the third one.

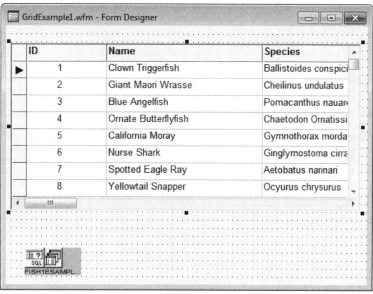

Figure 15-5

One of the first things that we can do, since we have set up the columns array, is to change the widths of the columns.

But before we get to that, how exactly do you set focus on the columns so we can access the properties in the Inspector? There are at least two ways of doing this, both are described below. You can use whichever means of giving focus to the grid that makes sense to you – dBASE doesn't care.

The first method of giving focus to the individual columns, is to click on the column in the Form Designer. This may require more than one click, but if you look at the Inspector, you should see the column get focus. You will know when you see something like: form.grid1.columns["column2"] in the Inspector's combobox.

If your table is empty, however, this method will not work. You cannot click on data that does not exist in the table. Do not despair however. You can get to the columns in the Inspector directly – by either using the combobox at the top and selecting under "grid" the word "columns", or by clicking on the grid and in the Inspector going to the *columns* object and clicking the Inspect button. This will show a listing of the columns available. Clicking on the column you wish to modify (they will be shown as "Column1", "Column2", etc.) then clicking the Inspect button, you will "drill down" to the column and can modify any properties, as if you had double-clicked on it.

In the current example, we have six columns. We ought to change the widths of several of these to make them easier to work with. The first column is the "ID" column. It's a little wider than needed, but watch what happens when you change the *width* property. This should be available in the Inspector by using the spinbox's down-arrow button. The name column just moves left and the numbers start to disappear:

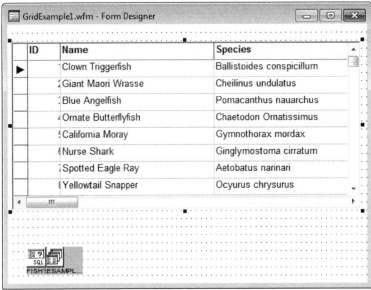

Figure 15-6

Obviously that's not very useful. The problem is that the column is really too large for the values displayed, but how do you control the display?

> **NOTE:**
> In build 2.61.4, the developers added the ability to modify the *width* of custom columns (ones where you have specified the fields displayed, as in this example) and the *height* of the rows (*cellHeight* property) in the designer. Move the mouse over the column (or row) headings and with the mouse between them, you should see the mouse cursor change shape – widen or shorten the width of the column by dragging the mouse left or right. For rows, the same, but over the row heading on the left. You can move a column by dragging it to a new location as well.

The field is an autoincrement field, which is a number. You can change the appearance using the *picture* property, but where is it? If you go to the Inspector, there is no *picture* property. This is because we are working on the column, not on the editorControl that is contained by the column. The column has a *width* property, but the editorControl has more properties that we can manipulate.

To get to the editorControl's properties, in the Inspector click on the *editorControl* object, then the Inspect button. Find the *picture* property here and set this to "9,999". (Type those characters in without the quotes, then press the Enter key.) Now if you click on the grid and the first column again, the Inspector will go back to the column, then using the spinbox you can reduce the width of the column and see the effect more correctly.

Change the column's *width* to about 50 (pixels) – you can type the value if you would rather, just make sure you press the Enter key after doing so, or when focus leaves the entry area of the Inspector, the width will not have changed. This should give enough room to see the number in the new format provided by the *picture* property of the editorControl and have a little space to the right between the number and the next column.

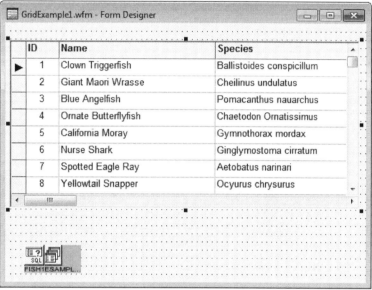

Figure 15-7

We will come back and revisit the editorControl object over the exercises and examples in this chapter.

Change the widths of the second column (Name) and third column (Species) to 150 pixels each, which should bring them down to a reasonable width for now.

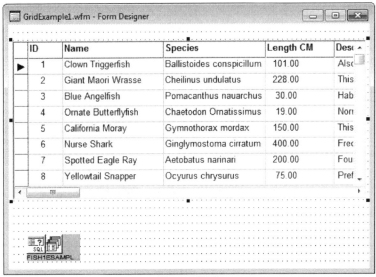
Figure 15-8

We could change the widths of the other columns, but for now let's leave things as they are. If you run this form, it should look something like:

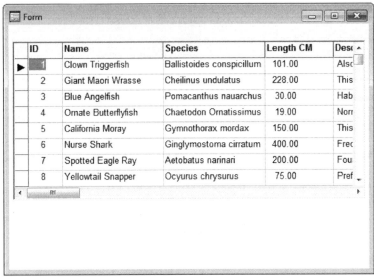
Figure 15-9

The Column's *editorType* Property

When you set the *dataLink* for the grid, the Form Designer evaluated the field types and determines what it should use for the different field types for the column editor. For example, use the Form Designer, the default control when you place a numeric value on a form is a spinbox control. The same type of thing is determined by the Form Designer when you use a grid. A character field, for example, will default to using an entryfield, a numeric or date field to spinbox, a logical value to a checkbox and so on. When dBASE Plus 2.2 was released, the R&D team added a new column type – the Editor – this is useful for longer character fields and for memo fields. We will examine this in a bit as it is quite handy. There is also a combobox, which can be used in the same way a combobox works outside of the grid – you can supply a dataSource, or use it with a lookupSQL or lookupRowset.

You can change the *editorType* for any column of the grid, as well as just using what the Form Designer assigns to your columns. This is useful if you don't like, for example, spinbox controls for numeric or date fields. You can change the control to an entryfield the spinbox buttons will no longer be there and the properties of the *editorControl* object will be updated.

In addition, the grid in current versions of dBASE assumes that a memo field will be displayed in an editor in the grid. If you prefer that your grids default to an entryfield, you can either manually change them, by changing the grid object's *defaultMemoEditor* property which defaults to "0 - Use columnEditor" to "1 - Use columnEntryfield" or the same for the grid column's *editorType* property. Finally, you can make a change in the dBASE Plus initialization (PLUS.INI) file, by adding these two lines:

```
[Grid]
DefaultMemoEditor=1
```

Changing this to 1 in the.ini file will tell dBASE to use the entryfield for all new grids (if a grid already has an editor set, you will need to manually change it).

With the grid form still running, let's take a look at the types. The first column is for a numeric field, so why is it not a spinbox control? Because autoincrement fields are read-only by definition and the ID field is an autoincrement field. Therefore this defaults to an entryfield and is not editable when the form is running. While you can give focus to the column, you cannot change the value. If you tab to the "Name" column, you will see that the text is highlighted and you can change it (don't, but it is possible) – by default data is "live" in a grid – meaning that you can change it and update it in the grid. You do not have to do anything special to make the data active. The "Species" column is also character and also an entryfield. However, if you tab to the "Length CM" column, you will see that this numeric value is displayed as mentioned in a spinbox. When the control gets focus, the buttons that are part of the spinbox control suddenly appear.

Pressing tab again will take you to the "Description" field, which is a memo field in the table, is defined by dBASE (by default) as an editor type for the *editorControl*. The tool button that appears will open a window the width of the column that will allow the user to view and edit the contents of the field to which the column is linked.

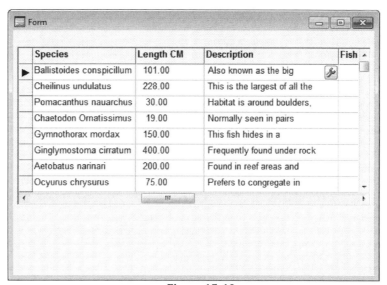

Figure 15-10

You might want to set a default row height when using an editor in a grid, so that the user can see more than one line of whatever is in the field that the control is dataLinked to. This can be done by modifying the grid's *cellHeight* property. I find it's generally best to experiment with this to find something that looks good to you. Setting the *cellHeight* property affects all rows of the grid. Also note that unless the *allowRowSizing* property is set to *false*, the user can change the height while viewing the grid (dragging on the bottom of a row in the indicator column on the left to make it taller or shorter).

If you tab once more you will end up on the "Fish Image" column. This column shows that it is an image by displaying a small picture:

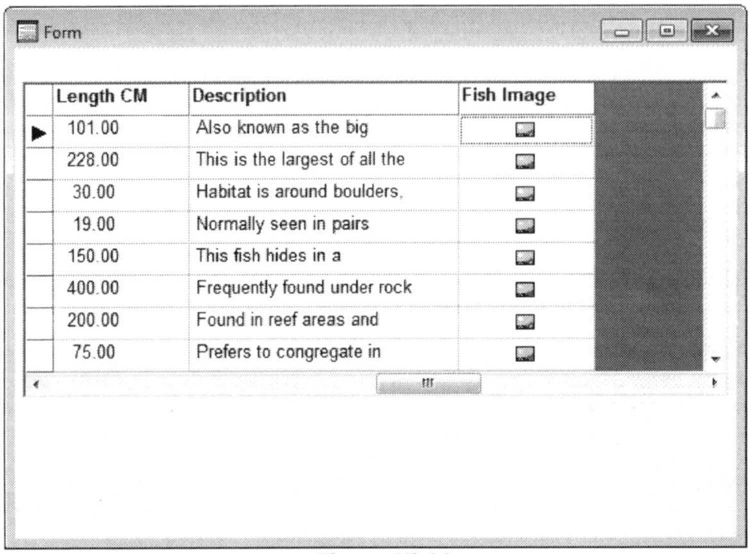

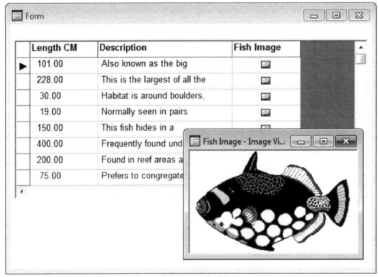

Figure 15-11

If you double-click on this, an image window will display outside of the grid itself. In the screen shot below, I moved the image over the grid, but it often displays off to the side of the form. You can of course move this and if you navigate to a new row with the window open, the image will change:

Figure 15-12

When you are on the last column, what happens if you use the Tab key? You move to the first column, but the next row of the table! This wrap-around is a standard feature of the grid. If you are on the last row and you tab off the last column, by default the grid will place you into the rowset's *beginAppend* mode – you will be adding a row. You can turn that off –

we will discuss it later, but by default, this is what will happen. You can also use the "Back Tab" that is built into Windows by using the Shift key with the Tab key (hold the Shift key and press Tab ...). This will back-tab or backward tab through the columns, and again, it will wrap around.

If you bring the form back into the Form Designer, you should examine the various properties that can be used to assist in editing data. For example, a spinbox control has some of the properties, events and methods of the regular spinbox in dBASE. A combobox has some of the properties, events and methods of the style 2 combobox and so on. This is important to note if you are creating a grid that you wish to allow your users to edit data in.

At this point, we've pretty much covered the basics. It is now time to delve into the grid in more depth and start looking at how to make this control really useful and at the same time, make it work for you and your users the way you need it to.

Checkboxes
The developers, in release 2.61.4 added a property of the grid to work with an issue that has been making developers a little crazy, the checkbox display. In the grid, if the editorControl is set to a checkbox, typically if the current row has focus the checkbox is displayed, if the row does not have focus, the checkbox is not displayed. Many developers felt this was odd. The developers added a new property to the grid: *alwaysDrawCheckbox* which defaults to *true.* If set to *true*, then all rows will display the checkbox, if you change it to *false* the grid will exhibit the behavior mentioned above.

Comboboxes
In the same release as above (2.61.4), the developers added the following properties and events to the combobox in the grid (the editorControl, actually), to match the stock combobox control:

- Style (options of 0 – Dropdown, or 1-DropDownList)
- AutoTrim
- MaxLength
- SelectAll
- BeforeDropDown
- BeforeCloseUp
- OnChange
- OnChangeCancel
- OnChangeCommited
- BeforeEditPaint
- OnEditPaint
- The columnCombobox auto adjusts its height to match the current grid *cellHeight* property.

Use of the Mouse with the Grid
In build 2.61.4, the developers updated the grid to handle passing appropriate mouse coordinates to the columnHeading mouse event handlers. If you click anywhere on the grid, as long as the appropriate mouse event handler has been created and is not overridden by a matching *columnHeading* or *editorControl* event handler, the appropriate event will fire. This includes column headers row headers, grid cells, or the grid background.

Editable or Not?
One of the first things you need to determine with a grid is if you want to allow your users to be able to edit data in the grid at all. Many developers have found that since the editorControl objects do not have all the properties, events and methods that their regular

form equivalents have, that their users can get into trouble editing data in the grid. This really boils down to a decision that you have to make and the more familiar you are with the abilities of the grid, the better your ability to make an informed decision will be.

In my own applications I seldom let the user edit data in a grid. However, once in a while I find the grid to be the best way to do something. In those cases, it is sometimes easier to let the user edit the data in the grid. So while most of the time I don't allow it, sometimes I break that "rule" in my application development.

Editable Grids

For a grid to be editable, there is not a lot you *have* to do as a developer. To allow your users to edit data, you might want to set properties of the editorControl object for individual columns, but otherwise the grid is editable.

Do you want to allow your users to add new data? If you do, again, there is nothing you need to do. If, however, you do *not* wish to allow this, you can set the grid's *allowAddRows* property to *false*. Doing so will mean that when the user gets to the last row of the grid, pressing the down arrow key, or tabbing to the last column and then pressing tab once more (wrapping around) will **not** place the rowset into append mode, adding a blank row to the table.

If you are allowing your user to edit the data that is displayed in the grid, here are a few things you should be aware of.

Read-Only Fields

Some fields are by their nature not editable – this includes autoincrement type fields – these can only be modified by the database engine. Others are calculated fields. However, you might want to set some fields as not being editable as well. For example, if you were displaying a customer record table and you had a customer number that is created in a special way, used to link the customer's data to other data in your database, you do not wish to allow the user to change the linking field, correct?

The simple method of handling this does not involve the grid at all, but actually involves the field object for the field in question. If you select the query object on the form (or in the data module), you can go to the rowset object and inspect it, then the fields array object and inspect that, then the individual field. Once you find the field and inspect that (this all assumes the use of the Inspector), there is a *readOnly* property, which defaults to *false* (because normally a field is not read only). If you set this property to *true*, then when the form with the grid is run, the field is not editable.

Another method of limiting the data that can be edited that can be useful in some special cases is if you have only one field you wish the user to be able to edit in the grid. Rather than setting the *readOnly* property for each field, you could go to the grid object itself and select the *frozenColumn* property – with this you must specify the name of the field you wish to "freeze". There is a tool button and selecting this, you can select the field. When you run the form, the only column that can get focus is the one that is selected as the *frozenColumn*. While this may have limited use in your applications, it is a good thing to know about.

Non-Editable Grids

A grid can be set up as a "display only" grid in several ways. The simplest is to set the grid's *allowEditing* and *allowAddRows* properties to *false*. Doing so means that a user cannot edit or add a row, therefore the data is not editable.

Another means of setting the grid into a read only state is set either the grid's *rowSelect* property to *true* or the grid's *multiSelect* property to *true*. Either of these will put the grid into a read-only state. However, it should be noted that the developers at dBASE, LLC have stated that using *rowSelect* doesn't *have* to force the grid to be read-only, so this may change at some point in the future.

The advantage to *rowSelect* is that it also highlights the current row in the grid. This makes viewing the grid easier, because the user can see the row that is selected better – it becomes much more obvious which row is selected. The screen below shows a grid with the *rowSelect* property set to *true*, and running:

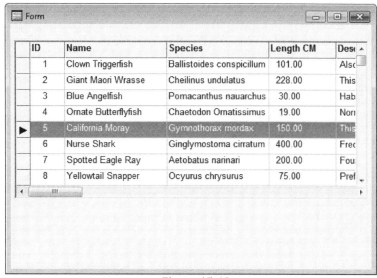

Figure 15-13

The *multiSelect* property works similar to *rowSelect* but it allows a user to select multiple rows at a time. The way this works is that once a row is selected, the user can select more rows by either using the Shift key and selecting another row (this selects all rows from the current one to that one), or by using the Ctrl key and selecting another row (this selects individual rows one at a time, but you can select as many as you might need). Once your user has selected multiple rows, what do you do with them? We will come back to actually working with the *multiSelect* property later in this chapter.

Display Issues

Display on the grid can get fairly complex, fairly quickly, so let's start with the basics. The first things to examine are the many *font* properties of the grid.

Fonts

The grid has the usual *fontBold*, *fontItalic*, *fontName*, *fontSize*, etc. properties. These affect all cells of the grid and are effectively a global property for all cells of the grid that are not set differently (note that the heading controls have a different set of font properties we will discuss shortly). What do I mean by this? If you set the *fontBold* property for the grid to true, all cells in the grid will be displayed with **bold** text. The same for changing the *fontName*, the *fontSize*, etc.

For the most part you are most likely to only want to change the *fontName* and maybe the *fontSize* properties for the whole grid. If you wanted to change font properties for individual columns of the grid, you can do this by modifying the properties of the *editorControl* for the individual column. We'll come back to this in a moment.

As well as the font properties for the cells of the grid, there are font properties for the heading controls that also default to the whole grid. For example, you might want to change the *headingFontSize* of all the heading controls to something larger or smaller. Again, these properties affect all of the heading controls for the grid – they are global properties.

Colors

The grid has quite a few color properties, similar to the font properties mentioned above, which also tend to affect the whole grid. We can affect individual column and cell properties but that is done differently. The color properties can use a variety of different color definitions. These were discussed briefly in the previous chapter and are discussed in full in the online help for dBASE under the heading "colorNormal". Most of the colors that will be used in this chapter will either be hexidecimal values or JavaScript color names (such as "white"). You can also use the Windows specific color definitions. If you examine the properties in the grid that we discuss here, you will see a mix of these. So you might see in one case "WindowText/Window", but in another you might see "silver".

The *bgColor* property affects the background ("bg" for background) of the grid – the area that is not covered by the cells of the grid. In order to see the area described, make the height of the grid taller in the example form:

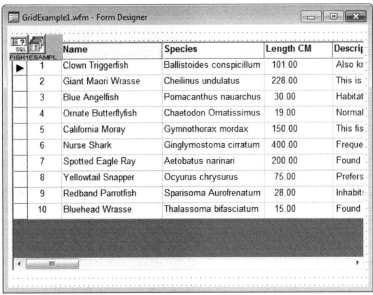

Figure 15-14

The dark gray area is the area affected by the grid's *bgColor* property. You can change this to some other color simply enough. The default is "gray". However, if you find the *bgColor* property in the Inspector, you can change this to a color such as "white". This would look like:

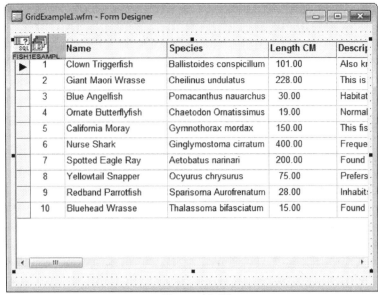

FISH1ESAMPL

	Name	Species	Length CM	Descrip
1	Clown Triggerfish	Ballistoides conspicillum	101.00	Also kr
2	Giant Maori Wrasse	Cheilinus undulatus	228.00	This is
3	Blue Angelfish	Pomacanthus nauarchus	30.00	Habitat
4	Ornate Butterflyfish	Chaetodon Ornatissimus	19.00	Normal
5	California Moray	Gymnothorax mordax	150.00	This fis
6	Nurse Shark	Ginglymostoma cirratum	400.00	Freque
7	Spotted Eagle Ray	Aetobatus narinari	200.00	Found
8	Yellowtail Snapper	Ocyurus chrysurus	75.00	Prefers
9	Redband Parrotfish	Sparisoma Aurofrenatum	28.00	Inhabit:
10	Bluehead Wrasse	Thalassoma bifasciatum	15.00	Found

Figure 15-15

Of course you can use lots of other colors as well, I just chose one that was dramatically different, which may be something you would want to use for your own applications.

You can change the colors of the lines in the grid that separate the columns. The default for the grid's *colorColumnLines* and *colorRowLines* properties is "silver".

The *colorNormal* property affects the cells in the grid, which is a global property – it affects all cells in the grid. The default value for this property is "WindowText/Window". This and several others require a foreground and a background – the foreground referencing the text displayed, the background being what it says. So you could use (for dramatic effect) "yellow/red" which would give you yellow text on a red background for the cells in a grid.

The *colorHighlight* property affects all cells in the grid, but only when the individual cell has focus. If you have a grid that you want your users to be able to edit, you might want to change the *colorHighlight* property to something that makes it obvious which cell has focus (this is particularly useful if the user ends up looking away from the screen for a moment and then looks back). If you used something like "WindowText/0x80ffff" for this property, when a cell gets focus, it will have (typically) black text on a yellow background.

The *headerColorNormal* property affects the column headings and the *colorRowHeader* affects the headings on the left side of the grid used to show the current row pointer.

If your grid has the *rowSelect* or *multiSelect* properties set to *true*, then the *colorRowSelect* will allow you to alter the color of both the text and background of the row that is selected. This can be used to fit in with a color scheme being used for your application.

Once you have set all these color properties (if you do) for your grid, you can make the grid look very specific to your application's needs. However, as noted these affect the whole grid, not individual cells and columns. We'll take a look at this in more detail in a bit.

Other Grid Appearance Properties

By default the grid displays column headings, the row selection header on the left and the lines between columns and rows. You can turn each of these settings on or off yourself, by using the appropriate properties of the grid. These properties all begin with the word "has" and are logical values, which all default to *true*. The *hasColumnHeadings* property will turn off the column headings of the grid if set to *false*, for example:

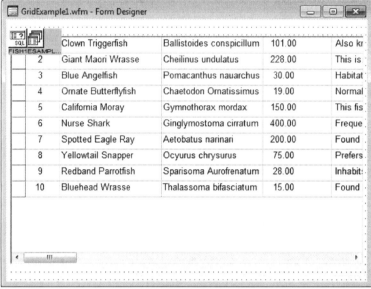

Figure 15-16

Row Height Issues

One concern with rows in the grid is when you reach the bottom – it is possible to see a partial row in the grid. Some developers are okay with this and others are not. Using the example form shown above for "GridExample1", if the height of the grid itself is small enough, you might see something like this (Figure 15-17):

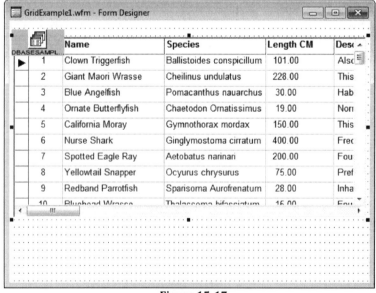

Figure 15-17

Notice how the last row is cut off. Some developers like this appearance, others do not. One way of resolving the issue is by use of the grid's *integralHeight* property. By default this is set to *false*, but changing this property in the form designer to *true* will cause dBASE to only display the row if you can see all of it in the grid:

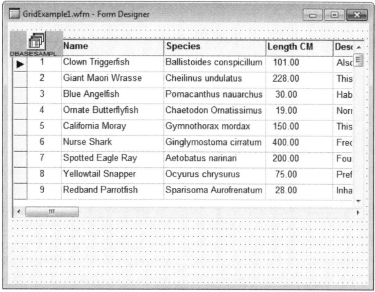

Figure 15-18

Note that the row that does not fit on the grid is not displayed. The only drawback to this is that a user may not know there is at least one more row at the bottom of the grid. *(That is the point of the vertical scrollbar on the grid, however, so one could make a case for this either way, or the programmer could design the grid to be just tall enough for the last displayed row, and not worry about it …)*

Changing the Appearance of Individual Columns

As noted above, the font and color properties discussed affect the whole grid. What if you wish to affect individual columns of the grid?

First, to make the following discussion relative to the sample form we've been working with, you might want to set the FISH1 query object's rowset's *indexName* property to "Name".

What if you wish to affect individual columns of the grid? This is done by modifying properties of the *editorControl* or the *headingControl* for the specific column. For example, if we wanted to show that the data displayed in the grid is sorted on the Name column, we might want to alter the appearance of the name column. In our example form, for example, clicking on the Name column in the grid to give it focus and then the *editorControl* object in the Inspector and clicking the Inspect button will show the properties of the *editorControl*. You can change the font properties, or more dramatically the *colorNormal* property. So you might do something like set the *colorNormal* property to "WindowText/lightblue". *(For some reason this does not always automatically display when you change the property in the Form Designer. Running the form will display it, and if the property is set, bringing the form into the Form Designer will also display the color.)*

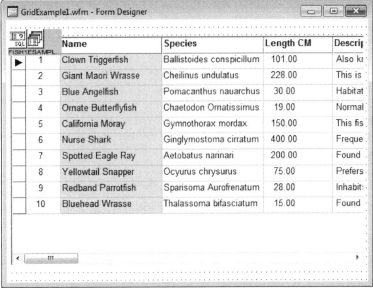

Figure 15-19

Similarly, you can modify the heading color or font properties. If you wish to wish to, you could bring the form back to the Form Designer, click on the grid, then the column and in the Inspector select the *headingControl* object, the Inspect button. From there you have access to the font and color properties of the column's heading control.

Enhancing the Grid's Abilities

The rest of this chapter is going to delve into using code to alter the way the grid works. You can follow along if you wish, or skip the rest of the chapter, that's up to you. The details are here to cover areas that many developers have requested assistance with over the years.

Multiselect Grids

A multiselect grid is useful for situations where you might wish to allow your users to select more than one row for some sort of processing.

The difficulty really comes about in addressing the rows that the user selected and doing something with them. What you need to do might be something such as printing a list of information, changing a value, selecting a series of rows for deletion, or pretty much anything.

In order to understand this better, let's make a copy of the first grid example form. If the form is in the Form Designer, press Ctrl+W and close the designer saving any changes. If the form is running, click on the 'x' in the titlebar of the form to close it. In the Command Window, type:

```
copy file GridExample1.wfm to GridExample2.wfm
```

To be sure the form works as expected, open it in the Source Code Editor (right click on it in the Navigator and select "Open in Source Editor" or press F2). Change the number 1 to 2 as shown below, there are two places you need to do this:

```
parameter bModal
local f
f = new GridExample2Form()
if (bModal)
   f.mdi = false // ensure not MDI
   f.readModal()
else
   f.open()
endif

class GridExample2Form of FORM
```

Save this and exit the Source Code Editor by pressing `Ctrl`+`W`. Open the form in the Form Designer.

The first thing to do is set the grid's *multiSelect* property to *true*. It may not appear anything has happened. Now let's set the *colorRowSelect* property to "WindowText/LightBlue", to give us a color other than the default, which will be whatever the default highlight colors are for your Windows settings.

Next we want to place a pushbutton on the form under the grid. Change the *text* property of the pushbutton to read "Process Selected Rows". You will want to experiment with the height and width of the pushbutton (use the mouse to drag the edges), so there's enough room for the text on the pushbutton. This should end up looking similar to the following:

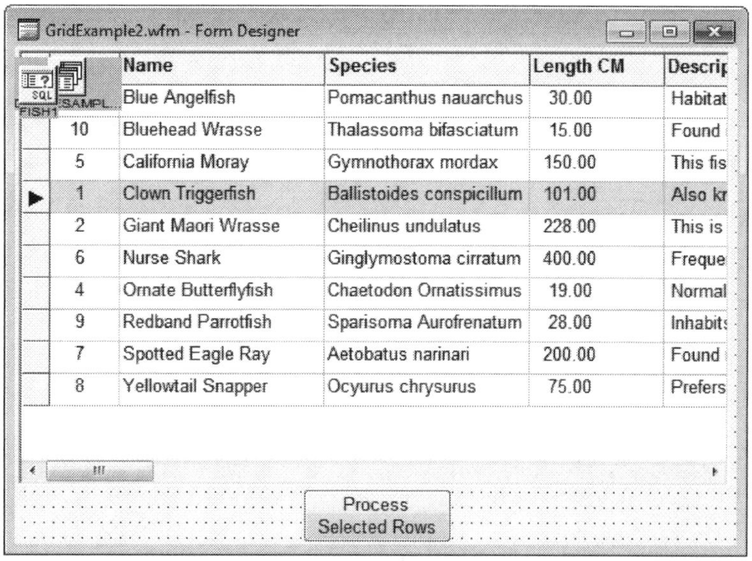

Figure 15-20

Before we start writing code, let's briefly discuss the concept of what we are going to do.

When the grid's *multiSelect* property is set to *true*, you may use the grid's *selected* method to return an array of bookmarks to the selected records. This is similar, yet different, from the way a listbox object works. A listbox object's *selected* method returns the text of a single item if the *multi* property is set to *false*. The grid's *selected* method does not fire if the *multiSelect* property is set to *false*. The grid's *selected* method always returns an array object.

The array object for the grid's *selected* method is an array of bookmark objects. These have been discussed in earlier chapters, but to reiterate some important details – bookmarks are transient. If you change the index order (*rowset.indexName*), set a filter condition or a *setRange()*, the bookmarks you have set may be gone. Sometimes if you navigate before you copy the data from the grid's *selected* method, you will lose the array – this is a sort of nasty bit that if you're not aware of it, can make you a little crazy. Before you try to do anything with the bookmarks contained in the array, you will want to copy the contents of it to another array.

With all that said, let's build some code. The code below will be executed from the pushbutton's *onClick* event handler and in this particular case is only going to list the contents of the Name, Species and Length CM fields. There are a lot of comments embedded in the code in an attempt to make the code make sense. To create this code, in the Form Designer make sure the pushbutton has focus, and in the Inspector window go to the "Events" tab. Click on the *onClick* event, and click the tool button. Enter the code shown below:

```
function PUSHBUTTON1_onClick
    // see if the user has selected at least
    // one row:
    if form.grid1.selected().size > 0

        // copy the array:
        local aRows, i
        aRows = form.grid1.selected()

        // display the number of rows selected:
        ? "Number of rows selected: "+aRows.size

        // loop through the array:
        for i = 1 to aRows.size

            // the goto method of the rowset uses
            // bookMarks, which is what is
            // contained in the array:
            form.rowset.goto( aRows[ i ] )

            // display the contents of
            // some of the fields:
            ? i+" - "+;
              form.rowset.fields["NAME"].value.rightTrim()+;
              " - "+;
              form.rowset.fields["SPECIES"].value.rightTrim()+;
              " - "+;
              form.rowset.fields["LENGTH CM"].value

        next // end of looping through array

    else // user didn't select any rows

        ? "No rows selected"

    endif
return
```

Check your work for typos. When you run the form, use the Ctrl key as well as the mouse (Ctrl+mouse click) you can select multiple rows. This should look something like:

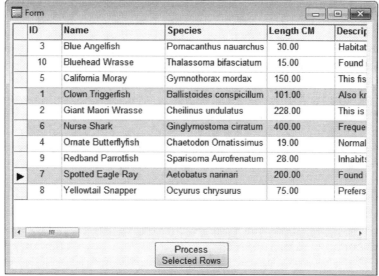

Figure 15-21

The output should look something like the following in the output pane of the Command Window:

```
Number of rows selected: 3
1 — Clown Triggerfish — Ballistoides conspicillum — 101.00
2 — Nurse Shark — Ginglymostoma cirratum — 400.00
3 — Spotted Eagle Ray — Aetobatus narinari — 200.00
```

The number that is displayed is not the ID field in the table, but the index for the for/next loop.

Go ahead and close this form. We're going to move on to another example.

Changing Rowset Sort Order

This example is actually going to show to different things – the ability to use the column *headingControl* to react to the mouse and the ability to change the colors of columns as needed to help make a visual cue to your users for what is happening.

Once again, we're going to copy the first example, and then modify it from there.
In the Command Window, type:

```
copy file GridExample1.wfm to GridExample3.wfm
```

To be sure the form works as expected, open it in the Source Code Editor (right click on it in the Navigator and select "Open in Source Editor" or press). Change the number 1 to 3 as shown below, there are two places you need to do this:

```
parameter bModal
local f
f = new GridExample3Form()
if (bModal)
    f.mdi = false // ensure not MDI
    f.readModal()
else
    f.open()
```

```
endif

class GridExample3Form of FORM
```

Save this and exit the Source Code Editor by pressing [Ctrl]+[W].

Open the form in the Form Designer and follow along. This one is going to be a little more complicated than the previous. We need to know which fields have index tags associated with them, for starters. For example, we know the Name field has an index tag. A quick check shows that the ID and Species fields also have index tags. These are the first three columns of the grid.

For starters let us set some properties to show the form's default – the Name column – is the one that the data is currently sorted on. The first thing to do is to click on the grid to give it focus, then on the Name column to give it focus. In the Inspector find the *editorControl* object and click on it, then click on the tool button. Click on the *colorNormal* property and enter "WindowText/LightBlue". Press the enter key after doing so. Again you will see that this change is not apparent. That's okay … it will be.

We want to use the asterisk character to show which columns can be clicked to change the sort order. We should also do the same for the ID and Species columns. In the Form Designer click on the ID column, go to the *headingControl* object, click the Tool button. Find the *value* property and add the asterisk after the letters "ID". Do the same for the Species column.

In order for the code we create to function properly, we must assume that columns 1, 2 and 3 are always "ID", "NAME" and "SPECIES" respectively. We could make this more flexible, but it takes a lot of work. In order to be sure that these columns are always in the same places, we are going to look at some properties of the grid we haven't yet. The first of these is *allowColumnMoving* – by default, a user can move a column by clicking on the heading and moving it left and right. This can allow for some great flexibility, which we will come back and examine later. However, we need these columns to remain static so set this property to *false*.

Other related options are *allowColumnSizing* and *allowRowSizing*. These default to *true*. You may or may not wish your users to be able to change the sizes of the columns and rows – that's completely up to you. If you do not wish to allow your users to change these, set these properties to *false*.

From here the code gets a bit more complicated. We're going to create some custom properties for the grid so that we can use them in the code that will be executed when the user clicks on the column heading. To do this, we will use the grid's *onOpen()* event. Find this event in the Inspector, and enter the code below:

```
function GRID1_onOpen
    // Grid's onOpen event handler
    // We need to set some custom properties of the grid:
    this.indexColumnColor      = "WindowText/LightBlue"
return
```

This could be more complex, we could try changing some of the font properties of the column when it is selected, etc.

The next thing to do is tell dBASE what to do when the user clicks on the *headingControl*. To do that, click on the Name column, once you see the Inspector recognizes it, click on the *headingControl* object, then the tool button. Go to the "Events" tab and find the *onLeftMouseUp* event. There is no *onClick* event that we can create an event handler for, but the closest to a standard left mouse click is to fire when the user lets go of the mouse button (mouse down, mouse up). Select the *onLeftMouseUp* event click the tool button and enter the following code. Check it carefully for errors. Note that this uses some properties of the grid that we have not discussed.

```
function headingControl_onLeftMouseUp(flags, col, row)
   // When the mouse is let up on a left mouse click,
   // we need to execute a bunch of code:

   // change color of column, set index ...
   private nColumn, aColumns, cField, oRowSet, i
   nColumn = form.grid1.currentColumn   // get current column
   aColumns = form.grid1.getColumnOrder() // returns an array

   // reference to form.rowset:
   oRowSet = form.grid1.dataLink

   try
      if nColumn == 1
         oRowset.indexName := "ID"
      elseif nColumn == 2
         oRowset.indexName := "NAME"
      elseif nColumn == 3
         oRowset.indexName := "SPECIES"
      endif

      // don't update the grid until we're done
      oRowset.notifyControls := false

      // change the color of the grid
      // to the standard colorNormal:
      for i = 1 to form.grid1.columnCount
         form.grid1.columns[ i ].editorControl.colorNormal :=;
             form.grid1.colorNormal
      next

      // change the color of the column we're changing
      // the index to to the specially defined color:
      form.grid1.columns[ nColumn ].editorControl.colorNormal := ;
             form.grid1.indexColumnColor

      // Tab to the column selected
      form.grid1.setFocus()
      if nColumn > 1
         // backtab to the first column (just to be sure
         // of where we are in the grid):
         keyboard replicate( "{Shift+Tab}", form.grid1.currentColumn-1 )
         // tab to the current column:
         keyboard replicate( "{Tab}", nColumn-1 )
      endif

      // allow updates to grid now:
      oRowset.notifyControls := true
```

```
         // ensure we update the grid:
         oRowset.refreshControls()

      catch( Exception E )
         if e.code # 239 // "Index does not exist"
             msgbox( "Unexpected error: "+e.code+" - "+e.message,"Error!", 16 )
         endif
      endtry
   return
```

There is one more thing that must be done for this to work properly. You have set the code above as the event handler for the Name column, but we really need the same code to execute when the *onLeftMouseUp* event occurs for the ID and Species columns.

We could duplicate the code – have a copy for each column, but that is definitely a case of too much code and is not very efficient. Instead, we have code that works (or should) in all three instances. Unfortunately the visual means of doing this in the Form Designer is limited and cannot handle what we need to do. So we need to save the form and exit the Form Designer (use Ctrl+W – you may need to do this twice, once to close the Source Code Editor, once to close the Form Designer). Next open the Form in the Source Code Editor. Find the constructor for the grid. The code will start with this statement:

```
   this.GRID1 = new GRID(this)
```

Once you have found this, move down in the code until you get to the constructor for the column headings. You should see this as part of the code:

```
      with (columns["COLUMN2"].headingControl)
         onLeftMouseUp = class::HEADINGCONTROL_ONLEFTMOUSEUP
         value = "Name *"
      endwith
```

You might see other properties, such as the *fontName* being streamed out, but you can ignore that. We want to copy the line of code that begins with "onLeftMouseUp" – just this one line. Highlight it and then use Ctrl+C to copy it to the Windows Clipboard. Then move your cursor up to:

```
      with (columns["COLUMN1"].headingControl)
         value = "ID *"
      endwith
```

(Again, this may have the *fontName* property streamed out.) Insert the statement shown above, so that this section code looks like:

```
      with (columns["COLUMN1"].headingControl)
         onLeftMouseUp = class::HEADINGCONTROL_ONLEFTMOUSEUP
         value = "ID *"
      endwith
```

Repeat for the "Species" column, so that it looks like:

```
with (columns["COLUMN3"].headingControl)
   onLeftMouseUp = class::HEADINGCONTROL_ONLEFTMOUSEUP
   value = "Species *"
endwith
```

Run the form once you have checked your code for errors. If you click on the *columnHeading* for the Species column, the grid should look similar to:

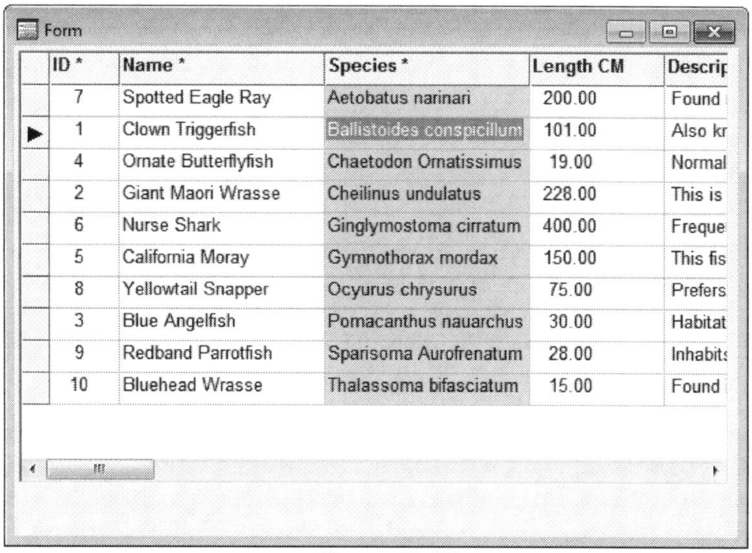

Figure 15-22

Conditional Colors of Cells and Rows

One feature of the grid that was often requested and finally delivered by the developers at dBASE (in dBASE Plus 2.5), was the ability to work with the individual cell of a grid, changing the color conditionally.

There are two events of the editorControl object called *beforeCellPaint()* and *onCellPaint()* that are used. The *beforeCellPaint()* event is used to set the color of a cell based on a condition and is executed, as the name sounds, before the cell is "painted" or displayed. The *onCellPaint()* event is used to re-set the color to the grid default, or some other color, depending on what your application needs.

WARNING: The code we are about to work with builds (each new section builds on the earlier) and you may find you only need part of it for a specific application – use what you need to.

You can of course use these events for other purposes, but the primary reason they exist is to give you control over how a grid is displayed.

To see how to work with this, copy the first Grid Example as we have done before. In the Command Window, type:

```
copy file GridExample1.wfm to GridExample4.wfm
```

To be sure the form works as expected, open it in the Source Code Editor (right click on it in the Navigator and select "Open in Source Editor" or press 🖭). Change the number 1 to 4 as shown below, there are two places you need to do this:

```
parameter bModal
local f
f = new GridExample4Form()
if (bModal)
   f.mdi = false // ensure not MDI
   f.readModal()
else
   f.open()
endif


class GridExample4Form of FORM
```

Save this and exit the Source Code Editor by pressing `Ctrl`+`W`.

Bring this form into the Form Designer. For our first example, we are going to set the "Length CM" field to display with a LightBlue background if the length of the fish is less than 100. To do this, click on the "Length CM" column, to give it focus. Click on the *editorControl* in the Inspector and click the Inspect button. Click the "Events" tab and then the *beforeCellPaint* event. Click the Tool button for this event, then in the Source Code Editor, enter:

```
function editorControl_beforeCellPaint(bSelectedRow)
   if this.parent.dataLink.fields["Length CM"].value < 100
      this.colorNormal := "WindowText/LightBlue"
   endif
return true
```

It should be noted that for a simple situation, the first statement shown after the "function" statement, you could use:

```
if this.value < 100
```

This is a lot less typing, but it means that for later examples we have to do more work. This code looks at the value of the "Length CM" field, if it is less than 100, sets the *colorNormal* property of the editorControl. The problem is that if we just do this, the first time a row is displayed that has a value of less than 100 in this field, then every row after it will change that editorControl to this color.

This is where we need the *onCellPaint* event – it fires after the cell is painted but before the next cell (and) row. In the Inspector window find the *onCellPaint* event, and click on it, then on the tool button. In the Source Code Editor enter this code:

```
function editorControl_onCellPaint(bSelectedRow)
   // reset the colorNormal property:
   this.colorNormal := ""
return true
```

This is simpler code because all we're doing is resetting the color to the grid's default.

If we were to run this form, it would not be obvious that anything was happening until we started navigating in the grid. This is because the grid does not evaluate the code for these events right away. We need to force this by telling dBASE to refresh the grid's display when the form opens. This is done using the form's *onOpen()* event. Click on the form surface to give it focus, and in the Inspector go to the "Events" tab, and find the *onOpen* event. Click the tool button and in the source code editor enter:

```
function form_onOpen
    // force the grid to display properly:
    form.grid1.refresh()
return
```

When you run the form, you should see something like this:

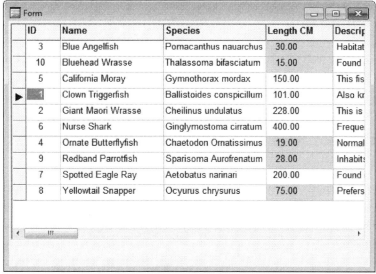

Figure 15-23

The Grid's *rowSelect* and *multiSelect* Properties and Colored Cells

If you set the grid's *rowSelect* or *multiSelect* properties to *true*, for the grid, the highlight may look a little strange, because the row that is highlighted has this cell the same color as it was before it was selected. This looks like:

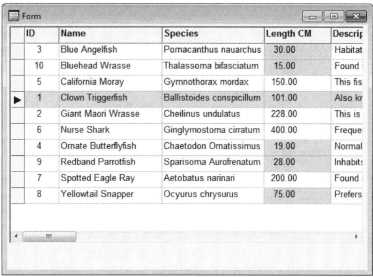

Figure 15-24

You can get fancier with your code, and change the appearance even further. For example, when a row is highlighted you can change the color of the cell to a different color. For this example we'll get a bit "artsy" in that I'm going to use some basic artistic concepts of blending colors.

We're using "LightBlue" for the cells that have a Length CM that is less than 100. Bring the grid into the Form Designer, set the *rowSelect* property to *true*, and then set the *colorRowSelect* property to "WindowText/Yellow".

Using this concept, if we change the places that the grid highlight intersects with the cells that are "LightBlue", we might want to change the color to a green color (basic color blending – yellow + blue = green).

We now need to go back to the "Length CM" column in the grid (click on it to give it focus in the Inspector) and then the editorControl for this column – click the Inspect button. Go to the "Events" tab and we're going to modify the code for the *beforeCellPaint* event handler, so click on the tool button for this event. We need to modify the code by adding the boldfaced code shown below. This uses the parameter built into the event called "bSelectedRow" – which is a logical value used to show if the current row is highlighted in the grid (selected).

```
function editorControl_beforeCellPaint(bSelectedRow)
    // set the colorNormal property based on the
    // length of the fish:
    if this.parent.dataLink.fields["Length CM"].value < 100
        if not bSelectedRow
            this.colorNormal := "WindowText/LightBlue"
        else
            this.colorNormal := "WindowText/LightGreen"
        endif
    endif
return true
```

This is all that is necessary. Save this and run the form. When you navigate over one of the rows that has a "Length CM" less than 100, you should see something like:

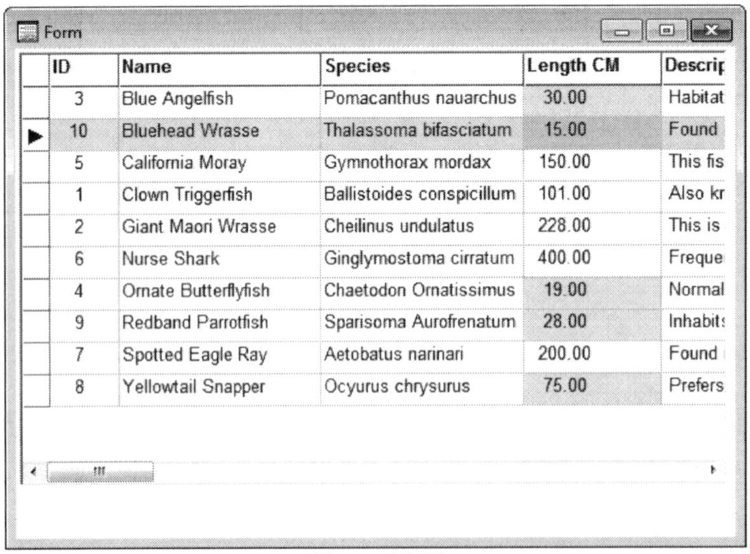

ID	Name	Species	Length CM	Descrip
3	Blue Angelfish	Pomacanthus nauarchus	30.00	Habitat
10	Bluehead Wrasse	Thalassoma bifasciatum	15.00	Found
5	California Moray	Gymnothorax mordax	150.00	This fis
1	Clown Triggerfish	Ballistoides conspicillum	101.00	Also kr
2	Giant Maori Wrasse	Cheilinus undulatus	228.00	This is
6	Nurse Shark	Ginglymostoma cirratum	400.00	Freque
4	Ornate Butterflyfish	Chaetodon Ornatissimus	19.00	Normal
9	Redband Parrotfish	Sparisoma Aurofrenatum	28.00	Inhabit:
7	Spotted Eagle Ray	Aetobatus narinari	200.00	Found
8	Yellowtail Snapper	Ocyurus chrysurus	75.00	Prefers

Figure 15.25

This could get more complicated. You might have a cell where you need different colors based on different values. If you are dealing with financial data you might want the cell to be red for values that are less than zero. There are many things you can do with this ... you are really limited to your imagination.

Coloring a Whole Row

What if, rather than an individual cell, you wanted the whole row to be a specific color? We could do this in two ways (at least). The more complex one is to copy the code for each column's editorControl – both the *beforeCellPaint()* and the *onCellPaint()* events, which is not very efficient coding. Instead you might want to just copy the references to the event handlers for the different cells.

Close the form, then open it in the Source Code Editor. In the grid's constructor code for the "Length CM" editorControl you should see:

```
with (columns["COLUMN4"].editorControl)
   beforeCellPaint = class::EDITORCONTROL_BEFORECELLPAINT
   onCellPaint = class::EDITORCONTROL_ONCELLPAINT
endwith
```

In order to reuse these two event handlers for the other columns, copy the two lines between "with" and "endwith" – highlight them and press `Ctrl`+`C` to copy to the Windows clipboard. Add these two lines to the other columns. If you do not see an editorControl entry in the streamed out code, add it so that you see something like the following in the Source Code Editor:

```
with (columns["COLUMN1"].editorControl)
   picture = "9,999"
   beforeCellPaint = class::EDITORCONTROL_BEFORECELLPAINT
   onCellPaint = class::EDITORCONTROL_ONCELLPAINT
endwith

with (columns["COLUMN1"].headingControl)
   value = "ID"
endwith

with (columns["COLUMN2"].editorControl)
   beforeCellPaint = class::EDITORCONTROL_BEFORECELLPAINT
   onCellPaint = class::EDITORCONTROL_ONCELLPAINT
endwith

with (columns["COLUMN2"].headingControl)
   value = "Name"
endwith

with (columns["COLUMN3"].editorControl)
   beforeCellPaint = class::EDITORCONTROL_BEFORECELLPAINT
   onCellPaint = class::EDITORCONTROL_ONCELLPAINT
endwith

with (columns["COLUMN3"].headingControl)
   value = "Species"
endwith

with (columns["COLUMN4"].editorControl)
   beforeCellPaint = class::EDITORCONTROL_BEFORECELLPAINT
   onCellPaint = class::EDITORCONTROL_ONCELLPAINT
endwith
```

```
with (columns["COLUMN4"].headingControl)
   value = "Length CM"
endwith

with (columns["COLUMN5"].editorControl)
   beforeCellPaint = class::EDITORCONTROL_BEFORECELLPAINT
   onCellPaint = class::EDITORCONTROL_ONCELLPAINT
endwith

with (columns["COLUMN5"].headingControl)
   value = "Description"
endwith

with (columns["COLUMN6"].editorControl)
   beforeCellPaint = class::EDITORCONTROL_BEFORECELLPAINT
   onCellPaint = class::EDITORCONTROL_ONCELLPAINT
endwith

with (columns["COLUMN6"].headingControl)
   value = "Fish Image"
endwith
```

Now when you run the form, you should see the complete row highlighted for any row that has a Length CM field with a value less than 100. In addition, if you navigate through the rows, the row that is highlighted will be green for those same rows. This should look like:

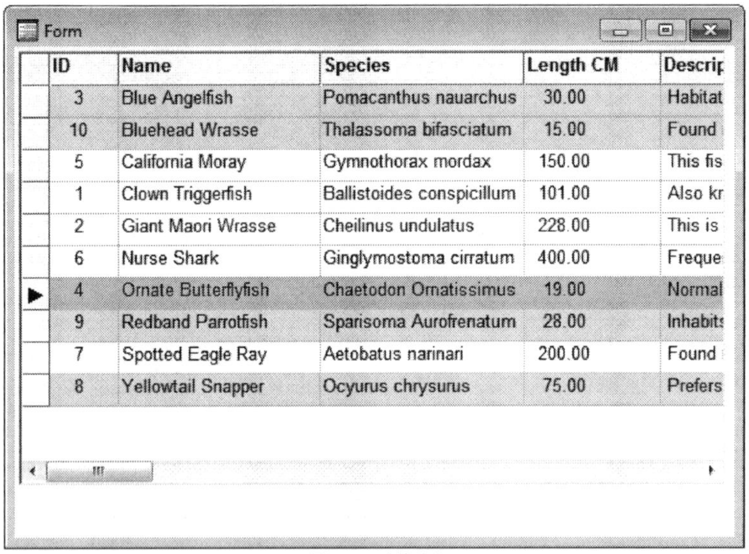

Figure 15-26

Saving and Restoring Column Positions

You (or your client) may wish to be able to move columns around on a grid, save them, then restore their position from where it was when the form closed the next time they view it, and more. This can get fairly complex, rather quickly.

However, the grid in dBASE Plus has some functionality that makes it easier to do this. We will be examining code that uses the following properties, events and/or methods of the grid:

- *columnCount* – the number of columns in the grid
- *getColumnOrder()* – a method that allows us to know the query (the table) and the field (for the column) for each column.
- *getColumnObject()* – a method that allows us to get access to the column itself and hence to the objects and properties of the column.

The code will also be looking at some techniques that we haven't dealt with in earlier chapters of this book, or at least not in the same ways we will be using them here.

As with previous examples, let's copy the first Grid form we created for this chapter. In the Command Window, type:

```
copy file GridExample1.wfm to GridExample5.wfm
```

To be sure the form works as expected, open it in the Source Code Editor (right click on it in the Navigator and select "Open in Source Editor" or press ⎙). Change the number 1 to 5 as shown below, there are two places you need to do this:

```
parameter bModal
local f
f = new GridExample5Form()
if (bModal)
    f.mdi = false // ensure not MDI
    f.readModal()
else
    f.open()
endif

class GridExample5Form of FORM
```

Save this and exit the Source Code Editor by pressing ⌃+Ⓦ. Bring this form into the Form Designer.

We need to add code in several places of this form. The basics of what is happening are that when the form opens, we need to check and see if there is a table that defines the grid layout. This table will contain some basic information – the name of the query object, the field object, the column *width*, the column *editorType* and the *value* of the column's *headingControl* object. If the table does not exist, the grid will be displayed the way it was designed (the constructor code for the form). If the table does exist, the columns are created in the sequence they are stored in the table, and the grid is then displayed. When the form is closed, the table is emptied out if it exists (and created if it does not), then the information is written back to it. This way if the user has changed the sequence of the columns, as well as the width of them and the next time the form is loaded, the columns will be restored the way they were when the form was closed.

Does this sound complex? Written out like that, it does, but if taken step-by-step it isn't too bad. The code in this section of the book is heavily documented to help explain what is happening.

The first thing we want to do is override the form's *open()* and *readModal()* methods, with a simple statement to use in either case. This will call a new method of the form that we will create called *init*. This concept has been discussed in earlier chapters of the book, so we don't need to explain it again. Give the form focus, and click on the "Methods" tab of the Inspector. Find the *open* method, and click the tool button. Add the code shown below:

```
function form_open
    // override the form's open method:
    class::Init()
return GRIDEXAMPLE5FORM::open()
```

Do the same for the *readModal* method:

```
function form_readModal
    // override the form's readModal method:
    class::Init()
return GRIDEXAMPLE5FORM::readModal()
```

After the return statement shown above, and before the "endclass" statement, add this:

```
function Init
    // code to execute before the form opens:
return
```

The Init method is one of several places we will be adding code to the form. The first thing we want to do is to modify the Init method by adding the code that is bold below:

```
function Init
    // code to execute before the form opens:
    local d
    d = _app.databases[1]
    // check to see if the table exists:
    if d.tableExists( "SaveGrid.dbf" )
        // it does, so we want to load the grid
        // based on the information in the table:
        class::LoadGrid()
    endif
return
```

This code looks to see if the SaveGrid table exists, if it does, calls another custom method of the form that we will create in a moment, that handles what is needed to build the grid.

With that typed in, after the return statement shown, and before the endclass statement for the form, add the following:

```
function LoadGrid
    // don't update screen
    form.rowset.notifyControls := false
    // release default grid
    release object form.grid1

    // recreate the grid:
    form.grid1 = new grid( form )
    form.grid1.dataLink = form.fish1.rowset
    form.grid1.bgColor = "white"
    form.grid1.height = 312.0
    form.grid1.left = 3.0
    form.grid1.top = 3.0
    form.grid1.width = 525.0

    // create query:
```

```
qSaveGrid = new query()
qSaveGrid.database := _app.databases[1]
qSaveGrid.sql       := "select * from SaveGrid"
qSaveGrid.active    := true

// loop through the table and set grid's Columns:
i=0
do while not qSaveGrid.rowset.endOfSet
    i++
    // create the column:
    form.grid1.columns["column"+i] = new GRIDCOLUMN(form.GRID1)
    // set the editorType before anything else
    form.grid1.columns[i].editorType := ;
        qSaveGrid.rowset.fields["ColumnEditorType"].value

    // set the datalink:
    cCommand = 'form.grid1.columns['+i+'].dataLink = form.'+;
        qSaveGrid.rowset.fields["QueryName"].value.rightTrim()+;
            '.rowset.fields["'+;
        qSaveGrid.rowset.fields["FieldName"].value.rightTrim()+;
            '"]'
    &cCommand.
    // Column header:
    form.grid1.columns[i].headingControl.value := ;
        qSaveGrid.rowset.fields["ColumnTitle"].value.rightTrim()
    // Column Width:
    form.grid1.columns[i].width := ;
        qSaveGrid.rowset.fields["ColumnWidth"].value

    // next row
    qSaveGrid.rowset.next()
enddo

// cleanup
qSaveGrid.active := false
release object qSaveGrid

// allow notification to occur
form.rowset.notifyControls := true
// refresh
form.rowset.refreshControls()
return
```

It is important to note that in the *datalink* part of the code there are places that have things that look like:

```
["'
```

That's a square bracket ([], double quote (") and a single quote ('). It's not easy to see the difference sometimes. The combination of delimiters is necessary to get just right.

The last bit of code we need is executed when the form closes. This is where we will save the configuration, so we have to see if the table exists, and if so, we want to empty it out, otherwise we want to create it. To add this code make sure the form has focus, in the Inspector click on the *onClose* event, and then the tool button. Enter the following code:

```
function form_onClose
    local aGridOrder, nRows, d
    // Store column order to an array:
    aGridOrder = form.grid1.getColumnOrder()
    // save the column widths and the editorTypes to the array:
    nRows = form.grid1.columnCount

    // create a shortcut:
    d = _app.databases[1]

    // save to a table
    if d.tableExists( "SaveGrid.dbf" )
        // it does exist, empty it!
        d.emptyTable( "SaveGrid" )
    else
        // it doesn't exist — save it
        cCmd = [create table SaveGrid ]+;
               [( QueryName char( 20 ),]+;
               [  FieldName char( 20 ),]+;
               [  ColumnWidth numeric( 5 ),]+;
               [  ColumnEditorType numeric( 1 ),]+;
               [  ColumnTitle char( 100 ) )]
        d.executeSQL( cCmd )
    endif

    // create query:
    qSaveGrid = new query()
    qSaveGrid.database := d
    qSaveGrid.sql      := "select * from SaveGrid"
    qSaveGrid.active   := true

    // loop through the grid's order and save it
    for i = 1 to form.grid1.columnCount

        // get column object reference:
        oColumn = form.grid1.getColumnObject( i )

        qSaveGrid.rowset.beginAppend()
        qSaveGrid.rowset.fields["QueryName"].value      := aGridOrder[i,1]
        qSaveGrid.rowset.fields["FieldName"].value      := aGridOrder[i,2]
        qSaveGrid.rowset.fields["ColumnWidth"].value    := ;
            oColumn.width
        qSaveGrid.rowset.fields["ColumnEditorType"].value := ;
            oColumn.editorType
        qSaveGrid.rowset.fields["ColumnTitle"].value    := ;
            oColumn.headingControl.value
        qSaveGrid.rowset.save()
    next

    // cleanup
    qSaveGrid.active := false
    release object qSaveGrid
return
```

If you check and double-check your code, then run the form, try moving columns around, changing column widths. Remember what you did, close the form, then re-run it. It should show everything the way it was when the form closed. One problem that may occur is that the ID column's editorControl has a *picture* property that we're not saving and restoring – see discussion below. This means you may want to widen the column a little.

After all that, there are still a few things you might be concerned with. This is a relatively simple example.

Multi-User?

One problem that might occur is in a multi-user environment, which many applications are these days. If the table that is used to store the grid layout is stored in the application's database folder, then the next user may change the first user's layout. This could get frustrating quickly.

Possible solutions:

- Name the table something different for each user. It would mean using the ID() function, or some other means of knowing who each user is, then using that to name the table. The code could get a bit tricky, but it could be done.
- Save the table to the same folder the user's copy of the .exe is in. *(This is not a good idea if your application is using the UAC.)* Along the same lines, you could save the table to the users' private data folders (if you are using the UAC).
- Use the INI file for the application. In many networked applications the executable and .INI file are stored on the local computers and the data (if using DEO, the object files) are stored on the network server. By using the local .INI file to store the settings rather than a table, the data will be available for individual users and not affect others. (The .INI file is discussed in later chapters of this book. With the UAC issues, this becomes more important ...)
- Similar to using the INI file, you could use the Windows Registry. There may or may not be a problem with user rights, depending on how the users are set up and which version of Windows is being used. (Reading and writing from/to the Registry is discussed in a later chapter of this book.)

Saving/Restoring More Properties Than Shown Here

The .INI and/or Registry options mentioned above also allow for you to save a flexible amount of data for each column. For example, what if the *colorNormal* property is set for one column's editorControl? Or one of the font properties, the *picture*, or ...? The code shown here does not take that into account.

For example, you should be able to use, the enumerate() function in dBASE to get a list of all the properties, events and methods of a grid column's editorControl or headingControl. You could save all the values, or just ones that make sense to save. Rather than using *enumerate()* you could just look at each editorType for the column and save the properties that make sense. For example, the entryfield, spinbox and combobox types have a *picture* property that you might want to save out. The spinbox has the *rangeMax*, *rangeMin*, and other related properties.

You might do something with the editorControl's properties, for example, by using:

- Column.editorControl.picture
- Column.editorControl.colorNormal
- Column.editorControl.colorHighlight

and so on for whatever properties you wish to store. You should be able to get events and methods, but that could be tricky ... so experiment. Have fun!

Using Multi Table Rowsets

When working in multi-table (parent/child or other) situations, you may want to handle your forms in a variety of fashions. For example, you might want to display a parent row on a form and the child data in a grid (this would of course assume a one to many relationship in the data). This kind of thing is easy enough to do.

You can also display just the fields that you want to, which actually includes fields from more than one table. If you are working with a parent/child relationship, you can display the parent data in the same grid as the child data.

There are many things that can be done with this, but you really just need to experiment to find the right combination. Generally I find it easier to display parent data in one grid (or just one row of the parent rowset) with the child data in a grid.

Building a Grid on the Fly

While I don't generally do this in my own applications, there may be times when you need to build a grid "on the fly". Perhaps you have an application that displays a table, but you don't know what the fields will be – it might be a "generic" table viewer form or something.

The code below is excerpted from a form that asks for the database, the table, the index tag to be used (if any), and then loads the data objects and a grid. The relevant code here to load the grid is shown below.

```
// ─────────────────────────────────
// Unfortunately while the columns array has a delete()
// method, it appears that it is not something we can
// use in our own code. So instead, we have to release
// the whole grid and rebuild it.
form.TableGrid.release()
form.TableGrid = new grid( form )
with (form.TableGrid)
    cellHeight = 22.0
    rowSelect = true
    colorRowSelect = "WindowText/0x80ffff"
    allowEditing = false
    allowAddRows = false
    anchor = 1  // Bottom
    height = 286.0
    left = 0.0
    top = 88.0
    width = 563.0
endwith

// set the datalink for the grid object:
form.TableGrid.dataLink := form.TVQuery.rowset

// now we have to loop through the fields array of the
// rowset object, and build the grid column-by-column:
local f
f = form.TVQuery.rowset.fields
// so we can work with a macro:
private cCmd
for i = 1 to f.size
```

```
    // create a new column:
    cCmd = 'form.TableGrid.columns["COLUMN'+i+;
        '"] = new GRIDCOLUMN(form.TableGrid)'
    &cCmd.
    //set the dataLink property:
    cCmd = 'form.TableGrid.columns["COLUMN'+i+;
        '"].dataLink = form.TVQuery.rowset.fields["'+;
        f[i].fieldName+'"]'
    &cCmd.

    // set the editorType to Entryfield (1), because
    // this is going to be a read-only grid anyway.
    // If you wanted to make this an editable grid,
    // you might want to check the field type
    // to determine what you wanted for the editorType
    // (entryfield, spinbox, checkbox, etc.).
    // As it is, we are going to check for a MEMO
    // type, and if a MEMO we will use an EDITOR control:
    if f[i].type == "MEMO"
        nType = 5
    else
        nType = 1
    endif
    cCmd = 'form.TableGrid.columns["COLUMN'+i+;
        '"].editorType = '+nType
    &cCmd.

    // set a default width:
    cCmd = 'form.TableGrid.columns["COLUMN'+i+;
        '"].width = 100'
    &cCmd.

    // by default the column's headingControl's value property
    // is set to the fieldName, so we don't have to do anything
    // with that.

next // i
```

As with the previous example, some of this code is a little tricky as the delimiters are nested using all three of the standard dBASE delimiters. Read the code carefully, and look for the difference between single and double quote characters.

A "generic" table viewer might look something like this when run, and after loading a table:

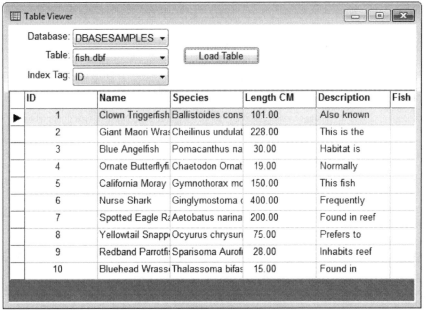

Figure 15-27

Restating Datalinks

Why would you want to restate the dataLinks of a grid? Most commonly you have a complex situation occurring where you need to change a table or something like that. The problem is that once you set the *active* property of a query (or database) object to *false*, all dataLinks are severed. This happens in code as well as in the Form Designer. In the Form Designer you can reset the dataLinks as needed. However, in code, this isn't something you can do visually.

If you change the table and it has the same fields as the original table, you would think that you would be able to restate your dataLinks once the query's *active* property is set to *true* as simply as:

```
form.grid1.dataLink := form.grid1.dataLink
form.grid1.columns["COLUMN1"].dataLink := ;
          form.grid1.columns["COLUMN1"].dataLink
```

and so on. This does indeed work. You can also explicitly set the dataLinks:

```
form.grid1.dataLink := form.rowset
  form.grid1.columns["COLUMN1"].dataLink := form.rowset.fields["FIELDNAME"]
     // or:
  form.grid1.columns["COLUMN1"].dataLink := form.rowset.fields[1]
```

Either way appears to work in some quick tests, so you have some options if you need to do this sort of thing in your application(s).

Cleanup

You may want to make sure that any databases that are open are closed, just to be safe, by going to the Command Window and typing:

```
close databases
```

Summary

As you can see, the grid is a very complex control in dBASE. We have seen much of what you can do, but there is a lot more. You may wish to examine examples provided by dBASE, LLC, or in the dUFLP, and if there is something you are not sure how to do, use the newsgroups and ask specific questions.

NOTES:

Chapter 16: Common Properties and Event Handlers of Form Controls

In chapter 14 we discussed (in some detail) the stock controls that are used with forms in dBASE applications. We briefly touched, in the case of some controls, on some very specific properties and events, but we haven't really looked at the "common properties and events" – the properties and events that are common to most of these controls. We haven't spent much time with areas that can be very important to a developer such as validation of data. This chapter will attempt to address some of these issues and make you more comfortable with these concepts.

Common Properties

The common properties of form controls are really mostly pretty basic – these include things like the size (*height*, *width*), positioning (*top*, *left*); *colorNormal*, *colorHighlight* and so on. There isn't much to say about these that have not already been said. There are other properties that mostly make sense such as *visible* – by default a control's *visible* property is *true* – normally it is there so the user can see and interact with it; but if you need to not display a control for some reason, setting *visible* to *false* can handle it. We are not going to examine *all* of the common properties, just a few that might need a bit of explanation.

Formatting Data –Picture and Function

There are a few properties that could use a bit more explanation, most specifically the *picture* and *function* properties used for several of the interface controls (Entryfield, Spinbox, grid column editorControl, etc.). These can be used to perform some basic formatting of the data as the user enters it. It can also be used to force the user to specific types of input.

An example of this would be if we used the first example form created for Chapter 13 and decided that all phone numbers used the same format (if your application is for a multinational organization, this can get more complicated). In the United States, phone numbers are displayed most commonly as:

```
(123) 456-7890
```

Where the digits in parentheses are the area code and then the rest of the number is displayed. Sometimes the format used is:

```
123-456-7890
```

And there are of course other ways of displaying the phone number.
To do this simply with an entryfield, you would set the *picture* property to something along the lines of:

```
(999) 999-9999
```

By definition, dBASE will understand when a phone number is entered into an entryfield that has this picture clause that the "9" is a placeholder for a digit. The parentheses, space and dash (-) characters will be inserted as literal values. What this means is that if the user saves this, the value will be saved with those characters as part of the value saved to the field in the table.

You may not wish to save those characters, in which case you could work with the *function* property and use a function such as:

```
@R
```

This tells dBASE to only display those literal characters, but not to save them as part of the field. What this really means is that rather than a value of:

```
(123) 456-7890
```

being saved to the field in the table, what would be saved is:

```
1234567890
```

This would require that the value be formatted again if you wanted to generate it in a report.

The following table displays some values for the *picture* property that you might find useful – it does not contain every possible combination, just some ideas:

Picture	Explanation
(999) 999-9999	This is one of several standard telephone number formats commonly used in the U.S. The area code is stored in parentheses and the rest of the number is as shown. The digit "9" in a picture allows only numeric input, while the literal characters "(", ")", space, and "-" are ignored and displayed as is.
!!!!!	Upper case – the exclamation mark is used to force characters to all upper case and they will be stored that way in a table. One "!" for each character you wish to force to upper case.
A9999	Would allow an alphabetic character as the first character, followed by ONLY numeric values.
L	Restricts the value to logical/Boolean (although normally I would suggest using a Checkbox control).

There is a lot that can be done with a combination of the *picture* and *function* properties of the controls that these belong to. For more details on the *picture* and *function* properties examine them in the online help, or in the dialog that appears (Template Property Builder) in dBASE if you use the tool button in the Inspector for either of these properties. dBASE will separate out the *function* from the *picture* template and place them in the appropriate properties if you use this dialog.

The *enabled* Property and the *when()* Event

The *enabled* property determines if a user may interact with a control at all. In the case of a Combobox, Listbox or Editor control this is more apparent than with some of the other controls, because the scrollbars or pushbuttons will be disabled. In the case of all controls the *colorNormal* property will <u>appear</u> to have been changed to a light grey – this means that the values displayed will appear in the setting determined by Windows for disabled controls. *(If you or your user has modified the settings for Windows, disabled controls may appear in a different color.)*

One aspect of the *enabled* property that can be frustrating for developers is that if you have a lot of controls you wish to disable or enable you have to create code that sets the *enabled* property for each control. There are ways to make this easier for you – the simplest is to place that set of controls on either a Container or a Notebook object (both of which are container objects). If they are contained by one of these objects, then setting the *enabled* property for the container will affect all (contained) controls. (This is more complex than it seems – if you set the *enabled* property to false for the container object, all controls are disabled; however, if you set it to *true* and some of the controls have their individual *enabled* property set to *false*, then those controls will not have the property changed and they will still be disabled.)

If you do not like the colors used when a control's *enabled* property is set to false, you may want to take a look at the *when()* event – if this is set to a codeblock such as:

```
{; return false }
```

dBASE will not allow the user to edit a datalinked field, etc. You could then set the *colorNormal* property to whatever you liked. Unfortunately, dBASE does not allow container objects to have this sort of functionality and indeed, some controls do not have a *when()* event. You would need to check in the Inspector or online help to make sure it is a member of that class.

It should be noted that the *when()* event can be used for more complex purposes. The point of this event is to enable or disable a control conditionally. This event returns a logical value (*true* or *false*), so you could do something where you only wanted a control to be enabled if another field in the table had a specific value or range of values:

```
function entryfield2_when
   if form.entryfield1.value => 3 and form.entryfield1.value <= 8
      return true
   endif
return false
```

Common Events

There are many common events for dBASE form controls, like the common properties, we are not going to discuss all of them here. There are a few that need a little more discussion, as they can be confusing

The mouse events are pretty clear for the most part (*onLeftMouseDn*, etc.), but there are some that could use a bit more explanation than what is in the online help.

Event Sequences

Probably the most confusing thing for any developer in dBL (and this includes the most experienced) is dealing with the sequence in which events fire. Taken in small numbers, events are not too difficult to work out. For example, any event that begins with the word *can* as part of the name will fire *before* the event (usually called from a method) itself – such as a form's *canClose* event. Before the form closes, any code assigned to the event handler for the form's *canClose* event will be executed and you can make a determination whether or not to allow the form to be closed. The form's *close* method will then be executed *if* the *canClose* event returns a value of *true*. After the *close* method is executed, the form's *onClose* event will fire, any code you wish to execute *after* the form has closed will be executed.

However, in a form with many controls, many of which have their own event handlers, this can start to get a bit confusing. In some cases your code in one event handler may assume that another event handler has fired – when instead, it may not have fired *yet*. When you add in the rowset events (if a user is editing and closes the form, the rowset's *canSave*, *save* and *onSave* may all attempt to fire, for example), this can add to the confusion.

One way that has been found to help is to insert some code that will show the developer when the event has fired so they can try things out; particularly if they are not sure when specific events are firing. Insert an output command (using the question mark) and some text that shows the name of the event:

```
? "Form.canClose() has fired"
```

If you do this for each event handler you are concerned with, when you attempt to perform specific tasks with the form and controls, you will find out what sequence the events fire in, then make sure your code is able to handle things in the way you need them to.

Example
If you would like to get an idea of how this works, try the following, which can be used to show the sequence for *onGotFocus*, *onLostFocus*, *canSave*, *save* and *onSave* events and methods of various controls, and the *canClose*, *close* and *onClose* events and methods of the form.

- Create a new form. Set the form's *metric* property to "6 - Pixels" and the *text* property to "Event Sequence Testing". Press ⌷Ctrl+⌷S to save the form, naming it "EventSequenceTest.wfm".
- Place a text control at the top of the form and set the *text* to something like: "Testing Event Sequences — Tab or use the Mouse to click on various controls"
- Click on the Navigator window, select the "Tables" tab, select the "DBASESAMPLES" database, then drag the "FISH" table to the Form Designer surface.
- Place an entryfield on the form. Set the following:

dataLink	Click on the tool button and select the NAME field. Click "OK".
onGotFocus *(event)*	Click on the tool button and enter:

```
function ENTRYFIELD1_onGotFocus
    ? "Entryfield1, onGotFocus()"
return
```

onLostFocus *(event)*	Click on the tool button and enter:

```
function ENTRYFIELD1_onLostFocus
    ? "Entryfield1, onLostFocus()"
return
```

- Place a second entryfield on the form, and set the following:

dataLink	Click on the tool button and select the SPECIES field. Click "OK".
onGotFocus *(event)*	Click on the tool button and enter:

```
function ENTRYFIELD2_onGotFocus
    ? "Entryfield2, onGotFocus()"
return
```

onLostFocus *(event)*   Click on the tool button and enter:

```
function ENTRYFIELD2_onLostFocus

    ? "Entryfield2, onLostFocus()"

return
```

- Click on the FISH query and *(in the Inspector)* drill down to the rowset (click on the *rowset* property, click the "I" button). Then on the "Events" tab of the Inspector:

  canSave   Click on the tool button and enter:

  ```
  function rowset_canSave
          ? "Rowset canSave()"
  return true
  ```

  onSave   Click on the tool button and enter:

  ```
  function rowset_onSave
          ? "Rowset onSave()"
  return
  ```

  save *(method)*   Click on the tool button and enter:

  ```
  function rowset_save
          ? "Rowset save()"
  return ROWSET::save()
  ```

- And finally for the form itself (click on the design surface), change the following:

  canClose   Click on the tool button and enter:

  ```
  function form_canClose
          ? "Form canClose()"
  return true
  ```

  onClose   Click on the tool button and enter:

  ```
  function form_onClose
          ? "Form onClose()"
  return
  ```

  close *(method)*   Click on the tool button and enter:

  ```
  function form_close
          ? "Form close()"
  return FORM::close()
  ```

- Save the form, and then run it. Click on the entryfields (or tab between them). Make a minor change in one of the fields (add a letter 'x' to the end of a name, for example). Try navigating. Close the form when you are done. Take a look at the output pane of the Command Window, and you will see output similar to:

```
Entryfield1, onGotFocus()
Entryfield1, onLostFocus()
Entryfield2, onGotFocus()
Entryfield2, onLostFocus()
Entryfield1, onGotFocus()
Rowset save()
```

```
Rowset canSave()
Rowset onSave()
Entryfield1, onLostFocus()
Entryfield2, onGotFocus()
Form canClose()
Rowset canSave()
Entryfield2, onLostFocus()
Form onClose()
```

Notice the sequence – it is not always what you might expect. For example, when you close the form, notice that if (as above) Entryfield2 has focus, the form's *canClose()* fires, the rowset's *canSave()* fires, the Entryfield2 *onLostFocus()* event fires, then form's *onClose()* fires. (It is interesting that no output from the form's overridden close method occurs.)

Before moving on, you may want to type the following into the Command Window, otherwise there may be some problems with tables later on:

```
close database
```

The *key()* Event

The *key* event fires for every keystroke the user types when the control has focus. This can allow code such as the custom class (discussed in another chapter) called *Seeker* to function – it reacts to each keystroke entered. The *key* event can also be used to create, for example, a "password" control, where each character typed is masked by another character. The difficulty is knowing what values are actually being entered. For example, in the case of a password control, you might want to pass along the delete or backspace keystrokes, to change or delete characters that were entered.

The *key* event passes along values that you can use for this purpose, specifically the numeric value associated with the character typed (nChar), the position of the character in the string (nPosition), whether the Shift key was held down (bShift), or the Control key was held down (bControl). The online help discusses this in more depth.

In addition to the idea of a password control, the *key* event can be used to perform some validation of an entry by checking to see what is typed, as it is typed, and only allow certain characters.

 NOTE

If you are considering creating a password control for your own application, you may want to take a look at the ones that are in the dUFLP (discussed in an appendix of this book) – a freeware library of code. There are a lot of concerns with this kind of control, as well as some pre-written versions that will save a lot of work.

The *onKey()* Event

What is the difference between the *key()* and *onKey()* events? The *key()* event fires as the key is pressed, which can be used to intercept the key, possibly changing the value of the keystroke, etc. The *onKey()* event fires <u>after</u> the key has been pressed. This may seem to be a really trivial/minor difference, but it is not.

Use the *key()* event to examine the keystroke *before* the value is displayed in an entryfield, or other control. Use the *onKey()* event after the value is displayed.

As noted in the discussion above about the *key* event, you can use it to validate what is entered into a control – not allowing some characters, etc.

Using the *onKey()* event you can tell dBASE to act on, for example, either the individual keystroke, or perhaps the complete value of what is associated with the control. The following simple example might be used to do something similar to the (more complex) custom class that ships with dBASE called SEEKER:

```
function LASTNAME_onKey(nChar, nPosition, bShift, bControl)
   form.rowset.findKey( upper( this.value ) )
return
```

The *onChange()* Event

The *onChange()* event can be useful to fire an event that, for example, might affect another control. To take this a step further, if you have a combobox of, say, States (or Countries), you might want to change the *dataSource* for another combobox that showed the available Cities.

You could use the *onChange*() event to fire specific code when a radiobutton's *value* property changes. The difficulty with this is that if you have more than two radiobutton controls, then you may want to hook several of them to the same event. This would mean that the event would fire twice each time a radiobutton was clicked, because one radiobutton's *value* becomes *false* at the same time another's becomes *true* – each of these is a change, so each change would cause the code to fire.

An example of a useful *onChange()* event handler for radiobuttons that would fire when each of the radiobutton's *value* property is changed would be a set of radiobuttons that were used to change the *language* property of the _app object:

```
function RadioButton1_onChange
   if this.value
      _app.language := this.text
   endif
return
```

> 📓 **NOTE**
> When changing the *dataSource* for a combobox (or listbox) control dBASE does not automatically refresh this information. So if you use *onChange* to modify the *dataSource* of a combobox, you might want to add code such as:
>
> ```
> form.CityCombobox.dataSource += ''   // two single quotes or
>                                      // two double quotes
> ```
>
> This will force a re-evaluation of the dataSource property and it will be modified to include any changes that your code may have made to it. This technique is called *restating* the *dataSource*.

Using the *onLostFocus()* Event to Force Navigation and/or Validation

When dBASE developers first started working with the various events associated with controls and forms, many of us *(I include myself in this)*, tried using the *onLostFocus()* event to force the user to navigate properly through the form. The difficulty is changing your mind-set when it comes to application development. In the DOS world, you could exactly control the sequence the user worked through the entry areas of a screen. However, with the advent of Windows, a completely new way of thinking has to be used – you, as the developer, should not be attempting to *force* the user into a specific path – they can just use the mouse and click on controls in whatever sequence they wish. And this is proper!

It is a bad idea to use the *onLostFocus()* event to attempt to force the user to go to another control when they leave the current control. It is also generally a bad idea to attempt to use the *onLostFocus()* event to perform validation of the value entered by the user. You can use the *z-order* of a form's controls to allow the user to move in an "orderly" fashion through the controls when they use the Tab key to navigate, but if they use the mouse, there should not be any attempt at "taking control" as it will only frustrate the user.

We will discuss validation in more depth later in this chapter.

All of the above is not meant to negate the fact that the *onLostFocus()* event for a control may have some very good uses.

The *onMouseOver()* and *onMouseOut()* Events
dBASE PLUS 2.5 introduced a couple of new events that are common to most or all form controls in dBASE. The purpose is to allow you to affect the appearance of a control when the mouse is over the control, then return its appearance to what it was before when the mouse leaves the control.

(Of course, you can do whatever you want to – for example, your code could count each time the mouse moves over a control and not show anything in a visual way at all.) This can be useful to make a form more dynamic in appearance. A simple example of this might be to change the color of a pushbutton when the mouse is over it, then when the mouse is not over it to return the color to what it was before. You might also change the pushbutton's *fontBold* property to true or false depending on whether the mouse was over the pushbutton. You would add the code like you do with other events if you are working in the Form Designer, by going to the Inspector, finding the event, and clicking on the tool button. For the pushbutton's onMouseOver event, you might include code like:

```
function DYNAMICBUTTON_onMouseOver(flags, col, row)
   this.fontBold    := true
return
```

And the *onMouseOut* event might look like:

```
function DYNAMICBUTTON_onMouseOut(flags, col, row)
   this.fontBold    := false
return
```

This is just a small sample of what might be done, but can hopefully give you some ideas (for example changing the border on an entryfield when the mouse is over it, the possibilities are endless).

Data Validation

Data Validation is one of the more important aspects of what a developer does when writing an application. If a database has mission-critical data the chances are good that it needs to have some form of validation performed to ensure that it is "good" data. If the user is allowed to just enter any old thing into a field in a table, somewhere along the line the data will become meaningless.

There are many ways a developer can code data validation into an application. We have already (in earlier sections of this chapter) discussed some, such as using the *key()* event of some controls to limit the data, or using the *picture* and *function* properties of some controls to either limit the data entered or modify the display of the data.

However, there are often times things that you must do such as requiring a value (not allowing the user to leave something blank), or checking to make sure the data is entered correctly, that takes more work than what can be done with those techniques. We will attempt to examine the various methods that might be used to perform data validation, including reasons to use, and possibly reasons to *not* use them.

Table Designer/Field Level Validation

When we discussed the Table Designer in an earlier chapter we took a brief look at the fact that you can, using the Inspector, set certain properties for individual fields when you design the table. These are specifically the *required*, *default, minimum* and *maximum* properties.

While it may seem like a good idea to do this, there are some drawbacks. The first drawback is that other table formats may not recognize this capability – so if you are writing an application you intend to upsize to another database (such as Oracle, etc.), then these properties may not carry across. In addition, if you use these properties, you have no direct control over any error messages that may occur if the user enters a value that does not meet the criteria. There are perhaps better ways to set defaults such as maximum and minimum values and even to determine that a field is required for a row to be valid.

Another issue – if you decide to set these properties after there is data in a table, you may get some odd results in the table, particularly if some of the values in the field do not meet the criteria set in these properties.

Control Level Validation

Another possibility for validating fields in a table would be in the form(s) used to enter/edit the data. There are several options, including as mentioned earlier with the *picture* and *function* properties, or the *key()* and *onKey()* events. In addition to these, you may wish to consider the following:

valid(), validRequired, *and* validErrorMsg

Some of the standard interface controls have the properties *validRequired*, *validErrorMsg* and a *valid()* event. These *can* be used to perform some data validation, but I have found that often these can cause more frustration for the user than they are worth.

The basic use of these properties and event handler, are:

For example, if you had an entryfield that you wanted the user to be limited to entering a value from 1 to 7, you could set the properties in this fashion:

validErrorMsg	Value must be from 1 to 7!
validRequired	true
valid()	Enter the following in the event handler:

```
function ENTRYFIELD1_VALID
   local bValid
   bValid = false // default
   if this.value => 1 and this.value <= 7
      bValid := true
   endif
return bValid
```

As a user I find that the way this works can be frustrating, because if you enter a value that is not considered valid by your code, you have to either enter a valid value, or you are stuck – you cannot take focus off the control at all. This means that you cannot even click on, for example, an "Abandon" button, that would abandon changes to the row. Instead you would have to enter a valid number, *then* click the "Abandon" button.

The when() *Event*
As noted in the discussion about the *enabled* property, the *when()* event can be used to disable a control.

However, you can do more than what was shown in the earlier discussion – the main reason this event exists is to allow access to a control (by default always) if the *when()* event returns a value of *true*. If you set up an event handler for this event, it must return a *true* or *false* value.

Why would you want to use this? You might have a situation where you only want a user to interact with a specific field (or control) if the value returned by another field (or control) meets some condition. If the event returns a value of *true* then the user will have access to the current control, if the *when()* event returns *false* the user cannot tab to the control, cannot click on the control – it cannot gain focus.

Spinboxes *and* rangeMax, rangeMin, *and* rangeRequired
Spinboxes are designed to handle numeric and date formats specifically, that can be set to limit entry (or using the buttons) to a specific range of values. The basic use, for example, if you wanted to limit a numeric value to a range of 1 to 7, would be:

rangeMax	7
rangeMin	1
rangeRequired	*true*

By setting these properties, if you ran a form with such a spinbox and tried to enter a value that was greater than 7, then the spinbox would change it back to 7; if you tried to enter a value that was less than 1 (0 or a negative number), the spinbox would change it to 1. If you tried to go past the boundaries using the pushbuttons on the spinbox, then you would be stopped and dBASE will beep at you.

Combobox – Limiting the Values Accepted
The combobox object has the ability to allow the user to enter new values that are not part of the *dataSource*, but what if you wanted to limit the user to just what was in the *dataSource*? The simple answer would be to set the combobox's *style* property to "2 - Dropdown List". This style of combobox does not allow the user to enter a value not already in the *dataSource*.

If you wished the user to be able to add new values, you might want to still use a dropdown list style combobox, but add a small pushbutton allowing them to add a new value – either by adding code directly in the current form (using a style 0 or style 1 combobox, and code to update the *dataSource*) or calling a popup or subform that would allow the user to add a new value. In any case you will want to restate the datasource, as mentioned earlier in this chapter.

Radiobuttons and Checkboxes

With radiobuttons and checkboxes data validation is sort of built-in. The user cannot select a value that is not there in front of them.

The one confusing factor with checkboxes and logical fields is one that actually is built in to the logical field itself.

A logical field is either *true* or *false* – at least, that's the way dBASE developers have believed for years. However, with the advent of the level 7 table format, there is a third option for logical fields –*null*. This can confuse developers' code. If you are testing to see if a value is not *false*, for example:

```
if form.rowset.fields["mylogical"].value <> false
    // do something
endif
```

In a case such as the above, if there are rows that contain a value of null in the logical field, then they would be selected. The obvious solution is to check for *true* in those cases:

```
if form.rowset.fields["mylogical"].value == true
    // do something
endif
```

The question that really comes up is "how do I avoid this situation?" This may be a case where setting a field's default property in the Table Designer is be a good idea – you could set the default to false, then the table would never contain a value of *null* for a new row. You might use either the command SET AUTONULLFIELDS or the rowset *autoNullFields* property. However, as we will see shortly, there are other ways to deal with this as well, to avoid the issue of upsizing the database, etc.

Form Level Validation

Form Level Validation is validation of the data that occurs when the user clicks a "Save" type button, or navigates, whatever is needed to call the rowset's *save()* method.

You can define this in the form, or as we will discuss below, in a datamodule – in either case the concept is to force validation of the data when an attempt to save the row is performed and not allow the save to occur if something is invalid in the data.

Sometimes, even if you have Record Level Validation *(see below)* created in, say, a datamodule, you may find that for a specific form you need to do more validation. If that is the case, the form has some events that you may wish to examine:

canClose()	Fires before a form is closed and can be used to save or abandon (*rowset.save()*, *rowset.abandon()*) changes that are pending.
canNavigate()	This can be used to disable navigation until the user has saved or abandoned changes.

onAppend()	This fires after the form's rowset has changed state to append mode. This can be used to set default values for specific fields.
onChange()	Fired when a changed control loses focus, might be used for specific field-level validation, but as noted elsewhere, this is not recommended for the most part.

We will take a look at similar control for the rowset, which is really the recommended way to handle data validation. However, there are times when you may wish to use a combination of the rowset methods and the form's methods to handle all permutations of the validation needed.

Note that the discussion of "Record Level Validation" below may be considered to be "Form Level Validation" if it occurs when running a form.

Record Level Validation

Record Level Validation is getting closer to the more appropriate way to handle validating your data. The reason for this is that we can define the validation required, then handle it in a form (Form Level Validation), or even better in a datamodule, which would allow any form that used said datamodule to automatically have any data validation that was defined.

The following events of the rowset can be used to perform various aspects of validation.

validErrorMsg	Set to an error message you wish to display if the value entered is not valid (the default message is "Invalid Input!" which is not very useful to the user).
validRequired	Set to *true* if you wish to force dBASE to evaluate the value in the valid event handler – the user will not be allowed to leave this control until the *valid()* event returns a value of *true*.
valid()	Insert code that will determine if a value entered is valid or not. This must return a value of either *true* or *false*, as it will not allow the user to leave the field if the validRequired property is set to *true*.

Setting Default Values

The rowset has the *onAppend()* event which is the most appropriate place to set default values for the fields in a rowset. This fires when the new record buffer is created – after the rowset is placed in append mode, the rowset's *state* property is set to 3 (Append).

It could be used to set logical values to *false*, set a date to today's date, or do more complex things such as setting the starting value from the *dataSource* array used in a combobox object.

Note that the values are in the row's buffer are not saved until the user causes a call to the rowset's *save()* method to occur.

Validating Data

There are several ways you could perform data validation, but it is recommended that you use the rowset's *canSave()* event. This event fires before the row buffer is actually saved to the table (whether adding a new row, or editing an existing row). If it returns a value of *false* the row buffer will not be saved.

If you use the rowset's *canSave()* event to perform validation, it is a good idea to do the following:

- Let the user know what is wrong, by using a message dialog (*msgbox()*);
- Return a value of *false* for the event;
- Optionally set focus to the appropriate control.

There is debate amongst the developer community as to whether the last bullet point is a good idea or not. Personally I find it useful if there is a problem in a field that is dataLinked to a control on the form, to set focus to the control, particularly since I usually use a different color for the control if it has focus (*colorHighlight*) where possible. However, this is a bit more tricky, as the rowset object does not know what a form is. A simple *canSave()* event for, say, the FISH table that we have used in some of the examples in this book, might look something like:

```
function rowset_canSave
    // Record-Level Validation for a form
    // using the Fish Table:
    if empty( this.fields["Name"].value )
        // let the user know there's an error
        msgbox( "The 'Name' field is required!",;
                "Data Entry Error!", 16 )
        // this            = rowset
        // first parent  = query
        // second parent = form
        this.parent.parent.EntryfieldName1.setFocus()
        // return a false value, otherwise we will
        // save changes!
        return false
    endif
    // return true if we get here, as it's valid ...:
    return true
```

If you wish to use rowset validation in a datamodule, it is a bad idea to set focus to specific controls because unless you are extremely consistent between forms you may name the same control on two different forms something very different (i.e., "EntryfieldName1", in another form "NameEntryfield"). This would cause difficulties because in one form the object would be found, in another it wouldn't.

One nice aspect of the use of the rowset's *canSave()* event is that this will fire even if a user tries to navigate in a rowset, although you may find some odd issues, such as the event firing twice (see "Halting Navigation").

Halting Navigation

It may be a good idea to use the rowset's *canNavigate()* event to avoid the user attempting to navigate while they are appending or editing a row (as noted above, the *canSave()* event may fire multiple times if you attempt to navigate while editing – which can resolve that issue). This event, like all events that begin with the word "can", is used to allow or disable the ability to actually perform associated methods of the object. In this case, any navigation attempts such as *next()*, *first()*, *last()*, *goto()*, etc. will be disabled if *canNavigate()* returns a value of *false*.

You could set this up easily enough by using the rowset's *state* property – which will be set to either 2 (for Edit) or 3 (for Append) if editing or appending a new row:

```
function rowset_canNavigate
   if this.state == 2 or this.state == 3
      if msgbox( "Save Changes to the current row?",;
                 "Cannot Navigate!", 1+32+256 ) == 2 // Cancel
         return false
      else
         this.save() // save changes
      endif
   endif
return true
```

There is no need to attempt to reset anything here, because this small amount of code will handle it – if the rowset's *state* property is anything other than 2 or 3, then navigation will be allowed, otherwise if the user clicks the "OK" button when the dialog appears the row will be saved and then navigation will be allowed.

You can get fairly complex with the code that is shown here, but this should give you a good jumping off place to look at options.

The advantage to form level validation, particularly if performed in a datamodule, is reusability of the code. Once you have defined the rules for the data validation, you never have to rewrite them. If something changes, you only have to change them in one place.

Drag and Drop

Drag and Drop capabilities have been available in dBASE for some time, but many folk are not very clear on how to use them. The ability to drag a file from the Windows navigator to an editor control might be useful, or to drag an image file to a form and display it; the ability to drag values from one listbox to another (a "mover" type class) can also be done. So, the question is, how does it all work?

The following is based on an article in the Knowledgebase by Tim Converse (*and used with his permission*).

There are two basic categories of drag and drop objects. Drop sources and drop targets. Some objects are both a drop source and a drop target.

Drop Sources are objects that initiate a drag and drop operation. These are the objects which can be "dragged".

Drop Targets are objects which accept a drag and drop operation. These are the objects which can have other objects "dropped on them".

Objects which can be drop sources all have:

- *dragEffect* property
- *drag()* method
- *onDragBegin()* event

Objects which can be drop targets all have:

- *allowDrop* property
- *onDragEnter()* event
- *onDragLeave()* event
- *onDragOver()* event
- *onDrop()* event

The allowDrop *property*
When set to false (the defaults is *false)*, objects which are being dragged will not be allowed to drop on them. The drag icon will not show any change indicating that this is a possible place to drop an object.

When this property is set to *true*, the mouse icon will change indicating that it is possible to drop on this object.

The dragEffect *property*
Defaults to "0 - None" but can be set to "1 - Copy" or "2 - Move".

- 0 - None - No dragEffect will be initiated with the object in question.
- 1 - Copy - A dragEffect will be initiated, but the object will remain stationary on the form. In this case you are "copying" data from one object to another.
- 2 - Move - A dragEffect will be initiated and the object will be moved. In this case you are "moving" the actual object on the form. *onDrop* is not fired when the object is released. (This would be useful if you were creating a designer of some sort.)

The onDragBegin() *event*
This event is fired when a drag event has been initiated.

The onDragEnter() *event*
This event is fired when the mouse pointer enters a possible drop target during a drag event.

The onDragLeave() *event*
This event is fired when the mouse pointer leaves a possible drop target during a drag event.

The onDragOver() *event*
This event is fired when the mouse pointer is over a possible drop target during a drag event.

The onDrop() *event*
This event is fired when a drag event is ended on a possible drop target.

The drag() *method*
This method is the heart of drag and drop in dBASE. It is called to begin a drag and drop operation. It takes the following three parameters:

- cName – a String of up to 260 characters long.
- cType – a String of up to 260 characters long.
- cIcon – Not currently implemented. It will be a string used to locate an icon to be used during the drag event.

The *drag* method is usually initiated inside the *onLeftMouseDown()* event of a drop source, though it can be initiated anywhere you choose.

The parameters are not enforced in dBASE. They can contain any information you need to accomplish the operation you are attempting.

An Example of Drag and Drop

This example will use drag and drop to move values between two listboxes. This is a simple version of a "mover" type control, which also allows moving multiple items, using pushbuttons as well. In this case we are keeping it simple to give you the basics of how drag and drop is used.

- Create a new form.
- Set the form's *text* property to "Drag and Drop Example", set the form's *metric* property to "6 - Pixels".
- Put two listboxes on the form.
- Modify the first Listbox as follows:
  name   SourceListbox
  dragEffect   1 - Copy
  onLeftMouseDown *(event)* Click the tool button in the Inspector, and enter the following:

```
function SOURCELISTBOX_onLeftMouseDown(flags, col, row)
   this.drag(this.name, this.value, "")
return
```

  dataSource   Click the tool button
                   and in the dialog click the tool button for the
                   dataSource again, add the following

                   Array Elements:
```
Red
Green
Blue
Yellow
White
```
                   Click OK for this dialog, and then click OK again for
                   the first dialog.

- Modify the second Listbox as follows:
  name   DestinationListbox
  allowDrop   true
  onOpen *(event)* Click the tool button and enter the following:

```
function DESTINATIONLISTBOX_onOpen
   this.DataArray = new array()
   this.dataSource := "array this.DataArray"
return
```

  onDrop *(event)*   Click the tool button and enter the following:

```
function DESTINATIONLISTBOX_onDrop(nLeft, nTop, cType, cName)
   this.DataArray.add( cName )
   this.dataSource += ""
return false
```

- Save the form as "DragAndDropExample", and then run the form. It should look something like:

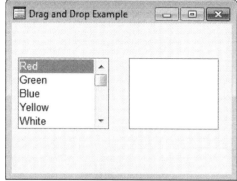

Figure 16-1

- With the form running, click and hold the mouse down on any item in the listbox on the left. Notice that the mouse pointer changes, showing that a drag operation is in effect. Move the mouse to the second Listbox and let up on the mouse button.

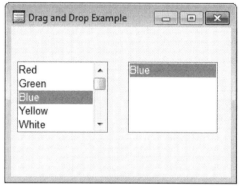

Figure 16-2

- If everything works properly, the item you selected from the first listbox is copied to the second listbox.

What did we do here?

In the *onOpen()* event of the second Listbox we created a new *(custom)* property of the Listbox called DataArray and then set the Listbox's *datasource* property to that array.

In the *onLeftMouseDown()* event of the first Listbox we initiated a drag operation, passing the parameters of the name and current value of the first Listbox.

In the *onDrop()* event of the second Listbox we took the value being carried in the drag operation and added it to the DataArray property of the second Listbox then refreshed the *datasource* of the second Listbox with that array.

In a real "mover" type dialog, we might remove the item on the left from the *dataSource*, and so on. This gets more complicated, but can be done.

What Else Can Be Done?

Drag and Drop is pretty versatile. As noted earlier you might want to make it possible to drag a text file to an editor control on a form, you could even allow the user to move controls around on a form with drag and drop. Indeed, dQuery, which is used in dBASE for creating datamodules, uses drag and drop quite a bit, dragging treeItems out of a treeView onto the design surface, creating new subforms to represent the query objects, etc.. With some effort you can add a lot of flexibility to your dBASE applications using this functionality. There is an example of a fully-functioning mover control (mover.wfm and movercontainer.cc) in the dUFLP (see the appendices for details).

Summary

This chapter of the book was really aimed at giving some examples of ways to use, or not to use, some of the more common events, to kind of open your eyes to possibilities. We could not possibly cover every single permutation of every event in this chapter – the complexities of the interactions between events can be bewildering. You should however be aware of the possibilities and be prepared for the fact that sometimes events may fire in sequences that you might not expect, because of the interaction between the various controls. We spent a bit of time examining ways to validate data – this is, as noted, often quite vital to an application to ensure the integrity of the data itself. In addition, you have taken a look at how Drag and Drop works in dBASE, because this is a very useful aspect of Windows applications.

Chapter 17: Custom Forms and Custom Form Classes

In this chapter we are going to take some time to look at designing your applications in an intelligent manner, making simple and easy changes that affect the application, by creating re-usable code. Notice that this chapter has some examples that might be a good idea to follow along with, to help you learn more about how these topics work. Part of this allows you to create easy-to-use libraries of code.

Source Code Aliases vs. Database Aliases, and Why They Are Important

Before we delve into creating custom forms and custom classes, we need to look at organizing our code. The best way to organize your code is to use what are called libraries of code. The concept is similar to the way that database aliases work.

When using local tables (as opposed to SQL Server tables, which work in a fundamentally different manner), a database alias points to a folder that contains multiple tables.

A library of source code works the same way. By creating folders on the hard drive that contain *only* custom code, you can make maintenance of your code easier. If you have a custom class that you use in all of your applications, keeping a copy of that class in one easy to find and use location makes sense, doesn't it?

Once you have a library of code, the difficulty then becomes accessing it. You could try to remember a path to the code and try to remember to load the appropriate files using a path, but after a while that can get confusing and what if you need to change the path for any reason? All of a sudden your application may no longer function properly.

The solution is to use what are called Source Code Aliases or simply "Source Aliases". These work in a similar fashion to database aliases, as discussed in earlier chapters of this book.

A source code alias is simply a way to tell dBASE to substitute an operating system path when it encounters the alias. A source code alias, just like a database alias, is delimited with colons (:). If you had a source code alias named "MyLibrary", and a file contained in the path pointed to by that alias called "MyTextClass.cc", using it is as simple as:

```
set procedure to :MyLibrary:MyTextClass.cc
```

If you change the path pointed to by "MyLibrary", you do not have to change your source code, where if you used a full path to the custom class file (.cc – we'll discuss these later in this chapter), you would have to modify your source code in every place you referenced the custom class file.

Source Code Aliases, while not required in dBASE, are a really good idea and you should get used to using them early in your application development.

You may notice that database aliases and source code aliases are used in the same way as each other – by using the colon as a delimiter. How does dBASE know what to do with them? Context – in a command such as that shown above ("set procedure ...") if dBASE sees the colon where it is shown, it knows to look for a Source Code Alias. In a command such as "open database ..." if dBASE sees the colon in the same place, it knows to look for a database alias instead.

One last note – some developers make the assumption that Source Aliases work in a deployed application. They do not. A Source Code Alias works for the *source code* – a dBASE executable does not use source code, nor does it look for your source code aliases. If you want similar functionality in your deployed applications you should take a look at DEO (Dynamic External Objects), which is discussed in a later chapter of this book.

How to Create a Source Code Alias
Way back in Chapter 1 we took a look at the Desktop Properties Dialog. To work with Source Code Aliases, you need to do a couple of things.

The first thing you need is to create the actual path where you will store your library or libraries of code. When dBASE is installed, there are some folders created that you *could* use. These fall under the folder:

```
C:\Users\<username\AppData\Local\dBASE\Plus\dBLClasses
```

If you are using dBASE Plus versions older than 2.7, or if you are using Windows XP and current versions of dBASE, the path to these will be slightly different:

```
C:\Program Files\dBASE\Plus\dBLClasses
```

These include folders named "FormControls", "Forms", "NonVisual" and so on. The advantage to using these is that they already exist, and there are already source code aliases for them.

The disadvantage is that if you install a completely new version of dBASE in a different folder (or on another computer), then uninstall the old one, deleting all files and folders, you will have just destroyed your source code library. In addition, if you don't back them up and a hard drive failure occurs, you have lost your library or libraries.

I always place my source code in a place on the hard drive I am likely to back up when I perform my regular hard drive backups *(you do back up your drive, don't you?)*, so if I uninstall the software or move to a new computer, I won't forget.

It is suggested that you create a folder on the hard drive, something like:

```
C:\My Company
```

Replace "My Company" with your own business name, application name, or whatever works for you. Then under that folder, create sub-folders for specific types of code. You could even use a structure similar to the one that is installed with dBASE:

```
C:\My Company\FormControls
C:\My Company\Forms
C:\My Company\Reports
```

And so on.

Once you have the folders created, the next step is to actually create the Source Code Aliases in dBASE. To do that, if dBASE is not currently running, start dBASE PLUS.

- Select the "Properties" menu, and then "Desktop Properties".
- Click on the "Source Aliases" tab.

Figure 17-1

- Click the "Add" button
    - Give a Source Code Alias name, such as "MyCustomForms"
    - Click the tool button by the entryfield for the path and select the appropriate folder.
- Click "Add" a second time, the new alias has been added, and will appear in the list.
- Repeat the steps from "Click the 'Add' Button" as needed.

You may find that you have multiple libraries of code, so you may want/need to create many source code aliases. This is not an issue – dBASE does not seem to have an upper limit to the number of source aliases that you can define.

If you need to change the path for a source alias, bring up the dialog, find the alias and change the path (either by typing in the entryfield or clicking on the tool button and changing it), then click the "Apply" button. The changes will be saved, and you will be fine. To remove one, simply use the "Remove" button.

When done, click the "OK" button.

NOTE

The Source Code Aliases are read when dBASE is loaded, and if you change them in the Desktop Properties dialog box as shown. When dBASE loads, these aliases are loaded into an Associative Array assigned to a custom property of the _app object, which is always available in dBASE. If you need to find a path associated with a source alias, you can do so by finding the alias in the associative array:

```
cKey = _app.SourceAliases.firstKey
cPath = ""
for i = 1 to _app.SourceAliases.count()
    if cKey.toLowerCase() == "mycustomforms"
       cPath = _app.SourceAliases[cKey]
       exit
    endif
    cKey = _app.SourceAliases.nextKey( cKey )
next
if not empty( cPath )
    // you have a path to work with ...
endif
```

It should be noted that you *cannot* do something like:

```
_app.SourceAliases[ "MyAlias" ] = "C:\SomePath"
```

You will be told "Property is read only."

Using Custom Forms

We are now going to start looking at working with and creating custom forms. dBASE PLUS does not come with any custom forms installed.

Why Work With Custom Form Classes?

A custom form is a template upon which you base other forms. In addition, once you have a basic custom form, you can subclass that to other custom forms. An example would be if you have a custom form with a specific color design and logo on it. You might then want to subclass that form for a data custom form and a non-data custom form. The data custom form might have a tabbox control, a grid and a seeker on one page for finding a record, the first page might have a set of navigation buttons and so on. The non-data custom form might have other purposes such as being used for lookup forms.

What if your customer wants you to change the color of your forms to green instead of lightblue, or change the company logo? All you would have to do is change the primary custom form's properties and both your subclassed custom forms and all forms that are subclassed from those will inherit the changes!

Changing Built-in Default Property Values

One really good use of a custom form is to change default property values to those you want or need in your own applications. For example, in an earlier chapter of this book, we discussed setting the *metric* property to Pixels, rather than the default setting of Characters. If you set this in your custom form(s), then any form that uses the custom form will automatically have the *metric* property set and you don't have to remember to set it when starting a new form.

Creating New (Custom) Properties for Custom Form Classes

One really useful aspect of creating custom forms is that if you have a custom property that you need to use in multiple forms, you can create it in a custom form and it will be surfaced in all forms that are derived from the custom form, as if it were a default property of the form class.

Why would you want to do that? One example *(of many that could be cited)* comes to mind, based on a project I did for a client. The users required a time-out to be built into forms, because often someone would lock a record and walk away from their machine for lunch. During that time, no one else could modify the record. So, I created a special set of routines to deal with timing out the forms after some amount of time (30 minutes, for example). In some cases, the timeout was not necessary, so I added a custom property called *useTimeout*. This property was set to a default value of *true* or set to *false* for the forms that did not need to use the timeout functionality.

This is just a single example and we will not delve into all the hows of doing the timeout option that I mentioned above *(hint, it used a the timer class)*, but it should start the gears moving.

Assigning Default Actions to Event Handlers

When working with a form you may want or need to have some specific action when something occurs with a form, such as opening it (the *onOpen()* event, for example) and you want it to happen with every form in your application. Creating event handlers for these events in a custom form means that you only have to create the code once, then all of your forms *(that are derived from the custom form)* will inherit the code and will automatically execute it when the event occurs. Even better, you can overwrite that code, add to it or just ignore the original code.

Creating Methods for a Custom Class

You can also create your own custom methods in a custom form, which again can be used and called as if they always existed in any forms derived from that custom form. Add to this the ability to override methods (such as the form's *open()* method) and you will find you can create a fairly powerful set of forms without having to copy code from one form to another.

Define Default Controls for a Form

You can create controls that will appear on all forms derived from a custom form. This is useful if you have a company logo, or specific text that appears on all forms, for example. You might need to have a timer object always available to all forms derived from your custom form. The real advantage to this is that if the company logo changes, changing the logo to a new image is as simple as changing the file reference in the image control placed on the custom form – this will automatically replicate through all of your other forms without having to do any more work.

The Complete Custom Form Class

Now after explaining all of the advantages to working with custom forms, it's probably time we created a basic custom form. We are actually going to create more than one custom form, so that we have a base form – one that all other custom forms are "based" on.

To do this, we need to tell dBASE we want to create a custom form. Start dBASE and make sure that the Navigator is set to the "Forms" tab.

We can create a custom form in the same way that we create normal forms, but rather than selecting the "Form" icon in the Navigator, all we need to do is to select the "Custom Form" icon – this one is yellow. If you doubleclick this icon, or use one of the other various means shown elsewhere in this book to open the Form Designer, you will start dBASE's Form Designer with a minor difference – dBASE knows that this is supposed to be a custom form and once you save it, it will stream code out a little differently.

Changing Built-in Default Property Values

We can set or change any properties we want to here, which will be reflected in any forms that are based on, or derived from, this form.

We are going to set a single property (this can be found under the heading "Miscellaneous" in the inspector):

metric   Change this to "6 - Pixels"

For the moment, this is all we need to do. This is our base form and we want all of the forms we create for our application(s) to use this metric.

Save the custom form by pressing Ctrl+S or one of the various other means of saving in the forms designer (using the "File" menu and selecting "Save As ..." or "Save", or the toolbutton in the toolbar). When the filename dialog comes up, enter the word "Base", then click the "Save" button. You should see something like this:

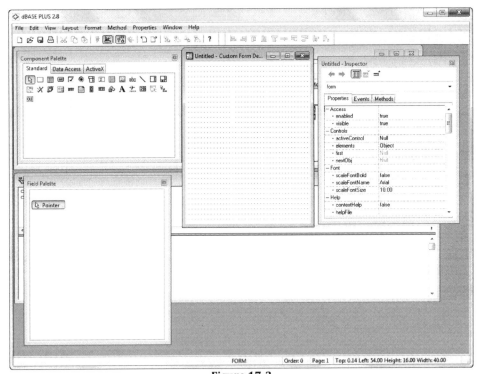

Figure 17-2

This doesn't look like we did much, however if you examine the source code for the custom form (press F9 to bring up the Source Code Editor), you will see that the code looks a little different than a regular form:

```
** END HEADER -- do not remove this line
class BaseCForm of FORM custom
   with (this)
      metric = 6 // Pixels
      height = 352.0
      left = 378.0
      top = 0.0
      width = 280.0
      text = ""
   endwith
endclass
```

Notice that the *metric* property is set, but that's really about it. The *height*, *width*, *top* and *left* properties are set at default values, but if we had moved the form or resized it in the designer, the values would have been streamed out differently. The *text* property defaults to being empty.

To get a better idea of what can be done, close the form designer (Ctrl + W , use the "x" in the titlebar of the form, or some other means of closing).

Next, we are going to create a new form. This form will be derived from the custom form we just created, and is just going to be a simple example of what we can do.

To create a new form, select the *white* icon for forms and bring up the form designer again. Go to the Inspector window, then find the *metric* property – notice that the default setting is "0 - Chars". In order to see the real power of custom forms, we need to tell dBASE that this form is going to be subclassed or derived from the base custom class form we just created. To do that, you need to select the "File" menu, and then select "Set Custom Form Class …".

This will bring up this dialog:

Figure 17-3

To set dBASE to use a custom form class, you need to first tell it what file contains the class. Click on the tool button by the entryfield for "File name containing class:" and select the file we just created called "Base.cfm". The combobox for "Class name:" shows that we could have more than one custom form class in the same file, but this can confuse the Form Designer sometimes and is not really a good idea.

Click "OK" and you will have told dBASE that our current form must be derived from the custom form "BaseCForm" in the file "Base.cfm". dBASE will close and reopen the form.

To see that this really worked, go to the Inspector window and find the *metric* property again. Notice that it now shows as "6 - Pixels". This is a small example of the abilities of using custom form classes.

To get an even better idea, drop a text control onto the design surface of this form, then set the following properties:

text	This Form is derived from BaseCForm *(widen the text control so that it is all on one line)*
fontSize	14
anchor	2 - Top
colorNormal	Navy/BtnFace

You may want to play with the form size a bit (widen it) and the *height* and such of the text control by dragging things around a little. Once you are satisfied, save the form (`Ctrl`+`S`) and call it "TestForm1".

If you run the form, it will look pretty much like it does now, so while we can do it, let's move on.

We should take a look at the class constructor code for the form "TestForm1.wfm". To do that, close the form (if it is still open) and open it in the Source Code Editor (right click, then select the option "Open in Source Editor"). Notice the line of code that starts the class description for this form:

```
class TestForm1Form of BASECFORM from "Base.cfm"
```

Notice that dBASE streamed out, rather than "of FORM", the name of the base class form and the file that contains the base form. This can be useful to know. For example, what if you wanted to change the custom form you are deriving your own form from? You could simply change it in the source code!

Close the Source Code Editor and let's re-open the custom form "Base.cfm" in the designer again.

This time we're going to make a more dramatic change for the purpose of seeing how easy it is to change all of your forms in an application. Find the *colorNormal* property of the custom form, which should show "BtnFace". Type the word (no spaces or quotes) "LightBlue" and press the Enter key. Notice that the form surface is now a light blue color. Save the custom form and exit the designer (`Ctrl`+`W` will do this easily).

Next, run the form "TestForm1.wfm" by double-clicking on it in the Navigator, you will notice that the form is light blue! How simple was that? If we had 100 forms that were derived from "BaseCForm" in the "Base.cfm" file, all 100 of those forms would now display a light blue background!

Clearing Out the Custom Form Class

One thing you should know early on in the process of working with custom forms is once you tell dBASE to use a custom form, it will always use it until you tell it not to, or you tell it to use another one.

This fact is very important, because if you do *not* tell dBASE to stop using a custom form, it will continue to do so, even if you don't want it to. This can also cause confusion if you delete or move the custom form class from its original location.

How do you tell dBASE to stop using your custom form? Well, you can change the custom form, but that may not be what you desire. The simple solution is to bring up the form designer (open a new form) – this will be based on your custom form. Select the "File" menu, and then "Set Custom Form Class ...". The dialog should look like:

Figure 17-4

If you click the button "Clear Custom Form Class", then click "OK", dBASE will clear out the custom form class and set the current form back to defaults. If you then close the form designer without making any changes, you will have cleared out that setting and not created a new form. This is useful for starting a new project, or whatever you need to do. Unless you know for certain that you will be working on the same project for some time, before you close dBASE it is probably a good idea to close your custom form, otherwise you may be surprised the next time you start the form designer.

Back to Using Custom Forms

For our purposes I am going to suggest that you change the *colorNormal* property of the Base.cfm file back to the default. The simplest way is to open the file in the Source Code Editor (click on it in the Navigator, then right click, select "Open in Source Editor") and delete the line that says:

```
colorNormal = "LightBlue"
```

Save this and close the Source Code Editor ([Ctrl]+[W]). The next time you work with this form or any form derived from it, the color will be the default (*BtnFace*).

A Data Custom Form

Next we want to create a custom form that is derived from our base custom form. This custom form might be one that we used for working with data and we could add a lot of custom code to this form that would only be useful on forms that had data.

We want to create a new Custom Form, by double-clicking on the yellow (Untitled) Form icon in the Navigator. Next, we need to tell dBASE that *this* form is derived from a custom form, by going to the "File" menu and selecting the "Set Custom Form Class" option. Select the Base.cfm file as we did before, and click "OK".

Next we may want to add some controls to this form that will appear on all data forms used by our application. For example, some title text might be useful. Drag a text object to the design surface, and set the following properties:

text	A Data Form
fontSize	14
anchor	2 - Top
colorNormal	Navy/BtnFace
borderStyle	1 - Raised
alignHorizontal	1 - Center
name	TITLETEXT

You will want to change the height of this text control a little so that it looks okay. This should look something like:

Figure 17-5

We could put a lot of controls on this custom form, for example in an earlier chapter we created a set of buttons down the right side of a form that dealt with navigation in a rowset, editing, appending, saving and so on. For now we're trying to keep things relatively simple – but it is possible to put all kinds of controls on a custom form that will appear on all derived forms.

We might want to add some code that made sure that when the form was opened, the user was always placed at the first row in the rowset. (In a real application you may not want to do this – for example with a lookup form where you want the lookup to show the current row, rather than the first row in the rowset) To do this we have a couple of options. One is to use the form's *onOpen()* event. The difficulty of using the *onOpen()* event is that it actually is executed **after** the form has opened. Why is this a problem? Consider that if the form opens and it is not on the first row already, then your *onOpen()* event fires and the form is told to navigate to the first row of the rowset – this causes the screen to sort of flash, which doesn't look good and may actually confuse a user.

It is suggested that you override the form's *open()* method, which can be set to execute specific code **before** the form opens then to open the form. This means that the navigation would occur before the form opens, when it does open, the user will be shown the first row of the rowset with no "flashing".

To override the form's *open()* method, we need to go to the Inspector window and select the "Methods" tab. Find "open", and click on it. Now click on the tool button, notice you are placed in the Source Code Editor and a method is created for you:

```
function form_open

    return BASECFORM::open()
```

We have two options here as well. We can put the code we want to execute directly in this method, *or* we can create a new method of the custom form, which can be called from other places as well.

One way of handling this is to call the method Init (short for "Initialize"). In the form's open method place a call to the soon to be created "Init()" method:

```
function form_open
    class::Init()
    return BASECFORM::open()
```

Then create the new *(custom)* method:

```
function Init
    // do any startup code I want to occur before the form opens:
return
```

Why would you want to do this in two steps like this? Well, at the moment you do not know which method you will use to open the form. There are two ways to start a form – one is with the *open()* method, the other is with the *readModal()* method. Do you want to duplicate code in both of those methods, when it isn't necessary? What if you also override the *readModal()* method and tell it to execute the form's new *Init()* method? This means that no matter which way you open the form, the *Init()* method is called and you don't have to duplicate more than a single line of code. To do that, go to the Inspector, find *readModal* and repeat what we did for the *open* method, giving us code that looks like:

```
function form_open
    class::Init()
    return BASECFORM::open()

function form_readModal
    class::Init()
    return BASECFORM::readModal()

function Init
    // do any startup code I want to occur before the form opens:
return
```

With this done, all our forms based off of this custom form class will always execute any code in the *Init()* method before the form opens, no matter if we open it as a modeless form, or as a modal form.

If you recall, we started this part of the exercise to create some code that navigates to the first row in the form's rowset before the form opens. To do that, we need to place some code in the new *Init()* method. However, what if the form does not have a rowset? It is possible – if we do not plan for this, running a form derived from the custom form class will generate an error message, which we don't really want!

So we want to add code that checks to see *if* the form has a value assigned to the *rowset* property, if it does, we then want to do our navigation, otherwise we do not want to do anything. This is pretty simple code, and should look like:

```
if form.rowset # null
   form.rowset.first()
endif
```

If you place this in the *Init()* method, the method might look like:

```
function Init
   // do any startup code I want to occur before the form opens:
   // Check to see if the rowset property is not null
   if form.rowset # null
      // if we have a rowset, go to first row:
      form.rowset.first()
   endif
return
```

It is a good idea to save your custom form – save it as "Data". If you press ⌨Ctrl+⌨S, dBASE will ask for a filename, enter "Data" (without the quotes) and dBASE will save this form. Exit the form designer. *(Before moving on to the next exercise, go through the steps to clear out the custom form, otherwise you may run into errors later.)*

Placing Custom Forms in Source Alias Folder

At the beginning of this chapter we discussed the concepts of using Source Code Aliases and creating libraries of code.

It is a good idea to get into this habit, so we are now going to start looking at putting your custom forms into a library. This will mean modifying the source code just a little, but is not a difficult thing to do. If you did not do this at the beginning of the chapter, you should do the steps below now.

The first thing is that you need to create the folder(s) that you want to store your library of custom code. You should create something like:

```
C:\My Company\Forms
```

You could change it to "My Project" and make a different library for each project that you do, or perhaps even put a different project folder under the "My Company" folder, etc.. The actual structure can be very flexible, and by using Source Code Aliases, you can come back and change it later – the only place you need to change things in dBASE is in the Desktop Properties dialog.

Once you have your folder created, move the two .CFM files that we created into the new folder (use the Windows Explorer). These are "Base.cfm" and "Data.cfm". You can (and probably should) delete the .CFO files (compiled custom forms) from wherever you had them before moving them.

Next, start dBASE PLUS up if it isn't already open, select the "Properties" menu and then the "Desktop Properties" menu.

Select the "Source Aliases" tab, then:

- Click the "Add" button
- Enter "MyCustomForms" in the Alias entryfield
- Click the "Tool" button next to the Path entryfield and select the folder that we created a moment ago (C:\My Company\Forms, or whatever you chose to use), click "OK".
- Click the "Add" button again
- Click "OK" (to save changes and close the dialog – if you wanted to add more aliases, you could do it now by repeating the steps above)

For our examples we're using the generic name of "MyCustomForms" for our source code alias, but again you can use whatever you wish for your real applications.

Now we need to modify the source code of two different files. The first is the custom form "Data.cfm". How do we open that? Well, it's actually easy – type the following in the Command Window, and you will see the form's source code in the Source Code Editor:

```
modify command :MyCustomForms:Data.cfm
```

The line we need to change is:

```
class DataCForm of BASECFORM custom from "Base.cfm"
```

Which needs to look like:

```
class DataCForm of BASECFORM custom from ":MyCustomForms:Base.cfm"
```

(Add the Source Code Alias, shown in boldface in the line above.) This tells dBASE to use the file "Base.cfm" from the source code alias "MyCustomForms" to get the custom form "BASECFORM". Save the changes and close this file (⌂Ctrl+⌂W).

That's all that is necessary for dBASE to understand this. Next, we need to do something similar, but for the form we created called "TestForm1.wfm". If dBASE is currently pointing to the folder that form is in, you can open it with the command (or any of the other options for opening a file in the source editor):

```
modify command TestForm1.wfm
```

We need to do the exact same thing we did with the Data.cfm file, changing this line:

```
class TestForm1Form of BASECFORM from "Base.cfm"
```

to look like this:

```
class TestForm1Form of BASECFORM from ":MyCustomForms:Base.cfm"
```

Add the Source Code Alias, shown in boldface and save and exit the Source Code Editor (⌂Ctrl+⌂W). We have now set our forms and custom forms to use the source code alias and we have just made our application development a bit easier (in the long run – it may not seem like it now, but this really does make a difference!).

It is important to note that if, while using the form designer, you tell dBASE to use a custom form that can be referenced by a Source Code Alias, dBASE will insert the Source Code Alias into the appropriate location. This is a nice feature.

We're doing the steps we've just taken only because we started in a different sequence. If the custom forms were placed in a folder referenced by a Source Code Alias, we would not have had to do a thing to tell dBASE to use the alias.

Using the "Data" Custom Form

Now that we have this custom form how do we use it? In theory you would use "Data.cfm" as the custom form for any new forms you create that work with data.

We are now going to start a more complex example form that will be based on something that was done in an earlier chapter of the book. We're going to use this for both a sample of the custom *form* as well as, later in this chapter, where we will start looking at custom *controls* as well.

In an earlier chapter we created a form that used the table "Fish" from the samples that are installed with dBASE PLUS. We will do something similar, but we're going to start over. The reasons will make themselves clear as we go. We are also going to start out fairly simply, then add more fields and controls later in this chapter.

To start, we need to create a new form. If dBASE is not open at this point, start it, making sure you are pointing to a good work folder (check the folder in the Navigator window).

Click on the "Forms" tab, double-click the first "(Untitled)" icon which will bring up the form designer. Next we want to tell dBASE that this new form is going to be based on (or derived from) our custom data form. To do that select the "File" menu, then "Set Custom Form Class". Select the file (which will be under the folder we created earlier – note that the dialog here does not understand Source Code Aliases, but all will be fine, really!) "Data.cfm". Click "OK" and you should see your new form now change just a little.

First, let's take a look at the text at the top of the form. The text control says "A Data Form", which seems a bit silly for an actual working form. Since we plan on using the Fish table from the samples, we should reset the text. To do this, click once on the control to give it focus, then a second time (notice that this is not a "double-click" – it is two separate clicks with a pause between them) and we can change the text. Type the words "Some Fish", then click anywhere on the form.

What did we just do? We changed the *text* property of a control that is derived from the custom form "Data.cfm". Notice that we cannot delete this control, so if we didn't want it to display we would have to set the *visible* property to false. The reason we cannot delete this control is that it is part of the custom form, not actually a part of this form, at least not directly. We have changed this *instance* of the text object named "TITLETEXT" at the top of the form.

It is a good idea to save your form at this point, so press Ctrl+S. dBASE will ask for a filename – call this form "SomeFish" and click "Save".

Before we do much else, we need to tell dBASE that we want to use a table with this form. To do that, click on the Navigator to give it focus (if you don't see it, select the "Window" menu, and "Navigator").

- Click on the "Tables" tab
- Select "DBASESAMPLES" from the "Look in:" combobox
- Click on the "Fish.dbf" table
- Drag it to your form

Your form should look something like:

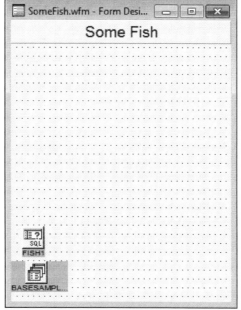

Figure 17-6

If you do not see the Field Palette right click on the design surface for your form and select "Field Palette" from the popup menu. To get started, we are going to do this simply, then later we will add more fields.

📝 **NOTE**

If you created the datamodule "Fish.dmd" in the chapter about dQuery, you could use this instead of following the steps to get the Fish table from the samples folder. Instead of the instructions given above, follow these:

- Click on the "Datamodules" tab
- Find the "Fish.dmd" datamodule
- Drag it to the form

If you want to be really organized, you could place your datamodules in another library folder and create a Source Code Alias for them.

Drag the Name field to the design surface:

Figure 17-7

Notice, if we have the data sorted properly, that the row shown is not necessarily the first in the table. If you are using the table, rather than a datamodule (see NOTE inset above), we want to change the *indexName* property of the rowset. Click on the "SQL" icon that says "FISH1" on the form. In the Inspector window, find *rowset*, then click on the Inspect button (it has the letter "I" on it). This will "drill down" to the rowset object of the query. Find the *indexName* property and in the combobox (click the "down arrow") find "NAME" and select this.

You won't see a difference in the form designer, but when you run the form, rather than starting on "Clown Triggerfish", you should see "Blue Angelfish". Why is that? Because we are using the custom form which we created some startup code that is executed before the form opens, which moves to the first row in the table.

To see this, run the form by clicking on the "Lightning Bolt" button in the toolbar (hold your mouse over it, you will see a speedtip that says "Run Form"). You should see:

Figure 17-8

There is one thing we haven't really looked at and that is the text that appears in the titlebar of the form. The form itself has a *text* property. If this property is "empty" dBASE places the word "Form" there when the form is executed. We can change this easily to whatever text we want. Click on the toolbutton in the toolbar next to the "Run Form" button (the one with the lightning bolt) that says in the speedtip "Design Form". This will bring the form back into the form designer.

Go to the Inspector window, find the form's *text* property (this will be under the "Miscellaneous" heading) and enter "Chapter 17 - Sample Fish Form", then press the `Enter` key. We have now changed the text that will display in the titlebar when we next run the form. In an application, changing the *text* property for the form is a good idea, as the user can tell what the form is easily if they have multiple forms open.

At this point we are nearly done so save the form, and exit the form designer (`Ctrl`+`W`). There is one more thing we need to do and that is to clear out the Custom Form that is in use, otherwise we might cause ourselves some confusion and frustration.

Start the Form Designer (double-click the first (Untitled) icon in the Navigator), then select the "File" menu and "Set Custom Form Class". Click the "Clear Custom Form Class", then click "OK" and close the Form Designer. The next time we start the Form Designer, we won't start with a form derived from a custom form class.

Creating Classes for Control Objects

The rest of this chapter will focus on creating custom classes for form controls and then putting them to use on the form we started toward the end of the section on Custom Forms. In order to do this, we need to understand custom classes.

It is important to note that like nearly everything created by dBASE design surfaces, Custom Controls are simply text files that have a special file extension, can be opened in the Source Code Editor like anything else (Forms, Datamodules, etc.).

dBASE PLUS itself ships with several custom classes that you may want to use in your own applications, but we will take a look at those in another chapter of this book.

Why Create Your Own Custom Classes?

Custom classes are ways of making reusable code. Some custom classes are written with *very* specific purposes in mind, others tend to be more "generic" (in that they can be used in many situations, rather than a specific field or field type, for example). We will be focusing on visual classes, but you can create non-visual custom classes for similar reasons.

You could create an entryfield that was designed to be a "generic" entryfield that had a specific color when it got focus and that was all that it did. This may not seem like much of a reason to use a custom class, but it is actually quite handy.

On the flip side, you could create another entryfield class that was designed specifically to validate date fields, and handle the errors for you in a way that is different from the way dBASE handles them. You could even add code to bring up a calendar form and more. This is a pretty specific purpose entryfield, but if written properly, it could be useful on more than one form, so making it into a custom class makes a lot of sense.

In either case, we are going to be looking specifically at visual classes, the ones used on forms, often specifically to work with data *(although not necessarily)*. Some of the concepts here were covered in earlier chapters where we looked at object-oriented programming in dBASE.

Custom classes that are used for forms are quite useful to a developer in many ways. In some cases, you may wish to change the way a specific type of object behaves and have that change available every time you use that type of object. You may wish to change the way an object *appears* and always use that change. By making these changes in custom classes, you have complete control over these behaviors and appearances application-wide. In addition, if your users decide that they want something to behave or appear differently, rather than having to change every occurrence of the entryfield object on every form in an application, by using a custom control you only have to change the custom control. All controls that are derived from that custom control will automatically take on the new behavior or appearance.

If you consider a large application you can see how useful this might be. If your application has 100 forms and each form has 20 or more entryfield controls, the last thing you want to do is modify each one, one at a time. By using custom controls you make it that much easier to develop and modify an application.

Methods of Creating and Modifying Custom Classes

There are at least two ways to create custom form classes. The first is by using the Form Designer, the second is by using the Source Code Editor and of course, you can always combine them. Once you have created a custom class in the Form Designer, you will most likely need to modify it using the Source Code Editor, so we will look at doing both here.

In addition, we could put each custom class in its own file, or we could put several custom classes in a single file. One of the great features of dBASE is that you have a lot of options.

For the purposes of the exercise here, many of our controls will go into a single file and others will go into a second file. In addition, we need to create a folder to store our form controls (if you haven't already), and a Source Code Alias to go with that folder.

Using the Windows Explorer, go to the same folder that the "Forms" folder is stored in and create a new folder. This folder should be named "FormControls".

In dBASE, start the Desktop Properties dialog ("Properties" menu, "Desktop Properties") and select the "Source Alias" tab.

Click the "Add" button. Type "MyFormControls" in the Alias entryfield, use the tool button to find and select the folder for this alias (the "FormControls" folder we just created). Then click the "Add" button again, then "OK" to close the Desktop Properties dialog.

Creating a Custom TextLabel Class

The first custom class we will create is a custom TextLabel class, because it doesn't use as much memory as the Text class does *(as mentioned in another chapter)*, as we don't need the HTML interpreter that is built in to the Text class.

We are going to start in the Form Designer and create the basic TextLabel control. To get started, we're going to create a new form.

When the form designer comes up, the first thing to do is to set the form's metrics to Pixels (find the *metric* property and change it to "6 - Pixels"). If we do not do this, dBASE will assume that we are working with Characters and the position and size properties will have values that will be incorrect for this control on a form that uses Pixels for the metric (while dBASE handles some conversions well, sometimes the conversions don't work – it's better to plan for the metric used for your forms).

Next, find the TextLabel control on the Component Palette (the icon looks like "abc" without the quotes). Drag this to the design surface. Next we want to change a few properties – you will want to look in the Inspector for these, and change them:

name	MyTextLabel
alignHorizontal	2 - Right
fontBold	true
text	MyTextLabel:
	(For the text property, notice the colon (:) at the end of the text.)

We gave this a name so that the name will be streamed out when we save it. However, we are not going to save this in the usual fashion. We could just save the form, but then how would we use the custom class we are in the process of creating?

We need to go to the "File" menu, and select "Save as Custom ...". This brings up a dialog that looks like:

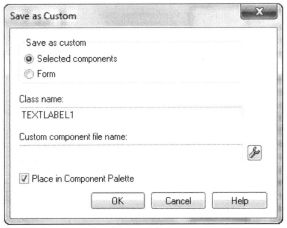

Figure 17-9

We could save the form as a custom form, but we don't need to *(this is a useful thing to note)*. We want to tell dBASE to save this as "MYTEXTLABEL" and we need to give a location to save it in. If we just type a filename it will go in the current folder, so click the tool button and select the "FormControls" folder.

Type "MyFormControls" in the Filename entryfield, and click "Save".

Before you click the "OK" button, we want to uncheck the "Place in Component Palette" checkbox. This option is useful in some cases, but many developers have found it can be frustrating as well – it tells dBASE to always load custom controls when dBASE starts, which you may not want it to do each time it starts. There are other ways to make your custom controls available for designing applications, this is just one. It is suggested that you always uncheck this.

Now click "OK".

Some dBASE developers suggest that you save the form you designed your custom class on, so that if you need to make changes to it in the designer you can. You can do that if you really wish. It's not 100% necessary most of the time unless you expect to be modifying the custom class' appearance in the Form Designer.

Now that you have saved your custom class, you can close the form you were using to design it, with or without or with if you wish) saving it. If you want to edit or examine the source code for your custom class, how do you do that? It does not appear in the Navigator, unless you change your working directory to the folder we saved it in. Simple – in the Command Window, type:

```
modify command :MyFormControls:MyFormControls.cc
```

You should see something like the following in the Source Code Editor:

```
class MYTEXTLABEL(parentObj, name) of TEXTLABEL(parentObj, name) custom
   with (this)
      height = 22.0
      left = 25.0
      top = 44.0
      width = 111.0
      metric = 6 // Pixels
      text = "Textlabel1:"
      fontBold = true
```

```
      alignHorizontal = 2 // Right
   endwith
endclass
```

Because of the way the Form Designer works with custom classes, you should remove the "name" parameter in the first line:

```
class MYTEXTLABEL(parentObj, name) of TEXTLABEL(parentObj, name) custom
```

The name parameter tells dBASE to pass along a name, but it doesn't pass along the name you would expect. If you remove this parameter, it actually does what you would expect. When you place an instance of your new class on the form, if you remove the "name" parameter, dBASE will name the first instance "MyTextLabel1", which is useful for knowing what you are looking at and working with.

The class statement should now read:

```
class MYTEXTLABEL(parentObj) of TEXTLABEL(parentObj) custom
```

The parameter "parentObj" is necessary, although the actual name of the parameter does not need to be specifically "parentObj". I often use "oParent" when I create my own custom classes, for example. The purpose of this parameter is to provide for dBASE a parent for the control, because the interface controls cannot exist outside of a form or container of some sort. When you place this on a form (or on a container on a form), dBASE looks for this parameter and will automatically assign the correct parent to the control.

> **NOTE**
> If you do not remove the "name" parameter, when the Form Designer streams out the *name* property of any instances of your control, it will ignore the name of the class you have given your control and instead stream out the *baseClassName* property. The first instance of your textlabel control on a form would have a *name* property of "TEXTLABEL1", rather than "MYTEXTLABEL1", which is what you want – especially if you have more than one custom textlabel control that you might wish to use on a form.

The *top* and *left* properties are not really necessary, but they don't hurt and sometimes the *height* and *width* properties are very important – this will depend on what you are doing with your forms. The *metric* property is streamed out, so that if you try to use this on a form with different metrics dBASE will know what to do with it *(or try – as noted earlier this doesn't always work)*. The other properties that are shown in the source code (above) are the ones that we changed (*text*, *fontBold*, and *alignHorizontal*). If these had not been changed, they would not have been streamed out to the control.

We will come back to this control in a bit, when we start putting the form together that we need it for.

> **NOTE**
> While we created this control visually, we could do it manually as well and just create a custom class file in the Source Code Editor, entering the code needed to define the class. The advantage to designing a custom class visually is that you can set the appearance exactly the way you need it to be before saving it.

Creating a Custom Entryfield Class

To create our custom Entryfield class, we will do something similar to what we did with the TextLabel class. So, the first thing we should do is start the Form Designer by opening a blank form and set the form's *metric* property to "6 - Pixels". Then we want to drag an Entryfield object onto the form.

Once the Entryfield is on the form, you may want to widen it a bit – I generally do, as the default width is seldom what I need anyway. Then you need to set the following properties:

name	MyEntryfield
value	MyEntryfield
colorHighlight	WindowText/0x80ffff

Why this particular setting for the *colorHighlight* property? Largely as a way to see that when the Entryfield gains focus, which field the user is currently working on. Changing the color that way is a useful visual cue to the user. *(There is a discussion about colors in the appendices of this book.)*

That's all we really need to change, at least for now. This is going to be a "basic" Entryfield, as opposed to a specific purpose one. So, we need to save it. As before, use the "File", "Save as Custom" options. Notice that the last file that you saved to is selected. For our purposes, this is perfect, as we want to store multiple form controls in the same custom class file. The only thing you need to do is uncheck the "Place in Component Palette" checkbox, and then click "OK".

We will come back to this in a bit, as well. We will want to remove the "name" parameter, but there isn't anything else we should need to do. When we created the custom TextLabel control, we closed the form, but we don't really need to do that, so we will leave the Form Designer up for now.

Creating a Custom Spinbox Class

Place a Spinbox control onto the form. Then change the following properties:

name	MySpinbox
colorHighlight	WindowText/0x80ffff

We need to save it. As before, use the "File", "Save as Custom" options. The only thing you need to do is uncheck the "Place in Component Palette" checkbox, then click "OK".

As you may have guessed we're going to create several custom classes now, and then come back to them all.

Creating a Custom Editor Class

Place an Editor control onto the form. Then change the following properties:

name	MyEditor
colorHighlight	WindowText/0x80ffff
evalTags	false

Why are we setting the *evalTags* property to *false*? Because for now we do not need the editor attempting to create, interpret or insert HTML tags into our text. You may want this behavior for some cases, but most of the time it can be frustrating. By turning this off for our "standard" Editor class, we don't have to remember to do it later.

We need to save it. As before, use the "File", "Save as Custom" options. Uncheck the "Place in Component Palette" checkbox, then click "OK".

Creating a Custom Image Class
Place an Image control onto the form. Then change the following properties:

name	MyImage
alignment	3 - Keep Aspect Stretch

Why are we setting the *alignment* property to "3 - Keep Aspect Stretch"? Because we want the image to resize if we resize the object, but we do not want it to be distorted, which is what will happen with the default setting.

We need to save it. As before, use the "File", "Save as Custom" options. Uncheck the "Place in Component Palette" checkbox, then click "OK".

NOW we're done (for the time being) creating new custom classes with the Form Designer, so you can close the form (use the "x" in the titlebar, for example) without saving (when asked, click "No").

Cleaning up the Custom Class Code
As we noted with the TextLabel control we created earlier, we need to remove the "name" parameter that is automatically generated by the Form Designer.
In the Command Window, type the following:

```
modify command :MyFormControls:MyFormControls.cc
```

With the custom class file open in the Source Code Editor, you will see that each of the classes we created has been saved to this file, one after the other, in the order we saved them.

To remove the "name" parameter, there's a simple way to do it in one shot:

Press Ctrl+R – this brings up the "Find and Replace" dialog in the Source Code Editor. In the "Find what" entryfield, enter (without the quotes): ", name"

That's a comma, a space and the word "name". In the "Replace with" entryfield, enter *nothing* – no space, no characters, just leave it empty.

Click "Replace All", you will see that ", name" is now gone. It is important that we remove the comma, the space and the word "name". If we don't, we leave the comma, this will confuse dBASE as it will be expecting a second parameter after the comma. This would cause errors when we try to use these classes.

This is the only thing that we *have* to do and you should see something along the following lines in your custom class file:

```
class MYTEXTLABEL(parentObj) of TEXTLABEL(parentObj) custom
   with (this)
      height = 22.0
      left = 25.0
      top = 44.0
      width = 111.0
```

```
        metric = 6 // Pixels
        text = "MyTextLabel:"
        fontBold = true
        alignHorizontal = 2 // Right
    endwith
endclass

class MYENTRYFIELD(parentObj) of ENTRYFIELD(parentObj) custom
    with (this)
        height = 22.0
        left = 41.0
        top = 79.0
        width = 119.0
        metric = 6 // Pixels
        colorHighLight = "WindowText/0x80ffff"
        value = "MyEntryfield"
    endwith
endclass

class MYSPINBOX(parentObj) of SPINBOX(parentObj) custom
    with (this)
        height = 22.0
        left = 45.0
        top = 128.0
        width = 56.0
        metric = 6 // Pixels
        colorHighLight = "WindowText/0x80ffff"
        rangeMax = 100
        rangeMin = 1
        value = 1
    endwith
endclass

class MYEDITOR(parentObj) of EDITOR(parentObj) custom
    with (this)
        height = 88.0
        left = 33.0
         top = 178.0
        width = 140.0
        metric = 6 // Pixels
        value = ""
        colorHighLight = "WindowText/0x80ffff"
        evalTags = false
    endwith
endclass

class MYIMAGE(parentObj) of IMAGE(parentObj) custom
    with (this)
        height = 88.0
        left = 35.0
        top = 269.0
        width = 84.0
        metric = 6 // Pixels
        alignment = 3 // Keep Aspect Stretch
    endwith
endclass
```

You should save these changes and close this file (pressing is the simplest way).

Putting These Custom Classes to Work

Now that we have a small library of custom classes, how do we actually use them?

The first thing we will do is to modify the form we had started to create (SomeFish.wfm) earlier in this chapter, so that it uses these classes. This can be done in the Source Code Editor, by typing the following in the Command Window:

```
modify command SomeFish.wfm
```

When the form opens in the Source Code Editor, we will need to make some minor changes in the code. Right after this line:

```
class SomeFishForm of DATACFORM from :MyCustomForms:Data.cfm
```

we need to tell dBASE to open the custom class file and make the classes contained in it available to the form. We do that by inserting this line of code directly after the line above:

```
set procedure to :MyFormControls:MyFormControls.cc
```

You should now see:

```
class SomeFishForm of DATACFORM from :MyCustomForms:Data.cfm
set procedure to :MyFormControls:MyFormControls.cc
```

> **NOTE**
> If the custom controls already existed, then you could just go to the Command Window and issue the SET PROCEDURE statement as shown above. Creating a new form would automatically recognize these controls and you could move on from there. The sequence we are doing things now is *only* due to the sequence of events we are using to learn how it all works.

The next thing we will do is tell dBASE to use our custom controls for ones that are already on the form. Find the line:

```
this.TEXTNAME1 = new TEXT(this)
```

And change it to read:

```
this.TEXTNAME1 = new MYTEXTLABEL(this)
```

Find this line:

```
wrap = false
```

and delete it. The reason we are deleting it is that the Text control has a *wrap* property, but the TextLabel control does not. Leaving it here might cause errors when we run the form. If there is an *alignVertical* property in the constructor for this control you may want to remove it as well *(which is not really necessary)*.

Find this line:

```
text = "Name"
```

and add a colon to inside the quotes after the word "Name", so that it looks like:

```
text = "Name:"
```

We are now done with the text control, let's move to the entryfield – this should be even easier. Find this line:

```
this.ENTRYFIELDNAME1 = new ENTRYFIELD(this)
```

And change it to read:

```
this.ENTRYFIELDNAME1 = new MYENTRYFIELD(this)
```

Save the form and exit the Source Code Editor (⌈Ctrl⌉+⌈W⌉).

To see that the changes worked, and we are now using our custom controls, run the form – it should look something like:

Figure 17-10

Notice that the TextLabel is boldfaced and that the background of the entryfield is yellow – when we ran this before, the Text was not bold and the entryfield background was white.

Now we have the basics, let's add controls for the other fields in the table, using our custom classes!

Close the form, and bring reopen it in the Form Designer (you can do this by using the "Design Form" button in the toolbar).

One thing you may want to do is rearrange the TextLabel and Entryfield controls, so they are on the "same line" (as it were), possibly move them up and so on.

The next thing we need to do is to look at the Component Palette. A new tab should exist, that says "Custom" on it. You may need to use the arrow buttons on the notebook to see the new tab.

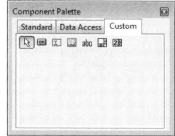

Figure 17-11

Adding fields to a form when you want to use custom classes is a bit more work than just dragging fields from the Field Palette, but you will find in the long run it is worth the extra effort.

For example, to add the "Species" field to the form, we need to drag two components to the surface, one for the text and one for the entry area. Then we need to modify a couple of properties.

If you hold your mouse over the controls shown on the Custom tab of the Component Palette, you will see that these have the names we assigned to our own controls. Drag an instance of "MyTextLabel" to the design surface. Using the inspector, change these two properties (in the Inspector):

name	SpeciesText
text	Species:

You may want to change the width of the control (shorten it, as it is actually too wide right now), in one of several ways. The easiest is to click on the control so it has focus, then use Ctrl (hold it down) and the left arrow key, until it is the size you want. If you go too far, you can use Ctrl and the right arrow key to make it larger.

Next, drag an instance of "MyEntryfield" to the form design surface. Change the following properties (in the Inspector):

name	SpeciesEntryfield
dataLink	Click on the Tool button, and in the dialog that appears, select the Species field, and then click "OK".

Once you have done this, you will see that rather than the *value* showing "MyEntryfield", it shows the species of the current fish in the table. This is not as difficult as it appears, is it? It is a bit more complex than simply dragging the controls from the Field Palette, but what you gain as a developer is much more flexibility and control.

You will probably want to widen the entryfield, again using the Ctrl and right arrow keys. You can do more manipulation once all the controls are set. I am going to now run you through placing the other controls on the form fairly quickly. If you follow along this will become easier and easier as you get used to it:

Drag an instance of "MyTextLabel" to the form and change these properties in the Inspector:

name	LengthCMText
text	Length CM:

Drag an instance of "MySpinbox" to the form and change these properties in the Inspector:

name	LengthCMSpinbox
datalink	click the Tool button, and select the "Length CM" field, then click "OK".

You will need to widen this control so that it has room to show four numbers to the left of the decimal point, and two to the right.

Drag an instance of "MyTextLabel" to the form and change these properties in the Inspector:

name	DescText
text	Description:

Drag an instance of "MyEditor" to the form and change these properties in the Inspector:

name	DescEditor
datalink	click the Tool button, and select the "Description" field, then click "OK".

Drag an instance of "MyTextLabel" to the form and change these properties in the Inspector:

name	ImageText
text	Image:

Drag an instance of "MyImage" to the form and change these properties in the Inspector:

name	FishImage
dataSource	click the Tool button, select "Binary" (for "Binary Field"), click the Tool button, and select the "Description" field, then click "OK", and then click "OK" a second time (there are two dialogs involved).

The next thing you will want to do is spend some time lining up your controls, changing sizes of controls, etc., so that your form looks good. You may need to widen the form a little, whatever works for you. When you are done, you should have something that looks something like the following:

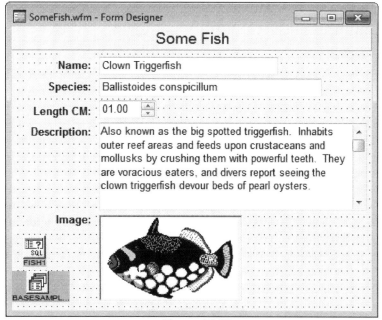

Figure 17-12

This doesn't look like all that different from what we did in an earlier chapter, but if you run the form, you will see some interesting differences. Click on the "Run Form" button in the toolbar and note that the background of the Name field is yellow. Now tab to the next field, and note that the background of the Name field is now white, but the background of the Species field is yellow. If you use the navigation buttons on the toolbar, and navigate through the table, you will see everything updates appropriately.

Creating a Custom Pushbutton Class

For an application, it is useful to have pushbuttons that do many things, although in some applications a toolbar at the top of the screen may be used instead of pushbuttons on a form. We are going to look at creating pushbuttons similar to what was done in Chapter 13, but we are now going to make them into custom pushbuttons. What does that mean? It means that like the other custom classes we've created so far, these will be reusable on many forms, while the pushbuttons we used in Chapter 13 can really only be used on that form.

To start, we will create a "base" custom pushbutton class, which we will then use for all of the pushbuttons we use.

Once again, we will bring up a blank form in the form designer. This is just going to be used to create our base form. Set the form's metrics to "6 - Pixels", now drag a pushbutton to the form surface. Change the following properties in the Inspector:

    name   MyPushbutton
    text   MyPushbutton

Select the "File" menu, select "Save as Custom ...", then uncheck the "Place in Component Palette" checkbox. Click "OK". Now close the form but don't save it.

We need to go into the custom form control class, and make the same change we did for the other classes, and now is the best time to do so. In the Command Window, type:

```
modify command :MyFormControls:MyFormControls.cc
```

Remove the text ", name" in the same manner as we did with the controls we worked with earlier:

```
class MYPUSHBUTTON(parentObj) of PUSHBUTTON(parentObj) custom
```

Now save this and exit the Source Code Editor ().

We could have done a variety of things with this custom class, but there isn't a lot we need to do. The pushbuttons we are about to create will rely on this base class and if we find we need to modify the base class, we can do so later.

The next thing we need to do is to create the pushbuttons that we are going to use for the form we've been creating (and as noted, for other forms as well), but we don't actually have to do this in the form designer. We can do the rest of this in the source code editor. We are now going to create a new custom class file that will contain just those custom pushbuttons we wish to use.

In the Command Window, type:

```
create command :MyFormControls:MyPushbuttons.cc
```

dBASE will bring up the Source Code Editor with a blank work area. We are going to create our custom pushbuttons by hand.

We have seen how the custom classes are created when using the Form Designer, we're just going to do this directly by typing what we need into the editor. We are going to take this in steps. The first buttons we will create are our navigation buttons – these buttons will navigate to the first row, the last row, the next row and the previous row.

To start, we need to create the first line of code for the definition of the first pushbutton. Type the following into the Source Code Editor:

```
class FirstButton(oParent) of MyPushbutton(oParent) ;
          from ":MyFormControls:MyFormControls.cc" custom
```

> **NOTE**
> The statement shown above could be entered as a single line, or if we use the semicolon character we can split it over multiple lines. dBASE understands that the semicolon character means that the command continues on the next line. This can help for readability of code and can reduce the width of statements if you want to print your source code.

We are telling dBASE that we want to create a pushbutton class that is subclassed from our own custom class called "MyPushbutton" and it tells dBASE where that class definition is. We are using the parent parameter as that is required for all visual controls, even if we are not using exactly the same one that is used by dBASE itself.

Now we need to define the text that will display. Add the line:

```
this.text := "First"
```

We do not need to give a *height* or *width* for the pushbutton, as these are defined in the base class.

The next thing that needs to be there is the set of instructions to be executed if the pushbutton is clicked. This will be different for each pushbutton.

```
function onClick
   form.rowset.first()
return
```

This could be more fancy, checking to see if we are already at the first row (using the rowset's *atFirst()* method), and letting the user know that we are already there, but for now let's keep it simple.

The last thing we need to define is the end of the class:

```
endclass
```

So all put together, we should have code that looks like:

```
class FirstButton(oParent) of MyPushbutton(oParent) ;
             from ":MyFormControls:MyFormControls.cc" custom
   this.text := "First"
   function onClick
      form.rowset.first()
   return
endclass
```

Before we move on to another class, I want to note that we did not write code that points to the *onClick()* event for this class, such as "this.onClick = ...". Why not? Because we used the same name as the event. If we had decided to call the code to be executed something like "*MyButtonClickCode*" then it would have been necessary to add a line in the code above that looked like:

```
this.onClick := class::MyButtonClickCode
```

However, we used the name of the event. Because we did, dBASE does not need to be told to look for it – it sees it automatically. It knows that when the pushbutton's *onClick()* event is fired, it needs to execute the code that we assigned to it.

Now that we have our first button, we can copy the code for the next button and only make minor changes. If you highlight everything we've done so far, use the Copy command (Ctrl+C) to copy this to the clipboard, putting the cursor on a line after the "endclass" statement, then paste (Ctrl+V), we can change the code to:

```
class LastButton(oParent) of MyPushbutton(oParent) ;
             from ":MyFormControls:MyFormControls.cc" custom
   this.text := "Last"
   function onClick
      form.rowset.last()
   return
endclass
```

Change the words that are in boldface above and we have our second custom button!

We're going to do the same thing, but make slightly bigger changes for the NextButton:

```
class NextButton(oParent) of MyPushbutton(oParent) ;
               from ":MyFormControls:MyFormControls.cc" custom
    this.text := "Next"
    function onClick
        if ( not form.rowset.next() )
            form.rowset.last()
            msgbox( "At end of rowset", "Can't Navigate", 64 )
        endif
    return
endclass
```

The biggest change is the code for the *onClick()* event. We only need to do this one more time for the PreviousButton, and we will have all of the navigation buttons completed. Copy the NextButton, and paste it at the end of the file, and then make the changes noted in bold:

```
class PreviousButton(oParent) of MyPushbutton(oParent) ;
               from ":MyFormControls:MyFormControls.cc" custom
    this.text := "Previous"
    function onClick
        if ( not form.rowset.next(-1) )
            form.rowset.first()
            msgbox( "At end of rowset", "Can't Navigate", 64 )
        endif
    return
endclass
```

It is important that you get the "-1" in call to the rowset's *next()* method.

The next five buttons are going to be the ones for adding, editing, saving, abandoning changes and deleting rows. The code will be very similar to that in an earlier chapter.

As before, copy one of the button class definitions we've already created and make the following changes to create your Add Row button:

```
class AddRowButton(oParent) of MyPushbutton(oParent) from ;
               ":MyFormControls:MyFormControls.cc" custom
    this.text := "Add Row"
    function onClick
        form.rowset.beginAppend()
    return
endclass
```

Repeat the copy/paste we've been doing and create the following:

```
class EditRowButton(oParent) of MyPushbutton(oParent) from ;
               ":MyFormControls:MyFormControls.cc" custom
    this.text := "Edit Row"
    function onClick
        form.rowset.beginEdit()
    return
endclass
```

```
class DeleteRowButton(oParent) of MyPushbutton(oParent) from ;
                ":MyFormControls:MyFormControls.cc" custom
   this.text := "Delete Row"
   function onClick
      if msgbox( "Delete this row?", "Delete Row?", 36 ) == 6
         form.rowset.delete()
      endif
   return
endclass

class SaveRowButton(oParent) of MyPushbutton(oParent) from ;
                ":MyFormControls:MyFormControls.cc" custom
   this.text := "Save Row"
   function onClick
      form.rowset.save()
   return
endclass

class AbandonRowButton(oParent) of MyPushbutton(oParent) from ;
                ":MyFormControls:MyFormControls.cc" custom
   this.text := "Abandon Row"
   function onClick
      if msgbox( "Abandon changes to this row?",;
               "Abandon changes?", 36 ) == 6
         form.rowset.abandon()
      endif
   return
endclass
```

The last button we are creating for this exercise will be pretty simple; it is one that closes your form. If you copy one of the button classes above and paste it into the file, then make the changes noted in bold, the button will be ready to go:

```
class CloseButton(oParent) of MyPushbutton(oParent) from ;
             ":MyFormControls:MyFormControls.cc" custom
   this.text := "Close"
   function onClick
      form.close()
   return
endclass
```

We could go in and create custom buttons for filter-by-form and locate-by-form, but you should have the picture now. You can copy that code and create those buttons if you wish.

We should consider creating a control like we did in an earlier chapter that displays the current row state, otherwise a user might lose track of where they are. Like these pushbutton classes, the code is actually pretty generic and we can use it on multiple forms.

The code for this looks like the following and is based on the code we did previously. Just add this to the end of the pushbutton classes and it will be available when you use your pushbuttons.

```
class MyRowState(oParent) of Entryfield(oParent) custom
   this.value := "State"
   this.borderStyle := 1 // Raised
   this.colorNormal := "maroon/BtnFace"
```

```
    this.fontBold := true
    this.fontItalic := true
    this.when := {|| false }
    function onOpen
        // if we haven't already defined the calc field
        if type('form.rowset.fields["Rowstate"]') # "O"
            // do it here
            local f
            f = new field() // create it
            f.states = new array() // build an array with the
                                    // possible states
            f.states.add("Closed")
            f.states.add("Browse")
            f.states.add("Edit")
            f.states.add("Append")
            f.states.add("Filter")
            f.states.add("Locate")
            f.fieldName := "Rowstate"
            f.beforegetvalue := ;
                {;return this.states[ this.parent.parent.state + 1 ]}
            form.rowset.fields.add( f )
        endif
        this.datalink = form.rowset.fields["Rowstate"]
    return
endclass
```

Now that we have all of this code, we should use it. first, you should save your work and exit the Source Code Editor. One thing that you will find useful after doing this much code, is that you can have dBASE compile the code without ever actually using it. This is useful, because you could easily have entered some typos in the code, and not seen them. In the Command Window, type:

```
compile :MyFormControls:MyPushbuttons.cc
```

dBASE will tell you if any errors are found and try to tell you what line in the source code. This is very handy! *(If errors are found, fix them …)*

Putting the Custom Pushbutton Classes to Work

Now, let's put those custom pushbuttons onto a form, so we can see them in action. Before we start the Form Designer, we need to tell dBASE to load the custom pushbutton classes we created. This is simple … at the Command Window, type:

```
set procedure to :MyFormControls:MyPushbuttons.cc
```

Now open the form we were working on earlier called "SomeFish.wfm" in the Form Designer (the simplest method is to click on the "Forms" tab of the Navigator, click on the file, then right-click on it and select "Design Form", there we go).

If you click on the Component Palette now, and scroll to the "Custom" tab, you should see something like:

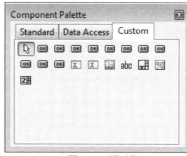

Figure 17-13

If you hold your mouse over the various pushbuttons, you will see the appropriate names ("Addrowbutton", etc.).

To add these to our form, we will need to make the form a little wider, drag the right side of the form to provide more room. Let's drag these pushbuttons and controls to our form in the following sequence, then work on lining them up and making the form look good:

Drag the "MyRowState" control to the right, and place it near the top of the form.

Drag the "FirstButton" pushbutton so it is under the "MyRowState" control.

(Note: when you drag custom pushbuttons to the form, sometimes the Component Palette shifts back to the "Standard" tab, which can be frustrating, but it happens ... just click back over to the "Custom" tab ...)

Continue with the pushbuttons under each other on the right, in the following sequence:

    PreviousButton
    NextButton
    LastButton
    AddRowButton
    EditRowButton
    SaveRowButton
    AbandonRowButton
    DeleteRowButton
    CloseButton

Next, we will use a feature not mentioned earlier in the chapter on using the Form Designer – the "Lasso" – which is a simple way of grabbing multiple controls and selecting them all at once (we could do the same, using the Ctrl key, holding it down, then clicking on each control we want to work with, but this is a little faster).

Click on the design surface of the form above and to the left of the "FirstRowButton", then drag while holding the left mouse button down, to below and to the right of the "CloseButton". Make sure all of your pushbuttons are included in the rectangle, let go of the mouse button and they are now all selected. This is handy when doing things such as aligning components.

Now that they are selected, find the button in the toolbar at the top of the screen to "Align Left" – this will line up all of the controls selected on the left side.

Next, move the buttons up or down so that they are grouped, the first four (First, Previous, Next, Last) and the next five (Add Row, Edit Row, Save Row, Abandon Row, and Delete

Row), then the "Close" button should be by itself. I tend to click on a pushbutton and just use the up or down arrow keys to move it up or down, which gives some pretty fine control. You should have something that looks similar to:

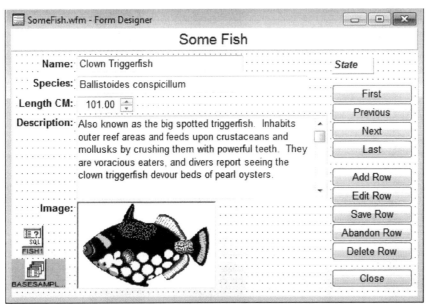

Figure 17-14

Readjust the form's right and bottom edges if needed.

Save the form ([Ctrl]+[S]), and let's run it (use the "Run Form" button in the toolbar). Try navigating, try clicking the "Add Row" button, notice that all the fields go blank, if you click the "Abandon Row" button at that point, you will be asked if you wish to abandon. Look at the RowState control as you click some of these buttons and note that it changes properly. This works really well!

The best part is that all of those pushbuttons that you just created can be used on other forms and you don't have to change a thing! You have just created a nice library of some basic controls that you can use over and over.

Modifying the Base Pushbutton Class

Why would you want to modify the base pushbutton class? Well, there are probably plenty of reasons. What if you wanted to change the color (the *colorNormal* property) of all the buttons you are using? Wouldn't it be easier to change it in the base class, rather than modifying each pushbutton? How about changing the *fontName* property?

To show something that works well in dBASE PLUS release 2.5 and later, we are going to work with a couple of new events: *onMouseOver()* and *onMouseOut()*. (NOTE: If you are *using a version of dBASE earlier than 2.5, then this will not work.*) The first is an event that fires when the mouse is over a control, the second fires when the mouse moves off of it. What we will do is change the *fontBold* property of the pushbutton to *true*. When the mouse moves off the button, we need the *fontBold* property to change back to what it was before. Seems simple enough, right?

On order to do this and have it affect *all* of the pushbuttons we are using, we only have to modify the base pushbutton that is in the file "MyFormControls.cc". So, we want to open this in the Source Code Editor:

```
modify command :MyFormControls:MyFormControls.cc
```

Go to the bottom where the "MyPushbutton" class is, we're going to insert some code before the "endclass" statement and after the "endwith" statement:

```
function onMouseOver
   this.fontBold := true
return

function onMouseOut
   this.fontBold := false
return
```

This should give a custom control that looks like the following in the source code editor:

```
class MYPUSHBUTTON(parentObj) of PUSHBUTTON(parentObj) custom
   with (this)
      height = 24.0
      left = 30.0
      top = 62.0
      width = 107.0
      text = "MyPushbutton"
      metric = 6 // Pixels
   endwith

   function onMouseOver
      this.fontBold := true
   return

   function onMouseOut
      this.fontBold := false
   return
endclass
```

Save the custom class file (Ctrl+W) and let's run the form again (click on the "Forms" tab in the Navigator if necessary, and double-click the file "SomeFish.wfm").

We could have set this code to change the font, or if we were using images on the pushbuttons, changing the image when the mouse is over it, but this will do as a simple example.

Run your mouse over the pushbuttons, you should see the text change to **bold,** and back to normal.

The great thing about this is that we only had to modify the base pushbutton class to get this behavior for all those pushbuttons!

Using Your Custom Classes for New Forms

In all the work we have done so far with these custom classes, we have not gotten into really making everything available for all the forms in an application. So far, we've really only looked at this specific form.

So, how do you make all this code available when you develop?

We could just type the SET PROCEDURE command for each custom class, when we start dBASE, but that can get tedious.

You could tell dBASE to load all of your custom controls when it starts, but if you have a lot of them, this slows the startup of dBASE and you may load controls you won't use, or don't need. But, if you want to do this, it can be done. To do it, open the Form Designer and select the "File" menu. Then select "Setup Custom Components ...". This should bring up a dialog that looks like:

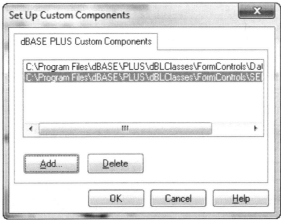

Figure 17-15

If you select "Add", you can add class files to the list – these will then always load when dBASE starts. You can also remove class files from the list by using the "Delete" button (which does not actually delete the file, but removes the file from this list, therefore not opening automatically when dBASE starts). As noted, the biggest drawback doing this is that if you have a lot of controls, you can slow down the start time of dBASE.

Another issue is harder to explain – if you have multiple copies of some controls with different properties, then start dBASE with one set of controls open, those controls are in memory. If you tell dBASE later to open another version of those controls (using SET PROCEDURE.) and they have the same names as the originals, dBASE will not actually replace what is in memory with the new versions. This can get a bit confusing and rather frustrating, to put it mildly.

So, what is the best solution? Well, there probably isn't a "best" solution. The usual recommendation is to create a startup program that you can use when you start working on your application. It might look something like:

```
set procedure to :MyFormControls:MyFormControls.cc
set procedure to :MyFormControls:MyPushbuttons.cc
```

Then, you could run the program by either double-clicking it in the Navigator, etc. Save it as something like "Setup.prg" or "LoadControls.prg", so that you know what it is and you'll be set to go. As you add more code to your library, you can add more files that get loaded as required.

Summary

In this chapter we did quite a bit of work in setting up source code libraries, using Source Code Aliases. We also created a useful set of custom classes that you can work with for now as well as other applications if you wish. However this is just a start. The longer you work with dBASE, the more functionality you will find yourself adding to your own custom code libraries and you will most likely find yourself relying heavily on other people's libraries. As is often stated in the dBASE user newsgroups, "Why reinvent the wheel?" If someone has created a particularly useful control and they make it available for everyone to use, why should you try to write your own? This is the whole purpose of the dUFLP *(a library of freeware dBASE code)* – discussed in the appendices.

In the first edition of this book the custom pushbutton classes shown here changed the *colorNormal* property of the pushbuttons when the *onMouseOver* and *onMouseOut* events fired. In dBASE Plus 2.6 and later, due to the default use of the Windows XP (and Vista) Themes, the *colorNormal* property doesn't work the same. The examples were modified to use the *fontBold* property which still works the same under XP (and later), and still gives a visual cue when the mouse is moved over the pushbuttons.

NOTES:

Chapter 18: Using the Custom Classes that Ship with dBASE

dBASE ships with a set of custom classes that can be used on your forms and applications. Some of them are ones you may have used without even realizing that they were custom controls.

This chapter will discuss the custom classes that ship with dBASE that can be used for forms – the visual classes. There are some others, including one that can be used with reports.

The developers at dBASE have not only included these custom classes with the software, they have included the source code for these classes. This allows you to see how they work and include them in your own applications. In order to access the source code you can use the Source Code Aliases shown in the chapter, but if you wish to include these in your own applications, it may be helpful to know the path to the files.

On Windows XP or with older versions of dBASE (older than dBASE Plus 2.7) the path to these is going to be (unless you installed to a custom path):

```
C:\Program Files\dBASE\PLUS\dBLClasses\FormControls
```

On an installation with the current versions of dBASE (2.7 or later) and current versions of Windows (Windows Vista or later), with a standard/default installation, the path that is being used by dBASE is:

```
C:\Users\username\AppData\Local\dBASE\Plus\dBLClasses\FormControls
```

If you are not sure where the files are, you can go to the menu in dBASE and select "Properties", followed by "Desktop Properties" on the submenu. From there, click the "Source Aliases" tab. Select any alias and the path is displayed.

Custom Pushbuttons

dBASE ships with a set of custom pushbuttons, which are actually opened by default when you start dBASE. When you examine the Component Palette in the Form Designer, it looks something like (by default, although you can rearrange it, make it larger, move it around, etc.):

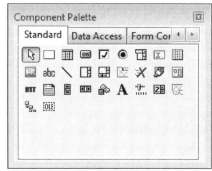

Figure 18-1

If you use the arrow buttons on the top right side of the notebook control on the Component Palette, you will see new tabs appear. For example, you can move over and find "Data Buttons". If you click on that, you will see:

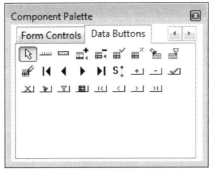

Figure 18-2

This tab shows a set of pushbuttons, including some toolbars (collections of pushbuttons), that can be placed on your forms. The names of these should tell you what you need to know, but the following is a quick summary:

- BarDataEdit – a "toolbar" of pushbuttons that include Edit, Delete, Save, Abandon, Filter and Locate buttons. (The toolbar is literally a container control with pushbuttons on it.)
- BarDataVCR – a "toolbar" of pushbuttons that are used to navigate in a rowset – First, Previous, Next, and Last.
- BitmapAppend – a pushbutton object that can be used to append a new row.
- BitmapDelete – a pushbutton object used to delete a row.
- BitmapSave – a pushbutton object used to save changes to a row.
- BitmapAbandon – a pushbutton object used to abandon changes to a row.
- BitmapLocate – a pushbutton that puts your form into "Locate by Form" mode.
- BitmapFilter – a pushbutton that puts your form into "Filter by Form" mode.
- BitmapEdit – a pushbutton that puts your form into "Edit" mode.
- BitmapFirst – a pushbutton for navigation to the first row in the table.
- BitmapPrevious – a pushbutton to navigate back one row in the table.
- BitmapNext – a pushbutton to navigate forward one row in the table.
- BitmapLast – a pushbutton to navigate to the last row in the table.
- RowState – a text control that shows the current state of the rowset on the form.
- ButtonAppend – a pushbutton with the text "Add" on it, same code as "BitmapAppend".
- ButtonDelete – a pushbutton with the text "Delete" on it, used to delete a row.
- ButtonSave – a pushbutton with the text "Save" on it, used to save changes to a row.
- ButtonAbandon – a pushbutton with the text "Abandon" on it, used to abandon changes to a row.
- ButtonLocate – a pushbutton with the text "Locate" on it, that puts your form into "Locate by Form" mode.
- ButtonFilter – a pushbutton with the text "Filter" on it, that puts your form into "Filter by Form" mode.
- ButtonEdit – a pushbutton with the text "Edit" on it, that puts your form into "Edit" mode.
- ButtonFirst – a pushbutton with the text "First" on it, for navigation to the first row in the table.
- ButtonPrevious – a pushbutton with the text "Previous" on it, to navigate back one row in the table.
- ButtonNext – a pushbutton with the text "Next" on it, to navigate forward one row in the table.

- ButtonLast – a pushbutton with the text "Last" on it, to navigate to the last row in the table.

The pushbuttons that start with the word "Bitmap" are smaller buttons that have an image on them, rather than text, the ones that start with the word "Button" have text, but no image. If you worked through the examples in the previous chapter, then you don't *really* need these pushbuttons.

There is one frustrating thing with this set of pushbuttons – if there is no rowset on a form and you run the form, the pushbuttons have code that sets their *visible* property to *false*. What this means is that if you place them on a form and the form's *rowset* property is null or empty, when you run the form the pushbuttons do not appear at all. This can be a little confusing.

These can be dragged to a form and used with your own application if you wish. Note that if you use these you will have to include the file :FormControls:DataButtons.cc with your application.

If you wish to examine the source code for this file, you can do so by going to the Command Window and typing:

```
modify command :FormControls:DataButtons.cc
```

If you want modify the source code, you should do so by copying the file to another location, before modifying it. The reason? The next time you install an upgrade to dBASE, it is possible that your modifications may be overwritten. If you end up having to move to a new computer, your modified version of the source code might not go to the new computer, if you do not place it in a location where you are likely to back it up.

Custom Controls on the *Form Controls* Tab

The Component Palette has a tab that you should take a look at titled "Form Controls". If you click on it, it should look something like:

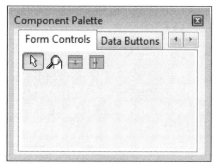

Figure 18-3

This has three controls, which are really only two – one of them is a variation on the other. The first is one that has been used by members of the dBASE Community for many years, and we will spend some time looking at this.

Seeker

The Seeker control (the one with the magnifying glass in the icon), appears as an entryfield if placed on a form, but is much more than that.

Seeker is designed to work with a character index for a table and perform what is called an *incremental search*. What this means is that if you have a large amount of alphanumeric data and you type the letter "C", the seeker control will move to the first row that begins with the letter "C". If you then type the letter "e", the seeker will move to the first row that begins with the letters "CE" and so on.

Some caveats: Seeker assumes that you are using an index that was created with the *upper()* function *(it converts the characters to upper case for the purpose of the index only)*. Seeker will not tell you if a match is found or not. Seeker is commonly used on forms that have a grid, which is useful to view the data as you "seek" through it.

The form shown below gives some idea of how you might use this. We are not walking through the steps to create this form in this chapter, although if you have worked through earlier chapters in this book, you should be able to do this yourself.

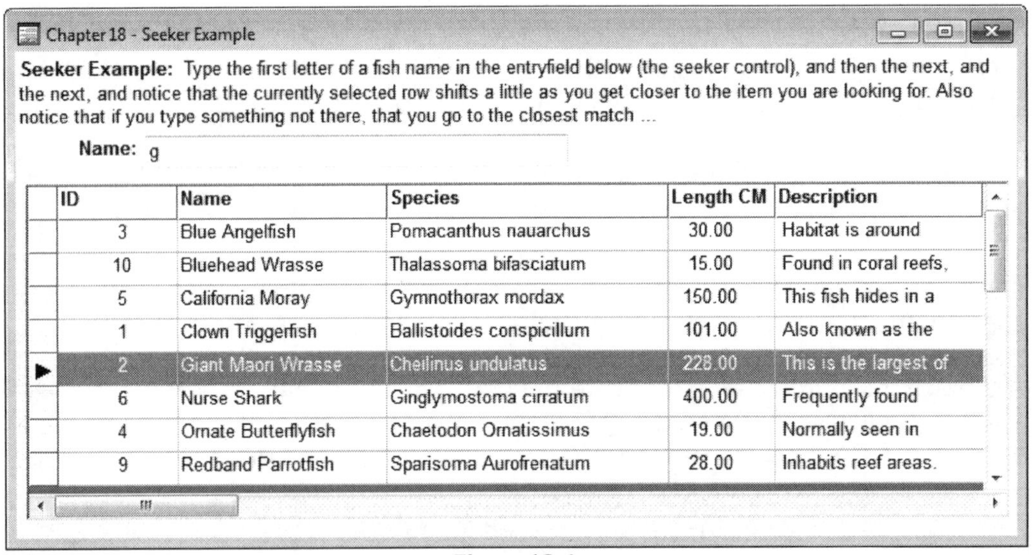

Figure 18-4

The only difficulty is that the Fish table that ships with dBASE PLUS in the samples does not use the upper() function on the name field for any of the index tags it has. The code in this form takes care of this by checking for it and creating an index if necessary, using a combination of the TableDef, DBFIndex and Database objects.

Using Seeker with Numbers?

Seeker itself was written to only work with character fields. However some time ago Peter Rorlick posted in the dBASE newsgroups a way to subclass the seeker control so that it can work with numeric fields instead of character fields. The way you do that is to copy the code below to a new filename such as "NumSeeker.cc".

```
CLASS NumSeeker( fArg ) of Seeker( fArg ) from;
                        :FormControls:Seeker.cc CUSTOM
   FUNCTION normalizedValue
      // Here we override the super class' method.
      // Instead of returning upper( trim( this.value )),
      // we'll convert this.value to numeric
   RETURN val( this.value )
ENDCLASS
```

If you want to use this, then all you have to do is (very similar to other examples):

```
set procedure to NumSeeker.cc
```

And you will find this new control on the component palette. Make sure that the form's rowset is set to an index that is based on a numeric field. Otherwise this should work exactly like the normal version of seeker.

It is probably a good idea to store this subclassed version of seeker in your own code library, with your own source alias and use it that way. With a bit of work you might be able to use seeker for dates, or other field types, but we will leave that exercise to the reader.

Using Seeker With Multiple Rowsets?

If you have multiple rowsets on a form that you might want the seeker control to work with, there are ways to force it to do this.

- The simple solution is to place two (or more) seeker controls on the form – but as you might imagine, this will clutter up your form.
- The next is that when you (somehow) move focus to another rowset, you change the form's *rowset* property (this will also allow any pushbuttons that use "form.rowset" to work on that rowset).
- The last is to set the seeker object's *rowset* property when you change the rowset on your form that you want to work with. This property is not necessary – by default seeker will use "form.rowset", but if you change the seeker object's *rowset* property you can work with a different rowset.

Important Note:

One last thing: You should **never** set a dataLink for the seeker control. If you do, you might inadvertently change data in your table. Seeker is designed to find rows that match what is typed into it, that is its only purpose. *(In addition, the property is protected so that you cannot set it in the Form Designer, so you would get an error if you tried.)*

Splitter

There are two forms of the Splitter Control, HSplitter and VSplitter, where "H" is for "Horizontal" and "V" is for Vertical. The examples given here will be done using the HSplitter control, but the options are the same, as internally the big difference is that one is subclassed from the other.

What is a splitter control and why would you want to use one on a dBASE form? A splitter is used to split a screen or form and when dragged left and right, or up and down (depending on the splitter being used), the screen updates and changes the surface available on that part of the form.

This control may not appear on the component palette. If it does not, all you have to do is go to the command window, and type:

```
set procedure to :formcontrols:Splitter.cc
```

The Splitter classes are based on the stock rectangle class. When dragged to a form, they appear exactly as rectangles. You will need to size them, and perhaps work with the *borderStyle* property to get the appearance you want for your splitter control (for example, the splitter used on the dQuery form uses the "raised" option for the *borderStyle*).

The splitter classes have two methods that can be used to update the form – *onMoving()*, and *onMoved()* – the first one fires as the splitter is moved by the user, the second one fires when the move is complete.

There is a property called *AllowDoubleClickMove*, which defaults to true – this allows the user to double-click on the splitter and have it move to a default position using the *DoubleClickPosition* property (the position is based on the form width or height, it defaults to 50%). If you do not want the user to be able to double-click on the splitter and have it shift to the default position, set the *AllowDoubleClickMove* property to *false*.

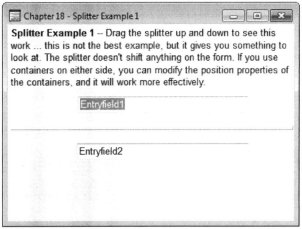

Figure 18-5

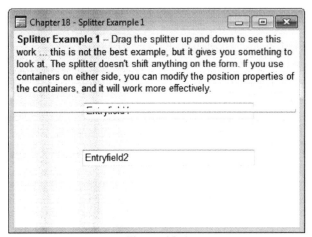

Figure 18-6

The code that is set in this sample form to work with the splitter is:

```
function HSPLITTER1_onOpen
   // we are overriding the Splitter's onOpen event here:

   // For this example, I'm turning this off:
   this.allowDoubleClickMove := false

   // Tell it what to do:
   this.onMoving := class::SplitterMoving
   this.onMoved := class::SplitterMoved

   // create custom property to handle "current"
   // position of control
   form.nCurrentTop = this.Top
return
```

```
function SplitterMoving
   ? "SplitterMoving event"
   ? form.hSplitter1.top
return

function SplitterMoved
   ? "SplitterMoved event"
   ? form.hSplitter1.top
return
```

The two methods at the end show what is happening as the splitter is moved, but the output is to the results pane of the Command Window.

HINT: It is probably a good idea to use containers to hold the controls on either side of a splitter. If you do, then when the splitter moves, you only have to update the properties of two controls (the container on either side of the splitter). If you chose NOT to use a container on either side, then when the splitter moves you have to update the position properties of every control on either side of the splitter, which can make for a difficult job coding. See the example below:

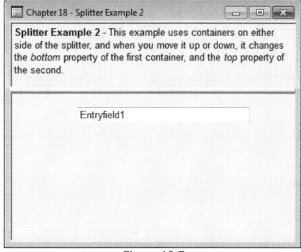

Figure 18-7

In this case, since we have containers on either side of the splitter, when the splitter is moved, we are changing the properties as mentioned earlier for the container objects. The code that does this is (it's quite a bit more complicated):

```
function HSPLITTER1_onOpen
    // If allowing the double-click to reset,
    // you can set the doubleClickPosition here.

    // For this example, I'm turning it on:
    this.allowDoubleClickMove := true
    this.DoubleClickPosition := 50

    // Tell it what to do:
    this.onMoving := class::SplitterMoving
    this.onMoved := class::SplitterMoved

    // create custom property to handle "current"
    // position of control
    form.nCurrentTop = this.Top
return

function SplitterMoved
    class::MoveIt()
return

function SplitterMoving
    class::MoveIt()
return

function MoveIt
    local nTop, nMove
    // the current position
    nTop = this.Top
     // did we move toward the top or the bottom?
    if nTop < form.nCurrentTop
       lTop = true
    else
       lTop = false
    endif
    // how far do we shift things?
    if lTop
       nMove = form.nCurrentTop - nTop
    else
       nMove = nTop - form.nCurrentTop
    endif

    // change the height of the Top container:
    if lTop
       // Make sure we're not setting the height to an
       // "out of range" value:
       if ( form.TopContainer.height - nMove <= 0 )
          form.TopContainer.height := 0
       else
          form.TOPCONTAINER.height -= nMove
       endif
    else
       form.TOPCONTAINER.height += nMove
    endif
    // change the top position AND the height
    // of the right container:
    if lTop
       // Change top position by 'nMove' units
```

```
      form.BOTTOMCONTAINER.top -= nMove
      // Change HEIGHT by 'nMove' units
      form.BOTTOMCONTAINER.height += nMove
   else
      // Change top position by 'nMove' units
      form.BOTTOMCONTAINER.top += nMove
      // Make sure we're not setting the height to an
      // "out of range" value:
      if ( form.BottomContainer.height - nMove <= 0 )
         form.BottomContainer.height := 0
      else
         form.BOTTOMCONTAINER.height -= nMove
      endif
   endif

   // update current left to where we are now:
   form.nCurrentTop := this.Top
return
```

If you were to use a vertical splitter, the properties you would be concerned with would be *left* and *width* for the container objects, rather than *top* and *height*, and so on, but the code would be quite similar.

Animate

This control may not appear on the component palette. If it does not, all you have to do is go to the command window, and type:

```
set procedure to :formcontrols:Animate.cc
```

When you go to create a new form now, this control will be on the Form Controls tab of the Component Palette.

So, what does it do? It is used to display a "single stream" .AVI file on a form. dBASE PLUS ships with a series of .AVI files that can be used on a form, in the "Media\Movies" folder (referenced through the Source Alias :Movies:).

There are some example files that you can examine that use this and these are what were used to give the details on how to use this control. Check the folder: ".\dBLClasses\Forms" and you will see "AnimateDisp.wfm" and "AnimateAbout.wfm". You can run these from anywhere using the source alias :Forms: in the Command Window:

```
do :Forms:AnimateAbout.wfm
   // or:
do :Forms:AnimateDisp.wfm
```

In addition, in the samples folder is a form that can be used to examine these .AVI files frame-by-frame or to run them.

```
do :Samples:AnimateDemo.wfm
```

The Animate control appears on the Component Palette as a Paintbox object, and if you drag it to a form's design surface, all you see is a square.

To use the Animate control on your own form, follow these steps:

- Create a new form, set the form's *metric* property to "6 - Pixels"
- Place an Animate control on a form (this is on the "Form Controls" Tab)
- Widen it a bit, otherwise it won't display properly
- In the Inspector, click on the "Events" tab
- Click on *onOpen*
- Select the Type button (has a letter "T" on it)
- Select "Codeblock"
- Click on the Tool button
- Enter the following:

```
this.open(":Movies:dBASESmall.avi")
```

(Note that you can use the name of any of the .avi files in the folder ".\Media\Movies", there are quite a few interesting ones there.)
- Click "OK"
- Run the form and see what happens.

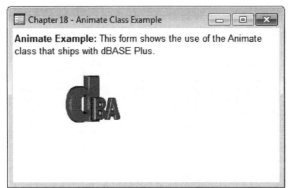

Figure 18-8

You could use this kind of control on a form that displays while performing a long process, so the user feels like something is happening *(some developers have found that a background process may slow the display of the AVI file, if not halt it, however)*. There are quite a few interesting.AVI files in the movies folder, and it's worth looking them over. These little movie files include ones that show data transfer, moving files (to a box, a trashcan, a shredder, etc.), sorting and a lot more.

Calendar

A calendar class ships with dBASE PLUS, and can be placed on the component palette (if it's not already there) in the same way that other controls can be used.

```
set procedure to :FormControls:Calendar.cc
```

To use this control, the steps are like this:

- Create a new form, setting the form's *metric* property to "6 - Pixels"
- Go to the Component Palette, select the Form Controls tab, then drag the Calendar control to the form's surface
- That's the absolute basics, if you do nothing else, the calendar will start at today's date.

However, if you want to set the date to a specific date, you can do this when opening the form, or do this in code in one of several ways.

- Using the Calendar control's *onOpen()* event (click on the form, in the Inspector select the Events tab, select onOpen, then click the tool button – when asked if you want to over-write the code, click "Yes"), you can set the date to any specific date:

```
function CALENDAR1_onOpen
   // the second parameter tells the control to repaint
   this.setDate( date(), "Y" )
return
```

Note that the value placed inside the parenthesis must be a date, but it can be a variable that references a date, a property of a form, or just about anything, as long as it evaluates to a date.

The cool thing about the calendar is that you can select a date using it, then return the date to some code.

There is a method of the calendar control that allows this, called *getDate()*. To use it, place a pushbutton on the form that has the control (outside the calendar's container), that might be a multi-purpose button, for example, that closes the form but also returns the date. In the *onClick()* event for the pushbutton, you could do something like:

```
function pushbutton1_onClick
   dDate = form.calendar1.getDate()
   msgbox( "Date selected: "+dDate )
return
```

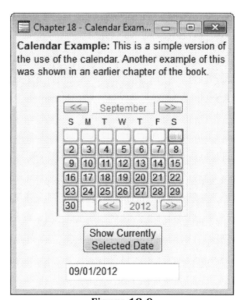

Figure 18-9

In addition, the calendar class is set up to allow you to "hook" into a method of the class, but only if you "register" the form with the class. This is done by overriding the form's *open()* event and calling the calendar's *registerOwners()* method:

```
function form_onOpen
   // register form controls with Calendar
   ///// Register dateFields with calendar
   this.calendar1.registerOwners(form)
return
```

When the user selects a date, you can get that value and work with it, with little effort. This requires that you create a method of the form (just add a section of code like the following), in this case, it requires an entryfield named "dateef" on the form:

```
function setDate(dDate)
   // This is called automatically by the
   // calendar class, but ONLY if you use the registerOwners
   // method, as shown above in the form_onOpen event.

   // set defaults for missing params:
   dDate = iif(empty(dDate),date(),dDate)
   // set value of dateef:
   form.dateef.value = dDate
return
```

You might want to create an event handler or add the lines in bold below to the form's *onOpen* event handler to ensure that the entryfield has a value when the form opens:

```
function form_onOpen
  // register form controls with Calendar
 ///// Register dateFields with calendar
    this.calendar1.registerOwners(form)
    // call the code when the form opens
    // so we have a date in the entryfield:
    class::SetDate()
return
```

This should give you some ideas for using this control.

It should be noted that in the dUFLP there are several other calendar classes with different appearance and in some cases different abilities. If you need a calendar for an application there are a few options.

Form Viewer

The Form Viewer class is used specifically for the purpose of viewing forms – note that the form displayed is not actually running in an interactive way. This is not the same thing as subforms, which is a totally different topic. As a developer of your own applications this is probably not a very useful tool.

This class is used in *(and was created for)* the Project Explorer in dBASE PLUS, but if you need to use it, it is available for use in your own applications. The control is in the dBLClasses\FormControls folder, and can be accessed using the :FormControls: source alias:

```
set procedure to :FormControls:FormViewer.cc
```

Once you have done that, the next time you design a form, the control will appear on the Component Palette's "Form Controls" tab as a container object.

To display a form, you use the class's method: *Display(cFormName)*, where "cFormName" is the name of the form file (formname.wfm or formname.cfm) that you want to display.

For example, in a form's *onOpen* event, you could decide to display the test calendar form that is shown earlier in this chapter. To do so (assuming the same folder that the form is in), place a formViewer control on a form, then go to the Inspector and select the form's *onOpen()* event, then enter:

```
form.formViewer1.display("CalendarExample.wfm")
```

When you run the form, you will see that the form appears, but you cannot interact with it as it is not running. This might look something like:

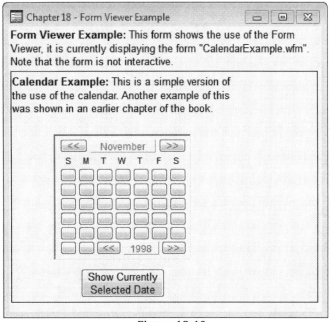

Figure 18-10

You can close the currently displayed form by using the control's *closeCurrentForm()* method (form.formviewer1.closeCurrentForm()). This would be useful if you needed to display different forms – close the current one and then display the new one.

Summary

This chapter was aimed at giving you an overview of the custom classes that ship with dBASE, so that if you find a need for them you can use them in your own applications. Probably the most commonly used control of the ones listed here is Seeker, followed by the Calendar class. However, these others can give you some great ideas for you to examine and learn from just by examining the source code.

NOTES:

Index

453

G

M

N

O

P

T